May the Lor,
contents of this
spiritual nouri;
edification.

Elder Ralph E. Harris

MW00806721

DAY BY DAY

365 DAILY READINGS ON BIBLICAL THEMES

ELDER RALPH E. HARRIS

❧

Sovereign Grace Publications LLC
Lexington, Kentucky

Day by Day: 365 Daily Readings on Biblical Themes
Published by Sovereign Grace Publications LLC
Post Office Box 23514
Lexington, Kentucky 40523
www.sovgrace.net
sgpublications@insightbb.com

Copyright © 2012 by Ralph E. Harris
All rights reserved. No portion of this book may be reproduced, stored in a retrieval system, or transmitted in any form or by any means, except for brief quotations in printed reviews, without written permission from the publisher.

ISBN 978-1-929635-15-3

Scripture quotations are from the *King James Version* of the Bible.

Printed in the United States of America.

CONTENTS

INTRODUCTION

A daily devotional is a useful resource to those of us who live in a fast-paced world. Although there is no substitute for the daily discipline of reading God's word, yet a book of brief devotional thoughts like the one you presently hold may serve a spiritually-beneficial purpose between opportunities for more intensive focus on the Scriptures.

I like to use a book of devotional readings early in the morning as a sort of springboard for meditation throughout the day, saving my daily Bible reading for the slower, less demanding hours of the early evening. Few of these devotional readings require more than four or five minutes of reading time; consequently, they are specially tailored for people whose daily lives are marked by one-hundred-one time demands.

Others may prefer to do their Bible reading in the morning and use the devotional to aid in a few moments of quiet reflection prior to retiring for the evening. Whatever particular format may be preferable to you as an individual, I would encourage you to devote the coming year both to reading through the Bible and reading each of the 365 daily entries in this devotional volume. I'm confident the two sources of material will complement each other.

I am grateful to Elder Ralph Harris and his dear companion, Melba, for supplying the content of these pages. I have long felt that Elder Harris was one of the most spiritually-minded ministers, as well as one of the premier and most articulate writers among our beloved Primitive Baptist people. It was my privilege to enjoy his fellowship on several occasions during the early days of my pastoral labors in south Georgia, and I have long admired his consistent Christian walk and commitment to the cause of Christ.

Elder Harris was born into a Primitive Baptist home on August 24, 1938 near Bonifay, Florida where he still makes his home. He united with Bethel Primitive Baptist Church April 19, 1959, was liberated to speak from the pulpit the following October 1, 1960 and was ordained to the ministry April 1, 1961. He met Miss Melba Jones in May of 1961 and was married to her the following December 24th at Mars Hill Church near Edison, Georgia. He baptized her on the first Sunday in April, 1962.

In 1976, at the request of the Board of Trustees, he assumed the editorship of *The Advocate and Messenger,* a Primitive Baptist periodical, and served in that capacity for 33 years until failing health required him to surrender those duties. He served several churches over the years but also had to give up that labor of love because of failing health.

He has written hundreds of poems over the years, most of which were published in *The Advocate and Messenger* during the time of his editorship. He has also written several spiritual hymns, including three that are in *The Old School Hymnal*: "Fear Not, Little Flock," "Hope Most Precious," and "Jesus, Blessed Jesus."

Several of the daily readings in this volume first appeared as articles in *The Advocate and Messenger*. I am thankful for this opportunity to preserve the writings of this humble servant of God in this more permanent form.

The daily readings are subdivided into three primary sections: *Nuggets of Truth* (which generally consist of an explanation of a particular verse of scripture), *Musings* (consisting of various random, Biblical thoughts), and *Bits & Pieces* (consisting of particular topical themes). The overwhelming majority of the entries are filed under the "Nuggets" subhead.

I have also found these readings beneficial in terms of stimulating my mind to thought and meditation in the conduct of my weekly pulpit responsibilities. On several occasions during the time that this volume was being prepared for publication, I have found a thought or two in one of the entries that has served as "sermon fodder" and led to my Sunday pulpit fare for the people I try to serve. I am confident that preachers, as well as church members, will derive benefit from this book.

Michael L. Gowens
Lexington, Kentucky
June 2012

PART 1

NUGGETS OF TRUTH

January 1

"In the beginning God created the heaven and the earth"
(Genesis 1:1)

Any other notions with regard to existence must necessarily contradict or fly in the face of the word of God. Hence, we are faced with a choice of either believing *God's* version of the matter or man's *theories* with regard thereunto. If He has given us faith we will believe *Him*, and if not we will believe *someone else*.

The main alternative to God and creation now being either ignorantly, deceptively, or dishonestly advanced as *fact* instead of *theory* is the idea of evolution. But we do not hesitate to say that this concept is absurd on the face of it.

In order for this theory to be true, any life form that came into existence would necessarily have to already be possessed of the ability to find and ingest nourishment. It would also have to be able to digest, assimilate and excrete that nourishment. Without any one of these abilities it would very shortly die.

It would also have to be able to reproduce itself, otherwise it would become extinct as soon as it died. It could not wait for weeks to evolve these abilities, much less millions of years. These things are so self-evident we marvel that anyone would actually think that the theory of evolution has credence.

The notion that any inanimate, lifeless substance could, of itself suddenly come to life, is simply too preposterous for words. But to argue that it then could live for millions of years before it evolved the ability to eat, breathe, see, walk, fly, etc., etc., insults the intelligence of reasonable people. It is amazing the lengths to which men will go in an effort to get around the existence of God.

The Bible clearly explains the existence of the earth and all the other heavenly bodies, as well as all life forms. This explanation may appear unbelievable to some but the alternatives are *far more* unbelievable.

☙❧

January 2

"Thou art a God that hidest thyself, O God of Israel, the Savior"
(Isaiah 45:15)

God has always hidden himself from the wicked so far as giving them a view of himself by faith. Not everyone possesses faith (2 Thess. 3:2) for God does not give it to all men, and therefore not everyone can see him with an eye of faith; see him so as to love him; or so as to trust him and find in him their all in all.

Ungodly men may see God in the works of nature and even go so far as to acknowledge his existence, but they despise him. They do not desire the knowledge of his ways and would prefer that he depart from them (Job 21:14).

God was for many centuries greatly hidden from the Gentile nations, and is yet but obscurely seen even by multitudes of those who profess to believe in him. Those who think they know *most* of him, actually know *least* of him. Some have such a dim concept of him as to think he is *altogether such an one as themselves* (See Psalm 50:21). But to entertain such an opinion of him is to have the *lowest* possible notions of his nature and being.

God often hides himself even from his own believing people. Bible readers will recall that David once uttered the following sad interrogatory; "Is his mercy clean gone for ever? Doth his promise fail for evermore?" (Psalm 77:8). And have we not often felt similar sentiments as we struggled under the hidings of God's face?

One of the characteristics of our corrupted nature is to begin to take even our greatest blessings for granted if we are given unbroken access to them over a period of time. God, in his wisdom, knows that it would not be in our best interest, in our present state, to enjoy uninterrupted communion with him or to always feel his presence with us. It is not for us to know now all the reasons why God hides himself from us from time to time, but we may be certain that all of his behavior toward us is in our best interest. May he give us grace to be reconciled to that fact.

෧ඏ

January 3

"If we say that we have no sin, we deceive
ourselves, and the truth is not in us" (1 John 1:8)

No man with any insight into his own corrupt nature, or even a head-knowledge of the letter of the Scriptures, could honestly think he has no sin. Not only have we all sinned (Romans 3:23; 5:12) but we all have a sinful nature (Isaiah 64:6; Eph. 2:3). "Who can say, I have made my heart clean, I am pure from my sin?" (Proverbs 20:9).

Those who say they have no sin not only deceive themselves and expose their ignorance, but they are pointedly contradicted by divine inspiration. Solomon put it very well when he said, "There is not a just man upon earth, that doeth good, and sinneth not" (Eccl. 7:20).

When a person makes the claim that they "have no sin" they are in effect saying that they have never sinned, neither personally nor in their father Adam, for that is the only way they could be without sin. But the apostle John says, "If we say we have not sinned, we make him (God) a liar, and his word is not in us" (1 John 1:10).

In other words, we would be tacitly accusing God of being a liar, for his word plainly shows that we have all sinned, both in Adam and by practice. In effect we would be saying that his word is *not true*, and who among us, who has any grace at all, would dare bring such an accusation against the Deity.

Christ died for the sins of his people and satisfied the demands of God's holy and righteous law in our behalf. Consequently we have been freed from the *damning power* of sin; but that does not deliver us from the *being* of sin within our old, corrupted nature. We will have sin in the flesh as long as we live, but in the resurrection these vile and corrupt bodies will "put on incorruption" (See Phil. 3:2; 1 Cor. 15:54). Then, and only then, will we "have no sin."

January 4

"When he dieth he shall carry nothing away" (Psalm 49:17)

Much is said in the Scriptures with regard to the deceitfulness of riches, yet multitudes still fall into the trap of thinking that material goods will solve all their problems. Many have even thought that gain is godliness, but from such characters Paul has taught the saints to withdraw themselves. Solomon had all that the human heart could desire and yet he ultimately confessed that it was all vanity. So have many others, to their ultimate sorrow, found that worldly wealth is far from being the most important thing in life.

The *love* of money is the root of all evil" (1 Tim. 6:10). That is, it is the root of all *kinds* of evil; and as a result of coveting after money many of God's people have "pierced themselves through with many sorrows," and some of them have even erred from the faith. Rather than gain being godliness, just the reverse is actually the case: "Godliness with contentment is great gain" (1 Tim. 6:6). Not just *gain* but *great gain*!

Worldly prosperity, in itself, is not contrary to godliness, but coveting after it *is*. It also carries with it great responsibilities that few people are ready or able to handle. The misuse of it has ruined many a man. It should not be *hoarded*, nor should it be *squandered*, but rather it should be used wisely, for the relief of others less fortunate and to the glory of the gracious Giver. If we think the proper thing to do with worldly goods is to build bigger barns in which to store them, and to take our ease, eat, drink, and be merry, God classifies us as a fool, and it may soon all be stripped away from us (See Luke 12:16-19).

Paul said, "We brought nothing into this world, *and it is certain* we can carry nothing out" (1 Tim. 6:7). To the covetous, especially, this should be a very sobering thought. "Take heed, and beware of covetousness: for a man's life consisteth not in the abundance of the things which he possesseth" (Luke 12:15).

≪∞≫

January 5

"This present evil world" (Galatians 1:4)

The world we live in is an evil world. If we fail to realize this we are in a very vulnerable position and will find ourselves often taken advantage of and misused. And even if we *are* aware of it we will still many times be a victim.

For instance, many times when we buy an item at a store we are overcharged in order to cover the store's losses from shoplifting and other misdeeds on someone's part. Even if stores never suffered such losses, some owners would still overcharge their customers.

I have many times been a victim of fraud at the hands of unscrupulous characters. They do such things because "there is no fear of God before their eyes" (Psalm 36:1; Romans 3:18). They *do* evil, because they *are* evil.

Christ prayed for his people, not that the Father would take them *out* of the world, but that he would "keep them from the evil" (John 17:15). We know not what calamities might befall us at the hands of this world if we were not "kept by the power of God" (1 Peter 1:5), and if we did not, by His merciful help, "save (ourselves) from this untoward generation" (Acts 2:40).

The apostle John tells us that apart from those who are "of God," the rest of the world "lieth in wickedness" (1 John 5:19). We will do well to keep this in mind and be careful not to conform ourselves to the world's much valued fashions and customs. Christ said, "That which is highly esteemed among men is abomination in the sight of God" (Luke 16:15).

Paul exhorts God's people to "do all things without murmurings and disputings," that they "may be blameless and harmless, the sons of God, without rebuke, *in the midst of a crooked and perverse generation*, among whom (they) shine as lights in the world" (Phi. 1:14-15). May he help us to do so.

∽∾

January 6

"What manner of man is this" (Matthew 8:27)

Even the winds and the sea obeyed our Lord. Such was never before seen among men, and it elicited from them the startling inquiry as to what manner of man he was. Well might they wonder at a man who could tell the wind to stop blowing and it would obey him; tell the waves to cease their raging and they would immediately become calm and serene; tell the lame to rise and walk, and they would take up their bed, and not only walk, but leap and run; tell the sick to be whole and they would there and then be free of their malady; and even tell the dead to arise and they would readily obey his command. Indeed, this was such manner of man as had never before been born of woman. This was God manifest in the flesh, and great is the mystery (1 Tim. 3:16).

Christ was the only man on the earth who was without sin; the only person to be conceived of the Holy Ghost, and born of a virgin. He was holy, harmless, undefiled, and separate from sinners (Heb. 7:26), and yet he who knew no sin was made sin for his people, that they might be made the righteousness of God in Him (2 Cor. 5:21). This is such a marvelous arrangement that it could only have been conceived in the mind of the Deity. It can only be revealed by the Spirit, and it can only be received by faith.

Christ never spent an idle moment, for he was ever in communion with his heavenly Father. He never spoke an idle word, never had an idle thought, and never did an idle deed. In a word, he always did those things that please the Father (John 8:29). He knew the thoughts of men before they spoke, for he knew all things (John 16:30; 21:17).

It was said of him, "Never man spake like this man" (John 7:46), and how true that was. What a man! And not just a man; he was the God-man, the Savior of his people. And he not only *was* but he *is*; "The same yesterday, and today, and forever" (Heb. 13:8). We hope to see him one sweet day, and be with him forever!

❧

January 7

"The devils also believe, and tremble" (James 2:19)

James shows us that true faith will be attended with works that are consistent with that faith. Anyone can make a *profession* of faith in Christ, but if they do not really possess it then their *works* will expose their insincerity. This is the primary means given to the church by which they may protect themselves from imposters and keep God's house pure from unregenerate men and women. "Ye shall know them by their fruits" (Matt. 7:16).

Even the fallen demonic spirit-beings believe there is a God because they have too much evidence to deny it. They even know that there is a day appointed for their torment (Matt. 8:29). But their belief is solely an *intellectual* matter. It is a far cry from the faith of God's regenerated people who love him and trust him and are willing to give their lives in his service and for his cause. God's people believe and are *comforted*; they believe and *trust*; they believe and *rejoice*; but the devils believe and *tremble*; they believe and *dread*; they believe and *quake*; they believe and fear a certain future punishment.

Demonic spirits were very active in the day when Christ walked among men, and they are still active today, but they, as well as Satan, are under his complete control. They can go no further than he *suffers* them to go (Matt. 8:28-34).

The devils could not remain in the wild Gadarene when Christ commanded them to come out, and neither could they go into the herd of swine without asking, and receiving, his leave. It should be of much comfort to us that he has such absolute control over them.

Yes, the devils *believe,* but they do not, and cannot, believe as do the saints. Their works are evil, and only evil, and that continually. And the best they have to say to Christ is, "What have we to do with thee, Jesus, thou Son of God? Art thou come hither to torment us before the time?" (Matt. 8:29).

January 8

"I was shapen in iniquity; and in sin did my mother conceive me"
(Psalm 51:5)

David here speaks of the corrupt nature he inherited from his first parent Adam. "By one man (Adam) sin entered into the world, and death by sin; and so death passed upon all men, for that all have sinned" (Romans 5:2). All of us are sinners by nature, *even from the moment of conception*, because Adam's polluted blood flows in the veins of our parents, and in their parents before them, and so on back to Adam. His sin is imputed to all those who were represented in him (the human family), just as the righteousness of Christ is imputed to all those who were represented in him (the elect family). This is shown very clearly by the apostle in Romans 5:19 when he says, "For as by one man's (Adam's) disobedience many were made sinners, so by the obedience of one (Christ) shall many be made righteous."

It is difficult to look into the face of a precious little infant, especially when it is smiling and cooing, and realize that all the existing seeds of evil dwell within its little breast, and that unless God in His mercy intervenes in the course of nature, hell will be its eventual doom. Paul tells us in Romans 6:23 that "the wages of sin is death." Therefore every little babe who dies in infancy is a testimony to the fact that they come into this world with a sinful nature. They could not have died if they had not been sinners by nature. And the fact that the others, who do not die in infancy, all grow up to be sinners, is likewise a clear testimony to the same thing. We all grow up to be sinners because of the fact that we are sinners by nature. We do not become sinners because we sin, but we sin because we are sinners. It is our nature to do so.

God visits his people in time and gives them a new nature that loves righteousness and hates evil. If he did not do this they too would go to their graves loving the world and its sinful ways. They would die in their sins just as do the wicked, or non-elect, and eternal torment would be their doom. If we have a sweet hope in Christ it is because we are among those upon whom he showed mercy, and we therefore owe him a life of service and praise.

January 9

"And at midnight Paul and Silas prayed, and sang praises unto God" (Acts 16:25)

For doing no more than obeying God's direction, Paul and Silas were beaten with many stripes and cast into the inner prison at Philippi with their feet bound firmly in the stocks. Consider for a moment what an uncomfortable position it would be to have the flesh on your back made raw and bloody from severe beating, and to have your ankles chaffed with iron stocks, while you sat on the cold, damp floor of a dark, lonely dungeon, wide awake at midnight. All this would be compounded by the fact that you were innocent of any crime, yet surrounded with some of the most vile and unprincipled characters on the earth. Normally speaking, one would think that there would not be much singing and praying going on at such a time, yet that was exactly what Paul and Silas were doing. The secret of their happiness on this occasion is well expressed by John Newton in the song, "How Tedious And Tasteless The Hours." He says, *While blest with a sense of His love, A palace a toy would appear; And prisons would palaces prove, If Jesus would dwell with me there.*

The key to being completely reconciled to the will of the Lord, no matter what our outward circumstances may be, lies in having the felt presence of the Lord. If we have that, nothing else matters. Again, to use the words of Newton, *It soothes our sorrows, heals our wounds, and drives away our fears.* Many of the martyred saints of old, even while tied to the stake with flames licking at their flesh, have been blest to breathe out their lives in joyful praise to the Lord.

None of us knows what lies ahead for us in this world, but of this one thing we may be assured: no matter what we may have to endure, if the Lord abides feelingly near us we will be able to face it in a way that becomes those who profess godliness.

Paul and Silas were in the way of duty when they were persecuted, and thus their consciences were clear. This alone is a great help to God's people in their times of trial, but when they can also enjoy the Lord's felt presence they too can pray and sing praises no matter how dark their outward circumstances may be.

January 10

"The words of the Lord are pure words" (Psalm 12:6)

Oh! blessed word, what a treasure thou art! We can never be thankful enough that the Lord has given us such a wonderful volume as is the Bible and that the words thereof have been kept pure through many centuries of time. David says, "Thou shalt keep them, O Lord, thou shalt preserve them from this generation for ever." And thus he has kept them and preserved them unto this day, and will do so for as long as the world shall stand.

Satan has vented all his power and wrath against the words of the Lord, from the time of his appearance to Eve in the Garden of Eden until now, and will continue to do so until that awful day when he and all is cohorts are cast into the lake of fire. But none of his efforts have succeeded in totally stamping them out, and in fact, the more he has sought to destroy them, the more they have been published abroad.

Speaking of the words of the Lord, Job expressed the sentiments of multitudes when he said he had esteemed them *more* than his necessary food (Job 23:12). At the time Job spoke these words he had very few, if any, of the words of the Lord on the printed page, but he no doubt had enough of them hidden in his heart that they were a source of great delight to him.[1]

David has a great deal to say in the 119th Psalm about the word of the Lord and of the value he placed upon it. In verse 105 he said it was a lamp unto his feet and a light unto his path, and in the 140th verse he said, "Thy word is very pure: therefore thy servant loveth it." Many others of God's people have likewise found it to be a continual help to them and have for many years treasured it and adsorbed themselves in its precious truth, some of them reading it through many times.

"Thy word have I hid in mine heart, that I might not sin against thee. Blessed art thou, O Lord: teach me thy statutes" (Psalm 119:11).

---

[1] *Job* is the oldest book in the Bible and the first of the poetical books.

January 11

"To whom then will ye liken me, or shall I be equal?
(Isaiah 40:25)

There is no being to whom we can liken God, for He is one of a kind. He is the *only* self-existent, uncreated and self-sufficient being in existence. *He only hath immortality, dwelling in the light which no man can approach unto; whom no man hath seen, nor can see"* (1 Tim. 6:16). No other being can, in the least degree, begin to approach this description. The gods of men die with them. Such gods are created in the depraved minds of men and dwell in darkness with them. They, like Dagon, fall on their faces unless propped up by their makers (1 Sam. 5:3).

There are religions in the world that declare God to be composed of flesh and bones the same as we, but numerous scriptures show this to be false. David said, "Whither shall I go from thy spirit? or whither shall I flee from thy presence? If I ascend up into heaven, thou art there: if I make my bed in hell, behold, thou art there." If God were composed of a body the same as ours, what would have prevented David from fleeing from his presence?

Moses said, "The Lord he is God in heaven above, and upon earth beneath: there is none else" (Deut. 4:39). Again, if God were confined to a body such as ours, how could He be in heaven and on earth at the same time? Indeed, who could we compare to him? Who could be thought to be his equal, or even *close* to his equal? Where could we go to find such an one?

Who but God can speak and it is done? Who but God can make a flea, to say nothing of a universe so large it defies man's feeble comprehension? Who but God is so great that he fills all space, and yet condescends to dwell within the hearts of his people? Who but God can quicken vile sinners, turn them from their iniquities, and make them his servants? Who but God can raise the dead out of their graves and carry them safely to heaven? Who but God can cast the devil and his angels into a never-ending hell? None! No, not one! "On earth is not his equal!" There is no one to whom we can liken Him! "Let the redeemed of the Lord say so" (Psalm 107:2).

January 12

"He must increase, but I must decrease" (John 3:30)

To those who envied the success of the ministry of Jesus over that of John the Baptist, John would have them to understand that he rejoiced in the works of Christ and was aware that he would soon pass from the scenes of time, but that Christ and his accomplishments in the redemption of his elect would endure forever, both in the courts of heaven and in the hearts and minds of those for whom he died.

John knew that his own influence among men would, for the most part, last but a short time after his departure, but that the influence of Christ, the effects of his work, and the continued benefits of his intercession for the saints after his ascension into heaven, would go on and on, and that the fame thereof would be spread to a greater and greater degree as time went along. John and his work as the forerunner of Christ would soon fade into the background and be little thought of among men, but Christ would be magnified more and more as the church of his founding took root and spread through the earth.

Among men there was not a greater than John the Baptist, with the exception of the one perfect God-man, Christ; yet, in comparison to him John was not worthy to loose his shoe latchets (Matt. 11:11; John 1:27). Though Christ, in human form, was born *after* John the Baptist, yet in his divine nature he was *before* John. In fact, as the Son of God, he existed from all eternity. John expressed it thusly: "He that cometh *after* me is preferred *before* me: for he *was* before me" (John 1:15).

Each one of us must *decrease*, but Christ must *increase*. Our life is quickly fading away, and when we are gone we will soon be forgotten of men, but Christ lives on from generation to generation, and the great mountain of praise that has been offered to him continues to grow as more and more of his people are born into the world and brought to the knowledge of him and his glory as the Savior and Intercessor of his elect family. The more his blessed name is magnified, the more it should please each of us.

❧

January 13

"The fool hath said in his heart, There is no God" (Psalm 14:1)

That there is a God is so plain a reality it is surprising that anyone would deny it. All creation declares the existence of the Creator, and in a passive sense it proclaims his glory. An unfathomable creation bespeaks an unfathomable God. "The heavens declare the glory of God; and the firmament showeth his handiwork" (Psalm 19:1). This is a wonderful truth, but not everyone will acknowledge it.

Those who say in their hearts, "There is no God," tell us some important things about themselves. We need not say anything with regard to what God calls them, but we can say with certainty that they are without excuse for their unbelief (Romans 1:20). And we can also say with equal certainty that they have no personal acquaintance with God. Fortunately I have not known very many people who were willing to openly proclaim their infidelity. It takes a person with no fear of God whatsoever to brazenly assert that the Deity does not exist. I tremble for those who tremble not for themselves.

It is a thing to be wondered at that anyone can observe the world around them and say there is no God. The intricacy of the human eye alone is enough to astound the wisest and most skilled of physicians. No man, no matter how far advanced in secular learning, can explain what life is. David said, "I will praise thee; for I am fearfully and wonderfully made: marvelous are thy works; and that my soul knoweth right well" (Psalm 139:14).

David was a man acquainted with God from His youth. He lived and died in faith, as did all the patriarchs of old (Heb. 11:13). This also is one of the most positive and unmistakable proofs of God and his work in their lives. The faith that would not fail them in life, did not fail them in death, and they could not relinquish it until it was swallowed up in full fruition. How blest were they! How blest have been millions of others, and how blest are we, if the Lord has made Himself known to us in covenant love!

January 14

"Stand ye in the ways, and see, and ask for the old paths..."
(Jeremiah 6:16)

The Lord speaks to his people and instructs them as to how they may find rest to their souls. There are many *ways* in this world, but there is but one *good* way, and it will only be found in "the old paths." If we choose that good way it will go well with us, and if not we will find that "the way of transgressors is hard" (Prov. 13:15).

With regard to this good way Israel said, "We will not walk therein," and consequently the Lord told them that he would bring evil upon them. "I will lay stumblingblocks before this people," said he, "and the fathers and the sons together shall fall upon them." And, true to his promise, he brought the sword of cruel enemies against them, and fear was on every side. Sadly, many today are following Israel's pernicious example.

Simply stated, the old paths consist of the way that the Lord has laid down for his people to walk in. It is a *good* way because it is the *Lord's* way. It is a *good* way because it is the *right* way. It is not sufficient merely to *ask* for the old paths wherein is the good way, but that way must be *followed;* it must be *lived.* It is a *narrow* way, and it is entered by a *strait* gate, but with all its difficulties it is still far better than any of the alternatives.

Many of God's people seem to have a strong propensity for growing tired of the old paths, and introducing new ways. But all they need is what God has given them. He equipped his church with everything it needed, and any additions to it are superfluous and will only do harm. The introduction of new things is an affront to God, for in effect it says he was not wise enough to know what his church would need through all ages of its history.

May the Lord help us to be satisfied with the goodness of his house (Psalm 65:4), and to walk in a "plain path" (Psalm 27:11), even though it causes us to be looked upon with contempt by the world. Only in this way will we find true rest for our souls.

❦

January 15

"Man is born unto trouble" (Job 5:7)

I have had many wonderful blessings during my life, but interspersed, all along the way, has been great trouble. It seems a great miracle to me that I survived childhood, for I suffered terribly with asthma from infancy. I was into my teen years before I had any medication, and its side-effects also gave me a lot of misery. Modern medications have given me a great deal of relief from that problem most of the time since I was about forty-five, but I still have to keep it in my system year-round. So that alone has been a lifelong battle.

Along the way I have encountered a great many other health problems and have had several surgeries. I have had stitches in at least thirteen different places, and more than once in one of those places. And in addition to these physical troubles which have been a continual source of distress all my life, I have also had a great many soul-troubles as I sometimes speak of them. Also the care of churches, and dealing with church-related problems, has often been a source of much heartache and grief. These and numerous other distresses of my own, as well as those I have observed in others of my acquaintances, have certainly proven to me the truth expressed in the above text.

Job said, "Man that is born of a woman is of few days and full of trouble" (Job 14:1). I have often heard unenlightened men preach that we can avoid troubles if we live right and have enough faith, especially if we send men like them enough money. But the Scriptures will not support such a notion. David said, "Many are the afflictions of the righteous: but the Lord delivereth him out of them all" (Psalm 34:19).

We are all great sinners by nature, and as Zophar told Job, "God exacteth of us less than our iniquity deserves" (Job 11:6). In all my troubles I have tried to keep in mind that things have been much better with me than they might justly have been. And too, I can always look around and see others in much worse conditions. I also try to remember that if I had never had difficulties, I would never have experienced the many sweet deliverances that have otherwise come my way. And who can say how much delightful communion with the Lord I might otherwise have missed?

January 16

"That we may be delivered from unreasonable and wicked men"
(2 Thessalonians 3:2)

The apostles of Christ had not been given a commission to go to ungodly men with the gospel, but rather they knew that "all men have not faith," and therefore they prayed, and desired others to pray, that they might be delivered *from* such characters. According to popular religion it is precisely these kind of people that need to hear the gospel so that they may have an opportunity to "get saved." However, as strange as it may appear to some, such an idea is never advanced in the Scriptures.

The "things of the Spirit of God" are foolishness to unreasonable and wicked men, and they can neither know them nor receive them, because they do not possess spiritual discernment or understanding (1 Cor. 2:14). Herein lays one of the main fallacies of Arminianism. It argues that all men have the ability to exercise faith if they will only choose to do so; that they *can* believe on Christ if only the gospel is preached to them. But this is clearly disproved by many Scriptures, such as the one just referenced.

Popular religionists will use such scriptures as Matthew 11:28 and apply them to all the unsaved, but that is a very obvious misapplication. It does not say, "Come unto me all ye that are ungodly and I will give you eternal life," but rather, "Come unto me *all ye that labor and are heavy laden, and I will give you rest.*" This does not describe those who are dead in sin, but it describes those in whose hearts the Lord has already performed a work of grace, and it tells them that Christ is the answer to whatever burdens of guilt, fear or distress they are laden with.

No, the gospel was never intended for wicked men, but for God's people who have a hunger and thirst for righteousness; those who have been stripped of self-righteousness and made "poor in spirit." "The poor have the gospel preached to *them*" (Matt. 11:5; Luke 7:22). No man can come to Christ unless he has been thus drawn by the Spirit (John 6:44). Christ does not bring *life* and *immortality* through the gospel, but He brings those things *to light* through the gospel. And they can only be *brought to light* in those who already have them. The gospel, as applied to the heart by the Holy Spirit, feeds and instructs the living. It does not raise the dead.

January 17

"If ye live after the flesh, ye shall die" (Romans 8:13)

The death the apostle speaks of here is not eternal death, for he was addressing *brethren* who were members of the church at Rome. God's people may fall so as to lose a close communion with Him, but they cannot fall so as to be eternally doomed and damned, for Christ has said that those to whom he gives eternal life *shall never perish* (John 10:28) nor be plucked out of his or his Father's hands. The death of the text is a death to the joys that accompany a life of godliness.

Once God's people are born of the Spirit they cannot go back into a state of unregeneracy or death in sins, but some of them have followed a fleshly course to the extent, and for such a length of time, that it has greatly blunted their spiritual lives and, at least for a season, stripped them of all heavenly joys and brought them into such a state of darkness and coldness that they lost sight of the blessedness they once knew and were left to wander in gloom and virtual hopelessness. This, to a child of God, is death of a grievous sort. Some have drifted so far away from God that they lost some of the gifts and abilities God had given them, and even though they later returned to the timely fold they were never again as useful in the militant kingdom as they could have been had they not strayed.

The only way we can avoid such an eventuality is to mortify the deeds of the body by the help of the Spirit. If we underestimate the corruption of our flesh and the danger we place ourselves in when we dally with sin, there is little chance that we will not stumble spiritually and be severely injured. We are the loser every time we walk after the flesh, but if we *live* after the flesh for any length of time there is a death awaiting us that will bring us much anguish of soul and can possibly even issue in *corporeal* death.

May the Lord help us to live close to him, seeking first his kingdom and his righteousness, for if we do not we will be on dangerous ground, and we will pay a high price for our folly.

࿇

January 18

"I would not live alway" (Job 7:16)

Job's severe afflictions caused him for a time to loathe life and to feel that his days were vanity. Many of us, under some of our most distressing adversities, have, for brief periods at least, had similar feelings. Generally speaking God's people do not have to dwell long in this "present evil world" before they realize that it is not a place they would want to live forever. They soon find themselves to be "strangers and pilgrims on the earth" (Heb. 11:13), and that there are many things worse than death.

When Job said, "I would not live alway," he was, of course talking about life on earth. He, like all God's people, had a sweet hope of living *forever* in the glory world after this life. Who among us do not desire to "live always" with the Lord after the sorrows of this present life have ended? That is the great object of our hope, and we look forward to it with sweet anticipation.

I believe it was more of a mercy than a judgment to Adam that he was prevented from returning to the Garden of Eden and partaking of the tree of life. How distressing is the thought of living forever in a fallen state and facing a never-ending stream of resultant calamities, heartaches and miseries! "It is appointed unto man once to die" (Heb. 9:27), and those of us who have a hope in Christ should be thankful that it is so. We have been crucified to the world, and the world unto us (Gal. 6:14), and while the ungodly find their chief delight in worldly things, we "desire a better country, that is, an heavenly" (Heb. 11:16).

Shortly after I began writing this piece I received a letter from an old brother in Texas in which he related hearing a preacher say, "Everyone is afraid to die." The old brother stated that he disagreed with that assertion, and so do I. I have some dread of the sufferings I might have to endure *before* I die, but dying itself I do not dread. And by dying I mean the moment when life leaves the body. I have a "good hope through grace" that when life leaves this body all my troubles will be over and I will be happy forevermore. But so far as this present world is concerned, I most certainly "would not live alway."

January 19

"He shall see of the travail of his soul, and shall be satisfied."
(Isaiah 53:11)

We have often heard this verse quoted with the little word "of" left out; but this changes the meaning altogether and misses the central point. If all Christ had seen had been the *travail* involved in his soul-sufferings without seeing "of" that travail, or what it would accomplish, there would have been nothing to be satisfied with. But he saw that his sufferings and death would result in the eventual housing of every member of the elect family in heaven, and this was a source of great satisfaction to him. His travail, as considered in the abstract, would have brought him nothing but grief, but as viewed in the broad scope of its purpose and intent, he was satisfied with what he saw.

It is certain that he did indeed foresee the sufferings that lay ahead of him before he went to the cross, and in his human nature he would have avoided that travail if there had been any way agreeable to the Father for him to have done so, but he was perfectly submissive to his Father's will. We see him in the garden of Gethsemane as he "began to be very sorrowful and very heavy" and said, "My soul is exceeding sorrowful, even unto death." He then prayed, "O my Father, if it be possible, let this cup pass from me: nevertheless not as I will, but as thou wilt" (Matt. 26:37-39).

The end or outcome of his travail is spoken of in Hebrews 12:2 as "the joy that was set before him." It was because of this joy that he "endured the cross, despising the shame." But if he had seen that even one of those for whom he suffered would be eternally lost, he could not have been "satisfied."

If you had ten children drowning and you saved all of them but one, would you be satisfied? No, indeed! You would be too grief-stricken over the loss of the one! Even so, if Christ had saved all of his children but one, he too could not have been satisfied. Praise be, he finished the work his Father gave him to do, and as a result he will, in the last day, raise up all those the Father gave him without the loss of one (John 6:38-39).

January 20

"Lovers of pleasures more than lovers of God" (2 Timothy 3:4)

The description the apostle gives of "the last days" seems to fit our own present day very well; but by "the last days" I do not know whether Paul is speaking of that period shortly before the return of Christ, or of the same "last days" mentioned in Acts 2:17, Hebrews 1:2, or of the "last time" spoken of by John (1 John 2:18).

Job said Christ (the Redeemer) would stand upon the earth "at the latter day" (Job 19:25), and there is disagreement among Bible readers as to whether this refers to the gospel day (age), or to the second coming of Christ. Whichever way that may be, he has already stood upon the earth in the latter day, because we have been in the latter day ever since His first advent. Whether he will "stand upon the earth" when he comes again does not seem relevant to me. The thing that appeals to me most is the fact that his people will be caught up together in the clouds, to meet him in the air, and so shall they ever be with him (1 Thess. 4:17).

I am sure that in every age of time there have been those who have met the description given in 2 Timothy 3:1-5. However, it seems to me that the things mentioned there apply to a time when such characteristics will be prevalent throughout society. It should be our concern that we not be found among those who are guilty of these things, for they constitute a list of iniquities that are very abhorrent to God.

How awful is the condition of an individual who loves worldly pleasures more than he loves God, to say nothing of being guilty of all the other things mentioned in the text! It seems to me that loving pleasures more than loving God is a product of self-love. It stems from a desire to fulfill the lusts of the flesh or the selfish cravings of carnal nature. The world is full of such pleasures, and here in America that is true on a much larger scale than ever before.

There are endless temptations to lure God's people away from the strait and narrow way that leads to life. There is only one other way, and it leads to destruction. May the Lord help us to avoid it as we would the plague.

January 21

"The heart of the sons of men is full of evil" (Ecclesiastes 9:3)

The doctrine of Total Depravity is so clearly taught in the word of God that it is a wonder more people do not see it. But the hearts of men are so blunted and blinded by this very depravity that they do not have a proper concept of the actual depths of their own native corruption nor of the "exceeding sinfulness of sin." Even Job desired to know how many his iniquities were, and prayed, "Make me to know my transgressions and my sin" (Job 13:23). Jeremiah said, "The heart is deceitful above all things, and desperately wicked," and then asked, "Who can know it?" Only God can truly, accurately, and fully see and know the unvarnished depths of man's wickedness by nature.

No one can go very far in understanding the Scriptures unless he has a reasonably clear concept of the native depravity of mankind. The apostle Paul, in writing to children of God who had been quickened into divine life, said, "We all (*without exception*) had our conversation in times past in the lusts of our flesh, fulfilling the desires of the flesh and of the mind; and were by nature the children of wrath, even as others" (Eph. 2:3). What a profound and enlightening statement this is! Oh, that all those who are presently in bondage to popular religion would let it sink down into their hearts and learn its invaluable lesson!

All of Arminianism's claims in favor of man's innate abilities and virtues are a product of its ignorance of man's depravity. Christ said no man could come unto him except they be drawn by the Father (John 6:44), but Arminianism says all men already possess all the abilities they need to come to him at any time they may choose. These two positions are poles apart, but Christ was right and popular religion is wrong. May God enlighten his people who have been led astray by false doctrine.

ھஜ

January 22

"Let not the wise man glory in his wisdom" (Jeremiah 9:23)

I suppose most of us have seen men who gloried in what they were, or at least in what they *perceived* themselves to be. Truly wise men are not very apt to glory in their wisdom, but some men, because they have considerable formal education, equate that education with wisdom, and consequently glory in this perceived quality. Many men who have achieved some degree of authority or position in society, tend to be at least to some degree swelled with pride because of it. And many of those who have come into great wealth are quite apt to let that advantage affect them adversely and to become somewhat pompous. But neither the wise, the mighty, nor the wealthy have any just grounds to glory in anything other than the Lord.

In 1 Corinthians 4:7 the apostle Paul asks three very probing and sobering questions, and the correct answer to them gives us the greatest reasons why no one should glory in who they are, or in what their position is, or in what they possess. (1) "Who maketh thee to differ from another?" (2) "And what hast thou that thou didst not receive?" (3) "If thou didst receive it, why dost thou glory, as if thou hadst not received it?" The answer to the third question is, *Men glory in what they have received because they either do not **realize** they received it of God; or they do not **believe** they received it of God, or else they have lost sight of the fact that they received it of Him.*

A person who possesses wisdom, has it because God gave it. They did not produce it themselves. A person who has authority and position in the world, is in that place because God has so blessed him. And a person who has wealth, has it because God gave the increase. They may take credit to themselves and claim that it was because of their industry, good business sense, and diligent labor, and it is indeed true that these things play an important part in some people's riches, but ultimately God is due the credit for any good thing that any of us possess. It is very wrong for us to glory as though we had not received it from him. And we make a grave mistake if we think otherwise. Paul said, "He that glorieth, let him glory in the Lord" (1 Cor. 1:31).

January 23

"We will not serve thy gods" (Daniel 3:18)

When Shadrach, Meshach, and Abednego would not serve the gods of king Nebuchadnezzar nor worship the golden image he had set up, the king told them that they would be cast into a burning fiery furnace. "And who is that God," said he, "that shall deliver you out of my hands?"

These three Hebrews were very plain and forthright in their reply, that the God they served was *able* to deliver them from the furnace and that he *would* deliver them out of the hand of the king, but even if he did not, they would not serve Nebuchadnezzar's gods nor worship the golden image he had set up.

As all Bible readers know, the faithfulness of the three Hebrews was greatly rewarded and they came through the fire unscathed, while those who cast them into the furnace were consumed by the heat.

In all ages of time the Lord has *reserved unto Himself* a complete number of individuals who have not, and will not, bow their knees to the false gods of the world (1Kings 19:18; Romans 11:1-5). "Even so then at this present time also there is a remnant according to the election of grace," says the apostle.

It is good to know that God has not, and will not, leave himself without witness, even though in times past he suffered all nations to walk in their own ways (Acts 14:16-17). Though the vast majority of the world today is still shrouded in spiritual darkness and ignorance, the remnant of faithful followers still exists in the world, even though they dwell in relative obscurity in the earth and are not known by the world (1 John 3:1). They are *in* the world (John 13:1) but they are not *of* the world (John 15:19).

What a blessed privilege it is to have such a relationship with the Lord that we are willing to submit to the abuses of a perishing world, and to even give up our natural lives rather than bow down to their false gods! Happy is such a people. May the Lord give us grace to always stand firm in that number.

৯৶

January 24

"We were dead in sins" (Ephesians 2:5)

I once heard of a debate between a Primitive Baptist minister and a "Reverend" from one of the popular churches. The "Reverend" made his argument that the way the plan of salvation works is like a man falling into a well and the preacher coming along and letting down the gospel bucket. "The man can either accept the chance of salvation and get in the bucket, or he can reject it and be lost," said the man.

When it came the Elder's turn to speak and he got to the point about the so-called plan of salvation, he said, "There's just one problem with my worthy opponent's argument, and that is, when the man fell into the well, it killed him, and now he *can't* get in the bucket."

That is exactly the case with Adam in the Garden of Eden. When he ate of the forbidden fruit he fell from his innocence into a state of death in sins, so that even if it were possible to "let the gospel bucket down to him," he couldn't get in. In man's fallen state, while in an unregenerate condition, "there is none that seeketh after God," and "there is none that doeth good, no, not one" (Rom. 3:11,12).

When I was a boy we had a cat to fall in our open, dug well on a couple of occasions (not the same cat), and in neither case did the fall kill the cat. These cats were perfectly aware of their desperate situation, and they called for help rather loudly. In neither case did we have to try to persuade them to get in the bucket when we let it down. They were more than happy to get on board and be drawn up out of that horrible pit. But suppose the fall had killed them. Do you suppose they would have been interested in getting in the bucket?

Christ said, "No man can come to me, except the Father which hath sent me draw him" (John 6:44). A lot of people still haven't learned what that simple language means.

လ၁ၡ

January 25

"If God be for us, who can be against us?" (Romans 8:31)

This grand declaration follows upon the apostle's teaching on the doctrine of predestination and its accompanying adjuncts and consequences. The obvious conclusion to a person's being predestinated is that God is *for* them and therefore no one can be effectually *against* them. To draw any other conclusion from the context is to wrest the Scriptures, for the true meaning is crystal clear.

All the powers of hell are arrayed against the children of God, but that does not in the least degree change the fact that they were predestinated. That destiny is conformity to the image of God's Son (v. 29) and the calling, justification and final glorification that follows is just as certain as if it had already occurred, and therefore it is expressed in the past tense by the apostle.

The persistent harassment that God's people have to endure at the hands of Satan as long as they live in this world, will not and cannot prevent God from calling them at his own appointed time. It cannot hinder their justification nor thwart their glorification. All these works are performed by the Lord no matter how strong and bitter may be the opposition of Satan. The children of God are secure in Christ because they are "kept by His power through faith unto salvation ready to be revealed in the last day" (1 Peter 1:5).

The saints may so behave in this life as to lose *fellowship* with God and consequently to lose the *joy* of their relationship with him, but they cannot *destroy* that relationship. Just as our relationship with our natural father could not be destroyed no matter how disobedient we were to him, so our relationship with our heavenly father cannot be destroyed by our disobedience. Our *fellowship* with him can be interrupted or lost, but not our *relationship*. Any other arrangement would have resulted in the final and total fall of all men "for in many things we offend all" (James 3:2): that is, in many things we are all offenders. If our eternal standing with God depended on our faithfulness our case would be hopeless.

January 26

"I know that my redeemer liveth" (Job 19:25)

Some two thousand five hundred years before the incarnation of Christ, Job was assured that his Lord was indeed alive, and that he was his Redeemer. And not only was he assured of these great truths, but he also had knowledge of a number of other glorious realities, such as that Christ would one day stand upon the earth; that though his own skin and body should be destroyed by worms, yet *in his flesh* he would see God; and that he would see him *for himself,* with his *own* eyes and not someone else's. All this and much more Job had some clear knowledge of long before the Bible as we have it was written and compiled.

It is interesting to observe that some of the most precious truths that God's believing people of today hold so dear to their hearts were known and loved thousands of years ago by others to whom the Lord revealed them. Our Redeemer did indeed *stand upon the earth* in the beginning of this present latter day dispensation, and he did indeed *redeem* his people, including Job and all the other saints who lived in the long ago. And we of today who look for his second personal coming believe just as firmly as did the saints of old that though we may die before his return, yet we shall, in the resurrection, see him with our own bodily eyes in our own glorified bodies, not in an *exchanged* body, but in a *changed* body (Phi. 3:21).

Hundreds of years before Christ came into the world, the Psalmist David had the assurance that he would one day behold the Lord's face in righteousness, and that he would be satisfied when he awoke with the likeness of his blessed Savior (Psalm 17:15). This has been the hope of God's humble poor down through the centuries.

In perfect harmony with the saints of old the apostle John said, "Beloved, now are we the sons of God, and it doth not yet appear what we shall be: but we know that, when he (Christ) shall appear, we shall be like him; for we shall see him as he is" (1 John 3:2). Surely having this hope in us should make us want to purify ourselves, "even as he is pure," and live just as close to him as possible.

January 27

"As thy days, so shall thy strength be" (Deuteronomy 33:25)

To us as individuals the greatest proof of the truth of this promise is the fact that no matter how long we have lived upon the earth our strength has been equal to the demands of each day. The very fact that we are still alive proves the point. There was never a day when strength totally failed us and we did not have the grace to surmount the obstacles thereof. It did not matter how severe the trials nor how many of them there were, we survived them, and therefore the promise of God to Israel of old has proven true in our own case.

One of the greatest mistakes we make as poor, weak mortals, is to try to deal with tomorrow's troubles before they come. Sometimes our imaginations run away with us and we distress ourselves with peradventures. That is, we concern ourselves with what *may* be. We think that, at the present rate, such and such will surely transpire, and oh, what a grievous thing it will be! But when we do this we go counter to the instruction of Christ when he said, "Take therefore no thought for the morrow: for the morrow shall take thought for the things of itself. Sufficient unto the day is the evil *(trouble)* thereof" (Matt. 6:34).

In other words, today's difficulties are enough for us to deal with, without distressing ourselves about what may happen tomorrow. We need to take things as they come and not forget to ask the Lord's help as we attempt to handle them in a way that brings honor to his name.

Let us remember that the key to successfully facing what lies ahead, whether it be today or tomorrow, is not in our *own* strength, but in the Lord and the strength he has promised us. Let us also consider that the patriarchs of old, the great champions of faith, "out of *weakness* were made strong" (Heb. 11:34), and in *that* strength they "waxed valiant in fight," and "turned to flight the armies of the aliens."

We simply need not try to face life leaning upon the feeble and fickle arm of flesh. We are much too weak and our foes are much too strong and formidable. But rather, let us go forth *leaning upon our Beloved*, for it is in him alone that we will rise triumphant over the great mountains of trouble that lie in our path.

January 28

"Be not wise in your own conceits" (Romans 12:16)

A deceased friend of mine used to jokingly say, "The thing I admire most about myself is that I am not conceited." But in all seriousness, one of the strongest traits of fallen human nature is self-admiration and self-esteem. This attitude and disposition is highly promoted in our society. I have seen Jessie Jackson on T.V. in classrooms exhorting the children to repeat after him, "I *am* somebody," in an effort to build up their self-esteem. Much of the wickedness of men is now blamed, not on their corrupt nature, but on their lack of self-esteem, and much is made of the argument that if criminals can be taught to esteem themselves more highly they will quit being criminals.

The Lord is fully aware of the natural propensities of men, and instead of seeking to build up their self-esteem he inspired Paul to write and exhort his people not to think of themselves more highly than they ought to think, but to think soberly (Romans 12:3) and not to be wise in their own conceits. He saw that *low* self-esteem was not the real danger, but rather too *high* a self-esteem.

It is strange to the ears of men who know nothing of human depravity to hear anyone speak of themselves as did Paul when he said, "O wretched man that I am! Who shall deliver me from the body of this death?" (Romans 7:24), or when he said, "I am the least of the apostles, that am not meet to be called an apostle," or when he said he was less than the least of all saints (Eph. 3:8), or the chief of sinners (1 Tim. 1:15). All such expressions come from an understanding of what men are by nature. One cannot become too much enamored with his own importance and worth as long as he sees himself in the light of the pure and holy law of God. It drastically changes his whole perspective. "We are the circumcision, which worship God in the spirit, and rejoice in Christ Jesus, *and have no confidence in the flesh*" (Phi. 3:3).

Paul expressed the proper view of himself in 1 Corinthians 15:10 when he said, "By the grace of God I am what I am." Likewise, if there is any good in *us* God is due the credit. "The flesh profiteth nothing" (John 6:63).

January 29

"He that is mighty hath done to me great things" (Luke 1:49)

For Mary to be chosen from among all the women on the earth to carry the Christ child in her womb was a great thing, but it was an even greater thing to carry him in her heart. As outstanding and unique a blessing as it was for her to be the mother of Christ, I am sure Mary would have been the first to agree that her *spiritual* relationship with Jesus as her Lord was of far greater importance than was her *natural* relationship with him.

If the Lord has taken up his abode in our heart it is a great thing; a wonderfully great and glorious thing; yea, an unspeakably precious thing, for that means he is ours and we are his. It is *very* important that we so live as to have *fellowship* with him, but it is *vitally* important that we have a *relationship* with him. There can be no *fellowship* unless there is first a *relationship*. We have nothing to do with bringing about the *relationship*, but we do have something to do with enjoying *fellowship* with him after the relationship has been made manifest in regeneration. All God's elect have a *relationship* with him, but because of disobedience some of them have little *fellowship* with him.

All who have a hope in Christ could with propriety adopt the language of Mary and say, "He that is mighty hath done to me great things." Divine life is the *greatest* thing, but bringing that immortality to light so that we can enjoy the possession of it in this life is also a great thing. It would do us no good here in time to be a child of God if he never made it known to us.

It is a "great thing" to be able to see the kingdom of God (John 3:3), for that means we have been born again, or born of his Spirit. It is also a great thing to have a part in the militant kingdom here in the world and to enjoy the fellowship of other dear saints of like precious faith. And, in fact, every favor we receive at the hands of our merciful God is a great thing. There are some things we think of as *smaller* blessings, and as we have indicated, some blessings are indeed greater than others. But in reality they are all great, for they come from One who is mighty, and they greatly benefit us. May he help us to view them in that light.

January 30

"He is despised and rejected of men...he was despised, and we esteemed him not" (Isaiah 53:3)

This beautiful prophecy of Christ tells us that he both *is* and *was* despised. That being the case, we are left to ask why this is so. Why *is* he despised, and why *was* he despised? Why was, and is, the only perfect and holy, harmless and undefiled person who ever walked the earth despised and rejected of men? Popular religionists admit that he *was* despised and rejected, but they cannot assign a logical reason for it because they reject the doctrine of Total Depravity, and apart from *that* there is no logical reason for it. Arminianism argues that Christ loves all men, and that all men, even in a state of unregeneracy, possess the ability to love Christ, merely by a decision of their natural will. But if that is so, why do they all by nature choose to despise and reject him? Popular religion does not have the answer.

The apostle John says that those who have had the love of God bestowed upon them and who are consequently called the sons of God, are *not known* by the world, just as it *did not know* Christ (1 John 3:1). Not only are they not *known* by the world, they are also *hated* by the world. Christ said to his disciples, "If ye were of the world, the world would love his own: but because ye are not of the world, but I have chosen you out of the world, therefore the world hateth you" (John 15:18-19). From whence then cometh this hatred of Christ and his true followers? It comes from their native depravity, which they inherited from their fallen father Adam. Men in nature are not simply *indifferent* to God but "the carnal mind is *enmity against* God" (Romans 8:7). Paul tells the Roman brethren that it was when they were *enemies* that they were reconciled to God by the death of His Son (Romans 5:10).

The "reproach of Christ" goes as far back as his true disciples go (Hebrews 11:25). He has given his true disciples fair warning as to how they will be treated in the world. Some examples are Matthew 10:17 & 24:9, John 15:18-21 & 16:2, 2 Timothy 3:12. Christ is still despised and rejected of men, and the more we conform our lives to his teachings the more we likewise will be despised and rejected by the world.

January 31

"Call no man your father upon the earth" (Matthew 23:9)

This command must be viewed in a religious context, realizing that Christ is here cautioning his disciples against such a fascination with flattering names and titles as characterized the scribes and Pharisees. He was of course not teaching them to refrain from calling their paternal parent *father* but he was letting them know it was wrong to call any man father who presumed to exercise any authority over men in matters of doctrine and practice and/or who laid any claim to being the vicar or substitute of Christ. In that unique sense there is but one who is our Father, and that is God.

We have observed a great love of high-sounding titles among the religionists of the world, which they apply to their leaders, such as Reverend, The Right Reverend, The Holy Father, The Most Holy Father, Worshipful Master, Wonderful Grand Master, The Most Excellent Master, etc., etc., *ad nauseam*. These things our Lord would have his followers to turn away from with revulsion and have no part with, for they imply qualities and powers that only God possesses. We find only One Being in the Scriptures whose name is *reverend* and that is God (Psalm 111:9). All the titles mentioned above, as well as others in that category, have been invented by men and greatly appeal to the carnal pride of those who wear them or use them. That alone should put such titles off limits to the true followers of the meek and lowly Lamb of God.

Let us note carefully the words of Elihu (Job 32:21-22): "Let me not, I pray you, accept any man's person, neither let me give flattering titles unto man. For I know not to give flattering titles; in so doing my maker would soon take me away."

May we, as the professed followers of Christ, leave the use of such titles to others, and acknowledge our rightful place as "unprofitable servants" (Luke 17:10).

❧

February 1

"Say ye to the righteous, that it shall be well with him..."
(Isaiah 3:10)

In a world where God's believing people suffer so many afflictions (Psalm 34:19), are often tempted and distressed with doubts and fears, and are frequently the objects of abuse and persecution, it is needful that they be reminded, and assured, that it shall be well with them. During those times when they are suffering, when the whole world seems to be against them and providence seems to be frowning upon everything they do, it can be very difficult for them to believe that it shall be well with them, but in spite of their doubts it still remains true that God cannot fail them and they will ultimately prevail and join in victory's joyful song. He is as much their God in their perplexities as he is in their triumphs, and after awhile, by his grace and the merits of a crucified Savior they will have overcome sin, Satan, death, hell and the grave.

No matter what the temporal circumstances of the child of God, there is a sense in which it is well with him. Even when he makes for himself a hell on earth by his disobedience, there is still a sense in which it is well with him, for he is still embraced in the covenant of grace, the Father-Son relationship between him and God cannot be broken, and the promises of the covenant cannot be nullified. But on the other hand, no matter how much a wicked man may prosper in this life, no matter how easy a life he may experience and no matter how much it may appear that everything is in his favor, in the final analysis, "it shall be ill with him" (Isa. 3:11). In a sense, there is never a time with a child of God when is not *well* with him, and there is never a time with a child of the devil when it is not *ill* with him. "If God be for us, who can be *against* us?" (Rom. 8:31), and conversely, if God be against us, who can be *for* us?

God's people are kept by His power and there is a place reserved for them in heaven (1 Peter 1:4-5). They may possibly live a life here on the shores of time that is dominated by pain, affliction, hardship, and even persecution, but they are citizens of a better country, that is, an heavenly, and when the Lord himself shall descend from heaven with a shout, with the voice of the archangel, and with the triumph of God, then they will all be raised and fashioned like unto the glorious body of Christ. Then, indeed, it shall be well with them forevermore.

February 2

"Preach the word" (2 Timothy 4:2)

If anyone wonders why a faithful minister of the gospel so often preaches on practical godliness, and if they wonder why they frequently feel that they are in his line of fire, they need only read the Scriptures of the Old and New Testaments. Ministers are commanded to "preach the word," and the word of God is made up of approximately two-thirds preceptive teaching. How could they faithfully comply with our Lord's command and not spend at least some of their time dealing with those scriptures that tell us how we ought to live?

The apostle Paul's method, under divine inspiration, was to first lay down fundamental truths as the foundation for the obedience of God's people, and then set forth some of those works that are incumbent upon them as followers of Christ. This is a good example for ministers in all ages to follow. Of course this involves occasional reproof, rebuke and exhortation, but this is to be done "with all longsuffering and doctrine." It is vitally important that the truth be preached "in love" for if not it will be of little profit to the hearers.

God's ministering servants are not authorized to preach anything other than "the word," and they have no grounds to expect success in their preaching any further than they comply with that injunction. Paul said, "We preach not ourselves, but Christ Jesus the Lord, and ourselves your servants for Jesus sake" (2 Cor. 4:5). Much time has been wasted by ministers as a result of their preaching about themselves and setting forth their own opinions and speculations.

In order to *preach* the word a man must *know* the word, and he cannot know the word unless he studies to show himself approved unto God, a workman that needeth not to be ashamed, rightly dividing the word of truth (2 Tim. 2:15). The ministry of a man who properly applies himself and who preaches the word of God instead of the vain notions and ideas of men will not be in vain but will strengthen and edify those who are blessed to sit under the sound of it.

৵৹

February 3

"Truly this was the Son of God" (Matthew 27:54)

The Gentile centurion and those that were with him watching Jesus during his crucifixion acknowledged him to be the Son of God when they saw and felt the effects of the earthquake and the other extraordinary things that occurred. They were convinced of His sonship when the Jews were not. Even evil spirits acknowledged him to be the Son of God even though the Jews would not (Matt. 8:29; Mark 3:11; Luke 4:41). How clearly does this show the blindness and hardness of heart they had been given over to!

Jesus was called "the Son of God" by Mark, John, John the Baptist, Nathanael, Peter, Martha, the disciples, and by the angel Gabriel (Matt. 14:33; 16:16; Mark 1:1; Luke 1:32, 35; John 1:34, 49; 3:16, 18; 11:27; 20:31). The general recognition of His claim to being the Son of God can be seen in Matthew 4:3, 6, 14:33, 17:40, 43 & 54, and John 19:7.

One of the reasons the Jews sought to kill Christ was because he affirmed that God was his Father, and they knew that he was thus declaring himself to be "equal with God" (John 5:18). It is interesting to observe that the very thing they most hated him for is the thing upon which our hope most firmly rests, his eternal power and Godhead (Romans 1:2); for if he was not "God manifest in the flesh" we have no reason to believe our sins have been put away or that we will ever see heaven.

The fact that there are things said of and by Christ that can only be said of *man*, and also things said of and by him that can only be said of *God,* proves him to be both God and man. He is verily God and verily man. He said of himself, "Before Abraham was, I am" (John 8:58), and he prayed the Father to glorify him with the glory he had with him before the world was (John 17:5). He could not have said this if his existence had begun with his incarnation. How beautifully is this summarized by John when he says, "In the beginning was the Word, and the Word was with God, and the Word was God" (John 1:1)! The apostle Paul says that "without controversy" this is a great mystery (1 Tim. 3:16), but to deny the truth of it would be to deny the Scriptures.

February 4

"Unto them that look for him" (Hebrews 9:28)

God's people look with sweet anticipation for the return of Christ. They do so because they, as did Abraham, "look for a city which hath foundations, whose builder and maker is God" (Heb. 11:10). They do so because they realize that they are "strangers and pilgrims on the earth" (v. 13). They do so because Christ is precious unto them (1 Peter 2:7), and they desire to be conformed to His image. They do so because they know that when he shall appear he will change their vile body, that it may be fashioned like unto his own glorious body (Phil. 3:20-21). They look for him because he is their soul's chief delight and they long to be *with* him, to be *like* him, and to be satisfied.

It comforts me to consider that whether the second coming of our Lord is near or not, I will be with Him soon, for I have reached the evening time of life. If I should live to be eighty-years-old, it would only be fifteen more years before my soul would take flight and leave this vile world behind. But since we have no promise of tomorrow, none of us know but what we may breathe our last breath momentarily, or but what Christ may return before the next tick of the clock. Thus we always live, not knowing but what we may, the next moment, be in eternity. Indeed, "What manner of persons ought we to be in all holy conversation and godliness" (2 Peter 3:11).

The subject of the second coming of Christ was near and dear to the heart of the apostle Paul and he mentioned it often. It is interesting to note that in his first epistle to the Thessalonians he ends each of the five chapters with a reference to the coming of Christ. It is a subject that often occupies my mind, and I have long been looking for the Lord's return. Many years of waiting have not weakened my faith in the least that one sweet day Christ will return to gather his people to himself. For the saints, what a day that will be!

৵৶

February 5

"I am the Lord, I change not; therefore ye sons of Jacob are not consumed" (Malachi 3:6)

All mankind would be ultimately ruined and doomed if it were not for the immutability of God, for if he were changeable like we are he would not put up with us for a day. We are capable of changing from a quiet and docile state of mind to one of agitation and anger in an instant of time. We are so capricious, inconsistent and moody that we could never, of ourselves, stay in favor with God for long at a time, if at all, and an eternal relationship with him would be out of the question. Therefore, "It is of the Lord's mercies that we are not consumed" (Lam. 3:22). It is not because of any stability in us, but rather "because his compassions fail not" (Lam. 3:22).

God chose his people in Christ before the foundation of the world (Eph. 1:4) "that (they) should be holy and without blame before him in love," and he has saved them and called them, not according to their works, but according to his own purpose and grace which was given them in Christ Jesus before the world began (2 Tim. 1:9). This alone guarantees that they will not be consumed or wasted. The apostle confirms this very forcibly when he says he is confident of this very thing, "that he which hath begun a good work in you will perform it until the day of Jesus Christ" (Phil. 1:6). He will not change his mind and leave off the work, even though his people are often unfaithful to him, for if he did he would never complete the work in any of them. But "the foundation of God standeth sure, having this seal, The Lord knoweth them that are his" (2 Tim. 2:19).

Psalm 130:3 poses the question: "If thou, Lord, shouldest mark iniquities, O Lord, who shall stand?" And sure it is that if God should keep account of the sins of his people so as to bring them up against them in the final day and impute those sins to them, then all of them would be lost. The whole human race would be lost. Thank God our salvation is by grace, not by works of righteousness which we have done, but according to his unchangeable mercy and compassion!

February 6

"These that have turned the world upside down..." (Acts 17:6)

God so blessed the ministry of Paul that its effects were extraordinary; so much so in fact that the envious and unbelieving Jews at Thessalonica accused him of turning the world upside down. But if the world was being thus affected, it was not God's *ministers* that were doing it, but *God Himself.* They could have had no success at all if he had not attended their efforts with the power of his Spirit.

The true servants of God preach the same things today that Paul preached. They open and allege "that Christ must needs have suffered, and risen again from the dead," and that Jesus, whom they preach, is Christ. But God is greatly withdrawn from his church in this day when there is so much worldly-mindedness, coldness and deadness among his favored people. The preaching of even his most gifted and able ministers is not attended with the same degree of success that accompanied that of the apostles. No one today is accusing any Primitive Baptist preachers anywhere of "turning the world upside down" with their preaching.

Some of our ministers have thought that by adopting certain means, measures and methods their churches would automatically grow, spiritually and numerically, but they will find, if they have not already, that spiritual growth and prosperity do not come any other way than by the power of the Spirit of God. The key to enjoying God's favor as a people and as a nation lies in such things as true humility, earnest, heartfelt prayer, a sincere seeking of God and reliance upon him, and an honest eschewing of evil (2 Chron. 7:14). If those who have been shown the truth as it is in Christ Jesus were to collectively engage in these things they would see much improvement in the state of the churches. But until that happens there is no reason to expect the kind of growth and prosperity that some believe will be the result of more frequent church services, relaxing standards for membership, national preacher's meetings, church-sponsored entertainments, etc. Only God can "turn the world upside down."

February 7

"When my father and mother forsake me, then the Lord will take me up" (Psalm 27:10)

One of the things this verse teaches us is that the children of God are not immune to the possibility of being forsaken, even by their closest of kin. It has happened many times in the past and it will continue to occur as long as the world stands. It is strange behavior but it happens. Fathers and mothers have been known to sacrifice their children to idol gods, or even to murder them if their continuing to live stood in the way of their own selfish interests and ambitions. But no matter what God's little ones meet with in this life they are assured in his word that nothing can separate them from his love (Romans 8:31-39).

Hundreds of thousands of babies are deliberately killed each year, forsaken, at least by their mothers, but the fact that those who should have loved them most have cast them away does not mean that God forgets about them. They do not go away and cease to have an existence, but the Lord *takes them up*. Their souls return to God who gave them and their bodies will be raised and glorified at the second personal coming of Christ.

No matter how others may behave toward God's people, great or small, old or young, rich or poor, God is the one constant in their lives. He never leaves them nor forsakes them (Heb. 13:5). He never forgets *who* they are or *where* they are. "Can a woman forget her sucking child, that she should not have compassion on the son of her womb? Yea, they may forget, yet will I not forget thee" (Isaiah 49:15).

God's knowledge of his people is inseparably connected with his very *foundation*, and that foundation *standeth sure* (2 Tim. 2:19). How miserable is that doctrine that declares a god who may love his people enough today to count them among his sheep, but because of a misdeed on their part he may hate them enough tomorrow to cast them into eternal hell. That is not the God of the Bible.

☙❧

February 8

"I have given you an example, that ye should do as I have done to you" (John 13:15)

In washing the feet of his disciples Jesus gave them, and his followers in every succeeding age, an example which, if observed in the true spirit of it, would make a little heaven on earth in our churches. Jesus showed us, by a number of vivid examples, what the real spirit of Christianity is all about. The washing of his disciples' feet is one of the most striking and beautiful instances of this, and how sadly is the spirit of it being violated in our day!

There have been some in days past, and possibly still today, who have made the literal washing of the saints' feet a test of fellowship. There have been declared, and undeclared, divisions among our people over this issue in the past, but this kind of behavior is a blatant contradiction of the very example over which the divisions have occurred. Divisiveness and uncharitableness is the direct opposite of what the example teaches. It teaches a spirit of humility and servitude; a willingness to perform the most menial tasks and services in behalf of our brethren. It teaches us that we are basically to live at one another's feet, each of us esteeming our brethren better than ourselves (Philippians 2:3).

If we get embroiled in a dispute over whether or not this example is to be performed literally or figuratively, we miss the whole point of it. It is certain that even if we comply with it in a physical way it will not profit us unless we apply the spirit of it to our everyday lives. What are we profited by literally getting down at the feet of our brethren and actually washing their feet if we do not *live* at their feet in a spiritual sense, and if we are not willing to be their servant and to devote our lives to their welfare and upbuilding?

I personally believe God's people should *literally* follow the example of Christ in the matter of washing the feet of their brethren, but I do not, and would not, make it a test of fellowship. Those of our brethren who *do not* wash feet physically, yet comply with the spirit of it, are nearer right than those who *do* it physically but fail to live according to the spirit of it. Christ set us a wonderful example of humility and servitude. He was, and is, meek and lowly in heart, and that's the way each of us should be.

February 9

"To me to live is Christ, and to die is gain" (Philippians 1:21)

This one verse, if we had no other, would show us that the apostle Paul had all his priorities in proper order. He not only considered Christ the most important thing in his life, but he also viewed death from the right perspective.

Life carried the prospect of *serving* Christ, and death carried the prospect of ever dwelling *with* Christ. Hence he says, "Whether we live, we live unto the Lord; and whether we die, we die unto the Lord: whether we live therefore, or die, we are the Lord's" (Romans 14:8). It was his chief desire that Christ might be magnified in his body, "whether it be by life, or by death." Only the miraculous work of the Holy Spirit within the heart of a person can produce this kind of attitude toward Christ and these views toward life and death.

Paul considered Christ to be his life (Col. 3:4). To him there was no real living without Christ. To him Christ was all in all. This is the key to the fact that he had learned, in whatsoever state he was, therewith to be content (Philippians 4:11). The man or woman whose greatest love in life is Christ, always has Him to draw upon, to feed upon, to lean upon, no matter what their circumstances may be.

To have the fervent love of Christ in our heart is to have contentment even when all outward conditions appear to be against us. It was this love, in full exercise, that enabled Paul and Silas to pray and sing praises unto God even though it was midnight and they were behind prison bars for no other reason than serving Christ (Acts 16:25).

How indescribably blest, how richly favored, how wonderfully situated, are those to whom Christ is "the chiefest among ten thousand" (S. S. 5:10) and who enjoy close fellowship and communion with Him! They cannot be robbed of that which is hidden within their heart. Christ is *in them*, "the hope of glory" (Col. 1:27).

There can be no real and lasting peace and happiness without Christ. May he draw us into a closer companionship with himself. May he increase our love and devotion to him. May he so deal with us that we may also say, as did Paul, "To me to live is Christ, and to die is gain."

February 10

"He telleth the number of the stars; he calleth them all by their names" (Psalm 147:4)

What an amazing God we have! Not only did he *number* the stars but he *made* them also (Gen. 1:16), and even *named* them. What if you or I were called upon to give names to ten thousand stars? Do you suppose we would be up to the task? What about a *million* stars? What about *untold billions* of them? When we think of such things we are quickly caught up in a quagmire of incomprehensibility; our little finite minds fail us and we are lost in a sea of awe and wonder.

In Hebrew 12:22 we read of "an innumerable company of angels," and in Jude 9 and Revelation 12:7 we read of Michael the archangel, and in Luke 1:19, 26 of the angel Gabriel. And since these two angels are called by name, may we not safely conclude that *all* the angels are likewise named. It is my opinion that all the innumerable host of saints—each member of the elect family—has been given their own individual name by which they are, and will be, known in heaven.

I have personally known of several people by the same first and last name as my own, but in heaven I believe we will have our own unique names. "The sheep hear his voice: and he calleth his own sheep by name, and leadeth them out" (John 10:3). If the stars and the angels have their own distinct name, why should it not be the same with God's people, for even the very hairs of their heads are numbered (Matt. 10:30; Luke 12:7). "Rejoice, because your *names* are written in heaven (Luke 10:20). "My fellowlabourers, whose *names* are in the book of life" (Phil. 4:3).

God is a God of infinite variety. He makes each of us to differ from every other person who ever lived upon the earth. He gives us our own distinct features, our own fingerprints, our own unique personality and disposition. Would he then settle for the name given us by our parents, and which probably thousands of other people share with us, or would he not rather give us the name of *his* own choice? I like to think he would do the latter.

February 11

"An inheritance incorruptible, and undefiled, and that fadeth not away, reserved in heaven..." (1 Peter 1:4)

God's people take much comfort in the fact that a heavenly inheritance awaits them after this life. Among the glorious things that are said about this inheritance is that it is *reserved* for a specified people—those who are "kept by the power of God through faith unto salvation..."

Both the *power* and *faithfulness* of God are concerned in this *keeping* of the saints, for the end is salvation, *in every case*. Not one shall be lost. Not only is their inheritance *reserved* for them, but they are *reserved* unto it. It is *reserved* and they are *kept*. Nothing could be more sure than that all the saints will be ultimately conformed to the image of Christ, for it is *this* to which they have been *predestinated* (Romans 8:29).

Their inheritance is both undefiled *and* incorruptible. That is, it has never *been* defiled, and it can never *be* defiled. *Incorruptible* simply means it *cannot* be corrupted. It is impossible that it should lose the tiniest particle of its purity. Eternity is not long enough for it to be corrupted. It is safe and secure from any form of contamination. Those who inhabit it must be clothed with incorruption before they can be carried there (1 Cor. 15:53), so that *they* cannot corrupt it. Nothing impure can enter there. That is why it is necessary for their "vile body" to be "changed" and "fashioned like unto" the glorious body of Christ (Philippians 3:21).

Finally, their inheritance "fadeth not away." Thus when they leave this world they enter "into life eternal" (Matt. 25:46), a state of happiness that never ends. It is an "everlasting life." As the poet says, *"When we've been there ten thousand years, bright shining as the sun, we've no less days to sing God's praise than when we first begun."* The joys there not only do not *end*, they don't even *fade*. They will remain constant and unchanging---eternally. This is a soul-cheering message to those who love the Lord and whose hope is in His mercy.

February 12

"As then he that was born after the flesh persecuted him that was born after the Spirit, even so it is now" (Galatians 4:29)

Isaac was the promised seed of Abraham, while Ishmael was the product of a failed effort on the part of Abraham and Sarah to *produce* the promised seed. The only birth Ishmael ever experienced was fleshly. He was never born of the Spirit. His half brother Isaac *was* born of the Spirit, and because of this he became the object of Ishmael's hatred and persecution. And the apostle tells us that as it was *then*, so it is *now*. Put any two people together under these circumstances for any length of time and the unregenerate will persecute the regenerate. It is as certain as the sunrise.

Paul knew very well how this works. Those who are born of the Spirit *never* persecute those who are only "born after the flesh." It is *always* the other way around. There are two reasons for this. One is, that they have no *reason* to persecute unregenerates, and the other is, they have a principle of grace planted within their heart that deters them from willfully inflicting harm on others.

Cain is a good example of an *unregenerate* person persecuting a *regenerate* person. He was "of that wicked one" (the devil)—see 1st John 3:12—and slew his brother Abel. And why did he slay him? "Because his own works were evil, and his brother's were righteous."

It is always true, in every case, that the works of an unregenerate are evil. His *works* are evil because *he* is evil, and he highly resents the fact that anyone else is righteous. The wicked would soon do away with the righteous if they could. They would destroy them from the earth if it were not for God's providential restraints upon them. So the apostle says to the humble followers of Christ, "Marvel not, my brethren, if the world hate you." Under the circumstances it cannot be otherwise. Ishmael is still persecuting Isaac to this day.

February 13

"Some indeed preach Christ even of envy and strife..."
(Philippians 1:15)

We who are deeply conscientious about preaching the gospel find it difficult to believe that there are actually some who "preach Christ" for dishonorable reasons. But there *were* such characters in Paul's day and we would be naive to think there are not still some of that ilk around today. Judging by the fruits and effects of their efforts and activities, I believe I have perhaps known a few of them, even among the Old Baptists.

Paul said of these characters that there was envy, strife and contention associated with their preaching; that they were not sincere, and that they supposed they were adding affliction to his present imprisonment (v. 16). They were certainly not reflecting any love for him or for the cause of Christ.

A number of things I have witnessed among members of the Old Church have likewise reflected no real love for the brethren and no honest concern for the damage it was doing to individuals or to the cause. And such things have indeed added greatly to the burdens and cares I was already carrying. I am thankful that the Lord is the Judge in such matters. I would not be capable of determining what would be an adequate punishment for such behavior.

It is inconceivable to me that anyone could "preach Christ" and yet not be sincere about it. To me it is the most serious, sacred and solemn thing in the world, and yet I have seen those who approached it as though it were not much more than a theatrical performance.

Paul had to deal with "false apostles, deceitful workers" who transformed themselves into the apostles of Christ. And he said this was no marvel in view of the fact that Satan himself is transformed into an angel of light. "Therefore it is no great thing if his ministers also be transformed as the ministers of righteousness" (2 Cor. 11:13-15). If we do not believe there are still such characters around, we are sitting ducks for their deceptive works. Let us watch and pray.

February 14

"Marvel not that I said unto thee, Ye must be born again"
(John 3:7)

Regeneration, or the new birth, is the act of the Holy Spirit in taking up His abode within the heart of those who, until that point, have been dead in trespasses and sins. Notice that Christ did not tell Nicodemus, "Ye must *get* born again," but rather, "Ye must *be* born again." In other words, this is not something a person just decides they are going to have happen to them, but it is a work that God performs in the life of each one of His chosen people sometime between conception and death. It always occurs at *God's* appointed time, *not* when the individual decides it is going to happen. This is precisely why Christ spoke of it as a *birth.*

No one ever has anything to do with their *natural* birth, and neither do they have anything to do with their *spiritual* birth. Most people *think* they do, but they are mistaken. They misinterpret their experience, and do not understand that life must always precede action.

It is popularly believed and taught that unregenerate persons can *get* themselves born again by simply reciting a prayer that basically says they realize they are a sinner in need of salvation and that they accept Christ as their personal Savior. But the truth is that when people begin to feel themselves to be sinners and to desire salvation they are already born of the Spirit. In other words, they feel their sinfulness *because of* the new birth, not in order to bring it about. Those who are "dead in sins" do not have such feelings; they do not possess faith, they do not love Christ, and they have no interest in spiritual things.

Conviction for sin is an *evidence* of the new birth, not what produces it. Faith in Christ is an *evidence* of divine life, not what procures that life. Love for God is a product of His love for us, not the other way around. No one loves God except those to whom He has revealed Himself. There is no fear of God before the eyes of the others (Psa. 36:1; Rom. 3:18). Consequently the new birth is "of God" (John 1:13). "Not of blood, nor of the will of the flesh, nor of the will of man, *but of God.*" "You hath he (God) quickened (given life), who were dead in trespasses and sins" (Eph. 2:1,4,5). It can be no other way.

February 15

"A bishop then must be...apt to teach" (1 Timothy 3:2)

Those who are ordained to the ministry ought to be men who are adept at teaching, and none can meet this requirement unless they first have a good understanding of the basic doctrines and practices of the church and have a reasonably thorough knowledge of the Scriptures. No one can *teach* what he does not *know*.

But even knowledge, standing alone, will not qualify a man to teach if he has no God-given abilities to convey that knowledge to God's people. A man who cannot aptly communicate his thoughts to others in an understandable way can certainly not qualify for so demanding an office as the ministry. Even if a man had all the other qualifications for the ministry, without this one he should not be ordained.

No church is likely to grow in grace and in the knowledge of the truth if they are led by a man who is not capable of teaching them from the Scriptures. It is not enough that a man merely *preach* but he is to teach *and* preach (Matt. 11:1). And one of the reasons he must have a good knowledge of what is expected of God's people is because the requirement rests upon him to *teach them to observe all things, whatsoever Christ has commanded them* (Matt. 28:20).

Many good men have been treated very unfairly by being put into the pulpit when they had no gift to preach and teach. Permanent damage has been done to them and to the church by laying a weight upon them that they were not qualified, or able, to carry. I know of no other one error that has done the Old Church more damage.

Let us thoroughly familiarize ourselves with the scriptural qualifications of the ministry and strive as best we can not to ordain men to that office who do not meet the requirements. As a result of mistakes in this regard, many a useful gift has been buried and the men who possessed them rendered detrimental to the cause they sought to represent.

Paul told Timothy, "The things that thou hast heard of me among many witnesses, the same commit thou to faithful men, who shall be able to *teach* others also" (2 Tim. 2:2).

February 16

"They went out from us, but they were not of us..." (1 John 2:19)

Beginning with the early church there have been those who made a profession of belief in Christ and his truth for a time but soon fell by the wayside and apostatized. Even some of those who followed Christ in the early part of his ministry eventually reached the point where they "went back, and walked no more with him" (John 6:66).

It is still the same today. There are those who are not "of us" who, for one reason or another, join themselves to us, but they are united to us in name only, and with time the Old Church does not prove to be what they want. They find that the Biblical standards it upholds are too restrictive for their tastes, or they discover that it holds to doctrines which are repugnant to their carnal minds, which minds are all too enamored with the things of time and sense.

It is noteworthy that even in the apostles' day there were some that came among the true disciples who did not belong with them. Our churches have sometimes taken in people whom they feared were not well enough established to really know what they were doing, but for fear of embarrassing them or driving them away, they were questioned sparingly or not at all when they offered themselves for membership. No doubt with hindsight churches have felt that they should have been more careful in this regard, and doubtless in some cases they *should* have been more thorough in their examination of some candidates.

However, even the apostolic church (or the church during the days of the apostles), was bothered by some that *went out from them because they were never of them.* To me this shows that those who make up the old church have never been perfect. Their judgment was sometimes faulty, even in the days of the apostles.

I have always tried to pray that the Lord would so keep me, protect me and preserve me, that I would never so fall as to lose my place among the precious household of faith. I realize this requires me to "keep my body under and bring it into subjection," but I would never want to think I could do this merely in my own strength without the merciful aid of the Holy Spirit. May the Lord help us to heed the admonition of Hebrews 3:12 and 2 Peter 3:17-18 and to faithfully serve Him until He calls us home.

February 17

"You hath he quickened, who were dead in trespasses and sins"
(Ephesians 2:1)

In order to maintain their 'universal offer of salvation' doctrine, popular religionists have no choice but to deny the doctrine of Total Depravity and to argue that unregenerate sinners are not actually *dead* in sins. In fact they make little or no distinction between *dead* sinners and *living* sinners, for their doctrine implies that a *dead* sinner can function in the spiritual realm just as efficiently and effectively as a *living* sinner can.

They maintain that a person *dead* in sins can love Christ enough to "accept Him as their Savior," feel their need of Him, pray to Him, repent of their sins, or anything else the *living* sinner can do. But if that be true, what point is there in the new birth? If sinners can do everything *before* the new birth that they can do *after* the new birth, what is the difference between the regenerate and the unregenerate?

The advocates of popular religion argue that dead sinners can accept Christ as their Savior *before* he is their Savior. In other words, they can accept Christ as their Savior in order to get him to *become* their Savior. So, in effect they are advocating that sinners can accept a *falsehood* in order to make it a *reality*.

This is an unworkable theology, because it makes no sense. If a person is not saved until he accepts Christ, then Christ has not saved anyone who has not accepted him. Therefore He is not the Savior of those he has not saved. Consequently, if they must accept him in order for him to save them, then they must accept him as their Savior before he *is* their Savior in order that he may *become* their Savior. This is a tangled up doctrine that simply cannot be true.

According to the Scriptures those who are dead in sins cannot even *know* or *understand* the things of the Spirit of God (1 Cor. 2:14). They are enmity against God; they are not subject to the law of God, and neither indeed *can* be. "So then they that are in the flesh cannot please God" (Rom. 8:7-8).

If God did not irresistibly *quicken*, or give spiritual life to his people "even when" they were dead in sins, then none of them would ever be born again, for in that state of death they *would* not and *could* not come to Christ (John 6:44-65). This is both scriptural and reasonable.

February 18

"His compassions fail not. They are new every morning..."
(Lamentations 3:22)

From the context we learn that it is "of the Lord's mercies" that we are not consumed. And it is also because of the fact that his compassions toward us *do not fail*. The writer then asserts that these compassions are "new every morning,"—after which he reminds us of the greatness of God's faithfulness.

In Psalm 39 David expressed the desire that the Lord would so deal with him that he might know how frail he was. One of the most remarkable faults of fallen men is their ignorance of their innate frailty and weakness. They may not agree that they are their "brother's keeper" but they at least *act* as though they think they are their *own* keeper. Little do they realize how utterly dependent they are on the mercy of God to preserve their lives, to say nothing of keeping them from the myriad dangers each of us face daily.

We sometimes come to the close of day feeling that almost everything is drained out of us. At such times we may feel little ambition to even try to go on. We may feel greatly discouraged, distraught and downcast, and yet, after a night's rest we often find that the picture looks quite different; we feel a renewed strength and fresh resolve and determination; our faith seems stronger and our hope seems brighter. This is because God's compassions are indeed "new every morning" and they do not fail.

Paul says that though our outward man perish, yet the inward man is renewed *day by day* (2 Cor. 4:16). God does not give us tomorrow's strength today. We do not *need* tomorrow's strength today. We only need *today's* strength, and the Lord knows how much that is, or is going to be. We are to pray for our *daily* bread, not *tomorrow's* bread. "*This* is the day which the lord hath made" (Psalm 118:24), and it is *this* day that we are to be primarily concerned with. For all we know God may not *make* another day, so let us rejoice and be glad in *this* one.

☙

February 19

"Whom he did foreknow, he also did predestinate..."
(Romans 8:29)

From the standpoint of God's omniscience, or unlimited knowledge, He foreknew everyone who would ever live upon the earth, but from the standpoint of the covenant of grace He only foreknew *His people*. Hence they are referred to as "elect according to the foreknowledge of God the Father" (1 Peter 1:2). These He not only foreknew in a covenant sense, but He also predestinated them, in consequence of which they will all ultimately be called from nature to grace, justified and glorified. And when all this is completed they will have been fully "conformed to the image" of Christ.

Thus we see the hand of God in their salvation *from* all eternity *to* all eternity. The final destiny of His chosen family has never been uncertain from His standpoint, though they may, and often do, have their own questions and doubts about it.

What a vast expanse there is between what the elect are by nature and what they are, and will ultimately be, by grace! "They go astray as soon as they be born, speaking lies" (Psalm 58:3), yet, one day their vile body will be changed and fashioned like unto the glorious body of Christ (Philippians 3:20-21). They come into the world "dead in trespasses and sins," and until grace lifts them out of that state they walk "according to the course of this world, fulfilling the desires of the flesh and of the mind," and are, by nature, children of wrath even as those who are not God's people. In other words, they have the same fallen nature as the non-elect (Eph. 2:1-3). But one sweet day they will stand before the throne of God as pure and holy as if they had never committed a single transgression. All those who were "ordained to eternal life" (Acts 13:48) will not only be given the gift of faith but they will be given eternal life, and they shall never perish nor be plucked out of God's hand (John 10:27-28).

How wonderful is the grace of God! How glorious are His works and ways! And how marvelous is that method of salvation whereby Christ was slain in behalf of His people and redeemed them to God by His blood *out of* every kindred, and tongue, and people, and nation (Rev. 5:9)! These shall all be with Him in Glory and shall praise His name forever. Wonderful is His name!

February 20

"I know that in me (that is, in my flesh,) dwelleth no good thing"
(Romans 7:18)

You have no doubt heard it said that there is a little good in everybody, and I can see where those who are ignorant of what the Scriptures have to say on the matter would think so, but the truth is that there is *nothing*, absolutely *nothing*, good in those who have not been born of the Spirit of God. I realize that many people would revolt at such a statement, but I speak of the way *God* views unregenerate men—not the way *others* view them.

If the words of Paul are carefully examined it will be observed that he did not say there was no good within him, but he said there was no good *"in his flesh."* There was indeed good in him, for he had been born of the Spirit, but that *good* was not *in his flesh.* Our flesh, or our body, will remain a *"vile body"* until it is raised and fashioned like unto the glorious body of Christ (Philippians 3:20-21). Paul referred to his natural body as "the body of this death," or, as we might say, "This body of death." The reason we live in a *dying* body is because it is a *sinful* body (Romans 6:23). It is a *corrupt* body and will be sown, or buried, in corruption, but if we are a child of God it will be raised in incorruption (1 Cor. 15:42-44).

Those who have not been quickened by the Spirit of God into divine life have no principle of grace within their hearts. They have not been made partakers of the divine nature (2 Peter 1:4) and therefore they possess nothing but a *fallen, corrupt* nature, in which there is no good.

This is not to say that corrupt men cannot do anything that is deemed good in the eyes of the society around them, nor that they cannot do anything that issues in good to others, but they cannot do anything good in *God's* sight, for He knows their *hearts* and He knows that all they do is motivated in one way or another by the flesh.

"So then they that are in the flesh (unborn spiritually) cannot please God" (Romans 8:8). *"A corrupt tree cannot bring forth at the same place sweet water and bitter?"* (James 3:11). Yes, there are some people in whom there is not even a *little* good. These are the kind Paul prayed to be delivered from (2 Thess. 3:2).

February 21

"I am in a strait betwixt two, having a desire to depart, and to be with Christ, which is far better: nevertheless to abide in the flesh is more needful for you" (Philippians 1:23-24)

The two conflicting yearnings expressed here by the apostle Paul are both high and noble, and they are both characteristic of the true servants of God. Only those who love God and His people and who live "in hope of eternal life" know anything about the "strait" to which the apostle here refers. The wicked never experience Paul's *strait.* They neither experience his desire to be with Christ, nor his longing to be of service to the saints. They miss his conflicts, but they also miss his comforts.

Christ was the center of Paul's life (Philippians 1:21). To him, Christ was synonymous with life and with real living. In his mind and heart there was no life apart from Christ, and thus it is with all true Christians. There is no joy greater than *serving* Christ Jesus, and no happier prospect than being *with* Him. *"To live is Christ, and to die is gain."* Happy is the man, or woman, who has this view of living and dying. Satan has no darts in his arsenal that can penetrate this blessed shield of faith.

Paul's *strait* lay in the fact that there was at one and the same time a strong desire within him to leave this old sinful world behind him and to be through with trouble and sorrow, and also an unselfish longing to remain among his beloved brethren in Christ "for their furtherance and joy of faith" (v. 25). The great passion of his soul while he remained on earth was to strive for the benefit and upbuilding of the saints, and no man ever went about that labor of love with any greater fervor, faith and dedication than did he. He "labored more abundantly than they all" (1 Cor. 15:10).

How fearfully does the life of Paul shame those slothful servants who love their leisure and who find greater delight in material pursuits than they do in serving the Lord and His people!

(There is a part of me that wants to go on and be with the Lord, but as I have said from the pulpit a few times, I carry pills around in my pocket to try to stay alive as long as I can. These are conflicting desires, but they seem to be consistent with Paul's.)

February 22

*"The vessels of wrath fitted to destruction...and...the vessels of
mercy...afore prepared unto glory"* (Romans 9:22-23)

One of the major stumbling blocks that prevents many people from
arriving at a proper knowledge of the truth is their inability or
unwillingness to accept the fact that the final destiny of all men was
determined before they were born. The thought of such a thing conjures
up all sorts of false ideas in the minds of most people.

However, the Scriptures very clearly teach this great truth. Jacob
and Esau are a perfect example (Rom. 9:9-14). Jacob was loved of God,
and Esau hated, before either of them were born or had done any good
or evil. This quite clearly illustrates the doctrine of eternal election and
emphatically shows that salvation from sin is "not of works, but of him
that calleth." No man on earth, no matter how learned or skilled in
semantics, can successfully explain this away or make it mean anything
other than what it says.

God "afore prepared" the vessels of mercy "unto glory," and Christ
redeemed them "to God" by His blood "out of" every kindred, and
tongue, and people and nation (Rev. 5:9). Notice, he did not redeem
every member of the human family, but he redeemed a people "out of"
every nation and race. Again election is plainly taught.

The vessels of wrath were not "afore prepared" unto destruction, but
each of them are "fitted" by their own corruption for destruction, and
they were "before of old ordained to this condemnation" (Jude 4). The
vessels of mercy were "ordained to eternal life" (Acts 13:48), and true
believers will be found among no other class.

Election, as taught in the Scriptures, does not do any damage to the
vessels of wrath, for it is not the cause of their condemnation. They are
condemned for their sins and for nothing else, and their unrelenting
rejection of God and godliness clearly shows that their being appointed
to wrath is just and right. All men would have perished eternally if
none had been elected and predestinated.

All of human experience clearly testifies to the existence of two
distinct families or classes of people upon the earth—vessels of wrath
and vessels of mercy. Even the first two people born into this world

illustrate this point. Abel was righteous (Matt. 23:35; Heb. 11:4) and Cain "was of that wicked one" (1 John 3:12). One was a vessel of mercy and the other was a vessel of wrath. These two classes never exchange places, and neither class ever desires such an exchange.

৩৯৫৬

February 23

"Good Master, what good thing shall I do that I may have eternal life?" (Matthew 19:16)
"Master, what shall I do to inherit eternal life?" (Luke 10:25)

Christ was asked this question only twice that we have any record of, although the incident involving the rich young ruler was recorded by more than one writer. Both the ruler and the lawyer who put this question to Jesus exposed their ignorance as to how sinners come into possession of eternal life. They, like the vast majority of religionists today, or any other day, thought eternal life could be obtained by something they could do. The lawyer appeared to ask simply because he thought he might entangle Christ in an inconsistency, while the rich ruler seemed confident he could easily measure up to any requirement Christ might set before him. Both were wrong. Without the light of the Holy Spirit men are always wrong about anything religious.

It has been interesting to me over the years to observe that when you ask Arminians what they think a person must do in order to have eternal life, the number of answers you get will be just about the same as the number of people you ask. But none of them will give you the answer that Christ gave the only two people we read of who asked Him this question.

Christ told the ruler that if he would "enter into life," he must keep the commandments of the law, and if he would "be perfect" and "have treasure in heaven" he would have to go and sell what he possessed, and give to the poor, and also he would have to follow him. He also told the lawyer to keep the law, and said, "This do, and thou shalt live." We are told that the young ruler "went away sorrowful: for he had great possessions." But it is my opinion that the lawyer had no real interest in the subject of eternal life one way or the other. He was only "tempting" or testing Christ. But Arminianism, or popular religion, did neither of them any good, just as it does no one else any good so far as their obtaining life by it.

The apostle Paul made it very clear that "no flesh shall be justified by the works of the law" (Gal. 2:16; 3:11). Therefore it is very obvious that Christ was not telling the ruler and the lawyer that they could "have" or "inherit" eternal life by keeping the law. But if they had done what he told them to do they would have entered into a "life" that would have brought them much more joy and satisfaction than they had ever known before. Very few find the "narrow" way that leads to this kind of life (Matt. 7:14).

February 24

"It pleased God by the foolishness of preaching to save them that believe" (1 Corinthians 1:21)

The reason the apostle uses this terminology, "the foolishness of preaching," is not because there is any foolishness in the gospel, but because unbelievers *view* it as foolishness. Gospel preaching only saves *believers,* and even then it does not save them in an *eternal* sense. Eternal salvation is *by grace,* not by the gospel.

In order for unbelievers to be saved eternally by a message, if such a thing were possible, that message would have to be one that appealed to them; one that pleased the ears of unregenerate men and women. But the message contained in the gospel of Jesus Christ is *foolishness* to those who are in a perishing state (1 Cor. 1:18), and *a stumblingblock* to the unbelieving Jews (v. 23). Therefore the gospel of Christ cannot be the means of saving anyone, in any sense, who looks upon it as foolishness. It cannot even save them in a *timely* sense, for they will not embrace it. None of us believe, or benefit from, a message that we consider foolish or nonsensical.

The true gospel brings tidings that are good only to those who have been made "meek" by the inward work of the Holy Spirit. To those whose hearts have been broken and softened by a felt sense of their own wretchedness, unworthiness, and spiritual poverty, the gospel has the effect of "binding up" or healing. It proclaims liberty to those who have been held captive to the bondage of religious ignorance and error. It deals with the spotless life of Christ and His propitiatory sacrifice for the sins of His people, and it comforts those who mourn (See Isaiah 61:1-2). It is a preparation suitable only to those who have been graciously fitted to receive it. "The *poor* (the poor in spirit) have the gospel preached to *them*" (Matt. 11:5 & Luke 7:22). Unto those *who are saved* (already eternally saved) the gospel is *the power of God* (I Cor. 1:18), and unto *them which are called* (already called of God) it is "the power of God, and the wisdom of God" (ver. 24). The others reject it, because to them it is nothing but foolishness.

Christ does not bring life and immortality through the gospel. He only brings these "to light" through that means (II Tim. 1:10), and thus the gospel instructs "the man of God" in righteousness and thoroughly furnishes "him" unto all good works (II Tim. 3:16). There is "another gospel" that the unsaved will receive but they will have no part of the gospel of Christ.

February 25

"Rightly dividing the word of truth" (2 Timothy 2:15)

In order for the Scriptures to be properly understand they must be "rightly divided". No man can arrive at any just and accurate doctrinal conclusions unless he is able to distinguish between *proof* texts and *reference* texts. Proof texts are those scriptures that state doctrinal and practical truths in such language as is not open to interpretation. In other words, they can have but one meaning, and that meaning is made as plain as words can state it. Reference texts are those scriptures that must be interpreted in the light of their context and often must be taken in a limited or restricted sense.

Such reference texts are frequently taken out of context and misapplied. Thus the application that is placed upon them is in total disagreement with the proof texts that deal with the same subject.

One of the plainest instances of this is the popular application of John 3:16. This is a *reference* text that is frequently used as a *proof* text, and is taken to mean that God loves everybody. But if we take this verse to have that meaning, then we place it in direct opposition to other scriptures that clearly show that God does *not* love everybody (Psalm 5:6; Mal. 1:3; Romans 9:13).

Not only that, but if we take the "world" of John 3:16 to mean every member of the human family, then we make it to contradict the statement of Christ in John 17:9 that He prayed *not* for the *world*. The only way we can make John 3:16 harmonize with Romans 9:13 is to recognize that John 3:16 speaks of the "world" of God's elect rather than the "world" of all humanity.

May the Lord help us in our study of His word. May he give us light, wisdom and understanding so that we may make a proper application of those precious truths that he has left on record for us.

February 26

"Unto him that is able to do exceeding abundantly above all that we ask or think" (Ephesians 3:20)

This is one of those scriptures that conveys to us something of the vast difference between us and our great Creator. Someone has said that we can't outdo God in giving, and that is true, but it is also true that we can't even come *close* to God in giving. His power to *do*, far exceeds both our power to *ask* and our power to *think*. There is no small gulf between *our* thoughts and ways and *His* thoughts and ways

(Isaiah 55:9). The difference is too vast for us puny mortals to conceive or comprehend.

There has never been a prayer that went unanswered because the petition was greater than God could fulfill. Oft-times he withholds things we ask of him because he knows they would not be in our best interest, but *never* does he withhold *anything* from us because of a lack of ability on his part to grant our requests.

Our problem is that our prayers are often limited to small things because our unbelief restrains us from asking for larger things. It is quite characteristic of God's people to limit God in their own hearts and minds (Psalm 78:41). Consequently they often fail to ask, and therefore fail to receive, many things that they otherwise could have had.

Many far higher and more God-honoring things are often not ours simply because we do not ask for them. The Lord exhorts his people to open their mouths *wide*, and assures them that if they do so he will fill it (Psalm 81:10). Oft-times we barely part our lips for His blessings, and therefore receive comparatively little.

How blest we are that God has not limited his mercies toward us merely to the things we have asked or thought! For instance, I am convinced that we have all received many deliverances that we didn't even know to ask for, without which we would have suffered great harm or even death. Anyone who has eternal life received it without asking for it. They didn't ask for it because they didn't want it. No one wants it until they have it, and then if they ask for it, they only ask for what they already possess.

"And it shall come to pass, that before they call I will answer; and while they are yet speaking, I will hear" (Isaiah 65:24). What an amazing and wonderful God we have!

February 27

"For Christ also hath once suffered for sins, the just for the unjust" (1 Peter 3:18)

We all too commonly speak of the sufferings of Christ without giving a great deal of thought to their unfathomable depths. And we are also much too prone to think of his sufferings primarily in terms of his *physical* pains on the cross. But as great as those sufferings were they were the least of His anguish. What bore most heavily upon him, infinitely so, was the soul-sufferings he endured at the hands of divine justice. He stood as the sinless substitute for all the multiplied millions of his people, those who were given to him by the Father in the covenant of grace before the world began. And as their Mediator and Redeemer he took upon himself all their transgressions and bore the equivalent of eternal death and damnation in their behalf, all in the space of a few hours.

The weight of this infinitely great load began to come down upon him in the Garden of Gethsemane before his betrayal and arrest. Who among us mere mortals can begin to comprehend the slightest particle of what he felt when he "began to be sorrowful and very heavy" and said to Peter, James and John, "My soul is exceeding sorrowful, even unto death" (Matt. 26:37-38)? What can we poor, ignorant souls know of the awful anguish he was going through when he was "in an agony" and prayed earnestly, "Father, if thou be willing, remove this cup from me"? Or how could we know anything of an inward distress and agitation so great that his sweat came out in droplets as large as if it had been blood? And then the ultimate agony, far surpassing all expression or human understanding, came when he cried with a loud voice, "My God, my God, why has thou forsaken me?"

Oh what an awful debt we owed, that such an infinite penalty was required at the hands of the very Son of God in order to absolve us of our guilt, put away our sins and deliver us from the wrath to come! And what a debt of gratitude and praise we now owe him for his great mercy toward us. Let us not forget to thank Him daily and to honor him with lives of service and devotion. I believe that in heaven we will understand the greatness of his sacrifice far better than we do now.

February 28

"Is not this the carpenter's son?" (Matthew 13:55)

What a cruel foe is unbelief to the world in general and to God's people in particular! What great blessings it forfeits and what great miseries it fosters. Merely because of the parentage of Christ those of His own country were quick to conclude that there could be nothing extraordinary about Him. Simply because they *knew* His parents they assumed that He could be neither prophet, priest nor king, much less the eternal Son of God. Very truly was it said of Him that "He was in the world, and the world was made by him, and the world knew him not" (John 1:10). Those who had seen Him grow up in their midst viewed Him merely as the son of Joseph and Mary. Little did they know, and far they were from believing, that this lowly carpenter's son was none other than their promised Messiah, verily God manifest in the flesh.

Many a God-called minister of the gospel has found himself receiving little or no honor or respect in the area where he grew up and even among some of his own kin. They have sometimes found much truth in the old adage, "Familiarity breeds contempt." Many circumstances may contribute to this phenomenon, but much of it may be traced to a simple unwillingness on the part of the locals to believe that God would call one to the ministry whom they know from personal observation to be a man full of frailties and shortcomings. This is very unfair to the object of their disrespect, but it is often one of the distressing burdens a servant of God must endure. He often suffers because of his faithfulness to a calling for which he did not volunteer, and sometimes goes with heavy heart as he sees little evidence that his labors are either profitable to, or appreciated by, those to whom he essentially devotes his life.

Those in Christ's own country were great losers by their failure to acknowledge Him for *who* He was and *what* He was, for as a result of their unbelief, "He did not many mighty works there" (Matt. 13:58). How many others have suffered similar losses as a result of the way they have treated the servants that God sent them? Only He knows! *"A prophet is not without honour, save in his own country, and in his own house"* (Matt. 13:57).

March 1

"The ways of the Lord are right" (Hosea 14:9)

Many a time during my life I have heard men, and even a few women, charge God with cruelty, unfairness and injustice. But there has always been something in me that was greatly repulsed by such accusations against the Deity, for I have always known that God is in all respects holy and just and good. If God could make a mistake or if he could do *anything* amiss, he would not be God.

On many occasions I have heard the advocates of popular religion say that the doctrine of Election is a dangerous doctrine. It has always astounded me to hear so-called professors of religion make such a God-dishonoring statement. By saying such things they clearly imply that God made a major blunder when he inspired men to include information on the doctrine of Election in the Bible. It is ludicrous on the face of it to think that an all-wise God would leave information on record by divine inspiration that would be dangerous for his people to know. I feel sure that people often just do not stop to think about what they are saying.

The very thought of God doing anything that was not right was very abhorrent to the apostle Paul. In anticipation of the negative reaction of unenlightened men to his teachings on the subject of Election, he asks, "What shall we say then? Is there unrighteousness with God?" And then he answers his own question with a resounding, "God forbid."

No! God's electing love is so far from being an instance of *injustice*, that it is, in every place, shown rather to be an instance of great *mercy*. The Scriptures are very clear in maintaining God's divine prerogative, and right, *to do what he will with his own* (Matt. 20:15).

David says, "The Lord is righteous in all his ways, and holy in all his works" (Psa. 145:17). It couldn't be stated any better or any clearer. We as poor, weak mortals may not understand what God does, and often we do not, but of this we may be fully assured, "The ways of the Lord are right," whether we understand them or not.

❧

March 2

"That they which have believed in God might be careful to maintain good works" (Titus 3:8)

Faith in God carries the great responsibility of conforming our actions to our profession. No actual good can be expected from unbelievers, even though they are under the same obligation to obey the precepts of the moral law as are believers. However, the very fact that one "believes in God" shows that God has dealt with him in mercy, and this mercy brings him under the special duty of *maintaining* good works "for necessary uses, that (he) be not unfruitful" (Titus 3:14).

In the context we see two major reasons for the maintenance of good works by believers. The first is that it is "good and profitable unto men," and the second is, it keeps them from being unfruitful. The foremost concern of believers in maintaining good works should be the glory of the Lord, and they cannot glorify him if they are not bearing fruit to his honor. But there is an inherent "good" and "profit" that also comes to them as a result of following his example and adhering to the instruction he has laid down for them in his word.

The duty of believers to maintain good works is one of the "faithful sayings" that Paul referred to in four separate places and it is something that should be "affirmed constantly." Good works play no part in the obtaining of eternal life, for that is by the grace of God alone, but they do play a very important part in the peace and happiness of the saints while they live here in the world.

They are to "maintain" good works. That is, they are to remain constant in the performance of them throughout their lives, and they are to be "careful" in this regard. By so doing they *let their light so shine before men that they may see their good works and glorify their Father which is in heaven* (Matt. 5:16).

May the Lord graciously help all true believers to be "zealous of good works." He has before ordained that they should (*ought to*) walk in them (Eph. 2:10).

March 3

"Now we see through a glass, darkly; but then face to face"
(1 Corinthians 13:12)

Who better than the apostle Paul would know that in our present mortal state our vision of spiritual things is very dim compared to what it will be when we are glorified? He had seen enough of the glory of heaven to know that it could not be expressed in words. Even if it had been *possible* to have described the things he saw and heard when he was caught up to the third heaven, it would not have been *lawful* or *proper* for him to have done so (2 Cor. 12:4). These are things that are reserved for another day and another state of being.

There are many things we simply do not need to know in our present state and many things we could not now comprehend, even if it were told us. There were many things that Christ would later say to His disciples that even they could not bear in their immaturity (John 16:12). There are some "secret things" that "belong unto the Lord" only (Deut. 29:29). It is only the *revealed things* that belong unto us.

Oh how humble, contrite and subservient we poor benighted mortals ought to be before the Lord! His ways and thoughts are so much higher than ours that our concept of the difference is pathetically deficient (Isa. 55:8-9). How foolish men show themselves to be when they vaunt themselves and seek to appear wise (Rom. 1:22)! Even with as much divine revelation as the apostle Paul was given, he was still lost in wonder as he contemplated "the depth of the riches both of the wisdom and knowledge of God." And he could only exclaim in amazement, "How unsearchable are his judgments, and his ways past finding out" (Rom. 11:33)! What awe should possess us mortals! What admiration should grip us as we consider our standing before our Almighty Creator and Preserver!

But in spite of our ignorance in our present state, the Lord has still given us enough knowledge and information to thoroughly furnish us with all we need in order to perform all those works that *He* deems good. He has given us a great volume of truth; in fact, all that he would have us know. And if we rightly use it and apply it, not only will he be pleased with us but we will be greatly benefited. There will always be room for us to "grow in grace and in the knowledge of the truth." This we are instructed to do (2 Peter 3:18).

March 4

"That which is highly esteemed among men is abomination to God" (Luke 16:15)

If we had no Bible and no other statement from God than the above, it alone would go a long way toward guiding us as to what we should and should not involve ourselves in as followers of that which is good. Men, in their natural state, or their native depravity, love darkness rather than light (John 3:19) and therefore it is "the works of darkness" to which they are drawn and in which they find their greatest delight (Rom. 13:12; Eph. 5:11). They are not just *indifferent* toward the things of God, but they *hate* the light and will not come to it because it exposes and reproves their ungodliness (John 3:20).

Any time the followers of Christ find that something is popular with men in general they would do well to be very careful how they involve themselves in it, if at all. There is a wicked element out there that the apostle John referred to as "the whole world" (1 John 5:19) and for whom Christ said He would not pray (John 17:9) and the thoughts of their heart is "only evil continually" (Gen. 6:5). They are walking in a way that Christ said is *broad* and they entered it through a gate that is said to be *wide,* and this is where you will find the "many," all of whom are rushing madly toward destruction. Their ways should be carefully avoided.

The list of things that are popular among worldly-minded people is almost endless. And the number of things that are calculated to draw the minds and hearts of people away from God and godliness is likewise myriad. Satan does not care what form of worldliness he gets God's people mixed up in, nor how much religion they profess, just so long as they are not following and serving Christ. He hates those who bear the moral characteristics of their Lord and Savior, and one of his greatest delights is to lead them away from Christ and into the broad way.

May the Lord help us to avoid those things that are hightly esteemed among worldly-minded men and women. They promise pleasure, but they ultimately bring great pain.

March 5

"If any man preach any other gospel unto you than that ye have received, let him be accursed" (Galatians 1:9)

Paul expressed his amazement at how short a time it took some of the Galatians to be led off into error by false teachers and their perversions of the gospel. And we likewise marvel today that such vast numbers of God's people have been taken in, and deluded by, what the apostle called, "another gospel." How few, in our day, have access to the true gospel, and of those who do hear it, how rare are those who receive it and embrace it! "Who hath believed our report? and to whom is the arm of the Lord revealed?" (Isa. 53:1).

"Any other gospel" than that which was preached by Christ and the apostles is plainly and simply *a perversion of the gospel* (Gal. 1:7), and perversions of the gospel *trouble* God's people. Paul pronounced an anathema upon those who preach such perversions, which shows that he did not subscribe to the notion, so popularly held today, that it does not matter what we believe just so long as we are sincere. It *does indeed* matter, and it matters a great deal. "The truth shall make you free" (John 8:32) but error can make you extremely miserable, depending on what the error is.

There is just one *true* gospel. Paul ruled out *all* the "other gospels" besides the one he preached. I have always thought that common sense and reason should tell anyone that there can be but *one* true account of what Christ did and what he accomplished for his people. There can be but one set of accurate instructions for the saints to follow. There cannot be numerous conflicting gospels and all of them be true. Therefore Paul declared emphatically and without equivocation that "though we, or an angel from heaven, preach *any other* gospel unto you than that which we preached unto you, let him be accursed" (Gal. 1:8). It would be hard to state anything any plainer.

There are hundreds of different churches today, all preaching their own version of the gospel, and all claiming to have the truth, but unless they are holding to, and preaching, the same doctrines and practices Paul documented and preached, they are wrong.

March 6

"He had this testimony, that he pleased God" (Hebrews 11:5)

The true possessors of faith are the only ones who can please God (v. 6), and even they can only please him when they do the things he has commanded in his word. He will not settle for anything less than for things to be done exactly according to his instructions. He will give no sanction to that worship which deviates from the pattern he has given his people, and according to which their devotions are to be rendered. He will not accept less or more. Any additions to, or deletions from, his word are an affront to his wisdom and holiness and will be met with severe loss on the part of the guilty (Rev. 22:18-19). God's way is the only *right* way, and those who think otherwise are on a collision course with disaster.

There are multitudes today suffering all manner of distresses, heartaches and woes simply because they have absolutely refused to adhere to the plain teaching of Christ. There are a great many emphatic declarations in his word that are met with stubborn defiance, even on the part of many who profess to be his most devoted followers. And then they think it strange when trouble comes that their faith is so weak and their strength is so small.

Men have a strong innate tendency to think that God will take no offense if they change his pattern a little here and there, or if they adopt their own order of worship, just so long as *they* view it as worship. But that is a grave error, to say nothing of being a willful act of rebellion. We may be certain that if it is not "according to the pattern showed thee" (Heb. 8:5) then it is not pleasing to God. Why should he ever give tokens of approval to that which is in direct disobedience to his command?

If we would have the same testimony that Enoch had, that we please God, then we must reverence him and be willing in all things to conform our lives and activities to his revealed will. For all our "instructions in righteousness" the Scriptures are a thorough furnisher unto all good works (2 Tim. 3:16-17). Let us "search the Scriptures daily (Acts 17:11). They won't give us eternal life but they *will* guide us into those ways that please God.

March 7

"All their works they do for to be seen of men" (Matthew 23:5)

The works of the Pharisees were done in the name of piety and holiness, but those works were all a shameless pretense. Those hypocrites were total strangers to true humility and vital godliness. They loved positions of prominence and found all they desired in the mere externals of religion. Being called by high-sounding titles was extremely appealing to them. The applause and approval of men swelled them with even greater pride and reinforced their own high opinion of themselves. They prayed in public places, not out of any inward devotion to God nor with any felt sense of need, but merely to impress those that saw and heard them.

Among their many hypocritical proceedings was their habit of "making long prayers" for show, and for a pretense of close communion with God (Mark 12:40; Luke 10:47). Because of this, and because our Lord has revealed to us that people are not heard as a result of their "much speaking" (Matt. 6:7), I have always kept my prayers relatively short, particularly when called on to offer public prayer. The Lord has taught us not to imitate those who make long and wordy prayers, and he gives the following as the reason, "For your Father knoweth what ye have need of, before ye ask him." Sometimes I hear men pray as though they are trying to acquaint the Lord with various circumstances. This we cannot do, for *he knows all things* (John 21:17).

It has often amazed me that the Pharisees did not seem to realize that God could easily see through their pretended piety. Perhaps it was a case that they had deceived themselves into thinking that they were *actually* as good as they *thought* they were. Or perhaps they simply did not believe in God's omniscience and thought he could not see into their hearts.

What could be more vain than doing things merely to be seen of men? What an empty, meaningless and temporary reward that is! Men never appear more foolish and childish than when they seek such worthless and vaporous recognition, particularly in view of the fact that their hypocrisy is as obvious to God as the noonday sun is to us.

If we seek to please men we are not the servants of Christ (Gal. 1:10). If God *approves* of us, what does it matter if the whole world *condemns* us? And if he *does not* approve of us, what does it matter if the whole world *applauds* us?

ço⌉

March 8

"He that is mighty hath done to me great things" (Luke 1:49)

Happy are those who feel as did Mary when she uttered these beautiful and expressive words! And yet how inadequate do words seem when we think of how good the Lord has been to us and how great are the blessings that He has bestowed upon us! Who could begin to express the wonderful blessedness of possessing eternal life?

This alone far exceeds even the blessedness that was Mary's in being chosen to carry the precious Christ-child in her womb. As great as that blessing was, what would it have availed her if she had not possessed spiritual life? In actuality, what real meaning does life have to those who find their only source of joy in material things and who have nothing but contempt for God and godliness? To put it in Bible terms, "What doth it profit a man, if he shall gain the whole world, and lose his own soul?"

How blest we are if we have been brought by the mercy of God to love Him and to find our chief delight in Him! What a great thing this is! No life is so happy as that which is devoted to His worship and service. Oh that we all were more spiritual, more heavenly-minded, without being pharisaical! Oh that each of our hearts glowed with such heavenly love and humility that we constantly radiated the glory of God! Oh that our bosoms burned with holy zeal and we all yearned daily for the hallowed atmosphere of the house of the Lord! Oh that our minds and hearts were always deeply impressed with, and ever conscious of, the fact that "He that is mighty has done to (us) great things!" If it were so we would always go with hymns of praise on our lips and emotions of joy in our heart.

The Lord indeed has done great things *for* us and *to* us and when we properly reflect on it, and begin to enumerate our blessings, we find ourselves overwhelmed with a sense of His generosity and kindness. And, blessed thought, the best is yet to come. We will soon enter into the company of Abraham, Isaac and Jacob and all the hosts of the other departed saints, to say nothing of Christ Himself and "an innumerable company of angels." There our joys will never cease and sin will never annoy! "Bless the Lord, O my soul, and forget not all his benefits" (Psalm 103:2).

ॐॐ

March 9

"The tongue is a little member, and boasteth great things"
(James 3:5)

Have any of us ever had as much trouble with any other member of our body as we have had with our tongue? I have laid awake at night many a time grieving over words I wished I had never uttered.

I would estimate that the majority of what I would call my "soul troubles" have been a direct result of words that have rolled off my tongue with perfect ease. They came out so easily, but then it was impossible to put them back in my mouth. Some of the words I have spoken have sprouted wings as soon as they left my tongue, and the next thing I knew they had flown hundreds of miles in all directions with a little help from other tongues almost as unruly as mine. I don't suppose I have ever uttered an uncomplimentary word about anyone that did not sooner or later get back to them, usually with considerable embellishment, alterations and rearrangements.

Oh how hurtful our tongues can be, sometimes even when we mean no ill at all by what we say! How easy it is for our words to be misinterpreted or misunderstood, particularly by that class of people who wear their feelings on their sleeves and seem to almost wish to be offended! How careful we need to be to guard our lips, lest we needlessly offend one of God's little ones!

Great damage can quickly and easily be done to reputations by a loose tongue. What a dreadful evil is character assassination! Much of the good influence of many a worthy man has been maliciously weakened or destroyed by the unbridled words of liars and slanderers. There is ultimately, sooner or later, a just recompense that all such must pay, as surely as they live.

The tongue "boasteth great things," and how unbecoming! Boasting is a common fault of any unwise and unruly tongue. Everyone knows when it is being done, and no one cares to hear it. May we take great care to avoid this noisome sin.

There are a great many vices of the tongue, and many of them have issued in heartache, ruin and even death. Oft-times both blessing and cursing proceed out of the same mouths. "My brethren, such things ought not so to be" (James 3:10). Lord, help us to bridle our tongues. It is not necessary for everything that comes into our *brains* to come out of our *mouths*.

A Bridle On The Tongue

Ill-humored words have oft distressed
My mind and soul since I was young,
And I have learned there's constant need
To put a bridle on my tongue.

Harsh words have often pierced my heart;
O how, at times, those words have stung!
And thus I've seen how much we need
To put a bridle on our tongue.

Unguarded words, sharp and unkind,
Oft-times are quick and loosely flung.
O how much better if there'd been
A bridle put upon the tongue!

How often have we spoken words
Upon which little children hung!
And how we later on have wished
We'd put a bridle on our tongue!

How often had our Lord been pleased
If to His teaching we had clung!

Which tells each one of us that we
Should put a bridle on our tongue.

When tongues made pure are loosed in heav'n
Eternal anthems will be sung,
And there will be no further need
To put a bridle on our tongue.

- Elder Ralph Harris
Dec. 17, 1994

March 10

"Then they reviled him, and said, Thou art his disciple" (John 9:28)

As soon as Christ gave sight to the man who was born blind, that man immediately became the object of the Jewish leaders' contempt and scorn. And thus we also become the objects of the world's hatred as soon as we are brought out of the darkness of our native corruption into the light of God's grace and truth. We cannot be partakers of divine light without likewise, in some measure, partaking of the sufferings of Christ and insofar as we follow Him, just that far shall we meet with the world's contempt.

The gift of faith that the Lord communicated to Abel resulted in his death at the hands of his brother Cain, who did not possess that faith. And Joseph's coat of many colors, which was a gift from his father, earned for him the hatred of his brethren. By the same token, if God sees fit to bestow special gifts upon us we should not be surprised if some of those who do not possess those same gifts are at least somewhat resentful of our having them. As a result, we may very possibly become the objects of their contempt. Even some of our own kindred and brethren may treat us coolly and be jealous of the graces God has given us. Look at the sufferings the apostle Paul endured at the hands of his Jewish brethren as a direct result of the extraordinary gifts the Lord bestowed upon him.

The man who received his sight was immediately reviled and falsely accused by the Pharisees. And finally, as though they would pour upon him the ultimate charge of wretchedness, they accused him of being the disciple of Christ. Let each of us ask ourselves if we would qualify to have such an accusation brought against us. What greater honor could be bestowed upon us by an unfriendly world than to have it condemn us because of our efforts to follow in the footsteps of the meek and lowly Lamb of God?

Satan does not care how much religion we profess, just so long as we do not put Christ and His kingdom above all else. He will allow us all the external forms and empty religious rituals we may desire, just so long as we do not have the real substance of vital godliness. It is the humble, contrite, and faithful disciples of Christ that he detests, and it is against them that his strongest venom is directed.

March 11

"I am not worthy of the least of all the mercies and of all the truth which thou hast showed unto thy servant" (Genesis 32:10)

Jacob was greatly afraid and distressed at the time he spoke these words and we may marvel at his unbelief, particularly in view of his encounter with the angels a little before this. Nevertheless his words are beautiful and full of truth and instruction. Jacob was a man by whose name the whole family of the elect would thereafter be called (Deut. 32:9), yet he knew his place as a servant of God and felt his unworthiness of the least of God's mercies. We would that all of God's people were of a similar mind, and that they all occupied a like posture before the Lord.

No man has ever filled a truly significant place in God's service, or been of any real worth to the cause of Christ without humility. And no man is truly humble unless he is aware of the fact that in and of himself he is not worthy of even the least of God's mercies. Look how great a man John the Baptist was (Matt. 11:11; Luke 7:28) and yet he freely acknowledged that he was not worthy to stoop down and unloose the latchet of Christ's shoes (Luke 1:7). Look at the eminent apostle Paul as he refers to himself as "less than the least of all saints," and as *the chief of sinners* (Eph. 3:8; 1 Tim. 1:15). These men could never have been of any real use to God's people if they had not been made to know what they were by nature.

Jacob also gave credit where credit was due for what measure of divine truth he understood. He acknowledged that God *showed* it unto him. It was *revealed* truth---truth that he could not have known otherwise.

Again, he acknowledged his *servitude* to God, which is a further mark of his humility. All of those who have been blest to be a part of the household of faith are *servants*. They are not lords over God's heritage. Our Lord said to His disciples, "Ye know that the princes of the Gentiles exercise dominion over them...but it shall not be so among you: but whosoever will be great among you, let him be your minister; and whosoever will be chief among you, let him be your servant" (Matt. 20;25-27). We will have no difficulty heeding this instruction if our hearts are in harmony with the words of Jacob in Genesis 32.

March 12

"Godliness with contentment is great gain" (1 Timothy 6:6)

I am often struck by the enormity of the difference between what is actually true and what unenlightened men *think* or *suppose*. Where could we find this more markedly illustrated than in the fifth and sixth verses of 1 Timothy 6, where we find "men of corrupt minds, and destitute of the truth, *supposing that gain is godliness"* when in fact just the opposite is true—"Godliness with contentment is great gain"?

It should be carefully noted who it is that thinks *gain is godliness*. It is men of corrupt minds and destitute of the truth. Such characters are in no position to form *any* correct concepts of what constitutes godliness. Being in a state of wretchedness and ignorance renders them incapable of such a judgment. They are destitute of spiritual discernment, or understanding, and therefore they are as apt to view one thing as godliness as they are another, just so long as it is *not* godliness. *True* godliness is foolishness unto them (1 Cor. 2:14). Notice that they *supposed* gain was godliness. This was because they had no evidence or knowledge to base their ideas upon.

But those who have the mind of Christ do not have to *suppose* what godliness is. They know that godliness consists of living in harmony with God's word; according to the "instruction in righteousness" that is laid down there; and they know that this, along with contentment, is great gain. It does not matter how poor a man may be in material goods, if he has godliness with contentment he is wealthy beyond words, for not only does he have the comfort of communion with Christ here in this time world, but he is also an heir of heaven, a joint-heir with Christ. Hence all the riches of the Glory World are his jointly with Christ and with all the saints of God. What exceeding great riches indeed!

Contentment comes with a settled, firm and confident assurance that God will never leave us nor forsake us; that he will always do right by us, and that no matter how severe our trials and afflictions may become, all will ultimately be well. Who could ask for greater gain this side of heaven?

March 13

"Mary hath chosen that good part" (Luke 10:42)

Every habitual Bible reader is familiar with the circumstances that gave rise to this commendation of Mary by Christ. Rather than cumbering herself with much serving as her sister Martha was doing, Mary chose rather to sit at the feet of Jesus hearing His word. She put the spiritual ahead of the material, and in this she was an example that all God's people would do well to follow. The concerns of the soul should always take precedence over the concerns of the flesh, and an opportunity to feast the soul on the word of Christ should always be preferred over feasting the belly on the fruit of the ground.

Serving guests, like many other things, has its place, and is needful *in* that place, but when it conflicts with an opportunity to further our knowledge of Christ it will require a choice on our part. In choosing to be at the feet of Jesus, learning of Him, Mary did not neglect any pressing duty. She simply had her priorities straight, and rather than rebuking her, Christ said she had chosen that good part which would not be taken away from her.

Any time we are at the feet of Jesus hearing His word we stand to gain knowledge that may prove valuable to us in many circumstances throughout the remainder of our lives. If such an opportunity is missed or passed up who can say how great a loss it may constitute?

If I should be asked to give my opinion as to what Christ meant when He said, "One thing is needful," I would say it is that we should put first things first, and in the case before us that is what Mary did. In so doing she chose that "good part" which was never taken away from her. I am sure this was one thing she never regretted, for she carried precious memories of it to her grave.

May the Lord give grace and wisdom that we may always choose that good part. We will never be the losers for having done so.

March 14

"The heavens declare the glory of God: and the firmament showeth his handiwork" (Psalm 19:1)

Wherever we train our eyes we are beholding the handiwork of God. Everything around us bespeaks his power, wisdom and glory, whether it be in the intricate design of the lily or the brilliant colors of the rainbow, the tiniest grain of sand or the most gargantuan star. The one is as much his work as the other and is just as illustrative of his glory. Although the declarative voice of the heavens as it proclaims the glory of God is a passive one, just as the songs of birds passively glorify him, yet it is a wonderful declaration, and is of such a magnitude that it reaches to earth's remotest bounds and beyond. The immensity of the heavens speaks loudly and clearly of the greatness of

God. The stars of the sky are *innumerable* (Gen. 15:5; Heb. 11:12) and yet he even calls them all by their names (Psalm 147:4). Think upon this and marvel.

No matter how far the greatest telescopes peer out into space, they only discover more and more of God's handiwork, greater and more wonderful enigmas and marvels. And yet, the Bible speaks of the heavens as God's finger work (Psalm 8:3). What a gloriously incomprehensible Being he is, that he can merely *speak* and it is done! Such things are far too high for us.

The heavens declare that God is a God of infinite variety (1 Cor. 15:40-41). He has not created either men or stars so that they are mere clones of one another, but he makes them all to differ one from another (1Cor. 4:7). Among the untold billions of earthlings no two of them are exactly alike, either in appearance or personality. So also do the heavenly bodies each bear their own distinct qualities and characteristics.

The heavens are indeed a grand testifier to the glory of God, for they show him to be infinitely great and wise, a God of endless design and uninterrupted order, and a God of limitless power. Oh thou unbeliever! Dost thou seek a sign or proof of God's existence? Thou art without excuse, for they are all around thee, above they head and beneath thy feet. Were it not for thy blindness, it would be plain to thee!

March 15

"In the world ye shall have tribulation: but be of good cheer; I have overcome the world" (John 16:33)

The Lord has made no secret of the fact that His people will suffer while they live here in time, but neither has he left them without comfort. It is certain that they will have tribulation in this world, but it is equally certain that Christ has overcome the world, and that even amidst their troubles and trials there is reason for them to be of good cheer. We are informed that the afflictions of the righteous are many, but at the same time we are assured that if we are among that happy number, the Lord will deliver us out of them all (Psalm 34:19). Now, while we are confined to these tabernacles of clay (these mortal bodies), we often groan, being burdened, but we are also looking forward to the day when we will be "clothed upon" with a glorified body, that mortality may be swallowed up of life (2 Cor. 5:4).

Notice that when the Lord informs us of a difficulty that lies ahead of us, he also gives us a word of cheer and encouragement. "Beloved, think it not strange concerning the fiery trial that is to try you, as though some strange thing happened unto you: but rejoice, inasmuch as ye are partakers of Christ's sufferings," etc. (1 Peter 4:12-13). It is a principle that we may confidently rest in, that "as the sufferings of Christ abound in us, so our consolation also aboundeth by Christ" (2 Cor. 1:5). And one of the fringe benefits God's people reap from their sufferings for Christ's sake is that they learn to comfort others who are in similar troubles with the same comforts that they have received from God.

The children of God may sometimes wonder why their afflictions and tribulations are as severe as they are, but God is all-wise and he knows what is best for them. We may not always know why things are with us as they are, but he can see a "need be" that we sometimes endure heaviness for a season (1 Peter 1:17). If things were always easy and smooth for us our faith would never be tried, and if our faith was never tried it would never bring the praise, honor and glory to God that it would otherwise. May we learn, therefore, to glory in our trials, knowing that we will be better persons for having experienced them.

March 16

"His merciful kindness is great toward us..." (Psalm 117:2)

To those of us who feel that we can join with the apostle Paul in classifying ourselves as "the chief of sinners" the above words almost seem like an understatement. It is very distressing to me to think of the many times I have in one way or another violated God's holy and perfect law. And when we consider our own frailty and the wretchedness of human nature we are made to wonder how anyone could think that they do not daily transgress. In *many* things we all offend (James 3:2), and "if we say we have no sin, we deceive ourselves, and the truth is not in us" (1 John 1:8). All of us have sinned, (both by commission and omission) and we daily repeat the process (probably in many particulars) and yet the Lord's merciful kindness continues toward us. How great indeed is that kindness!

There are multitudes in the world who do not consider themselves to be *great* sinners, and some who do not view themselves as sinners at all. How then could they possibly feel that God *ever* shows them any *merciful kindness*? What would be the point in showing merciful kindness to those who never sinned, much less *great* merciful kindness? Only *great* sinners feel to need *great* mercy from the Lord, and only *great* sinners are able to view him as a *great* Savior.

Morally speaking the apostle Paul was as good a man as could have been found, both before *and* after his conversion. Yet after the light of the Spirit showed him what he was *by nature,* from that day forth he recognized the fact that he was a "wretched man" (Romans 7:24) and that deliverance from his sinful state could only come from God "through Jesus Christ" his Lord and Savior. He knew it could not be by his own works, because he understood that no amount of human merit and creature righteousness could ever overcome, or compensate for, the awful debt of sin he owed.

The reason why God's merciful kindness to his people is so *great* is because even at their best they are still *great* sinners and are entirely unworthy of the least of his favors. And those who are *forgiven* much, also *love* much (Luke 7:47).

March 17

"Thou couldest have no power at all againstme, except it were given thee from above" (John 19:11)

When the appointed time came for Christ to lay down his life for his sheep, he did not do or say anything from that point on that would have hindered or delayed his sufferings. When the great multitude came with swords and staves to Gethsemane to arrest him, he could just as easily have hidden himself from them then as he had done on numerous other occasions (Luke 4:28-30; John 8:59; 10:31, 39). That he had complete control over them is evidenced by the fact that they "went backward and fell to the ground" as soon as he spoke to them (John 18:6). As he told Peter on that occasion, he could have had twelve legions of angels and more come to his aid at any time he might have chosen. But the truth is, he didn't even need the aid of angels. It was he who had *created* the angels, and he could do just as well *without* them. He *needs* nothing, seeing that it is *he* who gives to all "life and breath and all things" (Acts 17:25).

What a pathetic sight is God's creatures bowing their necks against him! Poor, weak creatures thinking they can contend with their Maker! Pilate was like the rest of us in the sense that he was but a lowly worm of the dust, and could not have raised even a little finger against Christ if heaven had not consented. Oh, the marvel of the very Son of God incarnate suffering himself to be scourged by this godless governor! And yet, submit he must; not for lack of *power* to deliver himself, but because his very mission into the world required that he suffer, bleed and die for his people.

Of his life he said, "No man taketh it from me, but I lay it down of myself. I have power to lay it down, and I have power to take it again" (John 10:18). When the soldiers came to break his legs and hasten his death, they found to their amazement that he was already dead (John 19:32) for he had "given up the ghost" at *his* appointed time, not *theirs*. The Jews were charged with his murder because they had demanded it and intended it, but *he* was in control of the whole event, not they. Praise be to God for the sweet hope that he *laid down his life* for me!

March 18

"If ye then, be risen with Christ, seek those things which are above" (Colossians 3:1)

Those whom God has visited by the mighty power of his Holy Spirit and quickened into divine light and life are described as having "risen with Christ." This work of grace in the heart produces a resurrection from a state of death in trespasses and sins to a state of spiritual life in Christ. And unless a man has been thus raised, he consists of nothing but that which is *natural,* and in this fleshly state nothing good dwells in him (Romans 7:18). He does not receive the things of the Spirit of God, and not only that; such things "are foolishness unto him" and he cannot know them. The reason he cannot *know* them is because an understanding of spiritual things requires spiritual discernment, or understanding, and *this* he does not have (1 Cor. 2:14).

The great fallacy of popular religion is its contention that all men possess spiritual discernment, the spiritually *dead* as well as the spiritually *alive.* This is a grave and momentous error and it throws the whole arminian system totally off the Biblical track. It is only those who are, *already*, "risen with Christ" who are exhorted to "seek those things which are above." Extend this admonition to any of those who have *not* been thus born of the Spirit and it will be flippantly rejected, if not laughed at and scorned. "The carnal mind is enmity against God: for it is not subject to the law of God, neither indeed can be. So then they that are in the flesh cannot please God" (Romans 8:7-8).

But let us in no way downplay or underestimate the importance of God's "risen" people seeking heavenly things. Their eternal destiny does not in any way depend on it, but their spiritual health and well-being here in time does largely depend on it. If they live after the flesh they will *die* to the spiritual joys they otherwise could have experienced, but if they through the Spirit mortify the deeds of the body, they shall *live* in the sense of enjoying peace of conscience and happiness of soul (See Romans 8:13). May the Lord help us to humbly and sincerely walk in the paths of righteousness and to enjoy the sweet tokens of his love.

March 19

"Casting all your care upon him; for he careth for you"
(1 Peter 5:7)

Part of what is involved in humbling ourselves "under the mighty hand of God" is our casting all our care upon him. We must have the aid of his Holy Spirit in this, for it is contrary to our fleshly nature to "submit ourselves" to him (James 4:7), and that is what we are doing when we obey his precepts. Conversely, we are exalting ourselves and rebelling *against* him when we do not obey him.

It grieves me to think of the number of times I have failed to cast my cares upon the Lord. And any time I have ever been guilty of this failure it has resulted in distress of soul and anguish of mind and heart that I otherwise would not have had to endure. I rather suspect that each of us have experienced the difficulty involved in immediately submitting ourselves to God when distresses have arisen. I believe many times our initial reaction is to begin trying to figure out how *we ourselves* are going to work the problem out, and this results in sleepless nights and the weakening of our health.

This is not to say that there is never anything for us to do, for God always expects us to do what we can, but while we are doing *that* we should also be submitting ourselves to his will, trusting in his mercy and acknowledging within our heart that he is in complete control of all events and circumstances. We sometimes try to go ahead of the Lord and this invariably, and inevitably, gets us into even deeper trouble. Unbelief is a great foe to God's people. It has caused us all much suffering. We need to remember that nothing is too hard for the Lord and that one way or another, and in his own time, he will deliver us out of all our afflictions.

At any time we are troubled and distressed over anything, no matter what it may be, let us take our burden to the Lord, and if we cannot then and there cast it upon him, let us take even *that* to him. Eventually we *will* be able to cast it all at his feet and leave it there.

How wonderful it is that the Lord cares for His people and extends to them the blessed privilege of casting their cares upon him! May he help us to avail ourselves of this blessed opportunity.

March 20

"If any man will do His will, he shall know of the doctrine,
whether it be of God" (John 7:17)

There is a wonderful principle set forth in this text showing us that there is an undeniable connection between obedience to God and spiritual understanding and perception. "Any man" who has been quickened by the Spirit of God and given a desire to comply with his precepts, and who responds positively to that desire, will find his insight into divine things increasing as he goes along. God's people, in regeneration, receive *of* God's fullness, and are given "grace for grace" (John 1:16). Hence, if they properly use the grace he gives them it will result in their being given more grace (James 4:6). It is in this sense that the apostle Paul besought the brethren that they not "receive the grace of God in vain" (2 Cor. 6:1). "God resisteth the proud *(those who rebel against His precepts)*, but giveth grace unto the humble."

In regeneration he gives his people spiritual senses, and the "strong meat" of the gospel belongs to those of them who exercise those senses to such an extent that they develop a keener ability to "discern both good and evil" (Heb. 5:14). Without this exercise of the spiritual senses they will be in great danger of *calling evil good and good evil and putting darkness for light and light for darkness,* etc. (Isaiah 5:20). Good spiritual discernment is vital to God's people, but they are not going to have that discernment if their walk is contrary to God's will. And they are not going to know what God's will is unless they spend a lot of time in his word, hiding it in their heart and storing it in their mind. I don't think I have ever known of any church trouble that was not in some way a by-product of a lack of spiritual knowledge and discernment.

If God's people are not "growing in grace, and in the knowledge of our Lord and Savior Jesus Christ" (2 Peter 3:18) then they are losing ground. Paul besought the Thessalonian brethren that as they had received of him how they ought to walk and to please God, so they would abound more and more (1 Thess. 4:1). And he prayed for the Philippian brethren that their love might abound yet more and more in knowledge and in all judgment (Phil. 1:9). May the Lord help us to do his will, and to increase in knowledge and understanding.

March 21

"He that speakest of himself seeketh his own glory: but he that seekest his glory that sent him, the same is true..." (John 7:18)

Christ spoke these words to those Jews who accused him of being an imposter, and his argument against their charge is very powerful indeed. He shows that he sought the glory of the One who sent him rather than seeking his own glory. This would not be characteristic of an imposter. The same is true of ordinary ministers. Those who are true servants of Christ will seek to honor and promote *his* name rather than their own. If a man seeks his own recognition and advancement we may certainly conclude that he is not called of God. We may be sure that both his desire to preach and the message he brings is "of himself" in the sense that God has not given it to him.

The apostle Paul said, "We preach not ourselves" (2 Cor. 4:5). That is, true ministers of the gospel do not have themselves as the subject of their preaching, but rather "Christ Jesus the Lord." And they are faithful to show their hearers that they are no more than servants "for Jesus' sake." They are careful to promote the glory of Christ and not to seek any glory for themselves. Like the apostle Peter, they would have their hearers to fully understand that they also are but men (Acts 10:26). They would not in any sense knowingly promote idolatry but rather would strongly encourage men to "turn to God from idols to serve the living and true God" (1 Thess. 1:9).

The preaching of the true servants of God is not calculated merely to please men, and thus to promote their own standing and popularity, but their purpose is to please God by preaching that which he bids them preach (Jonah 3:2). If men are pleased with the preaching of the truth, that is well and good, but the servants of Christ are to preach the truth whether it is pleasing to men or not. Paul did not *seek* to please men for he knew that if he did so he would not be the servant of Christ (Gal. 1:10).

It was always been, and always will be the hallmark of the true servants of Christ that their greatest pleasure and highest ambition is to seek the glory of the One who sent them. "Ye shall know them by their fruits" (Matt. 7:16).

March 22

"Blessed are the poor in spirit..." (Matthew 5:3)

The poor in spirit, or those who are poor in a spiritual sense, are those who have been given a sufficient insight into their own native corruption and depravity to make them fully realize that *all their righteousnesses are as filthy rags* (Isaiah 64:6). They have been made to see and feel that "every man at his best state is altogether vanity" (Psalm 39:5) and that man's heart is, by nature, "deceitful above all things, and desperately wicked" (Jer. 17:9). They are such as have been stripped of all "confidence in the flesh" (Philippians 3:3) and laid low in the dust of self-abasement. They come empty-handed to the footstool of God's mercy and throw themselves entirely upon his compassion and kindness, pleading nothing but the imputed righteousness of Christ.

Such characters are indeed blest, for they have "received the Spirit of adoption" and by the leadings of the Spirit have been made to see themselves as "less than the least of all saints" (Eph. 3:8) and to esteem their brethren better than themselves (Philippians 2:3). And being thus dealt with by the Lord they have been placed in a position where the true gospel is perfectly suited to their circumstances and condition: "The poor have the gospel preached to *them*" (Matt. 11:5; Luke 7:22). Being *materially* poor does not, in itself, qualify one as a subject of gospel address, but being *spiritually* poor does, for only the spiritually poor have had the necessary experiences to make them receptive of the gospel. "They that are whole (*in their own perception of matters*) have no (*felt*) need of the physician" (Christ) says Mark 2:17.

As long as a person is still clinging to any work, or works, of his own, and depending in part or in whole upon those works to get him to heaven, he is not yet truly "poor in spirit." Until he lives, from day to day, at the feet of Jesus, and until he becomes a continual beggar at mercy's door, he still has not reached a state of spiritual poverty.

We cannot make spiritual paupers of ourselves or of others, but if the Lord has made us so we have much to be thankful for, for ours is the kingdom of heaven.

March 23

"He endured, as seeing him who is invisible" (Hebrews 11:27)

Moses was a man of great faith, and consequently he endured many things at the hands of those who had little or no faith. He was an humble man, "very meek, above all the men which were upon the face of the earth" (Num. 12:3), and by virtue of that meekness he was very probably more a target of Satan's hatred than any other man of his day. But his faith, which God had given him in great measure, enabled him to endure all the trials, discouragements and heartaches that came his way. That faith equipped him to do something very miraculous and wonderful—he could see him who is invisible to the natural eye. And thus seeing and trusting in the faithfulness and goodness of the Almighty, he pressed forward when lesser men would have fallen by the wayside.

Those who have never been visited by the Spirit of God and quickened into Divine life are void of faith and therefore "cannot please God" (Rom. 8:8; Heb. 11:6). Not possessing faith, they cannot see him who is invisible, and in spite of the overwhelming evidence that surrounds them, they do not believe anyone else can either. It makes no sense to the natural mind that anything invisible can be seen. But the apostle Paul shows in Romans 1:30 that they are without excuse, because the invisible things of the Creator, such as his eternal power and Godhead, may be plainly concluded, and known to exist, from the things that he has made, or created. In other words, they ought to know that there cannot be a creation if there is no *Creator*. The fact that there is a *creation* clearly shows that there is a *Creator*. Therefore the Scriptures speak of those as *fools* who say in their heart, "There is no God" (Psalm 14:1).

What a wonderful thing true faith is! It enables us to believe in, rejoice in, love, trust in, and render obedience to, him whom we have not seen with our natural eyes (1 Peter 1:6-9). It enables us to endure many things that otherwise we could not bear. Let us not complain when our faith is tried, for this is one of the primary ways God brings glory to himself and good to us. It brings joy to our souls and praise to our lips when we endure, "as seeing him who is invisible."

March 24

"Blessed are they which do hunger and thirst after
righteousness" (Matthew 5:6)

Hunger and thirst after righteousness denotes a sincere desire and longing for the things of God and godliness, and those are indeed wonderfully blest characters whose hearts continually go out to God with such spiritual cravings. The apostle Paul said, "Our conversation is in heaven" (Philippians 3:20), by which he meant that their whole life, both in word and in deed, was centered in and around "the things of the Spirit of God." Both the words of their mouth and the meditation of their heart were acceptable in the Lord's sight (Psalm 19:14), and they were always seeking first the kingdom of God and his righteousness, for these meant more to them than life itself.

The person who hungers and thirsts after righteousness not only craves new or fresh evidences that he is clothed with the imputed righteousness of Christ, but he sincerely desires to *be* right and to *do* right. He wishes to be led in paths of righteousness, with no other view than the glory of God. His soul hungers for the proclamation of the true gospel. He loves to hear the wonderful works and ways of the

Lord preached in the demonstration of the Spirit and of power. He delights in conversing with spiritually minded people on scriptural subjects, and is often found searching God's word for more comfort, greater enlightenment and a richer understanding of his will.

One of the many precious promises of God's word is that those who thus hunger and thirst, "shall be filled." He who *gives* the hunger and thirst also *satiates* it, so that there is a double blessing. And he who gives his people a spiritual appetite has also given them an Inspired Volume of truth to which a lifetime of study may be profitably devoted. It is an inexhaustible well from which living waters have been drawn for many centuries, and still there is no less supply than at the first. There are times with those who draw from this well when it *seems* that it is dry, but this too is for their good, for it keeps them always going back to it in hopes of another time of refreshing.

March 25

"In every nation he that feareth (God), and worketh
righteousness, is accepted with Him." (Acts 10:34)

God is no respecter of persons in the sense that the nationality of people has absolutely nothing to do with whether or not they are accepted with him. It matters not whether they be Jew or Greek, black or white, red or brown, high or low, rich or poor, if they have been quickened by the Spirit of God and are consequently God-fearing workers of righteousness, they are accepted with him.

Primitive Baptists have often been accused of having a narrow platform, but this is far from being true. In fact, it is those who make this charge who actually have a narrow platform, for they argue that none will be saved eternally except those who hear, believe and obey the gospel. This excludes most of the human race, to say nothing of those who die in infancy, the mentally incapable, and those who lived before the gospel dispensation. But Acts 10:34 well expresses the Old Baptist platform and it embraces all God-fearing people, even in the most remote regions of the earth where the sound of a gospel sermon has never been heard. It embraces a people "out of every kindred, and tongue, and people, and nation" (Rev. 5:9) and this is a "great multitude" that no man can number (Rev. 7:9). This is a much broader platform than popular religion has.

We have often heard other orders say that it is their goal to "take the world for Christ," and we Old Baptists would have no objection whatsoever if they could achieve that goal, but they have never done it, and they never will. There are those whom our Lord described as goats, and to whom he said, "Ye are of your father the devil, and the lusts of your father ye will do" (John 8:44). These do not fear God, and they never will. They do not work righteousness and they never will. But if it were possible for the religious world to convert them and turn them into sheep, what reason would we have to object? From our viewpoint, the more righteous people there are in the world, the more pleased we are. It's just that we Old Baptists understand that the only ones who will be brought to fear God and work righteousness are among the elect family of God. The doctrine of the Bible bars no one from heaven except those to whom heaven would be *hell*. And that's the way it *should* be.

March 26

"I shall be satisfied, when I awake with thy likeness."
(Psalm 17:15)

There are several scriptures informing us that the Lord's people will ultimately be like him, and regardless of the way, or ways, that they will be like him, their conformity to his image (Romans 8:29) will be unspeakably wonderful. When they reach that blessed state, in the resurrection, they will then, and ever more, be satisfied. This alone, if we had nothing else to base it on, would amply show us that heaven, and our state therein, will be everything we could wish it to be, for however it may be, we will be satisfied with it. Everything will be exactly as we would have it, and of course, exactly as it should be. If there was any sorrow there of any kind, it would not be heaven, and we could not be satisfied. If there was anything lacking that we desired, or anything superfluous that we did not like, we could never be perfectly content with our situation there and would probably not wish to stay there forever.

John tells us that in the glorified state we will be like Christ and we will "see him as he is" (1 John 3:2). And with this knowledge what does it matter that we are presently left lacking in details? To be like Christ and to have a clear spiritual sight of him, unmarred by the veil of nature, is enough. What more could we desire?

Paul tells us that when Christ returns he will "change our vile body" and fashion it like unto *his* glorious body (Philippians 3:20-21). And in that glorified body we will be able to enter fully into the joy of our Lord, seeing the glories of heaven with perfect sight and hearing the music of heaven with anointed ears. Sin will be left behind and there will be nothing to restrain or dampen our endless delight.

And though "it does not yet appear what we shall be," Job shows us that we will each have our own identity (Job 19:27). He said *he* would see the Lord for *himself*, and that *his* eyes would behold, and *not another*. Even though there will be a glorious sense in which we will be "like Christ," it will still be *us* in a glorified body. And though we have never been completely and totally satisfied here in this present world, we *will* be satisfied in the next. This is a soul-cheering thought to those who love the Lord.

March 27

"God hath chosen the foolish things of the world to confound the wise" (1 Corinthians 1:27)

How utterly contrary are the thoughts and ways of God to those of the carnal mind. According to Isaiah 55:8-9, there is an unfathomable gulf that lies between them. Hence there is a continual quarrel on the part of unenlightened men against the mind and purpose of God. If they had their way God would not have made any choices among men at all, because the thought that he should *do what he will with his own* (Matt. 20:15) is very abhorrent to them, even though they do the same thing. What else could we expect of those who are spoken of in our text as "wise" but that they should be greatly offended by the fact that God has done works for the express purpose of "confounding" them.

It should be noted that these "wise" men (*wise in their own eyes and in the eyes of the world*) are of such a character and disposition that they have a very high opinion of themselves and of their own intelligence. Consequently the thought of their being "confounded" with "foolish" things is very insulting to their greatly inflated egos. For them to be confounded by great and profound mysteries would not be anything to be wondered at, but God confounds them with the very things that they deem as "foolish." He puts them to confusion by the very things, and individuals, that they look upon as "weak," "base," and "despised," and even things that they consider beneath their notice, as though they "were not." God has "chosen" these things, "that no flesh should glory in His presence," just as he has saved his people "by grace" and "not of works" *lest any man should boast* (Eph. 2:8-9).

God's ways are constantly confounding the worldly-wise, yet they continue to profess themselves to be men of great wisdom. And in doing so they *become fools* (Romans 1:22). To those whom God has enlightened, such characters appear all the more foolish as they constantly attempt to explain away the works of God and totally discount the Biblical record. The Scriptures tell us that "the fear of God is the beginning of wisdom" (Psalm 111:20) and "of knowledge" (Prov. 1:7; 9:10). According to this, the "wise" of 1 Corinthians 1:27 have not yet even *started* down the road to true wisdom.

March 28

"In him we live, and move, and have our being" (Acts 17:28)

T hese words were not addressed to a church, but to a heathen group who were worshipping "the unknown God" and who mocked when the apostle preached the resurrection of the dead unto them. The apostle Paul would have the Epicureans and Stoics, and the Athenian philosophers to know that they owed their very existence and preservation to the One who created the world and all things therein, and that all their very actions were under his complete control.

Unbelievers are just as much the creatures of God as believers. They are, and must be, upheld by the same divine power, and fed by the same providence. The very breath by which they deny and blaspheme God is a product of his benevolence to them. Every day they blindly, thanklessly and uncaringly "bite the hand that feeds them." They are like the swine that feed upon the acorns under the oaks and never look up or give a thought to where their nourishment comes from. And in this wretched state of wretched thoughtlessness and ingratitude they will remain forever unless grace prevents.

We have often thought of our text as a very good example of the exactness and accuracy of the Scriptures. Contrary to popular religion, the text has life *before* action. "In whom we *live*" first, and then "move." The doctrine of the masses has it just the reverse, saying, "If the spiritually dead will *move* (accept Christ, or perform various other conditions) then as a result they will *live* spiritually." This is not only contrary to common sense, but it is a totally unworkable theology. In *all* cases *life* must precede *action.* God gives life to his people and *then* there is movement. This is true both in the natural and spiritual realms.

The false idea of the origin of the species through an evolutionary process also requires some kind of movement or activity on the part of some material or substance in order that it may come to life. This of course, like arminianism, makes no sense. God is the sole source of all life. An *enemy* of God deciding on his own to become a *lover* of God is about as likely as a rock deciding to become a tree.

March 29

"They have their reward" (Matthew 6:2-5)

Our Lord spoke these words with regard to those hypocritical professors of religion who sought the glory of men and were fond of having their religious exercises *seen of men*. When they had accomplished what they sought for, they therein received their reward, but what a pathetic and transitory reward it was. What a vain thing they sought, and what an empty bubble it was when attained! Both the seeking for it, and the giving of it to others, is equally abominable to God. Seeking glory of men is an attempt to usurp the throne from God and to receive that which belongs only to Him. The guilty parties seek to make little gods of themselves.

The Lord calls them hypocrites, and very aptly do they fit that description. What greater example of hypocrisy could be found than that of a man pretending to be serving God while in reality seeking the glory of men and desiring to have his devotions observed by the same? And how devoid of principle must they be who are not afraid to seek their own advancement under the pretense of serving God! They are indeed hypocrites and so are those who give them the glory they seek.

How abhorrent to the apostles of Christ was the thought of receiving glory of men (Acts 10:25, 26; 14:11-18; 1 Cor. 2:1-5; 1 Thess. 2:6). They were men of principle who sought nothing but the glory of God and the good of his people. They not only did not seek the glory of men for themselves but they also taught them that they should turn from such idolatrous vanities to worship and serve the living and true God. Like John the Baptist, they felt unworthy to stoop down and unloose their Lord's shoe latchets. And so it is with his true servants today.

What pathetic characters are those who desire the praise of men, and who desire it so much that they are glad to accept it, even if it must come from other hypocrites. May the Lord deliver us from all suggestions of idolatry and from all vestiges of hypocritical religion. May our chief aim always be the glory of God and the mortification of our flesh.

March 30

"Wherefore comfort one another with these words"
(1 Thessalonians 4:18)

The "words" with which God's people are to comfort one another are the words of the context, particularly verses 13 through 17. It should be observed that the apostle speaks of the coming of the Lord in each chapter of this book. It was a theme that brought him much personal delight and comfort, and it likewise comforts all those who have the same hope as did he. It comforts them because it marks the end of this "present evil world" and the beginning of joys unspeakable, joys that will never cease. It comforts them because they are looking forward with sweet anticipation to seeing Christ in all his glory and being with him forever in total peace, perfection and contentment.

It is a great comfort to God's people to have the sweet hope of being one day reunited with their deceased loved ones in the glory world. How distressing would be their loss if they were "without hope" and never expected to see those loved ones again! It is a comfort to have the sweet assurance that we will not only be in the visible and personal presence of Christ, but also in the presence of all his saints, which includes the patriarchs and apostles and all the others of his people that we read of in the Bible.

Another great source of comfort is the assurance that when we are "caught up together" with the rest of the elect "to meet the Lord in the air, we shall "*ever* be with him." The duration of that happy state is *eternal.* We cannot comprehend this now, for in our present circumstances everything, and every situation, that we see with our natural eyes has an end, but we will understand it better by and by when faith gives way to full fruition.

And again, it is comforting to consider that in the Scriptures the death of the body is compared to *sleep,* because it is a state from which there will be an awakening. David said he would be satisfied when he *awoke* with the likeness of Christ (Psalm 17:15). Everything we are told about the resurrection of the righteous and their future state is comforting to those who love the Lord and who are eagerly awaiting his second personal appearing. As we have opportunity, let us comfort one another with these gems of truth that he has left us in his word.

March 31

"Their shepherds have caused them to go astray"
(Jeremiah 50:6)

As a general rule when churches go astray it is because their pastors have led them in wrong paths. Every church division I have ever had any knowledge of has been the result of poor leadership on the part of one or more preachers. I have seen pastors encourage the receiving of members into their churches who had been excluded from orderly churches, and this has *always* caused division and always will. I have seen pastors encourage the receiving of members who were living in a state of adultery, or in some other form of ungodliness, and this sort of thing, if not repented of, not only causes division but will result in the eventual removal of the candlestick from the guilty church or churches. I have seen weak pastors bring innovations into the church, and this has caused the members to go astray. All these things and many others have caused division among our people and it has often grieved my soul and caused my heart to bleed.

Pastoring churches is an extremely solemn and serious matter, and I have good reason to believe that there have been, and still are, a number of ministers who have not taken that responsibility nearly as much to heart as such a high calling demands. This is a fearful thing to be guilty of, and the consequences are very grievous. Many of the pastors, or shepherds, have not sought to properly inform themselves of the historical beliefs of our people either doctrinally, practically or governmentally, and this has placed them in a dangerous position so far as their knowing how to lead the flock. One popular expression is that "ignorance is bliss," but where the pastorship of churches is concerned this is far from true. "It is required in stewards, that a man be found faithful" (1 Cor. 4:2). And if they are not faithful the example they will set for the flock will be very hurtful and destructive.

Pastors are not to be "lords over God's heritage" but "ensamples to the flock" (1 Peter 5:3) and *helpers of their joy* (2 Cor. 1:24). There is a vast difference between the two. I know of churches even now where the pastors have overstepped their bounds and the membership is consequently divided. There may be silent minorities who are perhaps afraid to express their discontent, but the division is still there. Oh, that all our pastors were humble men who would always put the peace and welfare of our beloved Zion above all their own interests and ambitions!

April 1

"Groanings which cannot be uttered" (Romans 8:26)

In my earlier years I would often hear ministers who were called to the stand to preach let out deep groans of seeming distress. Perhaps the groans that were emitted under those circumstances were sometimes tinged with a measure of hypocrisy, or with an unconscious appeal for sympathy (I cannot say), but I do not doubt that most of those old brethren groaned because they felt a great burden in their souls. If my own experience bears any resemblance to theirs, they groaned under a felt sense of their own inadequacy for such a solemn and weighty duty as is the proclamation of the gospel. And in conjunction with this keen awareness of their own weakness and insufficiency, they also sometimes felt a measure of inner fleshly rebellion against, or at least a strong dread of, preaching on the particular subject God had lain on their heart to deliver. I would describe some of these feelings and subsequent groans as being *unutterable*.

Have you not sometimes desired to pray and yet the feelings you wanted to express came forth from your breast more in the form of *groans* than *words*? The fact of the matter is that a human vocabulary often greatly limits us so far as being able to communicate audibly what we feel inwardly. There is indeed such a thing as "groanings which *cannot* be uttered;" not just groanings that we *refuse* to utter, or are *remiss* to utter, but groanings that we simply *cannot* put into words. I recall that on one occasion the apostle Paul was "caught up to the third heaven...and heard *unspeakable* words, which it is not lawful for a man to utter" (2 Cor. 12:2-4). In the center column of marginal Bibles you will find that the translators have given an alternate reading: "words, which it is not *possible* for a man to utter." So we see that there were some things that even the inspired apostle could not utter or express.

I am thankful that the Lord knows my innermost thoughts and feelings. I am glad that those deep and sincere supplications that have a place in my *heart* but cannot find a place upon my *lips* are all clearly understood by Him. The words of our Lord in Isaiah 65:24 seem very appropriate here: "And it shall come to pass, that before they call, I will answer; and while they are yet speaking, I will hear." In his intercession for us he can even take our groans of emotion and present them to the Father as prayers. "Thanks be unto God for his *unspeakable gift*" (2 Cor. 9:15).

April 2

"I have loved thee with an everlasting love" (Jeremiah 31:3)

It is a cardinal principle of God's word that there is nothing that can separate his people from his love, which is in Christ Jesus (Rom. 8:31-39). He will never leave them nor forsake them, and consequently they may boldly assert that he is their Helper and that they will not fear what man shall do unto them (Heb. 13:5-6). He has begun a good work in them and he will perform it until the return of Christ (Philippians 1:6). They were given to Christ in the covenant of election before the world began, and they will never perish. No man can pluck them out of the hand of Christ, nor out of the hand of the heavenly Father, for they are one (John 10:28-30). In a word, they are eternally secure in Christ.

An *everlasting* love is a love that will not end. There are those who contend that God may love a person today enough to give him eternal life, but if he transgresses tomorrow God will then despise him enough to "appoint him his portion with the hypocrites." But such a love is beneath the dignity of the Deity. It is unworthy of the infallible nature God. The essential love of God for his people, is, like himself, immutable or unchangeable, and it is because of this immutability that "the sons of Jacob," or God's elect, *are not consumed* (Malachi 3:6).

Anyone who has any spiritual understanding of themselves and of human nature knows that if God's love was not immutable then they would have no hope of the Glory world. By keeping the commandments of Christ they can abide in his love in an experiential sense, i.e. in the sense of their joy being full, etc. (John 15:10-11), but they could never abide in his favor very long if it depended on their never displeasing him. If he should mark iniquities in the sense of keeping a running account against us, none of us could stand (Psalm 130:3). It is a thing to be marveled at that any of us should be called the sons of God. It is owing entirely to the *manner* of his love to his people

(1 John 3:1). It is an *everlasting* love, and it is because of that fact that his people are drawn unto him with loving-kindness, not because of any merit on their part.

April 3

"Though he slay me, yet will I trust in him" (Job 13:15)

Job is a prime example of one who had a faith that would not fail. Satan did not understand this kind of faith and neither does the world. Satan had no idea that Job's faith would withstand anywhere near the kind of test it was put to, but he thought that under such trials Job would *curse God to His face* (1:11; 2:5). And even when his own wife would have had him "curse God, and die" (2:9), he did not and would not "sin with his lips." By virtue of the severity of his mental and physical anguish he said things that under normal circumstances he would have reproved others for saying, yet he retained his faith and his integrity.

We read in Hebrews 11:13 that the patriarchs of old, "all died in faith." And the reason they died thus is because their faith did not fail them, either in life or in death. Not only was it good enough to *live* by, but it was also good enough to *die* by. In fact, it was a great stay and staff in the hour of death and enabled them to breathe out their lives sweetly with their eyes toward that "city which hath foundations, whose builder and maker is God" (Heb. 11:10).

Elder J. A. Monsees, in whose good home I had the pleasure of visiting a number of times before his death some 30 years ago, composed a song that begins with the words, "Oh, for a faith that will not fail!" He did indeed possess just such a faith and consequently it saw him through to the end of his earthly journey. And so shall it be with us if we have, as he did, "that faith of our father Abraham" (Rom. 4:12).

It is a great comfort to this unworthy writer that after a great many severe trials and afflictions I can still say with Job, that though God should slay me, yet will I trust Him. The Lord has been very merciful to me, and I realize that there is no such thing as *deserved mercy*. If it should please him to crush me under his mighty hand of justice, my mind and heart forcefully tell me that I should humbly submit to his righteous will and readily pronounce him just in all his dealings with me. The same Book that tells me that the afflictions of the righteous are many (Psalm 34:19) also tells me that "the righteous shall hold on their way" (Job 17:9). Faith and experience tell me that both statements are true.

April 4

"If any man will come after me, let him deny himself, and take up his cross, and follow me" (Matthew 16:24)

Being a true disciple of Christ is not an easy matter, for it requires self-denial, cross-bearing and obedience to his word. Many profess to be his followers who know nothing either of sacrifice, soul-trouble, or of walking in his steps. Many want to be called by his name, but it is only to take away their reproach, for they will neither embrace his doctrine nor submit themselves to his righteousness. They do err, not knowing the Scriptures (in their true sense), nor the power of God, and consequently "they being ignorant of God's righteousness, and going about to establish their own righteousness, have not submitted themselves unto the righteousness of God (Isa. 4:1; Matt. 22:29; Rom. 10:3).

In order to be a bonafide disciple of Christ we must, as a way of life, deny ourselves anything that does not please God or honor him and we must be willing to humbly reconcile ourselves to the opposition and hardship that such a course exposes us to. We cannot deny ourselves the friendship of the world without experiencing this cross. If we are not willing to put the cause of Christ above everything else, even our own family connections if necessary, and our worldly possessions, we cannot be his disciples (Luke 14:26-27). This may seem hard to us sometimes, but if "coming after Christ" was as easy as popular religion tries to make it appear, then the "narrow" way would be the "broad way," overflowing with all sorts of people.

The requirements for true discipleship weeds out pretenders (*false professors*) as well as the "almost persuaded" and leaves room only for the truly dedicated and devoted. Not only is the path of obedience and self-denial called the *narrow way,* but it is entered by a "strait" or *difficult* gate. It is unpleasant and disagreeable to the flesh, and consequently no man will enter it, or faithfully remain there, unless the Spirit of God so deals with him as to make the narrow way more appealing than any other way and shows him that the alternative will ultimately be far more difficult.

May the Lord help us to sincerely come after him and to truly be his disciples. And may we so live as not to give the adversary any just cause to speak reproachfully of us.

April 5

"We brought nothing into this world, and it is certain that we can carry nothing out" (1 Timothy 6:7)

In the context the apostle speaks of those who equate worldly gain with godliness and tells Timothy that he is to withdraw himself from such. Then he shows what true gain really is, i.e. "godliness with contentment." And as for worldly gain he points out that just as we brought nothing into the world, neither will we carry anything out.

The psalmist says, "Be not afraid when one is made rich...for when he dieth he shall carry nothing away: his glory shall not descend after him" (Psalm 49:16-17). In death the rich man and the pauper are totally equalized so far as their material substance is concerned. No matter how great a fortune a man may amass, when he dies he leaves it all behind. He carries not one penny with him. This should certainly cause us to view our worldly possessions from a proper perspective. The most treasured idol a man ever held in his bosom had to be left behind in death.

The rich man mentioned in Luke 12:16 who thought to store his goods and take his ease for many years, died that very night and left all his riches to others. The Lord then drove home the point that "So is he that layeth up treasure for himself, and is not rich toward God." How true it is that "a man's life consisteth not in the abundance of the things which he possesseth"!

Many mighty kings of ages past have had their wealth buried with them, obviously believing that this would ensure that their riches would follow them into the next life. Thieves have plundered many of these tombs. Others have been uncovered by archaeologists with the bounty intact. None of the kings carried anything out of this world with them. Their hoarded wealth did them no good beyond death.

How wise is the instruction of Matthew 6:19 to "lay not up for yourselves treasures upon earth, where moth and rust doth corrupt, and where thieves break through and steal: but lay up for yourselves treasures in heaven, where neither moth nor rust doth corrupt, and where thieves do not break through nor steal: for where your treasure is, there will your heart be also." And, "Set your affection on things above, not on things on the earth" (Col. 3:2). Lord, help us to heed Thy words.

April 6

"Which were born, not of blood, nor of the will of the flesh, nor of the will of man, but of God" (John 1:13)

This verse shows very clearly that those who believed on Christ and who received him did not do so in order to be born of God, but because they already *were* born of him. In Scripture, God's act of giving divine life to his people is described as *regeneration*, a *quickening*, or a being *born again*. Neither flesh and blood, nor man's will, has anything whatsoever to do with it. In every sense of the word it is "of God." "You hath *he* quickened," saith Paul, "who were dead in trespasses and sins" (Eph. 2:1,5); not "You hath he quickened who willed, or desired, to be born again," for those who are dead in sins have no desire to be "born of the Spirit."

Not only do they not desire to be born of the Spirit, but they persecute those who *are* born of the Spirit (Gal. 4:29). "Because the carnal mind is enmity against God: for it is not subject to the law of God, neither indeed can be" (Romans 8:7). If people were born of the Spirit because they wanted to be, then the new birth would be "of the will of man," and "of the will of the flesh."

Both "the things of the Spirit of God" and "the preaching of the cross" are foolishness to them that perish (1 Cor. 1:18; 2:14). Therefore these things cannot be used as instruments in the spiritual birth of those who are dead in sins. "No man knoweth the Son, but the Father; neither knoweth any man the Father, save the Son, and he to whomsoever the Son will reveal him" (Matt. 11:27). It is clear, then, whose will is involved in the new birth—and it is *not* man's. Not "of the will of man, but *of God*."

ℬℯ

April 7

"O wretched man that I am! who shall deliver me from the body of this death?" (Romans 7:24)

This verse proves that the very best of men are sinners still. Paul, an apostle, yet a wretched man. This was not someone else saying this about him, but was what he himself acknowledged. He did not say, "O wretched man that I *used to be*," but "O wretched man that I *am*!"

When men become partakers of grace, they are not thereby made free from the *being* of sin. It will still dwell in their flesh (Rom. 7:20) but it shall no longer have *dominion over them* (Rom. 6:14). "If we say we have no sin, we deceive ourselves, and the truth is not in us" (1 John 1:8).

But though there is this sinful nature even in the child of God, and he cannot live above sin (Rom. 7:15-21), yet in regeneration he is given grace to fight against sin and to bring his body into subjection (1 Cor. 9:27). He is killed to the love of sin and commanded to let not sin *reign* in his mortal body, nor to obey it in the lusts thereof (Rom. 6:12). If we could live *above* sin, then Paul would have said, "Let not sin *exist* in your mortal bodies."

Paul also referred to himself as "less than the least of all saints" (Eph. 3:8), and as the *chief* of sinners (1 Tim. 1:15). He acknowledged that no good thing dwelt *in his flesh* (Rom. 7:18), and in the same context he was very candid about the warfare within himself between good and evil (cf. Galatians 5:17). It is only by the grace of God that a man can see this in himself and confess it to himself and to others. It is the nature of men to deny their faults and failings and to try to justify themselves in their sins. But when Paul was brought to see himself as he was by nature and to grieve over his sins, he could freely confess that he was the least of the apostles and was not meet (or fit) to be called an apostle, because he had been a persecutor of the church of God. He also gave *God* all the glory for the change that had been wrought in him (1 Cor. 15:9-10).

April 8

"I will be to them a God, and they shall be to me a people"
(Jeremiah 31:33; Hebrews 8:10-12)

The covenant of grace that God has made with *spiritual Israel* has no conditions in it for them to meet. From beginning to end it contains a declaration of what God will do *for* them. This includes, (1) the putting of his laws into their minds and writing them in their hearts, (2) His being to them a God, and their being to him a people, (3) their all being brought to the knowledge of him, from the least to the greatest, (4) His being merciful to their unrighteousness, (5) His forgiving their iniquity, and (6) His remembrance of their sins no more. All these things are secured in and by the new covenant and God's people have nothing whatsoever to do with their coming to pass.

The old covenant that God made with the natural Israelites was a conditional covenant, and in one way or another they all broke it. But the new covenant is *not according to that former covenant,* in which they did not continue, even though God was a husband unto them (Jer. 31:32). If it was conditional on their part then it would be according to the old, and *spiritual Israel* would break it just like *national Israel* broke the first. But this covenant will not be broken, for it was made between God the Father, God the Son, and God the Holy Spirit. They all have their office works to perform, and all those works will be carried out to perfection, the end result being that all spiritual Israelites "shall be saved in the Lord with an everlasting salvation" (Isa. 45:17). He will be to them a God, and they *shall* be to him a people—no uncertainty about it.

There is much for God's people (spiritual Israel) to be doing, for they are under law to Christ, and righteous living should characterize their everyday conduct and deportment. But in that eternal covenant that secures their final destiny, they have nothing to perform, for in order for the stipulations of *that* covenant to be perfectly met, God alone must carry them out and complete them, otherwise not one living soul would ever see heaven.

April 9

"All that are in the graves shall...come forth" (John 5:28-29)

In view of how plainly the Scriptures speak on the subject of the resurrection of the dead it has always seemed strange to me that anyone claiming to believe the Bible would deny it. How much plainer could language be? "All that are in the graves..." that is, dead people... "shall come forth." And why in heaven's name would they *want* to deny it. It was a central and beloved theme of the apostles of Christ, who had "hope toward God...that there shall be a resurrection of the dead, both of the just and unjust" (Acts 24:15). Paul dwelt at length on the resurrection of the dead in 1 Corinthians 15. His argumentation is powerful and irrefutable. Why would anyone *dare* to deny it? And again, why would anyone *want* to deny it?

Paul said to king Agrippa, "Why should it be thought a thing incredible with you, that God should raise the dead?" (Acts 26:8). And indeed, why should *anyone* think it incredible? If God could create a universe, what would stop him from raising the dead? If he could make a man out of dust, what could prevent him from raising him from a corruptible body to an incorruptible? (1 Cor. 15:58; Philippians 3:21).

All that are in the graves shall come forth. None shall be exempt. The righteous shall be raised to life and the wicked unto damnation. Though they "sleep in the dust," the first shall awake to everlasting life and the second to shame and everlasting contempt (John 5:28; Daniel 12:2).

To those who fondly await the Lord's return, the prospect of the righteous being raised and fashioned like unto the glorious body of Christ is most delightful to contemplate. And at the same time it is good to know that the justice of God will be magnified in the eternal condemnation and punishment of the wicked, who all their lifetime had nothing but contempt for him and his people.

April 10

"Is thy God...able to deliver thee from the lions?" (Daniel 6:20)

King Darius did not know whether Daniel's God was able to deliver him or not, but that was never a question with Daniel. This is the difference between those who have been given divine knowledge and understanding and those who have not. To Darius there were "gods many, and lords many," but to Daniel there was "but *one* God" (1 Cor. 8:5-6) and that was "the Father, of whom are all things, and we by him," etc. Darius was familiar with gods who were not able to deliver those who served them, and he thought Daniel's God might be one of them. But Daniel was acquainted with the one true and living God, and knew that he could not fail nor be discouraged (Isaiah 42:4).

We frequently hear people among the popular religions of the day talking about what their god *wants* to do, and what he will do if we will *let* him. They speak of what he is *trying* to do and of the frustration he feels because of the millions who are supposedly being lost that he would like to have saved but could not because they would not *allow* him to do so. Such a god is not the God of Daniel and neither is he the god of any other true believer.

The God of true believers is that Majestic Being described by Nebuchadnezzar in Daniel 4:35, who does according to his will in the army of heaven, and among the inhabitants of earth: and none can stay his hand, or say unto him, What doest Thou? He is the same whose works are truth, and his ways judgment, and who is able to abase those who walk in pride (Dan. 4:35-37).

What would be your answer, dear reader, if you were asked if your God was able to deliver you from the lions? My own reply would be a resounding, "Yes!" Not only is he *able* to deliver from the lions, but figuratively speaking I believe he has many times done so. There have been those who would have "swallowed me up quickly" if the Lord had "given me up as a prey to their teeth" (Psalm 124:3,6). How thankful we should be that he is not only *able* to deliver us but often *does* deliver us, no doubt many times when we are not even aware of it!

❧

April 11

"Hope that is seen is not hope" (Romans 8:24)

Hope that is seen is an oxymoron. As Paul says, "What a man seeth, why doth he yet hope for?" In other words, a man cannot hope for that which he already has in his possession. For example, if we were already in heaven we could not hope for it any longer. If we had already entered into the full fruition of that happy place, it would not just be *pointless* to hope for it, but it would be *impossible* to hope for it. We can and do hope for heaven now because we do not have perfect knowledge that it will be ours some day. If we had perfect knowledge that it would be ours, then we could not *hope* for it. We could only *look forward* to it. We might wish or desire that we were already there, but we could not *hope* that it would ultimately be ours.

Many people claim to "know beyond a shadow of a doubt that they are saved," by which they mean they *know* heaven will be their home. But in spite of their bold presumption, they cannot *know* beyond doubt but what they are deceived in the matter just as many others have been (Matt. 7:22-23). If others have been thoroughly convinced that they were children of God and yet were wrong, how can these know beyond a doubt that they are not likewise deceived? The truth is they cannot.

It has been my observation that those same people who speak with absolute certainty about their salvation also speak disparagingly or even contemptuously of hope. But those like the apostle Paul, who know something of their inner corruption by nature, cannot adopt the language of the self-righteous, but must speak of the hereafter in terms of hope. In more than one place the Scriptures speak of Christ as the *hope* of his people (Jer. 17:13; Col. 1:27; 1 Tim. 1:1). Therefore those who disparage *hope* disparage *Christ*. They also disparage *faith*, for "faith is the substance of things *hoped* for" (Heb. 11:1).

I have even heard people say that if all they had was a *hope* of heaven they would be ashamed. But the apostle Paul shows hope to be a product of Christian experience, and says, "Hope maketh not ashamed" (Romans 5:4-5). He lived *in hope* of eternal life (Titus 1:2) and I am certain he was not ashamed of it. Those who speak slightingly of hope are the ones who should be ashamed.

April 12

"Let nothing be done through strife or vainglory; but in
lowliness of mind let each esteem other better than themselves"
(Philippians 2:3)

We would live in an almost perfect world if everyone followed this instruction. Of course it cannot be expected that a God-hating world will follow such a holy and honorable course, but it is right and reasonable to expect it of God's regenerated and enlightened people. However, even *they* often fail to follow it as they ought.

Everything our Lord has taught us to do is contrary to the carnal flesh with which we were born into this world, and it is not always an easy matter even to esteem our brethren and sisters in Christ better than ourselves, but we are called upon to do it nonetheless. How closely do we measure up to this high standard when we are constantly criticizing our kindred in Christ and even mistreating them? How well are we fulfilling this divine requirement when we are treating them in ways we would not want to be treated?

Like all of the Lord's injunctives, this one must be performed sincerely, from the heart, if it is to be done acceptably. An outward pretense may deceive our brethren for a time, but God will not be deluded for a moment. True, heartfelt and humble obedience to any divine precept requires much grace on God's part and much prayer and diligence on our part. We would have neither the will nor the ability apart from the inner workings of the Holy Spirit (Philippians 2:12-13).

Let us think about it more seriously. Do we honestly and in actuality think of our brethren and sisters as being better than ourselves, or are we more prone to examine their faults, follies and failings and come to the conclusion that we are measuring up to a little higher overall standard than they? Would it not be much more fitting for us to always be carefully examining our own shortcomings and allowing that in many particulars our brethren may be greatly excelling us? I believe so. Let us pray over it.

৵৶

April 13

"The wicked, through the pride of his countenance, will not seek after God" (Psalm 10:4)

And thus with one stroke of his mighty pen God destroys the main thrust of popular religion; which is that Christians ought to get the gospel to the wicked so that they may have a chance to be "saved." If it were the primary purpose in a Christian's life to try to get the wicked to seek after God, then such a life would be a waste of time and energy seeing as how the wicked will not seek after him. Nowhere in the Scriptures can such a thing be found as that it is the responsibility of Christians to get the wicked saved. So far were the apostles from seeking to get the gospel to the wicked that they prayed rather to be delivered *from* such characters (Romans 15:31; 2 Thess. 3:2).

Not one single epistle was ever written to unregenerate sinners. When Paul wrote "to all that be in Rome" he made it quite clear that the "all" he had under consideration were those who were "beloved of God" and who had been "called to be saints" and whose faith was "spoken of throughout the whole world" (Romans 1:7,8). And so, likewise, in his other epistles, he addressed "the saints," "the brethren," "the church or churches," "the faithful in Christ Jesus," etc.

Never were the instructions and admonitions of the epistles ever directed to the spiritually unborn. In 2 Corinthians 2:15-16, Paul mentions the saved and the perishing and says, "To the one we are the savour of life unto life, and to the other the savour of death unto death." In other words, the gospel he preached was the savour of life unto those who were spiritually alive, but the savour of death unto those who were spiritually dead. And it is still the same today. "The preaching of the cross is to them that perish foolishness; but unto *us which are saved* it is the power of God" (1 Cor. 1:18). "The natural man receiveth not the things of the Spirit of God: for they are foolishness unto him: neither can he know them, because they are spiritually discerned" (1 Cor. 2:14).

In view of the above, how would you like to have the job of trying to get the wicked to seek God? How thankful we should be that God has not laid such an impossible task upon us! He told John to feed his *sheep* and *lambs* (John 21:15-17). Nowhere did he ever tell John or anyone else to feed the *goats*. The goats (*the non-elect*) can't eat gospel food anyway!

April 14

"By his knowledge shall my righteous servant justify many"
(Isaiah 53:11)

Who are the "many" that are justified by Christ? They are the *many* for whom his blood was shed and whose sins were consequently remitted (Matt. 26:28). They are the *many* that he shall make righteous by his obedience (Rom. 5:19). They are the *many sons* that he shall bring unto glory (Heb. 2:10). They are the *many* whose sins he bore (Heb. 9:28). They are the *many* who were ordained to eternal life (Acts 13:48). They are the *many* that were given to Christ by the Father (John 17:2). They are the *many* that "the Lord our God shall call" (Acts 2:39). They are the *many* that are led by the Spirit of God (Rom. 8:14). They are the *many* that He loves and chastens (Rev. 3:19). And in fact, they are so many that no man can number them (Rev. 7:9).

Thankfully, salvation will not be limited to those relatively few members of the human race who will have heard, believed and obeyed some man's version of "the gospel" but it will extend to all those described in the above verses. God has a people in every nation that has ever existed or that may exist in the future (Acts 10:35; Rev. 5:9). Some of those whom he chose in Christ before the foundation of the world (Eph. 1:4) have lived in the remotest regions of the earth, in places where the name of Christ was never spoken. But in the mind and purpose of God they were known and loved of him in the covenant of grace that was established in His eternal counsels long before any of them existed. Their life is hid with Christ in God; therefore before any eternal harm could come to them it would first have to come to God the Son and God the Father, and that can never be.

The "everlasting covenant" according to which God's elect are all saved and called is "ordered in all things, and sure" and he has so established it that it does not, and cannot, grow (2 Samuel 23:5). The number embraced in it does not grow *larger* and neither does it grow *smaller*. They shall all know God from the least of them to the greatest (Jer. 31:34; Heb. 8:11). The Scriptures will not allow that even one of them should be eternally lost. Thank God it is so!

"With God nothing shall be impossible" (Luke 1:37)

When the angel made this declaration he was speaking of those things that fall within the range of God's purpose and decrees, for it cannot be allowed that God would do anything contrary to his own eternal mind and will. It is within the *power* of God to sin, but it is not within his *character* or *will* to sin; consequently he has never sinned and never shall. The impossibility of his lying, for instance, does not reside in a want of power, but in a want of will or inclination. He does not have a nature contaminated with sin, as is ours; therefore all manner of sin is abhorrent to him and totally contrary to his holiness and perfection.

As pertaining to those things that God has *purposed* to do, and *promised* to do, nothing shall be impossible with him, for all such things are consistent with his holy and divine nature and the dignity of his Godhood. Even such extraordinary things as a virgin conceiving and bearing a perfect child by the Holy Ghost, and Elizabeth bearing a son in her old age, having always been barren, were not impossible with God. These events were in his eternal mind and purpose before all worlds and were brought to pass according to his determinate counsel and foreknowledge. So shall every other remaining aspect of his mind and will be perfectly fulfilled, regardless of how unlikely their fruition may appear to natural reason and logic.

Among the extraordinary and remarkable events yet to be brought to pass is the resurrection of the dead, the glorification of the saints, the casting of the wicked into hell, and the melting of the elements with fervent heat. And, as incredible as these things may seem to the wicked, they will not prove to be impossible with God. He tells us very emphatically in Isaiah 46:11, "I have spoken it, I will also bring it to pass; I have purposed it, I will also do it." And those of us who have experienced his power have no doubt but that he will.

April 16

"He showeth his word unto Jacob, his statutes and his judgments unto Israel. He hath not dealt so with any nation: and as for his judgments, they have not known them. Praise ye the Lord"
(Psalm 147:19-20)

How contrary is the above to the popular teaching of the religious world! How plainly does the Bible contradict the ideas and theories of unenlightened men! How foreign are their opinions and surmisings to God's revealed truth! His discriminating grace is plainly set forth in the text, and throughout the Bible, yet men persist in attempting to blur, or altogether eliminate, any and all distinctions between the elect and the non-elect; the church and the world; the righteous and the wicked; the called and the uncalled.

Under the Old Testament dispensation Israel was the *only* nation to whom God showed his statutes and judgments, and *national* Israel under the Old Covenant is figurative of *spiritual* Israel under the New Covenant. The only ones now to whom God shows his word, his judgments and his statutes, are *spiritual Israelites*. This truth is extremely unpopular with the religious world, but it is one to which we must faithfully and courageously cling if we are to be true to God's inspired word.

Who can honestly deny that "no man knoweth the Son (Christ), but the Father;" and "neither knoweth any man the Father, save (*except*) the Son, and he to whomsoever the Son will reveal him" (Matt. 11:27)? Who can deny that the God of heaven and earth hides some things from one class and reveals them to another (Matt. 11:25)? And who can deny that Christ actually *thanked* his Father for this and said, "Even so Father: for so it seemed good in thy sight"?

And what did David say when he spoke of God's word being shown only to Jacob or Israel? What did he have to say about God not dealing thus with any other nation? Did He complain that this was unjust or that it was unrighteous on God's part? Did he cry out, as does the religious would, against such discriminating dealings? No! No! But rather he follows immediately with, "Praise ye the Lord." Neither the Psalmist, nor Christ himself, had any problem with God *doing what he would with His own* (See Matt. 20:15), and neither should we. If we have a problem with anything God has said or done, it is *we* who need to get our thinking straightened out, not him.

April 17

"Evil men and seducers shall wax worse and worse, deceiving and being deceived" (2 Timothy 3:13)

I do not think this text is teaching that from generation to generation evil men and seducers will become more and more wicked, but rather that this kind of people will, in their own lifetime, become more and more insensitive to that which is evil and will give themselves over to the practice of it more and more as their days go along. One form of sin leads to other and greater forms of sin. Lying brings on the necessity for more and greater lies to cover the first lies, etc. Attempts to fulfill any lust of the flesh results in more and greater such attempts.

Sin always has a *downward* tendency. It never *elevates* but always *degrades and debases.* And men do not become more and more wicked by nature with each passing generation, for all men are fallen creatures and are born with as evil a nature as they will ever possess. We observe that even in the early history of the world "the wickedness of man was great in the earth, and that every imagination of the thoughts of his heart was only evil continually" (Gen. 6:5). This describes evil men just as they are today, no better and no worse, but nevertheless wicked to the core.

We also observe that evil men and seducers are always "deceiving and being deceived." Does this not emphatically point up the truth of the scriptural maxim, "whatsoever a man soweth, that shall he also reap" (Gal. 6:7)? The seducer will be seduced, the deceiver will be deceived, the liar will be lied to, etc. Any man who *sows* a crop of thistles will likewise *reap* a crop of thistles and he will, in time, be pricked by every one of the thorns.

But where sin abounds, grace will much more abound. For the sake of the elect, "the wrath of man shall praise (God)," and the remainder of wrath He shall restrain (Psalm 76:10). Wickedness shall never gain the ascendancy over His mercy, and until Christ returns, however distant that great event may be, there will be a few humble believers still kneeling at one another's feet and partaking of the ordinances that he instituted (1 Cor. 11:26). What a comfort!

April 18

"The preaching of the cross is to them that perish foolishness"
(1 Corinthians 1:18)

Consider for a moment how absurd, how powerless and impotent a crucified Savior must appear to those who have neither divine light nor spiritual discernment. Let an unregenerate sinner, with no understanding of what Christ came into the world to do, look upon him as he suffers and dies on the cross, and all he sees is a condemned man who could not even save himself, much less others.

One of the Jews in the times of Justin Martyr is quoted as saying, "We doubt your Christ, who was so ignominiously crucified, for our law styles every one that is crucified, accursed." This man rightly viewed Christ as having fallen under the most extreme curse of the law of God, but he did not have the slightest concept of why that curse lay upon him, for he said of the Christians, "We cannot sufficiently wonder that you should expect any good from God who place your hopes in a man that was crucified." Thus, to this day the Jews as a whole look upon Christ merely as a crucified and accursed malefactor who claimed to be "equal with God" and then died a shameful death, proving himself, in their eyes, to be a pathetic imposter.

But unto those who are saved, the preaching of the cross "is the power of God" (1 Cor. 1:18). Such preaching is not only delivered "in demonstration of the Spirit and of power" (1 Cor. 2:4), but it declares and proves that salvation in, through and by the perfect sacrifice of

Christ is in all respects one of the greatest proofs of God's power and wisdom. And additionally, it comes to God's believing people "not in word only, but also in power, and in the Holy Ghost, and in much assurance" (1 Thess. 1:5), which makes its authenticity undeniable to them.

There is a so-called gospel in the world that consists of an *offer* of eternal life to unregenerate sinners on the condition that they meet various and sundry requirements. This "gospel" of creature righteousness and human merit is of no value to those who have been brought to see and feel themselves to be "the chief of sinners" and altogether unworthy of the least of God's mercies. However, the true gospel is a message of comfort and hope to them, for it declares that by one offering Christ perfected forever them that are sanctified (Heb. 10:14). It shows them that they are saved and called with an holy calling, not according to their works, but according to God's own purpose and grace, which was given them in Christ Jesus before the world began (2 Tim. 1:9). What blessed news this is to those who have come to the end of their own strength!

April 19

"We know that we have passed from death unto life because we love the brethren" (1 John 3:14)

The Lord has mercifully provided his humble people with evidences that they are among his elect. Being omniscient, he naturally knows their propensity for questioning their sonship. They do this on the grounds of their awareness that they are unworthy and unfit, in and of themselves, to occupy so holy a place as is heaven. Therefore they are given such scriptures as the beatitudes, our text, and others, to provide them with assurances that they bear at least some of the marks of a gracious state. For example, no one hungers and thrists after righteousness unless they have passed from death (in sins) unto life (in Christ). Unregenerate sinners do not experience any feelings of spiritual poverty; they do not suffer persecution for righteousness' sake, and neither do they love the brethren. Consequently, if we truly possess any of these indicators of divine life we may draw comfort from the evidence that we are subjects of grace.

We are not told that we know we have passed from death unto life because we have "accepted the Lord as our personal Savior," or because we have professed faith in him, or submitted to baptism at the hands of some religious professor, or any other such thing. Any unregenerate in the country may simply *claim* to have "accepted the Lord" or profess to "have faith." They may be baptized into any of hundreds of different so-called "faiths." But those who do not have the law of God written in their hearts cannot truly "love the brethren" or feel themselves to be spiritual paupers, etc.

Even the children of God may sometimes wonder if they truly love the brethren, but if that love genuinely abides within their hearts they will not be able to deny it. Their concern for the welfare and well being of those brethren cannot be ignored but it will make itself manifest in some way. Those who really love the brethren will desire to be identified with them in some way and to have their company and fellowship. They will grieve with them in their sorrows and rejoice with them in their times of uplifting; they will have their best interest at heart; fear offending them, etc.

It is cheering to a child of God to find evidences in the Scriptures that they do indeed have a part with the precious children of grace. It comforts them when they can witness with the feelings, desires and hopes of the saints as set forth in God's word. Happy indeed are those with whom it is thus.

April 20

"I shall be satisfied when I awake with thy likeness"
(Psalm 17:15)

One of the certainties of the heavenly state is that the occupants of that happy place will be *satisfied*. And I have thought that this is all we really need to know about that glorious abode in order to make us desire it with all our soul. If we shall be *satisfied* in heaven then we will be perfectly happy and content with everything *just the way it is* and will not wish for anything to be otherwise. If there should be only one thing that we wanted to be different than it was, then we would not be satisfied.

Many people have various notions about how they desire heaven to be, but most of those ideas are sentimental in nature and fall far short of what heaven actually is. If and when we see heaven we will then have a much better understanding of what Paul meant when he said God is "able to do exceeding abundantly above all that we ask or think" (Eph. 3:20). In our present state we can but faintly conceive of the actual glory of heaven.

If we had *one* pain in heaven, that would destroy the perfection of the place and we could never be satisfied for we would not know but what there might be other and greater pains. If in heaven we were not perfectly assured that there would never be unpleasantness of any kind in that state then we could not be totally satisfied with it. In order to be satisfied in heaven there could not even be the *consideration* of any possible unpleasantness or distress. And if we were concerned in any way with those we had left behind here on earth we could not be satisfied. If we had any unpleasant recollections of our earthly life, no matter how small, we could not be satisfied. If we had the slightest fear or anxiety, we could not be satisfied. Complete satisfaction in heaven could only be ours if we were always totally delighted with everything just as we found it. And thus it must be.

The verse from which our text is taken not only tells us that God's people will be *satisfied* in heaven, but also that they will in some sense, or senses, be in the likeness of their Lord and that they will see his face in righteousness. First John 3:2 adds that they shall also "see him as he is."

None who have a sweet hope of heaven should ever entertain any notions that heaven will be any less than they are hoping for. They not only will not be disappointed, but they will find heaven to be far more wonderful than they could ever have imagined.

April 21

"None can stay his hand" (Daniel 4:35)

Unenlightened men are very prone to think of God as being such an one as themselves (Psalm 50:21). If we listen to their language we are apt to discover that they think there are some things he does not see (Psalm 10:11; Eze. 9:9) and that he cannot judge through the dark cloud (Job 22:13-14). There are ungodly men who question his knowledge (Psalm 73:11-12) as well as his ability to hear. Thus in their own mind and estimation they greatly limit him (Psalm 78:41).

We have often heard men speak of things they think God cannot do unless we allow him to do so. And we have frequently heard even professed Bible scholars question God's ability. The late Elder Robert Sanders of Georgia used to tell of a conversation he had with a local minister of another order. After some discussion as to how they were both personally saved, they agreed that it was all of grace, that they were not seeking God at the time he visited them in regeneration. Elder Sanders then said, "Well, brother, if he saved *me* that way, and he saved *you* that way, why don't we just leave it to him to save *all* his people that way?" The other minister then made the following amazing reply, "Well, I just don't know whether he is able!" This is a perfect example of what we mean when we speak of those who question, and limit, the power of God.

Our text says, "None can stay God's hand." But if it is a case that he wants to save us and we won't *let* him, then is it not a clear case that we have stayed his hand? If we have prevented him from doing something that he *wanted* to do, how can we escape the conclusion that we have indeed stayed his hand?

God teaches his people correctly in their *hearts*, but the religious ideas that are planted in their *heads* by misled theologians, and others, conflict with what their inner experience has taught them. The true gospel, if they ever hear it, may be the instrument in God's hands of reconciling their *heads* with their *hearts*. The Holy Spirit has never taught anyone anything that contradicts the truth, and the truth is that none can stay God's hand, or, in other words, prevent him from doing what it is his purpose to do.

❧

April 22

"I will be to them a God, and they shall be to me a people"
(Hebrews 8:10)

When it came down to their dying hour and they knew they were momentarily facing eternity, a number of famous, as well as little-known, infidels have renounced their infidelity and acknowledged that there is no other hope than that held by the followers of Christ through the ages. But in all the annals of history we do not have a single instance of a humble disciple of Christ renouncing his faith when facing death. To any thinking person this amazing truth bespeaks volumes. And to those of us who have long held dear the precious truths of the gospel it is no mystery. Untold thousands have died rather than renounce Christianity, but who ever heard of an infidel being put to death because he would not renounce his unbelief?

If no one else in the world believed in Christ and his gospel but me, I still could not lay down my faith in him. Even if I could bring myself to renounce it with my *lips* I could not renounce it with my *heart*. I did not take it *up* of myself, and neither could I lay it *down* of myself. I have never had any desire to lay it down and do not have any reason to think I ever shall. God puts His law in the inward parts of his people and writes it in their hearts and minds, and they are all made to know him (Jer. 31:33-34; Heb. 8:10-11; 10:16). They cannot erase or eliminate this inward work, and why should they want to? It is a work that, the effects of which, makes the objects of it "new creatures in Christ," so that they can never go back to their former state. Since they are made to realize that their new state is far superior to their former state, they can never even *desire* to go back to a state of darkness and debauchery.

God chose his people in Christ before the foundation of the world and predestinated them to be conformed to his image; therefore he can no more disown them than they can disown Him in their hearts. The promise is, "I *will* be to them a God, and they *shall* be to me a people." Their relationship is certain, for the very foundation of God standeth sure, bearing this two-part seal, "The Lord knoweth them that are his. And, Let every one that nameth the name of Christ depart from iniquity" (2 Tim. 2:19).

April 23

"Behold, what manner of love the Father hath bestowed upon us,
that we should be called the sons of God: therefore the world
knoweth us not" (1 John 3:1)

The point at which the world recognizes that we have a divine relationship with God, is the point at which we become a stranger to it. Just as it did not have a spiritual knowledge of Christ because of his divine nature, so neither does it know us when we are made partakers of that same nature (2 Peter 1:4). A person who loves the world and the sinful pleasures thereof is naturally not going to understand a person who has been killed to the love of those things. Light has no communion with darkness (2 Cor. 6:14-15). Those who have been spiritually enlightened understand those who are in darkness, for they were once in the same darkness; but those who are in darkness do not understand those who are in the light, for they have never been there.

It is an invaluable privilege and blessings to be placed among the sons of God, but we should understand and be aware that with that inexpressibly wonderful favor comes a crucifixion of us unto the world and the world unto us (Gal. 6:14). The change that is wrought within a person in regeneration, or the new birth, makes them not want to have any more to do with this sinful world, which in turn makes this sinful world not want to have any more to do with him. So it is a duel death, a death of *him* to the *world*, and a death of the *world* to *him*. It sets up a mutual barrier between the two. Friends whose company the newly regenerated person previously had most desired, he now wishes to avoid. Oh! What a marvelous change is wrought in this heavenly birth! And how vastly different is this change from the weak, wispy and frivolous notions of the religious world with regard to what constitutes regeneration.

Let us never resent any losses or hardships we may have to endure as a result of being called the sons of God, for our elevation to that lofty state is a product of nothing less than the *love* of God. It is an inexpressibly glorious blessing that will never have an end. Any difficulties attendant upon the possession of that designation are far exceeded by the joys and comforts that are part and parcel with it.

April 24

"Some said, He is a good man: others said, Nay; but he deceiveth the people" (John 7:12)

It is right and proper to conclude that Christ was a good man, but that conclusion also calls for a further acknowledgement that he was exactly who he said he was. One of the reasons the Jews sought to kill him was because he said that God was his Father, "making himself equal with God" (John 5:18). If this claim was not true, then neither was he a good man. A good man would not have acted as an impostor or knowingly sought to deceive the people. Christ was either who and what he said he was or else he was the greatest blasphemer and deceiver who ever lived. But unlike all the others who have claimed to be the Christ, he proved *his* claims by his *works*. He did that which no man had ever before done (John 9:32) and spake as no man had ever spoken (John 7:46).

Even a ruler of the Jews (Nicodemus) acknowledged that no man could do the miracles Christ did "except God be with him" (John 3:2). But the fact that God was with him proved unquestionably that he was not an impostor; and if he was not an impostor then he was who he claimed to be. The believers among the people posed a very pertinent question when they said, "When Christ cometh, will he do more miracles than these which this man hath done?" (John 7:31). If it were true that Christ was a deceiver and the true Messiah should come today, what could he do that would more convincingly prove his deity than what Christ did? He healed multitudes, stilled the tempest, raised the dead, and did many other miraculous things. What more could another Messiah do?

As a general rule, in every crowd where the general public is represented there will be found believers and unbelievers. All of us would have been unbelievers if it had not pleased God to lift the scales from the eyes of some. If we had been left in darkness as the majority of the Jews were, no amount of miracles, arguments, or anything else would make any difference with us. We would, as they did, remain in unbelief. It is not the outward signs and wonders that makes a man a believer, but the inward work of the Holy Spirit, and only *God* can do that.

April 25

"We are all as an unclean thing, and all our righteousnesses are as filthy rags" (Isaiah 64:6)

Divine inspiration does not paint a flattering picture of human nature. As we are, in and of ourselves, that is, in our old carnal flesh, there is nothing good about us (Romans 7:18), and all those religious performances that stem merely from fleshly motives are no more pleasing to *God* than are filthy rags to *us*. It was only "by faith" that Abel offered unto God a more excellent sacrifice than Cain (Heb. 11:4), and the fact that Abel possessed the gift of faith bore witness to the fact that he was a righteous person. If he had not been righteous (made so by the grace of God) his sacrifice would have been no more acceptable than Cain's. Cain was not only wicked, but he was "of that wicked one" (the devil; 1 John 3:12), and therefore both he and his sacrifice were rejected: "The sacrifice of the wicked is an abomination to the Lord" (Prov. 15:8; 21:27). "Even his prayer shall be abomination" (Prov. 28:9).

All those righteousnesses that are performed with a view to gaining or procuring a place in heaven, are no more than filthy rags in the sight of the Lord. The prayers, fastings, and other religious exercises that the scribes and Pharisees engaged in "that they might be seen of men" were an abomination unto Christ, and He taught His disciples not to be as those hypocrites were (Matt. 6:1-8). If what we do in the way of worship has no higher object than the praise and recognition of men, we may be sure that it will not receive God's sanction. The best it can earn for us is His censure. Christ said, "Except your righteousness shall exceed the righteousness of the scribes and Pharisees, ye shall in no case enter the kingdom of heaven."

Oh, may it never be that our services and devotions consist of no more than mere externals with no honest and sincere view to the glory of God and the advancement of his precious cause here in the world! May we never bring any of our "filthy rags" to his altar, but come humbly, pleading nothing but the perfect righteousness of Christ.

ॐ

April 26

"What shall we say then? Is there unrighteousness with God?
God forbid" (Romans 9:14)

The apostle Paul well knew the objections that would be raised by some with regard to the subject of election that he dealt with in this chapter. His reference to the cutting off of the greater part of the Jewish nation from the privileges and benefits of the gospel necessitated his showing that not all *national* Israelites were *spiritual* Israelites (v. 6); that some of them were children of God, while others of them were children of the flesh. This is instanced in Isaac, through whom the spiritual lineage of the elect would be counted (vs. 7-8) and in Jacob, who was loved of God while his twin brother Esau was not. And all this would be so profoundly disagreeable to the carnal minds of men that they would immediately raise the charge that in such a case God would be unjust, and consequently guilty of unrighteousness. The same objection is still raised today against the doctrines of God's distinguishing grace.

In Elijah's day the Lord reserved to himself a complete number in Israel who would not worship the false gods around them. He was not guilty of unrighteousness in so doing. With regard to this Paul says, "Even so then at this present times also there is a remnant according to the election of grace" (1 Kings 19:18; Rom. 11:4-5). And again there was no unrighteousness with God in electing that remnant. He chose his people in Christ before the foundation of the world (Eph. 1:4) without being guilty of any unrighteousness. He visited the Gentiles *"to take out of them* a people for his name" (Acts 15:14), and again, *"out of* every kindred and tongue, and people, and nation" (Rev. 5:9) without any unrighteousness for not redeeming them all.

On and on we might go in this way, showing the discriminating grace of God in his dealings with men. And should it be argued again that he is unrighteous in so doing, we could give no better answer than that of the apostle when he was faced with the same argument, "God forbid!" Perish the thought! It is abhorrent to reason and common sense! "Shall not the Judge of all the earth do right?" (Gen. 18:25). Yes, he shall! Always and in all cases, whether we understand what he does or not.

April 27

"Humble yourselves in the sight of the Lord, and he shall lift you up" (James 4:10)

Without humility there is no real Christianity, and no real walk with God, and all pretenses to godliness are a hypocritical sham. God's regenerated people are the only ones who can humble themselves in the sense of the text, but it is imperative that they do so if they are to enjoy the lifting up that results from compliance with the precept. Our Lord has taught us that "whosoever exalteth himself shall be abased; and he that humbleth himself shall be exalted" (Luke 14:11). This is a principle we have seen verified over and over through the years, yet many never learn the lesson.

Many people exalt themselves by never admitting a fault and always seeking to justify their faults and failings, no matter how obvious those shortcomings are to others. But at some point they will be abased. Whether in this world or the world to come, they will eventually be forced to face the consequences of their haughtiness and high-mindedness. It is an unalterable truth that "God resisteth the proud, but giveth grace unto the humble" (James 4:6).

It is a common fault among men to seek recognition and notoriety. It is to be feared that this spirit of pride and vainglory has sometimes manifested itself even among ministers, but wherever it may exist it is very unbecoming and is much opposed to the spirit of the meek and lowly Lamb of God. The approval of our Lord and Master is a treasure of immeasurable worth, but the applause of men is a very fleeting and illusory bubble that leaves those who pursue it empty and unfulfilled. The only truly happy people in the world are those who are content to abide in the place where the Lord has put them, no matter how obscure, and to humbly and quietly serve him out of love and without any view to advancement or promotion. These he will exalt in his own time and way, without their seeking it.

April 28

"These shall go away into everlasting punishment, but the
righteous into life eternal" (Matthew 25:46)

Both the positive and the negative aspects of this scripture should bring consolation to God's people for it shows that His *justice* will be honored as well as His *mercy*. Any serious Bible student knows that God is not only a God of mercy but He is also a God of wrath. His justice is glorified in the punishment of the wicked and His mercy is glorified in His gracious dealings with His elect. The latter are referred to as "the vessels of *mercy*, which he (God) had afore prepared unto glory," while the former are spoken of as "the vessels of *wrath* fitted to destruction" (Romans 9:22-23).

Sins against an infinite God require and deserve an infinite penalty. That penalty was borne by Christ in behalf of the vessels of mercy, but the vessels of wrath are justly left to bear it themselves. The vessels of mercy are consequently said to be *blessed* because their sins are not imputed to them (See Psalm 32:2 & Romans 4:8). *Their* sins were imputed to *Christ*, but the sins of the vessels of wrath are imputed to *themselves*.

Our text shows that the duration of the punishment of the wicked will be just as long as the happiness of the righteous. In this verse the word *aionion* that was translated *eternal* with regard to the life of God's people, is the same word used in the original with reference to the punishment of the vessels of wrath. To deny the *eternal* punishment of the wicked is to deny the inspired word of God and to pour contempt upon the awful sufferings that Christ endured to deliver His people from that punishment.

Several years ago a minister argued with me that there is no such thing as an eternal hell. I asked him what Christ died for. He answered that Christ died to save us from timely trials and tribulations. I replied that in that case Christ did not save us from anything, for in view of the fact that we all have trials and tribulations, He obviously did not save us *from* them. He was left with no further argument. If the death of Christ did not save His people from *timely* miseries and it did not save them from *eternal* miseries then what else is there that it could have saved them from? Error and unbelief always runs up against an impregnable wall.

April 29

"The God which fed me all my life long unto this day"
(Genesis 48:15)

This is one of those many portions of scripture that I have often spoken of as *"inserted gems."* While in the process of blessing Joseph's sons Jacob makes what, on the surface, would seem to be a passing reference to his Heavenly Father and describes him as "the God which fed me all my life long unto this day." In our reading the Bible it is easy to pass over such phrases without much thought, but we may be certain that they were not just thrown in to fill up space, but to present precious truths that call for prayerful meditation and reflection. Our text is no exception.

It matters not how much we may have attributed our daily maintenance and sustenance to second causes, it is nonetheless true that it is *God* who has fed us every meal we have ever consumed "all our life long." No matter what route it took to get to our table it is a product of God's merciful providence, whether he is given credit for it or not. Else why should we pray to him for our daily bread (Matt. 6:11)? It is he who even provides food for the raven and for his young ones who are said to "cry unto God" for lack of meat (Job 38:41). This reminds us of the "angels food" he sent down upon the camps of Israel in the wilderness (Psalm 78:25). It is he that causes the grass to grow for the cattle and brings forth food out of the earth (Psalm 104:14).

Three meals a day amounts to 1,095 meals a year; and over a normal life span this comes to over 80,000. That is a tremendous amount of food, and not only does God *provide* it but he spreads it over a lifetime and gives it on a *daily* basis. Few of us today have missed many meals, and most of us would be better off if we did miss a few. I have lived almost 66 years and have never gone hungry because of poverty. There have been times when I didn't have exactly what I would have preferred to eat, but there has always been plenty of food, even in the hardest of times when we were buying some of it on credit.

The subject of food is a very large one that is threaded all throughout the Scriptures. It is made abundantly clear that God is the Provider, and that this providence has cared for us "all our life long unto this day." May we ever be mindful of his goodness and mercy.

April 30

"A man's life consisteth not in the abundance of the things which he possesseth" (Luke 12:15)

It would be difficult to imagine a lesson more important than this one, and yet how few seem to grasp it. How many have we known who have sought more and more *things*, vainly thinking that these would bring them happiness and fulfillment? The wealthy seem particularly liable to fall prey to this deceptive notion, though they are by no means the only guilty parties. I would think that most people have a rather lengthy want-list when it comes to material things. Not many, I would suppose, have reached the point where they can honestly say with the apostle Paul that they could be content with the bare essentials such as food and raiment (1 Tim. 6:8). I suspect that about the only possessions Paul had with him most of the time were a cloak and a few books and parchments (2 Tim. 4:13), and I suppose even these writings would have been on spiritual subjects, if they were not actually Old Testament Scriptures.

Most of us have no doubt complicated our lives to one degree or another through our accumulation of possessions. Many of God's people have become so encumbered in this respect that they have little time for the more important things in life. It is not that the possession of material *things* is wrong or sinful in and of itself, but it is the pursuit of an *abundance* of such things with the idea that they will bring us peace, satisfaction and fulfillment, that we need to guard against. What good are our earthly belongings to us in our times of deep soul-trouble and distress? What comfort or consolation will they bring us when we are drawing our last breaths or when we are standing over the cold corpses of our precious loved ones?

The Lord has shown us what is good, as well as what he requires of us, and that is to do justly, and to love mercy, and to walk humbly with him (Micah 6:8). In a word, our whole duty is to fear God and keep his commandments (Ecc. 12:13). Without this no amount of material things will do us any real good. May the Lord help us to keep our priorities straight.

May 1

"Look ye out among you seven men of honest report, full of the Holy Ghost and wisdom" (Acts 6:3)

Oh, that our churches had always followed this criteria in setting aside men for the office of deacon! If we would be honest with ourselves we would surely acknowledge that this rule has often been violated, to the great detriment of our churches. Many times we have seen men ordained as deacons who have never even been good *church members*, much less having demonstrated that they were qualified to serve as *deacons*. Sad to say, some of the weakest men I have ever known have been ordained as deacons, and insofar as this has been done and the divine rule broken and ignored, the churches have suffered. "My brethren, these things ought not so to be."

The Scriptures are explicit with regard to the qualifications of a deacon, and if a church does not have any male members who meet the criteria it is much better for them to have no deacons at all than to have them in name only. Just as ordaining men to the ministry who have not been called of God to that office does not make preachers out of them, so also ordaining men as deacons who are not qualified does not make deacons out of them. Furthermore, if we ordain men to an office in the church who do not measure up to the Scriptural directives, we can expect nothing but God's disapproval of our actions, and we may be sure he will not prosper us in our disobedience.

If a man does not meet the qualifications in 1 Timothy 3:8-12 we may be certain that he does not meet the qualifications in Acts 6:3. Opinions as to the duties of deacons range all the way from their doing nothing more than serving at the communion table and counting money, to running the church. Of course neither idea is correct. If the former is true then there is no need for them to be "full of the Holy Chost and wisdom." If the latter is true then the Bible misinforms us when it declares Christ to be the Head of the church. I have seen the office of deacon sorely misused by men who had no idea what their duties were. No doubt much more needs to be taught on the subject, but common sense should tells us that if a man must be full of the Holy Ghost and wisdom in order to fill the office well, then there must be some very serious responsibilities associated with that post.

May 2

"It is easier for a camel to go through the eye of a needle, than for a rich man to enter into the kingdom of God"
(Matthew 19:24)

The text speaks of those who are rich in their own self-esteem; rich in what they view as good works; rich in supposed creature righteousness and human merit. In a word, they are not "poor in spirit." They have no place in the kingdom of God for it is made up of those who are Christ-like in their meekness and lowliness of heart. They must be converted (from their lofty estimation of themselves), and become as little children (in humility and dependence upon the Lord) or they will never enter into the kingdom of heaven (Matt. 18:3). "The Lord is nigh unto them that are of a broken heart: and saveth such as be of a contrite spirit" (Psalm 24:18). This kind of spirit, or heart, the Lord will not despise (Psalm 51:17) and these are the kind of characters with whom he dwells (Isaiah 57:15) and to whom he looks (Isaiah 66:2).

There is no place in the Lord's house for those like Diotrephes who *love to have the preeminence* (3 John 9), nor for those who desire to be "lords over God's heritage" (1 Peter 5:3). Such characters are simply not *in* God's kingdom. They may, and often do, get their name on a church book, but that does not deceive the Lord. Membership in a church, even the true church, is not what puts a person *in* God's kingdom. There is no more likelihood of a man rich in his own self-righteousness entering the kingdom of God than there is that a camel will go through the eye of a needle, and we all know how likely that is.

There could not be a true church kingdom here in this crooked and perverse world if God did not reach down his hand of mercy and so deal with some of his people that they are brought to feel they are "less than the least of all saints" (Eph. 3:8). It is only from a posture of this kind of humility that anyone will be willing to obey the precepts that Christ has given for the government of his church. One great reason, if not the main reason, so many of God's people are not in the church kingdom is because they feel that "the place is too strait" for them. The eye of the needle is still too small, for they have not yet "become as little children."

ભ≈ટ

May 3

"He which persecuted us in times past now preacheth the faith which once he destroyed" (Galatians 1:23)

We have known quite a number of Old Line Baptist preachers who used to despise the doctrine they afterward were brought to love, promote and proclaim. When this happens, as it did in the case of the apostle Paul, there can be only one conclusion, and that is that *the Lord* opened their eyes to see and understand that the faith they had desired to destroy was in reality the *true* faith. It was *after* his conversion that Paul began to worship God "after the way which they (organized religionists) call heresy" (Acts 24:14).

If when people started looking for the true church they would seek out the way that popular religionists call heresy they would be much more apt to find the right path. Those doctrines that are upheld by the religious world have never been in harmony with the doctrine of Christ and his apostles. For instance, nothing can be found in the word of God about obtaining eternal life on the basis of "accepting Christ." Nothing can be found about an "age of accountability" at twelve years old. Nothing can be found about Christ setting up a temporal kingdom here on earth and reigning a literal thousand years after the current gospel dispensation is finished. Such false notions are myriad, and they are very popular in the religious world. If a person seeks the Lord's church among those things that are popular with organized religion they will search in vain for as long as they may inquire.

The path of truth and right, that leads to real *living*, has always been a narrow one that only a few in any given generation find (Matt. 7:14). It is a "strait" or difficult gate that opens to that path. Consequently, those who seek the easy, more popular road will pass up the strait gate in preference to the *wide* gate and the broad way where they see the masses walking.

Christ, John the Baptist, almost all the apostles, and many other true servants of Christ were put to death because religious people hated what they preached. If they had been going along with legalistic Judaism or with idolatrous heathenism hardly anyone would have had any problem with them or paid them any particular attention. But they contended for the truth, and that didn't set well with the unenlightened masses. Those who faithfully follow God's word today will likewise meet with a negative reaction from professing Christendom.

ৼৣৎ

May 4

"The blessing of the Lord, it maketh rich, and he addeth no sorrow with it" (Proverbs 10:22)

Wealth that is obtained by ungodly means will ultimately have great sorrow attached to it, for the Lord will not allow men to escape the ultimate consequences of ill-gotten gain. But those riches that are gotten as a result of the blessing of the Lord, whether material or spiritual, are not accompanied with such sorrow. This is not to say that those who have been made rich by the blessing of the Lord do not have any sorrows, but rather it is to point out that it is not the riches themselves that bring the sorrow.

If we should become rich in a monetary sense by the blessing of the Lord, it would be for the purpose of our using it to his glory and to the good of others rather than merely for our own benefit alone, that we might consume it upon our own lusts. If we misused such riches then our behavior would bring much sorrow upon us. Spiritual riches can also be misapplied and neglected, and this too will *produce* sorrow, but such riches themselves have no sorrow added with them.

I believe our text refers primarily to spiritual wealth. Those are rich indeed who have been blest with spiritual light and life; who have been led into a comforting and saving knowledge of the truth as it is in Christ Jesus and who have been given access to the true church here in the world. Those who have no divine life in them can see no richness at all in these spiritual blessings, but to those who are the happy recipients of them they represent wealth indescribable. And God's people never have any reason to be the least bit ashamed of the way in which they came by their spiritual wealth. They never worry about such riches rusting or decaying or being snatched away by thieves. These are blessings "in heavenly places in Christ" (Eph. 1:3) and therefore completely out of the reach of those who would strip us of them.

Truly, the blessings of the Lord maketh rich, and we will never have reason to be sorry that we have such treasures. May he help us to put a proper value upon them and to give him due praise for them, for they did indeed come from *him*. May we never forget what *truly* makes us rich.

May 5

"What fruit had ye then in those things whereof ye are now ashamed? for the end of those things is death" (Romans 6:12)

Anyone who has been identified with the Primitive Baptists any length of time has probably had someone say to them, "If I believed as you do, I would go and take my fill of sin," or some such statement. It has always made me feel bad for those who have said such things, because they were tacitly admitting that they were still in love with sin. They were, in effect, saying that if it were not for their fear of eternal punishment they would be a prolific participant in sin and wickedness. But of course if a person actually believed as do the Primitives they would understand that regeneration, or the new birth, drastically changes a person's attitude toward sin. They can no longer sin with impunity and it is never again the sweet morsel that it previously was. They still have a sinful nature after the heavenly birth, but sin no longer has dominion over them as it did before (Romans 6:14).

When a person's heart is changed by the grace of God they are given an entirely different outlook on sin and wickedness. They are made to feel ashamed of the sinful things they used to participate in freely and without remorse, and are made to wish they could avoid sin altogether. They then see that they never bore any worthwhile fruit while in their former state of corruption, and that a life such as they led only results in death and destruction. Literally, they become "new creatures in Christ" (2 Cor. 5:17). "Old things are passed away; behold, all things are become new."

It has always seemed to me to be a strange way of thinking to say that if Christ has done wonderful things for us such as embracing us in the covenant of election, giving us spiritual life and keeping us by his power, then we ought to respond by "taking our fill of sin." I have always felt that just the opposite should be the case. We should show our gratitude by living in such way as to honor and glorify the One who showed such great love for us and who has done such great things for us.

May 6

"Whom the Lord loveth he chasteneth" (Hebrews 12:6)

There are many texts in the Bible showing that God does not love everybody, but this is one of the plainest. It is irrefutably clear that God does not chastise everybody (Heb. 12:8); therefore he does not *love* everybody, for he "scourgeth *every* son whom he receiveth." "What son is he whom the father chasteneth not?" (v. 7). In other words, *all* of God's people are partakers of his chastisement; therefore if a person is without chastisement he simply is not a child of God (Heb. 12:8). This is so plain it ought not to be missed by anyone.

All of God's people are chastised for the simple reason that *all* of them need it. There are no exceptions. None of them are without sin. All of them to a greater or lesser degree deviate from the path of righteousness, even though their transgressions would ordinarily be viewed by the world as insignificant and not worthy of any correction or rebuke. But a humble child of God views no transgression as trivial, and he will not "despise the chastening of the Almighty" (Job 5:17), for he knows it is for his good.

Note that it is *love* that prompts the chastenings of the Lord: "Whom the Lord *loveth* he chasteneth." His rebukes are given in order to draw his people back into the path of obedience, not to drive them further from it. They are given as tokens that he cares for them and to let them know that he is dealing with them *as with sons*.

It is a great mercy to feel the rod of correction and to be blest with feelings of guilt and condemnation when we have not behaved as we should. This lets us know that we still have a tender conscience and that the Lord has not given us over to a reprobate mind. It gives us renewed evidence of the fatherly relation in which he stands to us, and the relation in which we stand to him as his sons.

He would have his children to likewise take disciplinary measures with their own offspring when they are disobedient. And he would have them do it in love, with a view to their restoration and betterment. "He that spareth his rod hateth his son: but he that loveth him chasteneth him betimes" (Prov. 13:24).

May 7

"For we know in part" (1 Corinthians 13:9)

I am often vividly reminded of my great ignorance as compared to what there is to know. Even when I limit the field of knowledge to the spiritual realm, I still find myself coming up woefully short of the mark I would like to measure up to. After many long years of study I still don't seem to have advanced very far in the knowledge of the mysteries of the gospel. Even as wonderfully blest with revelation and understanding as was the beloved apostle Paul, he was still keenly aware of the fact that he only knew in part and that he saw things "as through a glass, darkly." He stood in amazement as he contemplated the depths of the riches both of the wisdom and knowledge of God, saying, "How unsearchable are his judgments, and his ways past finding out!" (Rom. 11:33).

The more a humble man learns, the more impressed he will be with the limits of his own knowledge. The more he learns of God, the more he will feel his own insufficiency and weakness. What an astounding revelation it is when we come to the understanding that as the heavens are higher than the earth, so are God's ways and God's thoughts higher than our own (Isaiah 55:9)! An awareness of this momentous truth will go far toward keeping us from thinking more highly of ourselves than we ought to think and enabling us rather to think soberly and seriously. If we keep these things in mind we will have no difficulty admitting that in our present state we only "know in part."

But though our knowledge and understanding are greatly limited here, there is a far greater degree of light and knowledge awaiting us when we are raised and glorified. Just how this will be, and to what extent, we have not been told, but it will no doubt be a wonderful elevation and will equip us with everything necessary to praise God in perfection. Isn't that all we could ever desire?

May 8

"Surely the wrath of man shall praise thee: the remainder of wrath shalt thou restrain" (Psalm 76:10)

This verse expresses a truth that is demonstrated throughout the Scriptures; namely, that God is in full control of the hearts, minds and emotions of men and that his providential restraints are exerted whenever and wherever he pleases. He can, and often does, overrule, thwart, and frustrate the evil designs of men and so order them or turn them that his own ends and purposes are ultimately accomplished instead. This in no wise excuses wicked men of their evil deeds, for it is no thanks to them that their actions are made to achieve just the opposite of what they had intended.

God's putting a stop to the building of the tower of Babel is a clear example of what we have in mind. The expressed purpose of the builders was to construct for themselves a city and a tower in order to make a name for themselves and prevent their being scattered abroad upon the face of the earth (Gen. 11:4). But God confounded their language and the result was that they neither made a name for themselves nor prevented their being scattered abroad. They did not consider the Lord in their plans but only sought their own selfish ends, and consequently all their purposes were totally frustrated and overthrown. God is still doing the same kind of things today, though perhaps not in so visible and discernable a manner to our sin-clouded eyes.

We can clearly see the wrath of man praising God in the case of Joseph's brethren, who sold him into Egypt. Joseph told them, "As for you, ye thought evil against me; but God meant it unto good" (Gen. 50:20). Thus is the greatness of our God demonstrated. Consider the evil that was intended against Israel by Pharaoh, and look how thoroughly his fiendish purposes were frustrated and how completely that word was fulfilled which says of him, "Even for this same purpose have I raised thee up, that I might show my power in thee, and that my name might be declared throughout all the earth" (Rom. 9:17).

If it were not for God's providential restraints upon the wicked, none of His people could or would survive for very long in this wicked world. Let us ever be mindful that the heirs of heaven are "kept by the power of God" (1 Peter 1:5).

May 9

"Every man at his best state is altogether vanity" (Psalm 39:5)

Man cannot see himself as he truly is in and of himself until or unless God reveals it to him. When the apostle Paul saw this he could say, "I know that in me (that is, in my flesh,) dwelleth no good thing" (Rom. 7:18). There are very few people who would agree that this is true of themselves, but it is nonetheless a fact. In their flesh *no good thing* dwells. If they have been born of the Spirit of God then they possess an *imputed* righteousness, but this is in what is called *the new man, the new creature,* and *the inner man* and is no part of the old carnal flesh.

By virtue of the fact that Adam was the federal head of all mankind, we all fell in him, and with him. We *together* (all at the same time) became filthy and unprofitable (See Psalm 14:3 & Rom. 3:12). Consequently we all come into the world with a corrupt nature that is void of all good. When God looks at men just as they are by nature He sees nothing that is pleasing to Him. Even His own elect people before regeneration "were *by nature* the children of wrath, even as others" (Eph. 2:3). That is to say that their *nature* was the same as the nature of the non-elect, or the children of wrath. And even after the new birth they are still possessed of this sinful nature, and there is a warfare between it and the new nature (Gal. 5:17).

This is not to say that carnal men cannot do anything that is considered good by the society around them, or that they cannot do anything that issues in good to others, but these things do not come from any right principle within themselves. What they do arises from motives that are purely selfish and not from a principle of grace within the soul. In one way or another carnal men are motivated by the flesh in all they do.

So far as their nature is concerned men are "altogether vanity," even at their best state. "Every imagination of the thoughts of their heart is only evil continually" (Gen. 6:5). It is no wonder that Paul would say, "By the grace of God I am what I am" (I Cor. 15:10). If he had not been made a new creature in Christ Jesus he could not have said this. God views His people as they are in Christ, not as they are in the flesh. If He had not made them accepted in the Beloved by His grace (Eph. 1:6), even they would be rejected by Him.

May 10

"Unto me, who am less than the least of all saints"
(Ephesians 3:8)

I have often thought that this part of this verse fits me far better than it did the beloved apostle Paul. I know for sure that I am far less than him in respect to knowledge and understanding, and I feel to be much less than him in every other respect. How wonderfully he was used of the Lord in expounding the gospel, particularly to the Gentiles. And what a profound influence for good his epistles have had down through the centuries and up to the present. For zeal and dedication who has been his superior among us mere mortals? Who has been his equal for faithfulness, patience and courage under all manner of privation, hardship, and persecution? Does he not put all of us present-day ministers to shame in that respect?

Truly, the apostle Paul was a great man. And, like all truly great man, one of the most outstanding aspects of his character was his humility. He truly felt to be the least of the saints. But still (and I bless God for this), as little as he felt, he could yet count himself among the *saints.* This makes me feel that it is not improper for me to feel very little and insignificant among God's people, and yet, at the same time, be so bold as to entertain a sweet hope that I am one of them. But, Oh, how appropriately do the words of Paul seem to apply to me when he spoke of being the *chief* of sinners (1 Tim. 1:15). Do these words not fit me much more accurately than they did him?

Again, how well I can witness with this dear man of God when he says, "O wretched man that I am! Who shall deliver me from the body of this death?" And then I know that if there is any hope for me it lies in the same One he trusted for that deliverance, as he continued, "I thank God through Jesus Christ our Lord" (Rom. 7:25). Of a surety, if there is anything about me that is pleasing to God, it lies in what I am in Christ, and not in what I am in myself.

May 11

"Arise, go unto Nineveh, that great city, and preach unto it the preaching that I bid thee" (Jonah 3:2)

Jonah is a good example of the fact that God's ministers had best preach what he lays on their heart. On the other hand, when he lays nothing on their heart they had best not tax the patience of their hearers. Profitable preaching is done when a God-called servant's heart and soul are wrapped up in his subject. If God gives a man a message he will also give him an audience. And the audience will never be the same afterward. They will either be the better for having heard and obeyed the gospel, or they will be the worse for having heard it and not heeded it. They cannot occupy a mutual ground in which there are no consequences.

God's servants are bidden to "Preach the word," and to "be instant in season, out of season" (2 Tim. 4:2), and in those "out of season" times the preaching may be done somewhat mechanically and without real conviction or emotion. But the preaching that is laid on the hearts of God's servants will burn there like coals of fire until it is delivered. Then there will be nothing cold or mechanical, or formal and unfeeling about it. It will accomplish its purpose and it will prosper in the thing whereto God sent it (Isaiah 55:11).

Those who have truly been called to the work of the ministry are keenly aware that there is no real peace of conscience until or unless they preach the preaching that God has bidden them. They also know that there will be no real power or unction in the preaching unless the Holy Spirit condescends to provide the fire and conviction that renders it effectual. And if he deals thus with the preacher it is most likely that he will also prepare someone in the congregation to receive it profitably. But whether it is received with joy, consternation, or indifference, God's word will not return unto him void.

May 12

"Never man spake like this man" (John 7:46)

C hrist spoke as no man had ever spoken because he possessed what no man had every possessed, Deity in union with a sinless, flawless and pure human nature. He was perfect in every particular, and therefore spoke with perfect diction and elocution. He never stammered, stuttered or searched for suitable words. Every utterance was to the point and distinctly articulated. He never spoke superfluously nor said less than he intended, but every word had a distinct place and importance. And in addition to all this, his speech was accompanied with Divine power and authority (Luke 4:32; Matt. 7:28-29). Even those who rejected Him could not but marvel at *the gracious words which proceeded out of his mouth* (Luke 4:22).

Although we have not experienced the high pleasure of hearing the audible voice of Christ and the moving and forceful inflections thereof, we can find great delight in the precious words he has left on record for us by Divine inspiration. How we should treasure every line, every phrase, and word, even as Mary who sat at his feet and listened intently to every utterance with a fervent desire to learn all she could of him (Luke 10:39)!

There was a very distinct difference between the speech of Christ and that of the religious leaders of his day: "The people were astonished at his doctrine: for he taught them as one having authority, and not as the scribes." A similar difference exists today between those who are called to preach his word and those who are not. Stephen was one of those who spoke with Divine authority, and consequently the false religionists who disputed with him "were not able to resist the wisdom and the spirit by which he spake" (Acts 6:10). Thus it shall ever be. Those who speak with a conviction arising from the unction and power of the Holy Spirit, have something that others can only imitate but never duplicate.

May 13

"But when thou doest thine alms, let not thy left hand know what they right hand doeth" (Matthew 6:3)

One of the definitions of *alms* is "a charitable gift." There are many such gifts made by various businesses and organizations, and even by a church or two, in the town where I used to work. Often I was contacted by the donors and requested to have someone cover the presentation. Of course they wanted a story about it in the newspaper along with photos of their good deed. I always thought of the above scripture when this happened and I was somewhat amused at the number of people who wanted their almsgiving publicized as much as possible. How childish this seems to me, and how contrary it is to the Lord's way!

When I make my charitable contributions I do it as quietly and privately as possible. If I could do it without *anyone* knowing about it, that's what I would do. The Lord knows about it, and if he is pleased with it that's all the recognition I desire. And even if it could be that *he* didn't know about it, I would still give, for I know there are those who are in need. The apostle John said, "Whoso hath this world's good, and seeth his brother have need, and shutteth up his bowels of compassion from him, how dwelleth the love of God in him?" (1 John 3:17).

I view charitable gifts, when they are given for the right reasons, as reflecting the love of God in the heart of the giver. I also view the sharing of our earthly goods with those less fortunate as a wonderful opportunity the Lord has afforded us to show our love for him. Our Savior said, "Inasmuch as ye have done it unto one of the least of these my brethren, ye have done it unto me" (Matt. 25:40). "God loveth a cheerful giver" (2 Cor. 9:7).

Who can say how many times words of thanksgiving have been offered to God by the recipients of our little alms? Who can say how many times their hearts have gone out to Him in praise because of some little offering we have made? May the Lord help us to give our alms from a heart of love, and to do it without expecting, or desiring, any notoriety, remuneration, or praise.

May 14

"And with many other words did he testify and exhort, saying, save yourselves from this untoward generation" (Acts 2:40)

These words were part of the reply the apostle Peter gave on the day of Pentecost to those who were "pricked in their heart" at his preaching and inquired as to what they should do. Peter did not tell them a single thing to do in order to save themselves from eternal hell, for he knew it was not in their power to do that, but he did exhort them to save themselves from the untoward (*perverse and wicked*) generation of people they lived among.

God's people are saved in an eternal sense entirely by the grace of God without any adjuncts or conditions of any kind on their part. But their salvation from the ungodly element around them depends to a great extent upon their separating themselves from that class and steering clear of their works and ways. This is not only something they *can* do but it is something the *must* do if they are to be saved in that sense. God is not going to do *for* them what he commands *them* to do.

The saints live "in the midst of a crooked and perverse nation" (Phil. 2:15), among whom they shine as lights in the world." But the extent to which their light shines depends largely upon their "doing all things without murmurings and disputings," for it is in this way that they show themselves to be "blameless and harmless, the sons of God, without rebuke." They are *in* the world but they are not *of* the world. Therefore they are exhorted to "love not the world, neither the things that are in the world" (1 John 2:15).

Nothing is calculated to bring more distress and misery to a child of God than for them to form close alliances and associations with the ungodly and to emulate their manner of life. They are strictly commanded to "come out from among them" and be separate...and touch not the unclean thing (2 Cor. 6:14-18). This is really the only way we can save ourselves from this untoward generation. Those who play with fire will sooner or later get burned.

May 15

"The Lord gave, and the Lord hath taken away" (Job 1:21)

Although Job became very wealthy and influential, he never forgot where it all came from. He knew that it was the Lord who had given it and the Lord who had taken it away.

Those with riches are very foolish and ungrateful who say in their heart, "My power and the might of my hand hath gotten me this wealth," for it is the *Lord alone* that gives power to get wealth (Deut. 8:17-18). "The blessing of the Lord, it maketh rich" (Prov. 10:22). He can prosper us, or he can strip us, whichever he chooses. But we will do well to always be mindful of his merciful providence, whether we are experiencing feast or famine.

The aged man Jacob acknowledged that it was God who had fed him *all his life long* (Gen. 48:15). It is the same with all men. Some are fed much more bountifully than others, but all nourishment, no matter how plentiful or how meager, ultimately must be traced to the providence of God. Just as it is God who clothes the lilies of the field with beauty, so it is he who clothes the people of his pasture with raiment, even though they often manifest little faith in his power and grace (Matt. 6:28-33). The same God who raised Joseph from the pit and the lowly prison to great usefulness and power is still on his throne, and he still cares and provides for his people as much as he ever has.

May we be as ready to say, "Blessed be the name of the Lord," when he is taking away as we are when he is giving. He has assured us that he will never leave us nor forsake us (Heb. 13:5).

May 16

"The Lord God omnipotent reigneth" (Revelation 19:6)

We often sing, "The Lord Jehovah reigns, and royal state maintains; His head with awful glories crowned," and thus we acknowledge his rulership and supremacy. The word *omnipotent* means *unlimited power or authority; all-powerful or almighty*. This can only apply to the one true and living God, the God of the Bible.

It is he who "made the world and all things therein" and who is "Lord of heaven and earth" and who cannot be confined to temples made by men. It is he who is not worshipped with men's hands and who does not *need* anything. It is he who has "made of one blood all nations of men for to dwell on all the face of the earth, and hath determined the times before appointed, and the bounds of their habitation." It is he "in whom we live, and move, and have our being." Consequently it is very improper for anyone "to think that the Godhead is like unto gold, or silver, or stone, graven by art and man's device" (Acts 17:24-29).

The Bible plainly describes the kind of being God is, and it has always amazed me that so many people can read the pages of that blessed Book and still come away thinking he is *altogether such an one as themselves* (Psalm 50:21). If anyone is willing to take the Bible as their guide they must realize that the little puny god of popular religion cannot possibly be the God therein described.

We cannot at one and the same time believe God is *omnipotent* and also believe he is *trying* to save people. We cannot believe that "none can stay his hand" (Dan. 4:35) and at the same time believe that people are refusing to *let* him save them. It is impossible to consistently hold both positions. He is in full control of all things and all people. If he were hungry (which is likewise an impossibility), he would not tells us, because the world is his, and the fullness thereof (Psalm 50:12). May he give his people higher views of himself.

May 17

"Pray without ceasing" (1 Thessalonians 5:17)

No doubt God has untold millions of children upon the earth at any given time, and probably there are numerous occasions when hundreds of thousands of prayers are being offered up unto him simultaneously. Yet he tells us that "men ought always to pray" (Luke 18:1). If he were such a being as we are, there is no way he could keep track of even *two* or *three* prayers at the same time, much less *thousands*. But he is omniscient, and it presents no difficulty for him to hear each of us individually, personally and instantaneously and to keep a clear accounting of all our prayers.

When we pray we do not merely acknowledge his existence but we show our faith in his ability to hear us distinctly and to single us out from all others as well as to supply all our needs, no matter how great or how numerous those needs might be. When we pray we honor him by acknowledging him as our loving and merciful Father and our gracious Benefactor, and also by confessing our utter dependence upon him for life, breath and being. And when we pray "without ceasing," or in other words, *frequently throughout each day,* we acknowledge that our need of him is constant and unremitting. Our prayers are also an acknowledgment of his ever-present compassion and love for us, and of his willingness to help us. In other words, it is an acknowledgment of the truth of the word which exhorts us to cast "all our cares upon him, for he careth for us" (1 Peter 5:7).

Our Lord is fully aware of the importance of prayer in the lives of his people, and he would have them take full and continuous advantage of it. It is their chief source of communication with him and is an emotional and spiritual outlet that nothing else can provide. The

Scriptures tell us that "the effectual fervent prayer of a righteous man availeth much" (James 5:16). And though we do not know what we should pray for as we ought, that should not discourage us, for we also have the assurance that the Spirit itself maketh intercession for us with groanings which cannot be uttered.

Satan also knows something of the value of prayer to God's people, and he will try to hinder it in any way he can (1 Peter 3:7). Therefore let us not forget to pray often. Whatever it is, "take it to the Lord in prayer."

May 18

"For God so loved the world, that he gave his only begotten Son, that whosoever believeth in him should not perish, but have everlasting life" (John 3:16)

This is one of the most misunderstood and misapplied verses in the Bible. Popular religionists place it in the category of a universal offer of eternal life to a lost world of unbelievers and they contend that anyone can believe in Christ, even those who do not *have the witness in themselves* (1 John 5:10). However such a position clearly contradicts the Biblical doctrines of grace. It denies the doctrines of Total Depravity, Unconditional Election, Special and Particular Atonement, and Irresistible Grace. It also contradicts the doctrine of Final Preservation for it advocates that men must not only believe in order to *get* life, but they must *continue* to believe in order to *keep* it.

In actuality the "world" of John 3:16 is the world of God's chosen family, those whom he foreknew and predestinated to be conformed to the image of his Son (Romans 8:29). The "believers" of John 3:16 are the same characters, for they shall all know the Lord from the least to the greatest (Jer. 31:31; Heb. 8:7-12). They are also the "every man" of Hebrews 2:9 and the "children" of Hebrews 2:13. They are the "church" for whom he gave himself (Eph. 5:25). They are the "sheep" for whom he lay down his life (John 10:11). They are the same ones who "were ordained to eternal life" (Acts 13:48). They are the "vessels of mercy" of Romans 9:23 that God "afore prepared unto glory." No one will ever understand John 3:16 until or unless they identify who the "world" is that is spoken of there.

If we say the *world* of John 3:16 is the whole Adamic race, then we say that untold millions will at last have to pay the same penalty Christ paid for them on the cross. Not only would this mean that God demanded payment twice for the same sins, but it would also mean that he shed his blood in vain for all those who are finally and eternally lost.

True belief in Christ is not what procures or achieves everlasting life, but rather it is one of the things that identifies those who already have it. In other words, no one can truly believe in Christ until after they are given divine life. The "believers" of John 3:16 are the "called" of Romans 8:30. To say otherwise is to hinge eternal life upon belief rather than hinging belief upon eternal life, and *that* is a huge difference.

May 19

"David encouraged himself in the Lord his God" (1 Samuel 30:6)

Ziklag had been invaded and burned by the Amalekites and the wives and children of David and his men had been taken captive. The men were so distraught that they actually spoke of stoning David. This brought him into great distress, not only because of the captivity of his wives but because of the unreasonable anger of his men toward him. We can only imagine the anguish of soul he must have felt, which had to have seemed unbearable. But then, after the initial shock and dismay had somewhat abated, he did what every child of God must do when overwhelmed with grief and pain: he encouraged himself in the Lord.

No doubt he remembered that God was still on the throne and was in full and complete control of all things and all events, and that if worse should come to worse he would yet see his loved ones again in the Glory World. He could take comfort in the fact that God's people will never see each other for the last time, but will at last be reunited in a far better place.

I suspect that after prayerful consideration and reflection, David also encouraged himself in the hope that God would enable him and his men to rescue their captured loved ones from the Amalekites, which ultimately proved to be the case. No circumstance is ever beyond the reach of God's power, and no eventuality can alter the fact that *his mercy endureth forever*. David could encourage himself, as we often do, in the fact that God will never leave nor forsake his people, no matter how bleak or distressing their outward circumstances may be, or appear to be (Heb. 13:5).

How often has this poor, unworthy writer been compelled to encourage himself in the Lord his God, for there was nowhere else to turn for relief! And how thankful he has been for that God-given strength that has always prevented him from totally despairing but has kept him leaning on the everlasting arms of Jesus! Praise be to his great and holy name!

May 20

"Be ye not unequally yoked together with unbelievers"
(2 Corinthians 6:14)

What an awful burden it is for a believer to be yoked with an unbeliever. It is often enough of a burden simply to be placed in the same company with unbelievers, but it is much worse to be "yoked together" with them. It is an *unequal* yoke indeed. A believer cannot in good conscience *lower* himself, or herself, to the level of the unbeliever, and the unbeliever has no desire, and no ability, to *raise* himself, or herself, to the level of the believer. Consequently the only way they can ever agree is on the unbeliever's terms, and this is what makes it an unequal yoke.

A believer, simply because he *is* a believer, has a conscience that will not allow him to employ any underhanded or ungodly means or methods in his dealings with an unbeliever or anyone else. The unbeliever, however, does not feel such restraints where right and wrong are concerned, and consequently the believer is not on a level playing field with him. So again, when they are yoked together it is a very unequal yoke.

Marriage between believers and unbelievers is a particularly unequal yoke. In such a case the believer desires to conduct the marriage on the basis of Biblical principles, while the unbeliever couldn't care less about such principles. If there are children involved, the believer will want to "bring them up in the nurture and admonition of the Lord" (Eph. 6:4), while the unbeliever will likely want to follow the world's philosophies and let the children "do their own thing" without any Scriptural guidance or discipline at all. Our country today is reaping the bitter fruits of its application of the world's godless philosophy where child-rearing is concerned.

All of God's believing people would do well to take the instruction of 2 Corinthians 6:14 very, very seriously and not bind themselves to any kind of an alliance with unbelievers. Our faithful old forefathers have always pointed out the "unequal yoke" of this verse as one of the main reasons for their objection to Primitive Baptists uniting with secret, oath-bound societies. It is a good reason. *Light has no communion with darkness.*

May 21

"By this shall all men know that ye are my disciples, if ye have love one to another" (John 13:35)

Since Christ is the epitome of love, yea, love personified, how could it be otherwise than that his disciples should be recognized for their love to one another? He taught the very highest and most noble principles and standards, both by word and example, and thus if we would be identified as his disciples those principles must in good measure be reflected in our everyday lives. We can never meet the perfect standard that he always maintained, but we *can* "press toward the mark" (Phil. 3:14). If we love in word only (1 John 2:5) then we are missing the mark, for we must love in deed and in truth. The text says we are to "have love one *to* another," which necessitates the *manifestation* of love, not merely the *profession* of love.

The kind of love that marks us as the disciples of Christ is described in 1 Corinthians 13. It is a longsuffering love that is free of boastfulness, pride, and all unseemly or inappropriate behavior. It is a love that is not self-seeking and not easily provoked. It thinks no evil of those who are its objects, nor does it ever rejoice in anyone's iniquities. It rather rejoices in the truth and is forbearing toward others; full of faith, hope and endurance. In a word, it is a love that can be depended on, through thick and through thin, through good times and bad. It is a God-honoring love that is characterized by all things decent, honest and true. Happy are those who possess, and manifest, such a love and who enjoy the company of others who are likewise blessed.

We are not manifesting love toward our brethren when we are doing things that cause unrest, distress and confusion among them; neither when we are gossiping about them or otherwise encouraging ill feelings one toward another. We are certainly not showing love toward them when we are in any way stirring up strife among them or when we are habitually absenting ourselves from their assemblies. And no one is apt to suspect us of being true disciples of Christ if they find us warring among ourselves. May the Lord help us to always esteem our brethren better than ourselves and to studiously avoid anything that would hinder their spiritual welfare or progress in any way. We owe it to them and to our merciful Savior.

May 22

"I am a companion of all them that fear thee, and of them that keep thy precepts" (Psalm 119:63)

This verse is one of a great many in the Bible that indicates a gracious state. If we desire the companionship of those who fear God and keep his precepts, it is another strong evidence that we are among his people. The old adage is, "Birds of a feather flock together," and this is very true, whether they be good birds or bad birds. If we have had the principles of grace planted within our heart, then we will not desire the companionship of evil men. We will find it far more preferable to be companions of those who fear God, even if it be in tribulation, than to be companions of the wicked in their ease and pleasure (Heb. 10:33; Rev. 1:9).

We have no greater example of this than Moses, who was in a position as a young man in Egypt to have possessed great wealth and to have "enjoyed the pleasures of sin for a season." But because of the divine principles God had instilled in his heart he chose rather to suffer affliction, and the reproach of Christ, with the people of God (Heb. 11:24-26). He endured tremendous hardship and trial as a result of his identity with Israel, but his conscience would not allow him to identify himself with those who knew not God, no matter how bright his temporal prospects may have otherwise been. And thus it is with every little child of grace in whose heart a work of grace has been performed. They will seek out, and join themselves to, those who are tenderhearted, kind, humble and loving, and who strive to follow the meek and lowly Lamb of God in precept and example.

Any time Israel joined in affinity with the wicked kings or nations around them they were great losers for having done so. It has always been so with God's people and always will be. Let us always seek out God-fearing companions in all aspects of our lives, men and women who *keep his precepts*. We are safe with this kind of people. There is far more trouble experienced in following any other course than there is in identifying with God's humble poor. And, one moment of joy in the Lord outweighs all the sufferings we might have to endure as a result of following him.

May 23

"Be sober, be vigilant; because your adversary the devil, as a
roaring lion, walketh about seeking whom he may devour"
(1 Peter 5:8)

From the viewpoint of a follower of Christ the devil is a strange being. There is no good in him and he has no capacity for good--- only evil. He is not capable, to any degree, of the feelings of love or compassion. The only use he ever has for anything good, or that appears good, is to cover or camouflage his wicked schemes. Most of his works are clothed in a garb of religion so as to more easily ensnare the weak and unsuspecting. All of the false religions in the world may ultimately be traced to satanic influence. The devil has never had any problem with people having all the religion they desire, just so long as it is not *pure* religion. The apostle Paul said, "Satan himself is transformed into an angel of light. Therefore it is no great thing if his ministers also be transformed as the ministers of righteousness" (II Cor. 11:15). And by this fraudulent pretense almost the whole world has been deceived.

Satan is the archrival of God's people, and as such he is spoken of as "the accuser of our brethren" (Rev. 12:10). His chief ambition is to devour them in the sense of leading them astray and ruining their lives. He knows he cannot cause any of the elect to lose eternal life, but if they are not sober minded and vigilant with regard to spiritual things he may very well be suffered to destroy their present peace and happiness. In fact, the only way they can "stand against the wiles of the devil" is to "put on the whole armour of God" as described in the sixth chapter of Ephesians.

Satan is not only an adversary, but he is a vicious, ravenous enemy and is compared to a roaring lion seeking his prey. He definitely will devour anyone whom the Lord suffers him to devour. This truth is implied in the words, "whom he *may* devour." Just as the devils could not go into the herd of swine (Matt. 8:30-32) without being suffered of the Lord to do so, Satan likewise cannot devour anyone unless God lifts His providential restraints enough to let it occur. May the Lord help us to be sober and vigilant, always aware of the fact that Satan is desirous of our downfall. "Submit yourselves therefore to God. Resist the devil, and he will flee from you" (James 4:7).

May 24

"They think that they shall be heard for their much speaking"
(Matthew 6:7)

Based upon my observation of the length of the public prayers of many of my brethren over the years I have had to conclude that their feelings about such prayers differ at least in some respects from my own. As far back as I can recall I have felt that many public prayers were much too lengthy and repetitious, and perhaps too mechanical or formal. Most Bible prayers are very brief and at a normal reading speed it takes about twenty to twenty-five seconds to repeat the model prayer that Christ gave to his disciples (Matt. 6:9-13).

I have heard prayers that sounded to me more like sermons than prayers and I have many times known them to go on for ten minutes or longer. Some seem to feel that public prayer should cover everything they can think of, but I believe short prayers that primarily address the immediate needs and circumstances are more effectual. I do not believe our public prayers on Sunday should include everything we ought to have been praying for all week. I have never heard any negative comments about a short prayer, but have *many* times heard such comments about unduly lengthy and repetitious prayers.

I recall the prayers of a poor publican who only spoke seven words, "God be merciful to me a sinner," yet he went down to his house justified rather than the Pharisee who prayed a more wordy prayer (Luke 18:10-14). Our Lord tells his disciples not to be like those who think they shall be heard for their *much speaking,* and gives the following as the reason: "For your Father knoweth what things ye have need of, before ye ask him." We should not pray as though we were acquainting God with our circumstances, for he already knows.

I believe we can learn to condense our public prayers so that they cover all they need to cover on any given occasion without being too lengthy. It is not the *length* our prayers that gains God's ear, but the *substance* and *sincerity* of them. May the Lord help us to always pray in the spirit, being careful to ask only for that which is honoring to his holy name, and desiring only that which is according to his divine will. "Not my will, but thine, be done" (Luke 22:42).

May 25

"Where is then the blessedness ye spake of?" (Galatians 4:15)

The Galatian churches had been called "into the grace of Christ" and had therein greatly rejoiced. Obviously they had often spoken of it as a blessed experience for it freed them from the burdensome works of the law and gave them rest in the finished work of Christ. But now many of them had been deceived by false teachers and convinced that the grace of Christ was not sufficient after all, but that they must incorporate certain requirements of the old law service in order to be saved. And this of course destroyed the blessedness they had previously felt and found comfort in. The apostle then expressed his amazement that they were *so soon* removed from that former blessed state and led off into teachings that troubled them and perverted the gospel of Christ (Gal. 1:6-7).

To our sorrow we have seen many of God's people who have been called into the grace of Christ but who later, by one device of Satan or another, have become disenchanted with the old church and thus lost the blessedness they originally had found. It is sad indeed to see those who become dissatisfied with the goodness of God's house and who seem to think they have become wiser than he as to what that house should be and how it should be conducted. When they first came to it, it was beautiful to them, but with time they began to see ways they wanted to change it, update it, and, to their way of thinking, rescue it from destruction. They forgot, if they ever knew, that the old church is as much the church when it is small in numbers as it is when it is larger in numbers, and that it is God who adds to it. Where, then, is the blessedness they formerly spoke of?

Sadly, it is an all-too-common thing for God's people to leave their first love and to become lukewarm. In so doing they lose sight of the blessedness they first felt in seeing, and identifying themselves with, the true church. We may well desire to see the church more spiritual and dedicated, but lowering the standards and trying to appeal to the world will not accomplish that goal. Walking in the old paths will. May the Lord help us to remain therein, or return to them if we have left them.

May 26

"Bless them that curse you, and pray for them which despitefully use you" (Luke 6:28)

How contrary are the teachings of Christ to human nature! Man's natural reaction to being cursed and despitefully used is to reciprocate in kind, to do unto others as others have done unto him. But how differently the followers of Christ are taught to behave, and how wonderfully does such behavior show the superior excellence of the religion of Christ to all others! Very rarely do we see a person so spiritually mature and so honorably disciplined as to react in an humble, Christ-like manner under abuse and ill-usage. Normally men will strike back when mistreated, and then the original abuser seeks to "get even," and so it goes, back and forth, to the detriment of both parties.

As we have watched the wars between various religious groups around the world, such as the Catholics and Protestants in Ireland and the Arabs and Jews in the Middle East, we have marveled at how far both sides were from showing a Christian spirit. If the opposing parties were to adopt Christian principles in their dealings with one another, all conflict would cease. There can be no war where true Christianity is in exercise all the way around. But carnal minds will not accept this truth, and therefore, just as Christ prophesied, we see that there are wars and rumors of wars (Matt. 24:6; Mark 13:7). There are those who "hate peace" (Psalm 120:6). While the righteous are "for peace" the wicked are "for war." And thus shall it ever be until the great day when Christ returns and brings an end to these temporal scenes.

There could be no serious troubles in our world or in our churches if everyone practiced the Christian principles of loving their brethren and esteeming them better than themselves. Christ taught us that all things whatsoever we would that men should do to us is what we should do to them (Matt. 7:12). These are very high principles indeed, and much grace is needed if we are to live by them. Let us strive to make the teachings of Christ the constant rule of our lives. The rewards will be great.

May 27

"I give unto them eternal life; and they shall never perish"
(John 10:28)

Jesus speaks here of his sheep, or in other words, his elect family, and declares that they shall never lose the eternal life he gives them. And he goes further and asserts that no man shall pluck them out of his hand. He makes it very clear that no man is able to pluck them out of the Father's hand either. And to even further show their eternal security he declares, "I and my Father are one." So in order for a child of God to lose eternal life he would have to first be plucked out of the hands of both the Father and the Son. And in order for that to happen there would have to be some power stronger than God.

Popular religion says the devil can pluck them out of God's hand and that men can pluck *themselves* out of his hand. But this is to say that both the devil and men are more powerful than God. We Primitive Baptists cannot bring ourselves to cast such aspersions upon the Almighty (Daniel 4:35).

Job said, "The righteous also shall hold on his way" (Job 17:9). But if the righteous can lose eternal life then Job was mistaken. Christ said, "All that the Father giveth me shall come to me; and him that cometh to me I will in no wise cast out" (John 6:37), and he goes on to show that he will not lose any of them but will raise them up at the last day (vs. 38-40). Is anyone so bold as to say Christ was mistaken? The apostle Paul said he was confident of this very thing, "that he which hath begun a good work in you will perform it until the day of Jesus Christ" (Philippians 1:6). But if God's people can lose eternal life then that good work will not be performed long enough. Shall we believe Paul or popular religion?

Many people get off track on this subject by taking those Scriptures that refer to temporal falls and backslidings as meaning the loss of spiritual life. For instance, they think the fall mentioned in Galatians 5:4 means a fall from eternal life, when in fact it refers to being led away from reliance upon the grace of God to relying upon their own works. It has nothing whatsoever to do with losing eternal salvation.

"But Israel (God's elect) shall be saved in the Lord with an everlasting salvation" (Isa. 45:17). If salvation could be lost it would not be everlasting. Again, the Lord's declaration is, "They shall *never* perish," and never means *never*.

May 28

"I have learned, in whatsoever state I am, therewith to be content" (Philippians 4:11)

The apostle speaks here of those circumstances and conditions into which he was providentially led and directed. His confidence in God was such that no matter what his outward situation was he could contentedly rest in the assurance that God knew all about it and had a purpose in it. He was not ashamed of the things he suffered for the gospel's sake for he had a spiritual and experiential acquaintance with the One in whom he believed.

Not only that but he was persuaded that that same God was able to keep that which he had committed unto him until the final day (2 Tim. 1:12). It is a wonderful thing when we can totally commit our all into the hands of the Lord with the full assurance that whatever path he lays out for us will ultimately be for the best, even if it be a path of trial and tribulation.

We were never meant to stay here forever. We are appointed unto death (Heb. 9:27), and as Abraham Lincoln wrote, "Our life is ever on the wing, and death is ever nigh; The moment when our lives begin, we all begin to die." God is fully able, and I believe will, reconcile us to our departure when that time comes. But for now we need to be reconciled to whatever may lie between now and death.

For this we need to be much in prayer, and if we have not done so before, we need to begin familiarizing ourselves with God's promises to his people. These will prove to be a great boon to our souls in our hours of adversity, and even more so as we approach the end of our earthly sojourn. They will also contribute much to our contentment in whatsoever state we find ourselves.

The text is not in any sense intended to encourage us in a state of lethargy and complacency with regard to spiritual things. It is rather intended to show us that a point may be reached in our spiritual growth and development, if we apply ourselves unto wisdom, where we can truly rely upon the Lord and commit our all to him no matter how distressing or disarming our circumstances may be. Let us strive to attain that blessed plateau, and like Paul, fight a good fight and keep the faith. If we do so, when the time comes we will be as ready to be offered up as he was (2 Tim. 4:6-7).

May 29

"Behold, happy is the man whom God correcteth" (Job 5:17)

It is a great instance of God's mercy to his people that he corrects and chastens them, and they should never entertain any negative thoughts with regard to that chastening (Prov. 3:11; Heb. 12:5). It is administered for no other purpose than their good and is a gracious manifestation of God's love for them (Heb. 12:6; Rev. 3:19).

Chastisement may come in various forms but it should never be viewed as being too severe or more than is appropriate. If God dealt with us strictly on the basis of justice our miseries would always be far greater than they are. But his dealings with his people are always accompanied with kindness and forbearance and with a view to their betterment and instruction. A wise man of the past expressed it very well when he said, "God cannot do an unloving thing to one of his children."

If God's children were always obedient in all respects and never deviated from the path of truth and righteousness, then they would never need correction and chastisement. But "all have sinned, and come short of the glory of God" (Rom. 3:23). "In many things we offend all," or, *we all offend* (James 3:2). We all have a sinful nature and this often results in our *doing* things that we desire to avoid, and *failing* to do things that we desire to do. The apostle Paul expressed this very well in Romans 7:14-21. Consequently, due to the fact that our flesh is so weak and we are so constantly assailed on every side by the forces of evil, we are prone to err and when we do, we need the correcting hand of the Lord to lead us back into right paths.

The chastening of the Lord is not pleasant while it is being administered, but after it has done its intended work it produces very valuable results (Heb. 12:11). It would be greatly to our hurt if God did not correct us, just as it is greatly to the detriment of children when their parents fail to administer proper discipline. We may count ourselves happy and blest indeed if we are among those who are chastened of the Lord, for this shows that we are among His sons (Heb. 12:7-8). And if we are among the sons, all will ultimately be well.

May 30

"For they loved the praise of men more than the praise of God"
(John 12:43)

I cannot witness with those whose priorities are so misdirected. The praise of men means little to me, but the praise of God means everything. It matters little what *men* think of me so long as *God* is pleased with me. And what good would it do me for *men* to praise me if I did not have *God's* approval? If all the people in the world should commend me I still would be ruined and undone if *God* did not commend me. When we seriously consider the matter, it appears very foolish to us that men would place more value upon the sanction and recognition of men than they do upon the approbation of God.

It has been my observation that the praise of men is very popular in our society. Almost every newspaper we pick up, and every newscast we hear, tells of the presentation of awards to various individuals for various things. It is true that some of these people have done very honorable deeds that are worthy of commendation, but if they have done these things for the right reasons they will neither need nor desire any worldly honors; the approval of God will be sufficient.

Many a plaque, trophy and crown that no longer has any meaning to anyone is stored in a trunk or attic somewhere, but the praise of God is of enduring worth. It is treasure laid up in heaven where moth and rust cannot corrupt and where thieves do not break through and steal.

Most any time I see a local announcement pertaining to preachers of other orders who are scheduled to "preach revivals," a long list of their accomplishments is given and we are told how outstanding they are as a person and what a dynamic and exciting preacher they are. If I were invited to preach somewhere and I learned that that kind of build up was going to precede me, I would politely refuse the invitation. After that kind of praise of men I don't think I would be able to preach a lick anyway.

May 31

"And confessed that they were strangers and pilgrims on the earth" (Hebrews 11:13)

God's precious servants of old "died in faith" with the full realization that this world was not their home. They not only *knew* it to be true, but readily confessed it, and we are told that "they which say such things declare plainly that they seek a country" (v. 14). That is, they desire that better, or heavenly, country or city that God has prepared for them (v. 16) for they know that they have no continuing city here (13:14).

Once we have been killed to the love of this world and given a sweet hope of one day dwelling in that "city which hath foundations, whose builder and maker is God," we can no longer feel at home in this greatly inferior environment called *earth*. Once we have died *to* sin we can no longer live in it and delight in it (Rom. 6:2) as do those who are dead *in* sin. Thus we become strangers to this world, and it becomes strange to us (Gal. 6:14). We are then *in* the world but cease to be *of* the world. If we were of the world, the world would love us, but because we have been chosen *out* of the world and are therefore not *of* the world, therefore the world hates us (John 15:19). Hence it is not possible that we should feel at home here.

We live in a world in which the majority of the people either do not love God or else they believe in a god that bears little resemblance to our God. "Their rock (small r) is not as our Rock (capital R), even our enemies themselves being judges" (Deut. 32:31). Consequently we cannot join with them in their religious observances, ceremonies and services. Much of what the world calls *worship* is either embarrassingly shallow, immature and sanctimonious or else downright sacrilegious, and our consciences will not allow us to identify ourselves with it.

All such things enable us to know something of what John must have felt when he said, "And we know that we are of God, and the whole world lieth in wickedness" (1 John 5:19). It is not that we *chose* to be strangers and pilgrims on the earth, but the Lord's dealings with us have *made* us strangers. And we would not go back if we could. We are citizens of a better country than this.

June 1

"Blessed are they whose sins are covered. Blessed is the man to whom the Lord will not impute sin" (Romans 4:6-8)

The apostle Paul points out David's description here of the blessedness of those unto whom God imputes righteousness *without works* (Psalm 32:1-2). And Oh, what blessedness it is—too great for words! The blood of Christ has covered their sins, and consequently God will not impute sin unto them because their sins have been imputed to Christ. And not only this, the righteousness of Christ is freely imputed to them.

To those who have spiritual discernment the Scriptures make it very clear that Christ laid down his life for no one but his people. They are described as his *sheep* (John 10:15), the *vessels of mercy* (Rom. 9:23), *the church* (Eph. 5:25) and in a number other places they are referred to as his elect, or his chosen (Luke 18:7; Eph. 1:4). They are also referred to by various other names and titles. These are embraced in the covenant of grace, and by virtue of that covenant relationship God puts his laws in their minds and writes them in their hearts. He makes each of them subjects of divine teaching, is merciful to their unrighteousness, and remembers their sins and iniquities no more (Jer. 31:34; Heb. 8:7-12).

In no instance is their final salvation spoken of in Scripture as being uncertain in any sense of the word. It is always declared to be sure, even more certain than the ordinances of heaven (Isaiah 45:17; Jer. 31:35-37; Matt. 1:21; John 17:2). There is no mention in the Scriptures of such things as "accepting Christ as one's personal Savior," or "getting saved" or "letting the Lord do thus and so." All such expressions are of human invention and imply that eternal salvation is not certain to anyone. But this cannot be, because the salvation of God's people is based upon what Christ did, not upon what *man* does. Their salvation is certain because of the fact that Christ is "made unto (them) wisdom, and righteousness, and sanctification and redemption" (1 Cor. 1:30). Hence every heir of promise will be saved without the loss of one (John 6:37-38). "Thanks be unto God for his unspeakable gift" (2 Cor. 9:15).

June 2

"Day unto day uttereth speech, and night unto night showeth knowledge. There is no speech nor language, where their voice is not heard" (Psalm 19:2-3)

Both day and night have a passive voice that speaks of the glory of God, just as does the starry heavens. Though it is not an audible voice, it is a voice nonetheless, and in every place on earth where people dwell there are those who have ears to hear its message. They look into the heavens and they see the handiwork of God gloriously displayed, and day by day they see the plain mark of the great Creator upon all things around them, and it speaks to them of his greatness and glory. There is no inhabited region in all the world so remote that this voice is not heard by someone.

The apostle Paul said, "That which may be known of God is manifest in them; for God hath showed it unto them (that is, unto those who hold the truth in unrighteousness). "For the invisible things of him from the creation of the world are clearly seen, being understood by the things that are made, even his eternal power and Godhead; so that they are without excuse" (Romans 1:19-20). This tells me that the invisible things of God, such as his eternal power and Godhead, are plainly manifest by his creation, or the things he has made. And consequently, those who deny his existence are without excuse for their ignorance. It is only a fool who will say in his heart, "There is no God" (Psalm 14:1; 53:1). The fact that there is a *creation* plainly declares that there has to be a *Creator*. And those who can look about them upon the precise order and design of that marvelous creation and yet deny its divine origin, are doing so in the face of overwhelming evidence to the contrary.

How blest are those who not only can see God by an eye of faith but who can also see his mighty hand in all the vast works of nature! The intricate design and beauty of the flowers, the tender care of mothers for their young, the faithful rotation of the seasons in their turn, all these things and manifold more, testify gloriously of the magnitude and majesty of the great Maker of the universe. The voice of nature declares to us continually, "All these things wondrously reveal to thee the glory and goodness of thy Creator. Trust in Him for all thy needs, for he is well able to supply all thou shalt ever require, and much more."

June 3

In thy presence is fulness of joy" (Psalm 16:11)

In an 1874 article written by Elder Isaac Vanmeter, he told of questioning a deaf mute with regard to the location of heaven. The lady had recently been baptized, and with a slate and pencil in hand Elder Vanmeter wrote, "Where is heaven?" She looked at the slate for a moment, then quickly wrote the word *God*. Elder Vanmeter said he was struck with the answer, as involving a glorious and beautiful truth. "Even while here in the body," he continued, "when and wherever the Lord manifests Himself to us as He does not to the world, whether in prison, or in church, whether among friends, or exiled on some lonely Patmos, we are in a heavenly place; and we often realize that we have a little earnest of the inheritance, a foretaste of the joy. But the incorruptible inheritance of the saints in light is reserved *in heaven* for them."

If we have ever once experienced the felt presence of the Lord, no matter how briefly, we can bear witness to the truth of the above words. There is nothing else on earth like it. One moment of that joy leaves us changed for life and confirms to us that some glorious something awaits us out there in the future that far exceeds anything our limited capacities can imagine or conceive. As Elder Vanmeter expressed it, "Everything in nature, and in art that is most ravishing and full of joy is used by Inspiration to represent the glory and joy of *heaven*. And yet, all fail utterly to convey to our finite minds, and to our depraved understandings, an adequate idea of the things which God hath prepared for them that love Him."

I often marvel at my own seeming deadness, coldness and dullness where spiritual things are concerned and at how prone I am to provoke the Lord to withdraw himself feelingly from me. Oh how I long for his gracious visits to my soul, yet I find, as did Paul, that "When I would do good evil is present with me"! I look forward with sweet anticipation to the day "when this corruptible shall have put on incorruption" and I shall no longer be cumbered with this old sinful flesh and the hindrances that so often keep me at a distance from my Lord. In heaven I shall see him as he is, and communion will be unbroken. I often long for that day.

June 4

"Having a desire to depart, and to be with Christ, which is far better" (Philippians 1:23)

To be in heaven is to be with Christ, and to be with Christ is heaven. The apostle Paul knew that this is far better than anything else that could be thought or imagined. Isaiah expressed it so beautifully when he said, "Since the beginning of the world men have not heard, nor perceived by the ear, neither hath the eye seen, O God, beside thee, what he hath prepared for him that waiteth for him" (Isaiah 64:4). The apostle quoted the essence of this verse in 1 Corinthians 2:9 and gave some enlightening additional information with regard to it. It shows that the things God has prepared for his people are far too wonderful to be conceived by the mind of man. The Holy Spirit must reveal unto us any knowledge any of us have of such things, and even then we only know in part. Job, David and Solomon, as spiritually enlightened as they were, yet all three spoke of things that were "too wonderful" for them (Job 42:3; Psalm 139:6; Prov. 30:18).

The text at the head of this little piece often comes to my mind, and the words "far better" frequently ring in my ear. What is the sweetest joy we've ever known in this life? To depart and to be with Christ is *far better*. What is the most pleasant and delightful music we've ever heard on earth? To depart and to be with Christ is *far better*. What is the greatest pleasure we've ever experienced, the most beautiful scene, the most powerful sermon, the most touching song, the most binding relationship? Whatever we might name and no matter how many things we might enumerate, it still remains true that to depart and to be with Christ is *far better*.

Who can rightly conceive of the joy of "being with Jesus" in perfection? And who can begin to fathom the depths of delight associated with dwelling in that blessed state eternally? Who can envision the resplendent glory of that place called heaven, or tell the millionth part of how it will be? Who can imagine a place where it is said we will be satisfied—a place where not only is there no unpleasant thing, but where there is "joy unspeakable and full of glory," and that forever? Truly, it will be *far better*.

June 5

"Who comforteth us in all our tribulation, that we may be able to comfort them which are in any trouble, by the comfort wherewith we ourselves are comforted of God" (2 Corinthians 1:4)

A great deal is contained in this verse, and it gives us much food for thought. God comforts his people, not just in *some* of their tribulations, but in *all* of them. This shows the great care he takes *of* them and the compassion he feels *for* them. He can be touched with the feeling of their infirmities (Heb. 4:15), and he comforts them, not merely for their sakes alone, but also for the sake of others. They *learn* in their tribulations, and what they learn is to be used to the benefit of others.

Their tribulation encompasses "any trouble" they may endure as faithful followers of the Lord, for how else could what they learn prepare them to comfort others in *all* their distresses? The work of God is never more beautifully reflected in the lives of his people than when they pass along to others some of the benefits of their own divine instruction. How many times have we received a word of comfort from other dear souls whose hearts have been made compassionate and empathetic by virtue of their own sufferings? And though that word of comfort came from the mouth of man, dare we say it was not of the Lord? Were they not comforting us with the very same comforts wherewith God had in days past comforted them?

Nothing can come forth from the heart with such sincerity and conviction as that which has been placed there by the hand of God. Nothing is so meaningful, and so filled with substance and utility as that which is the product of divine experience. Let us then not question or complain of our tribulations and testings. Not only are we assured that, "as the sufferings of Christ abound in us, so our consolation also aboundeth by Christ," but we also learn things in those sufferings that we cannot learn any other way. Our most valuable lessons are learned in the furnace of affliction. It is in this way that we are made serviceable to others, and the Lord, in turn, views this as service to himself (Matt. 25:34-40).

June 6

"All scripture is given by inspiration of God" (2 Timothy 3:16)

A companion text to this is 2 Peter 1:21 which reads: "For the prophecy came not in old time by the will of man: but holy men of God spake as they were moved by the Holy Ghost." Consider for a moment the consequences of the Bible not being divinely inspired. If it does not stand upon God's authority, then it does not stand at all. If it does not have divine authorization then man's only guide for belief and behavior is his own perverted whims and ideas, and the opinion of one is as good as another. Also, if God cannot give his word to us, and preserve and fulfill it, then of what use is such a god to us. Therefore, if the Bible is not what it purports to be, then mankind is simply adrift upon a rudderless sea and there is no real purpose to anyone's life. Such an arrangement may appeal ever so much to the carnal mind, but to an enlightened Child of God it is an unthinkable prospect.

To those of us who have long loved the Lord and delighted in his word, there can be no doubt but that it came from him. Our experience bears it out and testifies consistently to its inerrancy. It is the only source of infallible information on any spiritual subject. Let the world have its speculations and conjectures, its theories and guesses, its suppositions and uncertainties; we will take the unalterable "shalls" and "wills" of the Bible. Let men build their imaginary castles in the air; we will build upon the unchanging Rock of revelation. We find sweet rest in the assurance that "the words of the Lord are pure words: as silver tried in a furnace of earth, purified seven times, and He will keep them and preserve them from this generation for ever" (Psalm 12:6-7).

All our lives through we have seen that those who conform their daily conduct to the teachings of God's word lead exemplary, useful and honorable lives, but those who do not, ultimately make shipwreck of their lives. What greater proof should anyone need that the Scriptures of the Old and New Testaments are the inspired word of God? Even if they were not, it still would pay to adhere to their instruction and comply with their righteous precepts. We are saved from many hurtful things when we live according to their holy rule and are thus guided by their ennobling light.

June 7

"Lord, thou hast heard the desire of the humble" (Psalm 10:17)

Not only does the Lord *know* the desire of the humble, but he *hears* it as well. Humble souls through the ages have audibly expressed their desires to him in prayer and to one another in their private communications. Not only has he heard them with the ear of omniscience, but also with the ear of compassion. He knows that their desire is toward him and to the remembrance of him (Isa. 26:8) and that their desire is therefore honorable, and he delights in fulfilling their longing.

And what *is* the desire of the humble? I believe their *chief* desire is the tokens of God's love and approval, and a close communion with Christ. The Psalmist says, "Whom have I in heaven but thee? and there is none upon earth that I desire beside thee" (Psalm 73:25). And with a view to enjoying his gracious approbation they desire to be lead "in paths of righteousness for his name's sake" (Psalm 23:3). "Oh, for a closer walk with God," says William Cowper, over two hundred years ago. And to this end the humble seek to draw nigh unto God, that he may draw nigh unto them (James 4:8). Another poet says, "Say, what is there beneath the skies, Wherever thou hast trod, Can suit thy wishes or thy joy, Like fellowship with God."

I believe it is the desire of the humble souls to always do unto others as it is proper and right for others to do to them. They desire to behave themselves kindly and inoffensively in all their dealings with their fellow man. They desire to keep themselves clear of all unbecoming behavior, even the *appearance* of evil. They want to always conduct themselves in such way that their lives will reflect the fact that they have been with Jesus, and thus bring honor to his name. In a word, they desire that their life may manifest the work of the Lord in their hearts. In all this they realize that they are very imperfect, but it is their desire nonetheless. And ultimately, they "desire a better country, that is, an heavenly" (Heb. 11:16). Can you, dear reader, witness with such desires?

June 8

"Thanks be unto God for his unspeakable gift"
(2 Corinthians 9:15)

Paul began this chapter by saying it was superfluous for him to write to the Corinthian brethren as touching the ministering to the saints. He had just devoted the entire eighth chapter to that subject and had commended them for their attention to that matter. Hence, in concluding his comments on that subject what could he say to provoke them more to continued Christian giving than to direct their minds toward the magnitude of God's kindness toward us, particularly the gift of his darling Son?

There is a difference of opinion among men as to what the "unspeakable gift" is, but it seems to me that nothing measures up to such a description as appropriately and as fittingly as does Christ and the eternal salvation of which he is the Author. If the apostle was going to narrow one gift down and describe it as "God's unspeakable gift" what else could he have chosen that would have exceeded this or even equaled it? The temporal blessings God gives us are wonderful indeed and we thank him for them from the depth of our hearts, but which of those timely favors would we exchange for Christ and what he has done for us? Indeed, *all* our spiritual blessings are *in Christ* (Eph. 1:3) and are a product of his mediatorial work in our behalf.

God's gift of Christ to his people is far too great to be expressed with human tongue or with ink and pen. No words in the limited vocabulary of men are sufficient to describe it. The most gifted orator with the most flowery and ornamental language at his disposal cannot amply describe its magnitude. It may in great measure be *felt* but it cannot be portrayed in words sufficient to adequately convey a satisfactory concept of its greatness. It falls in the same category with those things the apostle saw when he was caught up to the third heaven. It is both unlawful and impossible to be uttered. How ill equipped are we poor finite mortals to rightly value and appreciate the *unspeakable* Gift of God. Glorification will far better prepare us to enter into the depths of these things. "Oh, happy time, long waited for!"

June 9

"I am the Lord, I change not" (Malachi 3:6)

The Lord here credits the preservation of his people to his own immutability, which shows us that if our salvation depended upon the stability of our own fickle flesh none of us would have any hope of heaven. We are creatures of change and are by nature "unstable as water." We are constantly exposed to change, both in ourselves and in our environment. Therefore it is difficult for us to conceive of a Being who never changes. Job said, "He is in one mind, and who can turn him?" (Job 23:13). And James tells us that there is no variableness with Him, "neither shadow of turning" (James 1:17). He always remains the same and his years shall have no end (Psalm 102:27).

God may change his dispensations toward men and vary his dealings with them, but his mind and purpose never change. Being omniscient and knowing the future as well as the past, nothing can ever take him by surprise. No contingency can arise that he has not already made provision for. "Known unto God are all his works from the beginning of the world" (Acts 15:18). Being omnipotent he rules and reigns (Rev. 19:6) and "worketh all things after the counsel of his own will" (Eph.

1:11). Hence there is no possibility of failure with him: "He shall not fail nor be discouraged" (Isaiah 42:4). If he were capable of failure and discouragement he would be no different from us. He would be capable of changing from one state of mind to another and there would be no constancy nor stability in him. And, in a word, he would not be God.

We have great cause to be thankful for God's divine attributes, for without any *one* of them our salvation could not have been secured. But due to his unchanging nature and his unflawed holiness and power, every member of his beloved family will all be with him in heaven one sweet day. I await that happy hour with sweet anticipation. But until then, "Change and decay in all around I see; O Thou who changest not, abide with me!"

June 10

"A day in thy courts is better than a thousand" (Psalm 84:10)

A very brief period of real communion with the Lord is far better than a lengthy season in any other employ. The text does not state any particular thing that a day in his courts is better than, for it is not necessary. A day in his courts is better than a thousand anywhere else. There are no exceptions, therefore no exceptions are mentioned or implied. If years were spent in naming a thousand of this and a thousand of that, nothing could be named that would equal a day, or even a moment, in the courts of the Lord.

I have found that one moment of feeling the presence of the Lord in my soul makes up for all the trials, conflicts and adversities of a lifetime. If I can truly say, "It is well with my soul," then all else is well around me, no matter how great the tumult. A lady was once observed shouting praises to God in the midst of a tremendous earthquake. Someone inquired as to the reason for her exuberance at such a frightful time. She replied, "I am just thankful that I have a God who can shake the earth!" No doubt she was at that moment experiencing a wonderful sense of his goodness and glory, and this is a good illustration of the fact that outward circumstances, no matter how dire they may appear, are no impediment to the Holy Spirit's comforting visits with his children.

A thousand days of the best pleasure the world has to offer pale in comparison to one day of sweet communion with the Lord, and those are to be pitied who have never known such delight. O, what must heaven be, when we consider that communion with our Lord in that happy place will never be broken or interrupted! Someone has said, "Heaven is incessant joy with eternal duration." That is a good description, but a better one is, "Heaven is being with Jesus forever in perfection!"

June 11

"If ye be reproached for the name of Christ, happy are ye; for the spirit of glory and of God resteth upon you" (1 Peter 4:14)

We may be sure that if our walk before men is such that it pleases the Lord there are those who will disapprove of us and seek to discredit us. This is called in Hebrews 11:26 "the reproach of Christ" and is shown to have been experienced long ago by those who turned their backs upon the world and its temporary pleasures. Paul tells us that "all that will live godly in Christ Jesus shall suffer persecution" (2 Tim. 3:12). "The carnal mind is enmity against God," and it resents those who live by a higher standard. After a person is illuminated by the Spirit of God he should not be surprised if he "endures a great fight of afflictions" (Heb. 10:32), for he then becomes a special target of the forces of evil. His divine illumination results in his becoming a companion of those who are "made a gazingstock both by reproaches and afflictions" (v. 33). We cannot be made partakers of the divine nature without also partaking of the world's hatred.

Christ said, "Blessed are ye, when men shall hate you, and when they shall separate you from their company, and shall reproach you, and cast out your name as evil, for the Son of man's sake" (Luke 6:22). Moses counted this reproach "greater riches than the treasures in Egypt," and so should we. If we "suffer for well doing" we should count ourselves greatly blest. We are in good company if for the sake of Christ men revile us and persecute us and say all manner of evil against us falsely. We should rejoice and be exceeding glad on two counts: *first*, because our reward in heaven is great, and *second*, because we are in good company—the prophets of old were likewise persecuted (Matt. 5:11-12). Being the object of the world's reproach by virtue of our Christ-likeness is one of the greatest honors we may receive.

May the Lord help us to live in such way that we will be clearly distinguished from the ungodly. And then when reproaches come for this cause, may we, like the apostles, rejoice that we are counted worthy to suffer shame for His name (Acts 5:41). The apostle John reminds us of the fact that this reproach resulted in Cain killing his brother. Then he exhorts us thusly: "Marvel not, my brethren, if the world hate you" (1 John 3:12-13). It hated Christ before it hated us, and why should we be exempt from the same hatred (John 15:18)?

June 12

"Keep yourselves in the love of God" (Jude 21)

This verse is not exhorting us to get ourselves *in* the love of God, for we do not have that ability. If we could get ourselves *in* his love we could also remove ourselves *from* it, and it would not be an *everlasting* love (Jer. 31:3). We can, however, conduct ourselves in such way as to enjoy the *manifestations* of his love and favor. By building ourselves up on our most holy faith and praying in the Holy Ghost, as we are told to do in the previous verse, we may *experientially* keep ourselves in God's love. In this sense we may *continue* in the love of Christ (John 15:9).

As for the intrinsic love of God, which he has had for his people from all eternity, there is no *power* and no *thing* that can separate them from it (Romans 8:35-39). They have an incorruptible, undefiled and unfading inheritance reserved in heaven for them and they are kept by the power of God through faith unto salvation ready to be revealed in the last time (1 Peter 1:4-5). The good work that is begun in them by the Holy Spirit is never discontinued (Philippians 1:6). However, they may so behave as to temporarily lose a *felt sense* of God's love. They cannot lose the love itself, but they may, and often do, lose the *manifestation* of it to their souls.

It is very much in the child of God's interest to live as close to the Lord as they can. This closeness is greatly facilitated by their taking much care to maintain good works, attending divine services, frequently reading, studying, and meditating upon, God's word, and being often at the throne of grace. When they are disobedient it results in their being deprived of blessings they otherwise would have enjoyed. But when they are obedient it results in the maintenance of a good conscience toward God and men, and God condescends to crown their efforts with tokens of his favor. Thus it can be said of them that they are keeping themselves in the love of God.

June 13

"The words of the Lord are pure words" (Psalm 12:6)

I have never found anything in the Bible that would lead anyone down a wrong path. If a person will conform his or her life, actions and thoughts to the words that the Lord has left on record for his people it will never serve them in a destructive or detrimental way. It will always tend to their good, betterment and upbuilding. "The word of the Lord is right" (Psalm 33:4), and if we continue in that word then we are his disciples indeed; and we shall know the truth, and the truth will make us free (John 8:31-32). The more of the truth we learn, the more we are set free from error.

There is an unfathomable gulf between the thoughts and ways of men in nature and the thoughts and ways of God (Isaiah 55:8-9). Therefore the carnal mind is always enmity against God. When men rely upon their own judgment and understanding they pursue a path that always leads to ultimate destruction, no matter how much temporal prosperity they may enjoy along the way. But when they acknowledge the Lord in all their ways he will direct their paths (Prov. 3:5-6). If we have any real concept of what is in our best interest we will desire above all else that the Lord always lead us in paths of righteousness for his name's sake. Any time we are out of those paths it will result in pain to us in some way, for "God shall judge the righteous and the wicked."

The fact that a correct interpretation of God's word never leads anyone astray, and the fact that obedience to it leads to peace of conscience and fullness of life, is one of the greatest proofs of its divine origin and authority. "Where there is no vision, the people perish: but he that keepeth the law, happy is he" (Prov. 29:18). The most contented and happy people on the earth are those who esteem the words of the Lord's mouth more than their necessary food (Job 23:12). And conversely, those who reject it and refuse to be guided by it make shipwreck of their lives and bring themselves into misery and destruction. What more convincing argument could be made in its favor?

June 14

"Great is thy faithfulness" (Lamentations 3:23)

When we contrast our own faithfulness with God's, it gives us a much better concept of how great *his* faithfulness is. He has never broken a promise, never failed to do what he said he would do, and has never let us down in any way or particular. How many of us can say the same with regard to our behavior toward him? How many times have we been unfaithful to him and failed to abide by our good resolutions with regard to keeping his precepts and serving him with zeal and dedication? How many times has our zeal towards him flagged and our devotions wavered? When we think upon these things we must hang our heads in sorrow and acknowledge that our loyalty to him has fallen far short of what it ought to have been. What if his faithfulness to *us* had been no greater than ours to *him*?

He has always been faithful to give us our daily bread and to give us grace sufficient for our trials. He has never left us nor forsaken us. His mercies have been "new every morning" and his compassions toward us have never failed. When we have been guilty of unbelief, he has remained faithful (2 Tim. 2:13), for since we are his body, if he were to cast us off he would be denying himself. He would be denying himself that which he has said is "his portion" and "the lot of his inheritance" (Deut. 32:9). He would be denying himself that which Christ declared was the "joy that was set before him" (Heb. 12:2), which partly consists of having all his glorified family with him in heaven at last. Great indeed is his faithfulness!

"Know therefore that the Lord thy God, he is God, the faithful God, which keepeth covenant and mercy with them that love him and keep his commandments to a thousand generations" (Deut. 7:9). "God is faithful, by whom ye were called unto the fellowship of his Son Jesus Christ our Lord" (1 Cor. 1:9). "God is faithful, who will not suffer you to be tempted above that ye are able; but will with the temptation also make a way to escape, that ye may be able to bear it" (1 Cor. 10:13). Let us strive to be more faithful to him.

June 15

"My days are swifter than a post" (Job 9:25)

As our head turns white and our years accumulate we learn by experience what Job expresses here. There was a period in my life, a period that seems very brief now, when I didn't give much thought to time, but now I am frequently reminded of the fact that time is running out for me in this present world. The greater part of my earthly journey is over and at best I do not have many days left. Whatever I expect to do before I leave this world must soon be done, or else I will never do it. The days I have left will be much fewer than the days I have already lived. Every time I look at the clock, the second-hand reminds me that time is hastening on. With every breath the future is becoming the past, and whereas the days of our youth appeared to go by so slowly, our days now have grown wings and seem to fly unimpeded by friend or foe.

In Genesis 47:9, a one-hundred-thirty-year-old Jacob speaks of the days of the years of his pilgrimage as "few and evil." And I am sure that if we should live that long it would still seem that our days had been few, and by then we would probably put the same negative slant upon them that Jacob did. As we grow older, new ailments seem to develop on a regular basis, and advancing years certainly do not insulate us from life's burdens and troubles, but rather seem to expose us to more of them.

The apostle James very aptly compares our life to "a vapor that appeareth for a little time, and then vanisheth away." David said, "Behold, thou hast made my days as an handbreadth; and mine age is as nothing before thee" (Psalm 39:5). And in his thanksgiving in 1st Chronicles he compares our days to a shadow (1 Chr. 29:15). Job said his days were swifter than a weaver's shuttle (Job 7:6). All such comparisons are of course used to show the brevity of life, and they should encourage us to use time wisely. Let us be up and about the things that the Lord would have us do. Time is running out on us quickly.

June 16

"God was manifest in the flesh" (1 Timothy 3:16)

The apostle John, in the first chapter of his gospel speaks of the Lord Jesus as "the Word" and tells us, in effect, that he not only already *existed* at the beginning of the creation of the world, but that, as God, all things were made by him. And in the fourteenth verse he tells us that "the Word was made flesh, and dwelt among us." This is truly the crowning facet of the great mystery of godliness, a mystery far too great for our present comprehension. Perhaps it will be fully divulged to us in the next life, but for now we simply embrace the truth of it by faith and glory in the fact that it is so.

It is with holy awe that we contemplate the fact that he was "justified in the Spirit" or proven to be sinless and pure in his Spirit; never doing or saying anything contrary to the law of God. We marvel as we consider His interaction with the angelic beings; not only *seen* by them but also *served* and *worshipped* by them. What a wonder it is that he *was,* and *is,* preached unto the Gentiles and that he should be believed on at all in an ungodly world such as ours! And how we rejoice that the Father expressed his complete satisfaction and approval of all he had done by receiving him up into glory when he had finished his redemptive work!

It was prophesied over seven hundred years before his birth that he would be conceived of a virgin and that his name would be called Immanuel or Emmanuel (Isa. 7:14). Then Matthew tells us the interpretation of the name, which is, "God with us" (Matt. 1:23). Can we poor, unworthy sinners, think of anything more amazing and mysterious than "God with us"? Indeed, indeed, "What is man that thou art mindful of him? and the son of man, that thou visitest him" (Psalm 8:4; Heb. 2:6)? Truly it is amazing that he would "become flesh" and "dwell among us" and even more so that he would suffer in the place of his people and provide all things for them as their Mediator and Surety that they could not do for themselves. Is it any wonder that one of his names is "Wonderful" (Isaiah 9:6)?

June 17

"Surely the wrath of man shall praise thee: the remainder of wrath shalt thou restrain" (Psalm 76:10)

That which man intends as dishonor to God or harm to their fellowmen, may be, and often is, so ordered and overruled by him as to result in his praise. It most certainly was never any part of Pharaoh's plan to do anything for the purpose of glorifying God, for he acknowledged that he did not know God (Ex. 5:2). Yet his obstinate rebellion against God and his hatred of God's people were so ordered and overruled that it issued in God's power being greatly displayed and his name being declared throughout all the earth (Ex. 9:16; Rom. 9:17). Thus Pharaoh's wrath was made to praise God while at the same time that wrath was being restrained by Divine power. Pharaoh could go no further and do no more than God suffered him to do. The same is true with all other men and demons.

Now, because the apostle Paul preached and taught this very thing, he was accused of saying, "Let us do evil that good may come" (Rom. 3:8). But such a notion was very abhorrent to him and he said the damnation of those who thus accused him was just. The fact that God overruled the wrath of Pharaoh did not in any sense excuse his wrath. Neither were the evil intentions of Joseph's brethren in the least mitigated by the fact that God "meant it unto good" (Gen. 50:20). In a word, evil is no less evil just because God sees fit to bring good out of it. Great good (unspeakable good) has come to God's people as a result of the life and death of Christ, but look what awful calamities have befallen that nation that cried out for his crucifixion and who arrogantly proclaimed, "His blood be on us, and on our children" (Matt. 27:25). How horribly has that self-proclaimed judgment been executed ever since it was uttered!

Bless God that he is in control of all things and "worketh all things after the counsel of his own will" (Eph. 1:11). How thankful we should be that even the devils are subject unto him (Luke 10:17) and that his purpose cannot be frustrated or defeated in any way, shape, form or fashion. "The Lord God omnipotent reigneth" (Rev. 19:6). That says it all.

June 18

"The Lord trieth the righteous" (Psalm 11:5)

The Lord does not try his people in order to learn how they will react, for since he *knows* all things he therefore cannot *learn* anything. But rather, he tries them so that *they* may realize the value, usefulness and stability of the graces he has given them. When they are tested, and they come through triumphantly, it fortifies them for further, and more severe, tests. It has been beautifully pointed out that David's conflicts began with a bear and a lion before they progressed to Goliath, king Saul, and then the Philistines. The Lord told Israel that as their days, so would their strength be (Deut. 33:25), and we also shall find it so. He will not put more upon us than we are able to bear. Paul told the Corinthian brethren, "There hath no temptation [or *trial*] taken you but such as is common to man: but God is faithful, who will not suffer you to be tempted above that ye are able; but will with the temptation also make a way to escape, that ye may be able to bear it" (1 Cor. 10:13). I have lived to see this wonderfully verified in my own life over many years of experience, as have a great many others.

As with David, we too shall find that God spaces out our trials so that they do not all come upon us at once. And he adapts our trials to our own individual measure of faith and strength. That which would be a relatively insignificant trial to someone with *great* faith, might be a very severe trial to another with *weak* faith, and the Lord knows just how to mete out our trials accordingly. We should never complain of our present trials, for they may well be preparing us to deal with greater trials ahead.

Another benefit of trials is that they reveal who is a true possessor of faith and who is not. Those whose profession cannot bear the test of trials and afflictions are exposed for the hypocrites they really are, and the true possessors of the graces of the Spirit shine forth brightly in contrast. Let us never rebel against our afflictions and trials, for they serve numerous ends that are for our good and God's glory. They are one of God's great channels of blessing to his people.

June 19

"We shall not all sleep, but we shall all be changed"
(1 Corinthians 15:51)

The apostle acknowledges this to be a mystery, even to him, though he was blest with an abundance of revelation (2 Cor. 12:7). But though it is a mystery, yet it is a glorious truth. Although there will be some of God's people who are "alive and remain" when the Lord returns, and consequently will not "sleep" in the sense of undergoing corporal death as we know it, yet they will be changed (1 Thes. 4:17). They will undergo a change that will be equivalent to death and they will then be "raised in incorruption" (1 Cor. 15:42) and placed in an *incorruptible* state (v. 52). And Paul says this will take place "in a moment, in the twinkling of an eye," and "so shall we ever be with the Lord." No wonder he exhorts God's people to "comfort one another with these words." What a glorious prospect to those who *love the Lord's appearing* (2 Tim. 3:8).

Even Job, who lived thousands of years ago, was expecting to live again after he died, and he tells us that he was awaiting the day when his *change* would come (Job 14:14), at which time he would see God *in his flesh* and not someone else's (Job 19:25-27). This is the hope of every Christian and is a great bulwark to their souls. Christ will change their vile body, "that it may be fashioned like unto his glorious body" (Philippians 3:21). David said, "As for me, I will behold thy face in righteousness: I shall be satisfied, when I awake, with thy likeness

(Psalm 17:15). And John said, "We know that, when he shall appear, we shall be like him" (1 John 3:2). This is what God's people were predestinated unto (Rom. 8:29).

Words cannot express the blessedness of that day when "the righteous shall shine forth as the sun in the kingdom of their Father" (Matt. 13:13) with a glorified body, and basking in spiritual conformity to Christ. May the Lord help us to serve patiently and faithfully till our change comes.

June 20

"We remember that that deceiver said while he was alive, After three days I will rise again" (Matthew 27:63)

By calling Christ "that deceiver" the Chief Priests and Pharisees again showed how incredibly blind and hard-hearted they were. After all the miraculous works he had done, and after all the public manifestations of his heavenly Father's love *for* him, and approval *of* him, they still maintained that he was a vile person who deserved the most horrible of deaths. Oh, how thankful we should be that we do not have the same opinion of our blessed Savior! Unto those of us who believe, he is precious (1 Peter 2:7). Is not the depth of man's depravity inexpressible, when he can actually hate and despise our adorable Lord? And is not his love and mercy toward his people amazing, that they have been brought to love his great name and count him dearer than life itself?

The same One who is our life, the Chief Priests and Pharisees looked upon as their greatest nightmare. They sought, with every means at their disposal, to prevent His resurrection. They remembered that he had said he would rise again after three days, and they viewed such an eventuality as disastrous. We reflect upon the fact that he *did* arise and view it as a confirmation of our justification. To them the empty tomb was the worst possible catastrophe, but to us it is a most wonderful reality. It is the basis for our hope, for if Christ did not rise from the grave then our faith is vain and we are yet in our sins (1 Cor. 15:17).

The Chief Priests and Pharisees had no problem with propagating the most obvious lie in order to try to cover the fact that they had crucified the very Lord of Glory. And neither did they have any qualms about paying a large sum of money to try to perpetuate that lie. But thanks be unto God it was all to no avail. Their lie was so ridiculously implausible that it stood no chance of any widespread survival. All their efforts to cover up the resurrection only served to make it the more obvious and to make its proof all the more undeniable. In the net which they hid, their own feet were taken (Psalm 9:15). Happy is that people whose God is the Lord and who rejoice in the fact that he arose from the tomb on the third day and is now seated at the right hand of the Father, making intercession for the saints according to the will of God!

June 21

"Even so Father: for so it seemed good in thy sight" (Mt. 11:26)

Christ gave the above as the reason why God the Father hides the mysteries of the kingdom of heaven from some and reveals them to others. It is also the answer to why God does anything that he does. When the disciples of Christ asked him why he spoke to the multitudes in parables, he answered, "Because it is given unto you to know the mysteries of the kingdom of heaven, but to them it is not given" (Matt. 13:10-11). And do we ask why he did this? The answer is: *because it seemed good in his sight.* This is all we need to know as to *why* God does what he does. He is possessed of supreme and infinite dominion and authority both in heaven and in earth, and therefore "he hath done whatsoever he hath pleased" (Psalm 115:3). He does his will both in heaven and in the earth and "none can stay his hand, or say unto him, What doest thou" (Dan. 4:35).

Do we ask why Christ only lay down his life "for the sheep," or "the church" and not others (John 10:15; Eph. 5:25)? The answer is: *because it seemed good in his sight.* Do we ask why he calls some to special places of service and not others? The answer is: *because it seemed good in his sight.* Do we ask why he created Adam in such a state that he was capable of falling? The answer is: *because it seemed good in his sight.* Do we ask why he leaves so many of the earth's population in heathen darkness? The answer is the same, and on and on we might go posing such questions, always with the same outcome. There are many things the Lord has not chosen to tell us. And why is this? Again, the same answer applies.

There are many terrible things that may come into our lives, and we may sometimes be tempted to ask, why is it thus? We know the Lord could easily *prevent* such things, so why does he suffer them to happen? Often times it may very well be that the only answer we have in our troubles is that *it seemed good in his sight* not to prevent them. But of one thing we can always be certain, and that is that whatever God does is best and it is right, for he can do no wrong. Let us rest in that fact, and never question him or quarrel with him. What good would it do us poor dust-worms to oppose him anyway?

June 22

"Oh how great is thy goodness, which thou has laid up for them that fear thee" (Psalm 31:19)

A llow me to propose a question, especially to those of you who have long sought to travel the Christian road. If you had been told when you first started out on this journey what great blessings you would experience along the way, could you have believed your good fortune? Could you have begun to conceive of such wonders of mercy as have come your way? I do not think so. In the words of Job, David and Agur, you would have found these things to be "too wonderful" for you (Job 42:3; Ps. 139:6; Prov. 30:18). You could not have thought of such things, or even known that they existed. But all the while they were "laid up" for you. They were in the future, but you knew it not.

This is confirmed by Isaiah 64:4 and 1 Corinthians 2:9: "Eye hath not seen, nor ear heard, neither have entered into the heart of man, the things which God hath prepared for them that love him." Not only could we not conceive of the *temporal* blessings that were ahead for us, and others that may yet come our way, but neither can we *now* conceive of the *heavenly* blessings that still await us. I doubt not but that we shall find them to be far greater and more glorious than we ever dreamed or imagined.

As long as we live there will yet be manifestations of the Lord's goodness to us. These "storehouse" blessings, as they might be called, will continue to be meted out to us in his own time and way. David expressed as much when he said, "Surely goodness and mercy shall follow me all the days of my life." And then, topping all this off, he follows with the ultimate blessing, "and I will dwell in the house of the Lord for ever" (Psalm 23:6). Truly, the goodness of the Lord is great beyond expression.

June 23

"Wherefore doth the way of the wicked prosper" (Jeremiah 12:1)

There was a time in the life of David when the prosperity of wicked people distressed him. During a time when he was personally suffering great abuse and hardship, he saw others who were of very low character enjoying great ease and prosperity and it troubled him. But later on, after he was blest to see and realize more fully the dreadful end that such people will come to, he confessed his former ignorance with regard to this matter (Psalm 73).

The same kind of concerns as David had have likewise troubled many others down through the years. In spite of their love for the Lord and their efforts to conform their lives to his word they have found themselves surrounded with continual troubles, while they have seen wicked men faring sumptuously and enduring little apparent hardship or distress. Only God can reconcile his people to such matters and enable them to see that even though the wicked do not experience the kind of troubles they do, yet they are in a greatly superior position to those vile persons.

The ungodly "have their portion in this life" (Psalm 17:14) and therefore the only good they will ever know is here in this present world. Ultimately they will be "brought into desolation" and "consumed with terrors," and their miseries will never end. There is nothing about the present ease, or the final end, of such characters that anyone should be envious of. "Say ye to the righteous, that it shall be well with him," but, "woe unto the wicked! It shall be ill with him" (Isaiah 3:10-11).

As for the afflictions of the righteous, and they are *many* (Psalm 34:19), the Lord has wise and good reasons for them which have to do with the spiritual growth and welfare of his people. Not only that but the glory of God is seen in each instance of his deliverance of them from those afflictions. David said, "Before I was afflicted, I went astray" (Psalm 119:67), and in the 71st verse he said, "It is good for me that I have been afflicted; that I might learn thy statutes."

One of the song writers said, "Afflictions, though they seem severe, In mercy oft are sent; They stopped the prodigal's career, And caused him to repent." The Lord's ways are often mysterious to us, but we may be certain that they are always holy, wise and good.

June 24

"Be not conformed to this world" (Romans 12:2)

The world spoken of here is the world of the unenlightened and unbelieving, the world of the wicked and rebellious. God's people are commanded to come out from among them and be separate (2 Cor. 6:17). There is nothing about the world's perverted attitudes and values that will do the children of God any good at all. No matter how appealing those ways may appear outwardly, they are ultimately the ways of death (Proverbs 14:12). The saints should be of an entirely different mind and heart. Any time they are yoked together with unbelievers they are in an *unequal* relationship (2 Cor. 6:14). This is true because an unbeliever has no scruples about using underhanded and unethical means and methods, while the Christian's conscience will not allow him to do so.

From the viewpoint of the world, what the Christian views as evil, they view as good. What the Christian views as darkness, they view as light. What the Christian views as bitter, they view as sweet (Isaiah 5:20). Their darkened mind has a twisted and perverted view of things. They have things backward and misdirected. They are like the wild Gadarene, before the Lord put him in his "right mind." They are not "right" in their thinking, and therefore they are not "right" in their conduct.

God's people have also sometimes shown a strong propensity for becoming enamored with the world in their *religious* teachings and practices. This too is very dangerous and destructive. The Lord has given his people all the necessary directives and instructions they need so far as the conduct and government of his church is concerned. These things are all calculated to keep his church markedly distinct from popular religion. The more God's people conform to the world in doctrine and practice the more that distinction is blurred and the more they lose their apostolic identity. Therefore when the Lord tells them not to be conformed to this world, he gives them one of the most valuable lessons in the Bible.

June 25

"My grace is sufficient for thee" (2 Corinthians 12:9)

We, like the apostle Paul, may sometimes pray for the removal of painful things, but we need not be surprised if the Lord chooses not to give us our request. He may very well choose rather to give us sufficient grace to deal with whatever the trouble or perplexity may be. He always knows best, and it may be that chronic distresses or infirmities in our lives serve a purpose that we are presently not aware of, or which we do not fully understand. One reason the Lord gave Paul for not removing his thorn in the flesh was that God's strength is made perfect in our weakness. That is, the strength he supplies his people is manifested and magnified in their weakness and need. If they had no need, where would be the stage for the display of His strength? He is glorified in sustaining and helping his people. If they had no weaknesses and infirmities, they would have no need of his grace and would never experience it.

Beyond what is taught us in 2 Corinthians 12:7, we have no specific knowledge of what Paul's "thorn in the flesh" was. It is useless to speculate, but we are told that it was a "messenger of Satan to buffet" (or harass or distress) him. However, from God's standpoint it was used to keep Paul from becoming "exalted above measure" because of the abundance of the revelations that had been given unto him. Keeping him humble was vital to his success as a gospel minister. He could never serve the Lord in an acceptable or profitable manner if he was not meek and lowly in heart. All God's servants must be kept feelingly aware of their own insufficiency in order to go leaning upon him. They must be made keenly conscious of the fact that their sufficiency is of God (2 Cor. 3:5), otherwise they will be leaning upon the arm of flesh.

Though the Lord did not see fit to remove Paul's thorn, yet he assured him of grace sufficient to bear it and benefit from it. Consequently we do not find Paul ever mentioning it again. If keeping the thorn meant having the power of Christ resting upon him, then he would rather *glory in his infirmities* and "take pleasure" in them. Let us likewise glory in those infirmities that God does not see fit to rid us of, for we may be assured that there is a worthwhile purpose for them, and that he will give sufficient grace for whatever sufferings are required of us.

June 26

"There is no peace, saith my God, to the wicked" (Isaiah 57:21)

For those of us who have a hope in Christ I suppose it is impossible to comprehend how it would be to *never* have any peace of mind or conscience, but that is exactly the continual state of the wicked. And what is true of the wicked is necessarily true of the Devil and all his agents: never, never any real peace. They are not of a peaceful disposition, and therefore they do not love peace nor seek it. In fact they *hate* peace (Psalm 120:6). The Psalmist says in that place, "I am for peace: but when I speak, they are for war." What a miserable life it must be where there is no true peace! Where there is peace there is calmness, harmony, rest and quiet, but where there is no peace there is turmoil, strife, disunity, unrest and clamor.

To the child of God there is great peace just in knowing that God exists and that he is a God of mercy. But there is the greater peace when there is some assurance of a personal relationship with him; when we can say, "My beloved is mine, and I am his" (Song of Solomon 2:16 & 6:3). The wicked know nothing of this, and they have the greatest of disdain and hatred for those who do. In fact, one of the greatest contributors to their lack of peace is the enormous hatred and resentment they harbor toward the righteous, both toward God and his people. They can never enjoy peace of conscience, for all their works are evil. "The way of peace they know not...they have made them crooked paths: whosoever goeth therein shall not know peace" (Isaiah 59:8). "The way of peace they have not known" (Romans 3:17).

The apostle Paul tells us that to be carnally minded is death; but to be spiritually minded is life and peace (Romans 8:6). There is a vast difference. In Galatians 5:19 he tells us that the works of the flesh are, adultery, fornication, uncleanness, lasciviousness, idolatry, witchcraft, hatred, variance, emulations, wrath, strife, seditions, heresies, envyings, murders, drunkenness, revelings, and such like things. There can be no peace in following after these things.

But the fruit of the Spirit is love, joy, peace, longsuffering, gentleness, goodness, faith, meekness and temperance. What an amazing contrast! One of the things Peter tells us we must do if we would love life and see good days is to "seek peace and ensue (pursue) it" (1 Peter 3:10-11). May the Lord so help us.

June 27

"If thine enemy be hungry, give him bread to eat"
(Proverbs 25:21)

Biblical injunctions are dramatically opposed to the natural instincts and inclinations of men, but if it were not so, what proof would we have that the Scriptures were divinely inspired? Any humanly devised document claiming to deal with the proper conduct of men toward one another and toward God would always favor man's natural propensities. But the Bible sets a much higher standard. It requires that of us which we will not and cannot do by nature alone. In order for any of our thoughts or activities to be acceptable in the sight of God they must be performed out of love to him and with no other design than his glory. This the natural man will not and cannot do (Rom. 8:7; 1 Cor. 2:14). "Unto the pure all things are pure: but unto them that are defiled and unbelieving is nothing pure; but even their mind and conscience is defiled" (Titus 1:15). Only quickened souls, acting in harmony with the principles of truth and righteousness implanted within their hearts, can please God. Hence it is that those who are "in the flesh" and those who are "without faith" *cannot* please God (Rom. 8:8; Heb. 11:6).

If the Scriptures instructed us agreeably to our corrupt nature, it would tell us that if our enemy is hungry give him *nothing* to eat. It would instruct us not to do *anything* for him except something hurtful and unkind. But Christian principles planted within the heart by the Holy Spirit tell us to *love* our enemies. Christ spoke to his followers of what they had *heard* from men as opposed to what *he* taught them. There was a vast difference. Men taught them to love their neighbors and to *hate* their enemies, but Christ taught them to love their enemies in the sense of doing good to them and praying for them (Matt. 5:43-44). In this way his disciples would "become the sons of God" in a manifest sense (John 1:12).

True Christianity involves much more than merely professing a belief in Christ. It is a life of faith in exercise. It is a life that distinguishes itself from the normal course of the flesh, and shows a much higher form of character and conduct. It requires much grace and a close communion with Christ, and for this constant prayer is essential. May the Lord help us to humbly follow his high and holy principles in all we say and do.

June 28

"Everyone that loveth him that begat loveth him also that is begotten of him" (1 John 5:1)

The text is saying that if we love God, we will also love those to whom he has given divine life. In other words, if we love God we will also love his regenerated people. If we have been made poor in spirit, we will love those who have likewise been made poor. If our heart has been tendered and softened, we will love those whose heart has likewise been mollified. We can detect those things in others that we ourselves have experienced, and it causes us to feel a special kinship with them. To our spiritual mind the fruits of the Spirit, namely, joy, peace, long-suffering, gentleness, goodness, faith, meekness, kindness and temperance, are very beautiful and desirable things and we seek out the company of those who possess such qualities. We desire to walk with them and to converse with them and to enjoy their fellowship.

One of the qualifications of a bishop, minister, or steward of God, is that he must be "a lover of good men" (Titus 1:8). And his love for them will arise from the fact that he sees in them the attributes that he most admires and which he desires to promote. The one thing in a person that will most quickly and effectively make him or her offensive to godly men and women is a spirit of haughtiness and high-mindedness. These qualities are diametrically opposed to the meek and quiet spirit that characterizes the humble followers of Christ. Those who display a spirit of arrogance and self-esteem will repulse tenderhearted, humble, and loving people.

One of the sweetest evidences that we have been begotten of God (born of God) is the fact that we love those who are begotten of him. The apostle John said, "We know that we have passed from death unto life, because we love the brethren." And how do we know this to be a fact? Because "he that loveth not his brother abideth in death" (1 John 3:14). Dear one, do you love the brethren? If so the evidence is clear that you have been born of God.

June 29

"I have learned, in whatsoever state I am, therewith to be content" (Philippians 4:11)

Every moment of our lives we are in some state and condition. Our circumstances are always changing, though much of the time it may be imperceptible to us. Our status is never constant. When someone asks us how old we are, we never attempt to tell them down to the second, because it would be impossible. Before we had time to get the words out of our mouth we would already be older than we had told them we were. The second hand on our watches and clocks is swiftly moving, but nevertheless we are always in some kind of state. A few moments from now, or possibly an instant from now our outward circumstances and our inner emotions may be altogether different from what they presently are. At any instant we might have an attack of illness, or we might receive news that would cast us into an altogether different state. Or, something might happen to immediately change us from a merely casual state into one of great happiness or joy.

I believe that in whatsoever state the apostle Paul was in, no matter how unpleasant it was outwardly, he had learned to be content that the Lord would take care of the situation in one way or another. He had learned to trust his all into the hands of the Lord with full confidence in his wisdom, his faithfulness, and his goodness. He knew that God would be true to His promises in all circumstances of life. He knew by experience that the Lord had never failed him nor forsaken him. He knew what it was to be "troubled on every side, yet not distressed...perplexed, but not in despair; persecuted, but not forsaken; cast down, but not destroyed" (2 Cor. 4:8-9).

Dear brother or sister, you are in some state as you read this. How is it with you at this moment? Are you content with your present lot in the sense that you are totally reconciled to the will of the Lord? Have you learned to fully trust your present situation into the hands of a merciful God? If you are presently surrounded with unpleasant circumstances are you content to wait on the Lord for deliverance? If not, may he bless you to find comfort in the fact that there is yet mercy reserved for you, and it will come in His own good time.

June 30

"These all died in faith" (Hebrews 11:13)

The apostle mentions such notable saints as Abel, Enoch, Noah, Abraham and Sarah, and points out that they all died in faith. Enoch did not die in the normal sense of the word, for he was translated without seeing death, but he necessarily underwent a change that was equivalent to death. Although he was a very righteous man, he still had a "vile body" that had to be *changed* that it might be fashioned like unto the glorious body of Christ (Phil. 3:21). Otherwise he could not have entered into that sin-free and magnificently glorious place called heaven. The dear saints mentioned above, as well as all others who have lived since their day, have all "died in faith." And the reason this is true is because the faith that God implants within the hearts of his people in regeneration will not cease until it gives way to full fruition in the glory world.

It has always been a comfort to me to observe the lives of the dear old saints and to see them standing firm in the faith unto the end, no matter how severe the trials and discouragements they may have met with in life. It strengthens me to see those dear souls who have lived long and godly lives come down to the end of the way still leaning on the everlasting arms of Jesus and fully trusting in his mercy. They die *in faith*, resting in a sweet assurance that where they are going is "far better" than anything they have ever known down here. And in so doing each of them proved beyond a doubt that there is such a thing as a faith that will not fail.

I have always believed in God, and very early in life I was blest with a sweet hope in Christ. I am now on the downhill side of life, but my faith is still strong. What a blessing that is! I have met with many discouragements along the way, and many afflictions have dotted my path. I have at times been persecuted, slandered, and otherwise ill used, but I can happily say with the beloved apostle Paul that "none of these things move me" (Acts 20:24). It cannot be long until I leave this world and I too have the sweet assurance that I will *die in faith*. The Lord is my all in all, and I would not think of casting away my confidence in him even if I could.

July 1

"Whatsoever ye do in word or deed, do all in the name of the Lord Jesus" (Colossians 3:17)

How many times do we consider this admonition before we act or speak? This is one of the many things I personally need to give more thought and attention to. When we combine this verse with the twenty-third verse it sets before us a very high standard by which to govern both our conduct and our conversation. The apostle says, "Whatsoever ye do, do it heartily, as to the Lord, and not unto men." Not only should all our actions and words be done in the name of the Lord Jesus, but they should be performed, and spoken, with a view to his glory and honor (1 Cor. 10:31). If we all did this, what a different world ours would be.

No one can even come close to complying with these directives unless they live close to the Lord and keep a careful guard upon their lives and lips. It is not something that we should expect to do perfectly, but it is a goal to aim at and strive for. We all have tongues that are extremely difficult to bridle, but James tells us that if we do not bridle them our religion is vain (James 1:26). This is a very sobering thought.

Years ago someone did an analysis of the lifetime of an average person. It appeared in *Ladies Home Journal* probably twenty-five years ago or longer. According to that analysis the average person spends six years eating; eleven years working; five and a half years washing and dressing; three years each for reading and education, eight years in amusement; three years conversing and *only six months in worshiping God*. I don't know how accurate those figures might be, but I suspect most people spend far too little time worshiping and serving the Lord. But if we would observe Colossians 3:17, 23, we would be acknowledging him and honoring him in all we said and did throughout every day. Let us always be striving to do better in these things.

∽∼

July 2

"And my speech and my preaching was not with enticing words of man's wisdom" (1 Corinthians 2:4)

With Paul's knowledge of words I suspect he could have impressed the most learned of men with his use of language if he had chosen to do so and the Lord had blest him, but his desire was not to put himself on display but rather the God of glory and his almighty power. Paul knew that it is only those words that are spoken from the heart "in demonstration of the Spirit and of power," that glorify God and point the hearers to Jesus. He did not want the faith of God's people to stand in the wisdom of men, but in the power of God, therefore he was careful not to put himself forward, but rather the One whom he preached. He did not preach himself, but Christ Jesus the Lord, and he acknowledged that he was but a servant for Jesus' sake (2 Cor. 4:5).

Paul was well aware of man's propensity for preacher worship and he was determined not to encourage such a thing in any way. He despised that spirit which says, "I am of Paul, and I of Apollos," etc., and was careful to condemn it (1 Cor. 1:10-15; 3:3-5). He knew he was not sent to preach "with wisdom of words," for he knew that if he should do so the cross of Christ would thereby be made of no effect (v. 17). He was faithful to show that though he might plant and Apollos might water, it was *God alone* who could and did give the increase (v. 6). No man can do that, and no man should ever get the credit for it. This is a very valuable lesson for us all.

We ministers, if we are not very careful, may put ourselves too much in the forefront in our preaching. We should labor very diligently to avoid doing this. Our old flesh can so easily get in the way and detract from our preaching, and lead the minds of our hearers away from the One we are supposed to be preaching. Some of us couldn't preach with "wisdom of words" if our lives depended on it, but if we are not careful we can temporarily forget what our main business is, and that is to preach Christ and him crucified. May He help us in our efforts to proclaim his wonderful name, to the end that the faith of our hearers may be directed toward Christ and strengthened in him rather than centering in the wisdom and abilities of men.

July 3

"Behold, I was shapen in iniquity; and in sin did my mother conceive me" (Psalm 51:5)

These words were a part of the confession David made to God after Nathan the prophet came unto him and he was deeply convicted of his sin with Bathsheba and his indirect murder of her husband. He spoke out of a heart smitten with profound remorse and godly sorrow and thus he humbly acknowledged his great transgression and confessed that it was against God, and God only. He traced his sin all the way back to its fountain and we learn from thence that he was well aware of the doctrine of original sin. He knew that he was *born* in sin, that he was polluted with the fallen blood of Adam *from conception.* Like the apostle Paul, he could see that in his flesh, his old corrupt nature, there dwelt no good thing. He was deeply ashamed and full of self-loathing and realized his desperate need of cleansing.

David was forgiven, but the sword never departed from his house and his sin was ever before him. We cannot delve into the divine mind and explore all the reasons why God would suffer one of his servants to fall into such awful sins as David committed. However, for the remainder of his days it no doubt served the purpose of humbling him and making him more cautious of straying so far from his God. We may be certain that from thenceforward he looked upon sin and its consequences in an entirely different light, having discovered a new respect for, and reverence of, God's holy law.

When God's children walk contrary to his word they make a great mistake if they try to cover up their transgressions or seek to justify them, acknowledging their sin with deep remorse, contrition, and godly sorrow is the only way back into communion and fellowship with God. "The Lord is nigh unto them that are of a broken heart; and saveth such as be of a contrite spirit" (Psalm 34:18) and such a spirit he will not despise (Psalm 51:17). He will revive the spirit of the humble, and the heart of the contrite ones (Isaiah 57:15). But "pride goeth before detruction, and an haughty spirit before a fall" (Prov. 16:18). May the Lord help us to always walk humbly with him.

July 4

"Little children, keep yourselves from idols" (1 John 5:21)

This exhortation applies as much to God's children today as it did in John's day, because one of the greatest flaws in our fallen nature manifests itself in our propensity for allowing material things to take a higher place in our affections than does the Lord. If we do not love him with all our heart, with all our understanding, with all our soul, with all our mind, and with all our strength, then we do not love him as we should. If we do not love him more than father, mother, wife, children, brethren and sisters, yea, and our own life also then according to his own words we cannot be his disciple (Luke 14:26). His kingdom and righteousness is to be sought *first*, above all things.

I have never known of anyone calling themselves a Primitive Baptist falling down to a graven image and worshipping it, but I have known many of them to put secular things above spiritual things and place more emphasis upon material things than upon heavenly things. I have seen many brethren who apparently thought nothing of missing their church services in order to go to a sing, or to attend some family function, or some other secular affair. This certainly gives the appearance of putting the Kingdom of God in a secondary or inferior position in one's life. I see nothing in his word that indicates that this kind of thing is pleasing to him. The apostle Paul said that Christ is the *head* of the body, the church: "who is the beginning, the firstborn from the dead; that in all things he might have the preeminence" (Col. 1:18). Does He hold the preeminent place in our hearts and minds?

We need to be careful lest we find ourselves failing to set our affection upon things above rather than upon things on the earth (Col. 3:1-2). The beloved and devoted apostle Paul tells us that in consideration of God's mercies to us we should present our bodies a living sacrifice, holy, acceptable unto God, which is our reasonable service. And he further exhorts us not to be conformed to this world: but to be transformed by the renewing of our mind, that we may prove what is that good, and acceptable, and perfect will of God (Rom. 12:1-2). May he help us so to do.

July 5

"Also of your own selves shall men arise, speaking perverse things, to draw away disciples after them" (Acts 20:30)

Those who have desired a following have caused the Old Church much distress, and such men have often arisen within the church. They accomplish their goals by the things that they teach, and these things are contrary to what Christ and the apostles taught. Some of the definitions of *perverse* are: "contrary, self-willed, insubordinate and headstrong." This kind of spirit is diametrically opposed to the attitude and disposition that Christ taught his disciples to have and to manifest. An humble man will not seek a following for himself, nor will he seek to lord it over God's heritage (1 Peter 5:3). The apostle Paul exhorted the saints to follow him as he followed Christ (1 Cor. 11:1). And this is as far as anyone should follow any man. "We ought to obey God rather than men" (Acts 5:29).

We should be very wary of men who manifest a desire to draw away disciples after them. This is a sure sign of an anti-Christian spirit and disposition. Those who are the true servants of the Lord will desire above all things that Christ always and in everything be shown to have the preeminence. John the Baptist said, "He must increase, but I must decrease" (John 3:30), and in the next verse he says twice that, "He that cometh from above is above all." Paul declared that Christ is Lord of both the dead and living (Rom. 14:9). Christ "was counted worthy of more glory than Moses, inasmuch as he who hath builded the house hath more honor than the house" (Heb. 3:3). God has put all things under the feet of Christ, "and gave him to be the head over all things to the church" (Eph. 1:22). He is "gone into heaven, and is on the right hand of God; angels and authorities and powers being made subject to him" (1 Peter 3:22).

When a man gains a following, what does he have? He has a vain thing that usually will not endure any longer than he does. The desire for such a thing is an empty bubble, and not only that, but it is highly displeasing to the God whose glory he will not give to another (Isaiah 42:8; 48:11).

July 6

"For God so loved the world, that he gave his only begotten Son"
(John 3:16)

Every time I hear anyone other than a Primitive Baptist say anything about this verse they apply it universally and say, "God loved everyone so much," etc. But I believe the word "so" here does not speak of the *extent* or *degree* of God's love but rather of the *"manner"* of His love.

God loved the world of his elect *in such a manner* that he gave his only begotten Son, etc. This application corresponds with 1 John 3:1, "Behold, what manner of love the Father hath bestowed upon us, that we should be called the sons of God." It shows that his love was such that it only applied to "the sons of God," and not to the whole Adamic world.

It did not apply to those who are "none of his," (Rom. 8:9). It did not apply to those who are "without chastisement," and who are "bastards and not sons" (Heb. 12:8). Nor did it apply to those who are "of their father the devil" (John 8:44). It did not apply to those who are "not of (Christ's) sheep" (John 10:26). But it *did* apply to those who were predestinated to be conformed to the image of Christ and who cannot be separated from his love (Rom. 8:29-39). These *shall not perish* but have everlasting life. They were given to Christ and shall all come unto him. He will lose none of them but will raise them up again at the last day (John 6:37-39).

This is the manner of love with which they are loved of God. But a manner of love that would have allowed untold numbers of them to be eternally lost would have been no love at all.

July 7

"We see Jesus" (Hebrews 2:9)

Speaking of Jesus, the apostle Peter said, "Whom having not seen, ye love; in whom, though now ye see him not, yet believing, ye rejoice with joy unspeakable and full of glory" (1 Peter 1:8). This does not contradict Hebrews 2:9, for there the apostle is speaking of seeing Jesus by faith, while Peter was speaking of seeing him in the flesh. None of us have seen Jesus with our natural eyes, but we are as convinced of his glory and blessedness and deity as if we had seem him face to face, for we see him with an eye of faith. He told Peter, "Blessed art thou, Simon Barjona: for flesh and blood hath not revealed it unto thee, but my Father which is in heaven" (Matt. 16:17).

Even when Christ lived on the earth it was only those who had faith who saw him for who he really was and worshipped him accordingly. To the blind Pharisees, seeing him in the flesh was no advantage at all, but rather, it only made their unbelief the more inexcusable. Neither their learning, nor their religion, nor their professed piety, enabled them to see him as his disciples saw him. The blind religionists looked upon him and despised him, while his enlightened followers looked upon him and adored him. The difference lay in the fact that the latter possessed faith while the former did not.

God's believing people are ever "looking unto Jesus" the author and finisher of their faith (Heb. 12:2). The Lord not only gives them faith, but he will also bring it to full fruition. Here in this time world they live and walk by faith, but at last their faith will end in sight. They shall not only be like him, but they shall see him as he is (1 John 3:2).

What a wonderful privilege it is to see him by faith now and to go from day to day and from moment to moment trusting in him, believing in him, and being allowed the unspeakable pleasure from time to time of supping with him and he with us! Millions in gold cannot begin to compare with it.

ॐ

July 8

"The race is not to the swift, nor the battle to the strong"
(Ecclesiastes 9:11)

Solomon speaks here of the Christian race and the Christian warfare, and shows us that in *that* race, and in *that* warfare, it is not the natural gifts and abilities of men that achieves the victory. In *that* arena we can only triumph in the strength of Christ. He did not tell his disciples that greatness in his kingdom was attained by superior physical strength or by an unusual intelligence quotient, but rather by servitude. What he recognizes as greatness in his kingdom is just the opposite of what men view as greatness in the kingdoms of earth. Any time a child of God endeavors to overcome his enemies in his own strength, he will fail in the effort. But when he goes forth clothed in the armor of righteousness he is assured of ultimate victory.

We are all familiar with the haughty and self-confident spirit in which Goliath went out to battle with David. Goliath came with sword, spear, and shield: but David came trusting in the name of the Lord of hosts. Goliath thought the conquest would be as easy as stepping on a grasshopper, but David was assured of victory through a power that the giant knew nothing of. One little stone from David's sling, directed by the great God of heaven, is all it took to slay the giant and to fill the hearts of the Philistines with fear and to bring about a great victory for Israel. And when the old church goes forth in faith, trusting in the Lord rather than in their own schemes, counsels and craftiness, they too may be confident of a victorious outcome.

The Lord has taught us to cast our cares upon him (1 Peter 5:7) with the assurance that he cares for us. But do we not often clench our cares to our breast as though we cherished them, rather than casting them upon the Lord? We should ever be mindful of the fact that our battles are too great, and our enemies too strong to be overcome by our own power and ability. Let us always trust in the Lord and in his strength, for his strength is made perfect in our weakness, and when we most feel our own weakness, then we are strongest in him (2 Cor. 12:9-10).

೨ഛ

July 9

"Thus saith the Lord" (Exodus 4:22)

I think this is the first time we find the words "Thus saith the Lord" in the Bible, but we find them many times thereafter in the Old Testament. What the Lord has said should be of great concern to us, and his word should be our guide in all we say and do.

Where doctrine and practice are concerned we had best have a "thus saith the Lord," or else we will find ourselves worshipping him in vain. Adding to, or taking from, the word of God is a serious offense with a strong penalty connected with it. The Lord told Israel, "Ye shall not add unto the word which I command you, neither shall ye diminish aught from it, that ye may keep the commandments of the Lord your God which I command you" (Deut. 4:2). And in this same book he says, "What thing soever I command you, observe to do it: thou shalt not add thereto, nor diminish from it" (12:32). Proverbs 30:6 says, "Add thou not unto his words, lest he reprove thee, and thou be found a liar" (cf. Rev. 22:19).

There is nothing that can be substituted for a "thus saith the Lord" when it comes to divine worship. Christ taught us that those who are guilty of "teaching for doctrines the commandments of men," are worshipping him in vain (Matt. 15:9). And it is those who desire to "draw away disciples after them" who speak "perverse things." No man will ever gain a following if he stays strictly with "thus saith the Lord," for God's word teaches us that we are to follow Christ, and "We ought to obey God rather than men" (Acts 5:29). The apostle Peter tells us of wicked men who allure others away from the truth by speaking "great swelling words of vanity" (2 Peter 2:18) and Jude speaks of the same characters (Jude 16).

It is of utmost importance that we put "thus saith the Lord" above everything else. The Lord will not allow his word to be tampered with without a just retribution. Many have shown great contempt for the things that the Lord has said, and they have found that "the way of transgressors is hard." Someone coined a good expression when they said, "The Lord said it, and that settles it, whether we believe it or not."

July 10

"...rich toward God" (Luke 12:21)

What a wonderful thing it is to be "rich toward God," and how awful is the state of those who have no riches of that kind! There are a great many things that might be mentioned in connection with spiritual riches, but I think all such things are summarized in the words of 1st Timothy 6:6, i.e. "godliness with contentment." According to the inspired apostle this is "*great gain.*"

How I wish I could keep this verse so fixed in my mind and heart that it would never be out of my consciousness for a moment! What wonderful words they are, and how instructive and meaningful— *"Godliness with contentment."* Could they not be used to describe heaven itself?

"Godliness" covers all that the Lord requires of us in his word, and "contentment" is the by-product of godliness. You will notice that when the apostle tells us what the kingdom of God is, he says "righteousness" comes before "peace and joy," (*"The kingdom of God is not meat and drink; but righteousness, and peace, and joy in the Holy Ghost"* - Rom. 14:17). There can be no true contentment, peace and joy without godliness or righteousness preceding it.

How rich are those who have the love of God abiding within their hearts and who "hunger and thirst after righteousness!" All the scriptural descriptions of those who are "blessed," such as in Matthew 5:3-12, are also descriptive of those who are "rich toward God." There are many of these "Blessed are ye," and "Blessed are they," and "Blessed is he," references in the Bible, and all of them are equally descriptive of those who are "rich toward God."

A good instance of this is Romans 4:6-8. How much richer could anyone be than to be numbered among those whose iniquities are forgiven and whose sins are covered? Such wealth cannot be taken away nor destroyed by rust and corrosion. Neither can they be diminished by inflation. These are the riches we should set our affection upon, rather than the worldly kind (Col. 3:2).

℘℘

July 11

"...throughly furnished unto all good works" (2 Timothy 3:17)

When the apostle Paul wrote this he was aware that no more scripture would ever be needed. He knew that "the man of God" would from thenceforth be thoroughly furnished with all the information he needed, both to know what good works are, and to perform them.

The poorest of the poor can yet comply with the Bible, and being aged and infirm is no impediment to the observance of its precepts and instructions. Some of the most devoted and spiritually-minded followers of Christ have been men and women who were confined to beds of affliction or to wheelchairs. Even if invalids cannot assemble with the saints at the Lord's house, ordinarily they can still have the saints come to them if they desire. There is always a way to comply with God's precepts and he is fully aware of our circumstances and has never required more of anyone than they were able to perform. He is not a hard taskmaster. His yoke is easy and his burden is light (Matt. 11:30).

Those since the days of the apostles who have claimed to receive further revelations from heaven beyond the Scriptures are clearly liars, for God's people have long since been provided with all the scripture they need to perform all that he accounts good and acceptable. If this were not true, how could they "prove what is that good and acceptable, and perfect, will of God"? If we were not, already, thoroughly furnished unto all good works, what point would there be in praying for our fellow man, and for all who are in authority, in order that we might "lead a quiet and peaceable life in *all* godliness and honesty" (1 Tim. 2:1-3)? How could we know for certain what constitutes *all* godliness and honesty?

Let us be everlastingly thankful that God has not left us without guide or compass. He has given us his word, so that his people—"the man of God"—may thus be perfect in the sense of having a complete instruction Book by which to govern their lives and to comply with everything the Lord would have them do. He has left them without excuse for any disobedience.

July 12

*"A little that a righteous man hath is better than the riches of
many wicked"* (Psalm 37:16)

I have often been struck with the contrast between the way things are
viewed by good men and the way they are viewed by worldlings.
The verse above is a good example of this. Who among the wicked
would ever think for one moment that a righteous man, poor in worldly
goods, is in a better position than an evil man with great riches? And
who among them would not much prefer to have the wealth of many of
their own kind than to have the "little" that a righteous man might
possess? Given a choice between that which is described above as
"better" and that which is *much inferior*, the worldling will always
choose the latter, for he *savors not the things that be of God, but those
that be of men* (Matt. 16:23).

Who among the sons of men, viewing things strictly from a carnal
standpoint, would ever have thought Moses made a good choice when
he preferred "to suffer affliction with the people of God, than to enjoy
the pleasures of sin for a season; esteeming the reproach of Christ
greater riches than the treasures in Egypt" (Heb. 11:25-26)? To the
natural mind this would appear to have been an extremely foolish
choice, yet it was the *right* choice, and by virtue of it Moses enjoyed
riches that the world knows nothing of. To him even "the reproach of
Christ," and great suffering for his sake, were "greater riches" than all
the vast treasures that were housed in Egypt in his day.

Those who have once had the great pleasure and privilege of "tasting
that the Lord is gracious" (1 Peter 2:3) are forever thereafter possessed
of an entirely different perspective on what constitutes true riches. They
are consequently made to realize that nothing is as precious as "a good
conscience toward God" and sweet communion with Christ, and that
when we have these things we are rich beyond measure. "A man's life
consisteth not in the abundance of the things which he possesseth"
(Luke 12:15).

It matters not how little we as God's people may possess in material
goods, our state is better than that of wicked men, regardless of how
much wealth they may have amassed. Their final end is eternal

destruction and misery, but ours will be unending peace and joy. Even the thought of it is great riches.

July 13

"Behold, I show you a mystery: we shall not all sleep, but we shall all be changed..." (1 Corinthians 15:51)

The "we" in the text are God's people, and the "change" will occur in the resurrection. This "change" is necessary because even though the saints have been born of the Spirit, they still have a vile and sinful body that cannot enter heaven without being "fashioned like unto" the glorious body of Christ (Phil. 3:21). "Flesh and blood cannot inherit the kingdom of God; neither doth corruption inherit incorruption" (1 Cor. 15:50). Therefore "corruption *must* put on incorruption, and this mortal *must* put on immortality (v. 53). As we presently are, in these frail and dying bodies, we could not bear the resplendent glory of God and his heavenly abode. Men have trembled in the presence of angels in human form. How *would* they quake if they could see them as they appear in heaven?

Not all God's people will sleep the sleep of death, for some will be alive when the Lord returns, but they, along with all the resurrected saints, will be changed from corruptible to incorruptible. The wicked will also be raised, but they will not be changed, for they will go to a place where no good shall e're be known. Their vile bodies will go to a vile place, suited only for those wretched characters that hate God and who never desired the knowledge of his ways (Job 21:14).

Job said, "All the days of my appointed time will I wait, till my change come" (Job 14:14), and, oh, what a change it will be! The very thought of being changed by the mighty hand of God so that in some glorious and unspeakably wonderful sense we will be like our precious Savior and be satisfied, is too marvelous for my weak mind to fathom. Yet that is what I and all God's enlightened children are looking for and hoping for—to be "changed, in a moment, in the twinkling of an eye, at the last trump." My soul longs for that glorious day. It seems like I have been waiting for a long time, but what are these few fleeting moments of temporal life compared to a happy and delightful eternity?

July 14

"He will not lay upon man more than is right; that he should enter into judgment with God" (Job 34:23)

We may be certain that God will never lay more upon us than is just and right, either in what he requires of us in the way of duty, nor in what he brings upon us in a way of punishment, nor in what he requires us to endure in a way of correction. If he should do so, then we would be justified in entering into judgment with him, but this can never be. Even if we *could* enter into litigation with God, our cause would always fall before his omnipotence and supremacy. He is in one mind and none can turn him (Job 23:13). "What his soul desireth, even that he doeth."

Our God is a God of truth, and is without iniquity. "Just and right is he" (Deut. 32:4). "The ways of the Lord are right" (Hosea 14:9). Therefore he can do nothing amiss, and we should never entertain the slightest notion that he is being too severe with us. No matter how trying our circumstances may become, God exacts less of us than our iniquity deserves (Job 11:6). We deserve nothing good at his hands, and therefore anything better than his wrath is a mercy. As the songwriter says, "If my soul were sent to hell, Thy righteous law approves it well."

When our load seems more than we can bear let us take comfort in the fact that God can never be charged with any degree of injustice in his dealings with us. He will not lay more upon us than is right. And this implies that he is *right* to lay certain things on us. He is a very merciful and compassionate benefactor, and when we look back upon the things he has laid upon us, we will be able to see that they were for our good. It may not seem so at the time we are enduring them, but ultimately they will yield the peaceable fruits of righteousness. The Lord always knows best, and He always deals with us accordingly.

July 15

"Let the brother of low degree rejoice in that he is exalted: but the rich, in that he is made low" (James 1:9-10)

There is a sense in which a work of grace in the heart of a poor man exalts him, for by it he is blest to see that he is rich in Christ. And the same work in the heart of a rich man debases him, for it enables him to see that he is a poor wretch by nature and that he has no righteousness to plead.

Of course this work of grace makes both a poor man *and* a rich man see their spiritual *poverty* as well as their spiritual *riches*. However, in our text the poor brother is taught to rejoice in the fact that the Lord has lifted him up and blest him to see that he is rich in Christ. But at the same time the rich man is taught to rejoice in the fact that he has been stripped of his own self-righteousness and brought low in that sense. The exaltation that comes as a result of one being able to see his blessed state in Christ, is indeed something to rejoice in. And likewise, the debasement that comes as a result of one being able to see himself as a poor sinner by nature, also calls for rejoicing.

Let me mention another facet of this subject. In an unregenerate state a financially poor man may be *rich* in his own self-esteem and in his estimate of his own merits and abilities. And by the same token, a monetarily rich man may be *poor* in the sense that he has no spiritual wealth. But when the Lord quickens them into divine life and shows them what they are by nature it will bring them both down in the dust of self-abasement. Then when they receive a sweet hope in Christ they are both made to feel that they are rich in him.

In effectual calling, the servant becomes the Lord's freeman, and the freeman become the Lord's servant (1 Cor. 7:22). Yet both are brought to the same point, for both are brought into servitude to Christ, and both are made free from the bondage of sin.

Do these things seem a mystery to you? Look to the Lord and ask for understanding. In the operations of the Spirit, the way up is down and the way down is up, "for whosoever exalteth himself shall be abased; and he that humbleth himself shall be exalted" (Luke 14:11).

July 16

"The Son of man...a friend of publicans and sinners" (Luke 7:34)

One of the things that irritated the Pharisees most about Christ was his familiarity with sinners, and his sympathy toward the penitent among them. His conduct did not agree with what they expected from the promised Messiah. These poor deluded wretches fancied themselves to be very pure and good, and so great was their pride and conceit that they verily thought they were too righteous to have any association with sinners. There was no doubt in their minds that when Messiah came he would identify altogether with such as themselves.

With such high esteem for themselves we may well imagine what their attitude was toward those who sought companionship with Christ and who felt the need of his grace. How disgusting it must have been to them to see those whom they considered to be vile, loathsome sinners falling down at Jesus' feet in tears and finding such a warm reception there! What poor, ignorant fools must they have thought them to be, and how much greater fool must they have thought Christ to be for allowing such characters access to himself! The intimacy between Christ and penitent sinners was, is, and ever shall be, a mystery of mysteries to the proud and lofty professors of religion.

But that which makes Christ most loathsome to the self-righteous is the very thing that makes him most precious to his meek and lowly followers. Where would they be were it not that he "receiveth sinners" (Luke 15:2) and sups with them?

Christ would do no good to anyone if he spent his time with those who feel no need of him and who feel to be as good as he is. His answer to those who questioned his disciples as to why he ate with Publicans and sinners was, "They that be whole need not a physician, but they that are sick." The Spirit of the Lord still dwells in the hearts of the same class as those to whom Christ showed himself mighty while he walked here upon earth, for the most part passing by the "wise men after the flesh" (1 Cor. 2:26), the mighty and the noble, and favoring the "weak and base things of the world and things which are despised." This has always confused, confounded and frustrated the "mighty" and it always will.

July 17

"Take therefore no thought for the morrow: for the morrow shall take thought for the things of itself. Sufficient unto the day is the evil thereof" (Matthew 6:34)

It ill becomes God's people, especially those who have had access to the true gospel, to fret themselves about what tomorrow may or may not bring, for it reflects a distrust in him and his providential care and keeping. The inordinate concern for food, drink and clothing that we are cautioned against in Matt. 6:25, indicates a heart not right with God (Psalm 78:37); a heart that is not steadfast in the promises of his word.

We should live one day at a time, be diligent in the things the Lord has taught us to do, and seek first his kingdom and righteousness; and in so doing we are assured by him that those things we have *need* of will be added. If we have a conscience "void of offense" (Acts 24:16), and if our ways please the Lord (Prov. 16:7), and if in his providence he sees to it that we have what we need, that is enough. If we do what we can toward providing for our own, then we should leave the outcome to the Lord, with perfect confidence that he will do his part and will fulfull every promise he has given us.

"Sufficient unto the day is the evil thereof." Each day of our lives will be loaded with enough troubles to keep all our graces sufficiently exercised without adding on the cares and concerns of the future. Those difficulties that we think may arise tomorrow probably will never materialize, and even if they do, the Lord will provide the grace we need *at the time it is needed*. We should not fret and worry over tomorrow's troubles, for the Lord will give us strength equal to each day's burdens (Deut. 33:35). "Trust in the Lord, and do good; so shalt thou dwell in the land, and *verily thou shalt be fed*. Delight thyself also in the Lord; and he shall give thee the desires (the *godly* desires) of thine heart. Commit thy way unto the Lord; trust also in him; and he shall bring it to pass" (Psalm 37:3-5). "Trust in the Lord with all thine heart; and lean not unto thine own understanding" (Prov. 3:5).

July 18

"Blessed are they that mourn: for they shall be comforted"
(Matthew 5:4)

I am sure I cannot get at all the depths of this verse, but there is much in it to comfort a trembling child of grace. To one who has seen something of the exceeding sinfulness of sin (Romans 7:13) and the wretchedness of his own nature (v. 24), there is much to mourn over. Should we not mourn over the pain we inflicted upon our Savior as he took our sins upon himself and bore them to the tree? And should it not be a source of grief to us that we have sinned, and do constantly sin against a pure and holy God, who has told us plainly in his word what he would and would not have us do? Should we not mourn over our weakness and instability, and our many faults and failings that manifest themselves in all we undertake to do? Should we not mourn when we see our beloved Zion being disturbed by designing men who seek to make it more appealing to an unbelieving world and turn it into a house of merchandise?

All these things and many more are things that the children of God should mourn over. This is a blessed kind of mourning because it is accompanied with self-loathing and repentance. It is a mourning that will be attended, in God's own time, with the comforts of his Holy Spirit. He comforts us when he blesses us with the manifestations of his love to us and for us, in spite of our great unworthiness of his grace and favor. He comforts us when he blesses us to see and feel his omnipotence, and to understand that he is in full control of all events and circumstances. He comforts us when he blesses us to contemplate the fact that he cannot do an unloving thing to any of his children, and that in all he does he is just and right in every particular. He comforts us when he blesses us to understand that his purposes for his church here in the world cannot and will not be defeated.

The Lord intends that we shall have occasional joys and pleasures in his service, and bestows many temporal benefits upon us all along through life, but in our present state it cannot all be peace and pleasantness. Our very nature and situation in a sin-cursed world requires that there be some mourning. And when this mourning is of a godly sort, it will be attended from time to time with comfort from on high. We may be sure of it.

July 19

"The dogs eat of the crumbs which fall from their master's table"
(Matthew 15:27)

This was the reply of the Canaanite woman when she pleaded with Christ in behalf of her daughter, who was grievously vexed with a devil, and was told that it was not meet to take the children's bread, and cast it to dogs (cf. Mark 7:25-30). What an extraordinary and suitable reply! It was so remarkable that it brought forth from our Lord a wonderful commendation of her faith: "O woman, great is thy faith."

The Lord tested her faith sorely. He could do that because he knew how strong it was and what the outcome would be. He did not test it for his own benefit but for the benefit of others. He at first "answered her not a word," and I fear that my faith might have at least faltered somewhat at that point, but not so this woman's. When she got no answer from Christ she appealed to his disciples, and then again to him. And when he further tested her faith by referring to the inappropriateness of casting the children's bread to dogs, she was not offended but rather acknowledged the truth of it and said, "Yet the dogs eat of the crumbs which fall from the master's table." How beautiful this is to me! And how I admire her faith! Though she considered herself no better than a dog, she yet believed Christ would show mercy to her daughter.

Notice well that when the Lord would commend "great faith" it is not in any way associated with any supposed "wonderful works in his name," human merit or creature righteousness, but it relates to an humble child of God who freely acknowledged her lowliness and unworthiness. This commendation came as a result of her persistently seeking the Lord's favor in behalf of a loved one in spite of the greatest imaginable discouragements. She sought nothing for herself, but for her dear daughter. And though she was a Gentile, and was looked upon by the Jews as on a level with animals, yet the Lord had not found this kind of faith among his own nation.

If the Lord has blest us to see what we are by nature we will not be offended by anything his word says about us in a negative way, even when it describes us as being altogether vanity even at our best state (Ps. 39:5). Our native corruption cannot be painted any worse or more severe than it actually is, and neither can God's glory be described any greater or more wonderful than it is. "How little a portion is heard of him?" (Job 26:14).

July 20

"Another Jesus, whom we have not preached"
(2 Corinthians 11:4)

I hear much said by the religious world about some man that they call *Jesus* and a few of the things they say about him sound as though they might be speaking of the Jesus I am acquainted with. But usually just about the time I think they are speaking of *my* Jesus they say something that makes me know they are talking about some other personality.

I hear some say *their* Jesus was just merely a good man, but this cannot be *my* Jesus, for he is both God *and* man (John 1:14). Others say *their* Jesus *wants* to save his people but he cannot do so unless they *let* him. This surely cannot be *my* Jesus because *my* Jesus has power over all flesh and gives eternal life to as many as his Father gave unto him (John 17:2).

They speak of *their* Jesus *wanting* to do this, and *trying* to do that, and they boast of *helping* him save people, *transporting* him where he wants to go, *preventing* him from doing his will, *frustrating* him, *hindering* him, and such like things. No! No! this cannot be *my* Jesus. This cannot be the Jesus of the Bible, for he is the Lord God omnipotent (Rev. 19:6), and he rules and reigns in heaven and earth. Nothing he has ever undertaken has been frustrated or brought to naught. He cannot fail nor be discouraged (Isa. 42:4).

I do not need a Jesus over whom I can rule, and who must conform to *my* will. I do not need a Jesus who can do no more than I will *let* him do. Such a savior is no savior at all, and he does not suit such a sad case as mine. I need that wonderful Savior who said, "I came down from heaven, not to do mine own will, but the will of Him that sent me. And this is the Father's will which hath sent me, that of all which he hath given me I should lose nothing, but should raise it up again at the last day." He had the power to do the work that his Father gave him to do, and when he had done that work he said, "It is finished." That's good enough for me.

July 21

"Jesus, when he had cried with a loud voice, yielded up the ghost" (Matthew 27:50)

Many times we have seen men and women who, when they lay dying, could barely speak at all so as to be understood. It seems that the voice is one of the first things to fail when people are approaching death, but not so in the case of our Lord. Only an instant before he "yielded up the ghost" he "cried again with a loud voice." This certainly verifies his assertion that "I lay down my life, that I might take it again. No man taketh it from me, but I lay it down of myself. I have power to lay it down, and I have power to take it again" (John 10:18).

He cried with a loud voice just before dying in order to show us that he did not die because the strength and vitality was all drained out of him, but because the work of redemption was completed. We may be sure that Christ did not *yield up the ghost* until he had finished all the work his Father had given him to do. He would not have stopped one moment short of it, and there was no need for him to go one minute beyond it. The soldiers came to him to break is legs and hasten his death, for they knew that, normally speaking, a crucified man would still be alive at that point, but they found that he was already dead (John 19:33). And Pilate marveled at the news that he had already expired

(Mark 15:44). But they did not realize that something very extraordinary had just transpired. The Son of God had just laid down his life for his people. No man had taken it from him but he laid it down of himself, voluntarily offering himself without spot to God, not to man (Heb. 9:14). God had accepted the offering, and three days later he received him back into Glory, testifying to his complete satisfaction with the work he had performed and declaring thereby that his people were fully justified.

July 22

"I have reserved to myself seven thousand men, who have not bowed the knee to the image of Baal" (Romans 11:4)

I take great delight in the fact that the Lord has always, in every age, "reserved to himself" a remnant who are so filled with the graces of his blessed Spirit that they will not worship the gods of this world. The apostle Paul, immediately following the above text, says, "Even so then at this present time also there is a remnant according to the election of grace," and I am sure the same could have been said in every age of time.

The Lord has always had his faithful followers, no matter how much they have been in the minority. Faithful Noah and his little family were greatly in the minority, but they survived the flood while all the rest of mankind was drowned. The fact that the masses were greatly in the majority was no advantage to them at all.

I love the dedication and courage that Shadrach, Meshach and Abednego displayed when Nebuchadnezzar made an image of gold and demanded that they fall down and worship it. They were not the least bit hesitant to let him know unequivocally that they would not serve his gods, nor worship the golden image he had set up, even if it meant their death. The threat of being eaten by lions could not persuade Daniel to stop praying and making supplication to his God three times a day. Like Hananiah, "He was a faithful man, and feared God above many" (Neh. 7:2). What a blessing such men are to the earth! The world is not worthy of such as these (Heb. 11:38). But if it were not for them, what a mass of turmoil, violence and total wickedness this world would be.

Oh, that we may be so blest of the Lord that we will always be found among the faithful! May he so keep us that we will never be found numbered among those rebellious ones who are unwilling to be guided by his word, but who seek out their own devices and inventions and bring in strife and confusion among his people. And if called upon to lay down our lives rather than deny him, may he give us the courage to say as did the three Hebrew children to Nebuchadnezzar, "We will not serve thy gods."

July 23

"By whom we have received grace and apostleship for obedience to the faith among all nations" (Romans 1:5)

Notice, Paul did not say that the grace and apostleship he had received from Christ were for obedience to the faith *by* all nations, but rather for obedience to the faith *among* all nations. According to Colossians 1:6 our Lord's commission to "Go ye into all the world and preach the gospel to every creature" had been complied with in the apostle's day. The gospel had been preached "in all the world:" that is, the *known* world, and among all nations. And it is obvious that the apostles and ministers of that day did not achieve obedience to the faith *by* all nations; but through the grace given unto them some *among* all nations were indeed brought into a proper compliance with the precepts of the gospel.

It is clear that one of the main objects of the gospel is "obedience to the faith." It is not sufficient merely to *acknowledge* the faith or to *profess* the faith, but it is necessary that we *be obedient* to it; otherwise we are not true disciples of the Lord.

The faith, that is, the true gospel of Jesus Christ, requires *obedience* on the part of his believing people. It is delightful and joyous to *hear* the "certain sound" of the gospel trumpet, but it is not enough merely to be *hearers* of the word; it is needful that we be *doers* of the word as well (James 1:22). We need to "obey the truth" (Gal. 3:1). Ministers of the gospel are to teach God's people to *observe* (put into practice) whatsoever things Christ has commanded in his word. It is only in this way of obedience that the children of God can enjoy fellowship (communion) with his servants, with him, and with Christ. Only in this way can their joy be full (1 John 1:3-4).

Obedience to the faith is God's ordained means by which we are to prove the sincerity of our discipleship. Christ says, "If ye love me, keep my commandments" (John 14:15); and His commandments are not grievous (1 John 5:3). If we love him as we ought, we will delight ourselves in his presence (Psalm 119:47) and serve him with all readiness of mind. May he bless us with greater zeal and devotion.

July 24

"God commendeth his love toward us, in that, while we were yet sinners, Christ died for us" (Romans 5:8)

The beginning of the Book of Romans tells us who the "us" are in the text: It is those who are beloved of God and called to be saints. There are those that the Lord does not love (one of the plainest proofs of this is in Romans 9:13, which was taken from Malachi 1:2-3), and he did not die for these. Rather, he laid down his life for "the sheep" (John 10:11, 15) and for "the church" (Eph. 5:25). These he has always loved. He loved them in eternity and chose them in Christ before the foundation of the world (Eph. 1:4), and has saved them and called them, not according to their works, but according to his own purpose and grace, which was given them in Christ Jesus before the world began (2 Tim. 1:9). He loved them with an everlasting love, and therefore with loving kindness he has drawn them to himself (Jer. 31:3).

All of God's elect fell in Adam, right along with the non-elect. They "all together," or all at the same time, *became filthy* (Psalm 14:3; 53:3), so that the elect are "by nature" children of wrath, even as are the non-elect (Eph. 2:3). God's people are *not* children of wrath, but they have the *same nature* as the children of wrath. Therefore, if they were never regenerated by the Spirit of God, they would die in their sins just as will the non-elect.

But even while they were in this fallen and ruined condition Christ died for them, and this is the ultimate commendation of the love of God for them. It is this act of taking their sins upon himself that most greatly magnifies and glorifies his love. If he had died for them because they deserved to be saved, they wouldn't have needed saving in the first place. If he had died for them because he was *obligated* to save them that would have been no commendation of his love at all. But his love is commended toward them in the fact that he died for them "while they were yet sinners," and "when (they) were enemies" (Rom. 5:8, 10). "Behold, what manner of love the Father hath bestowed upon us, that we should be called the sons of God" (1 John 3:1).

July 25

"The eternal God is thy refuge" (Deuteronomy 33:27)

Let us consider for a moment this One who is eternal. How could we comprehend a being who has no beginning and no ending? What words could we find to explain the mysteries or the depths of his divine nature and attributes? In addition to his being eternal, the apostle Paul adds that he is immortal and invisible (Col. 1:15; 1 Tim. 1:17; Heb. 11:27). How could we begin to form an image in our minds of One who is invisible to our natural eyes?

Moses was afraid to even look upon a visible representation of him in a flame of fire (Ex. 3:6). The very skin of his face shone from simply being in God's presence on mount Sinai and the children of Israel were afraid to come nigh him (Ex. 34:29-30). Oh, what must the actual glory of God be?

Peter says of this great Being that with him one day is as a thousand years, and a thousand years as one day (2 Peter 3:8), or as Psalm 90:4 expresses it, "A thousand years in thy sight are but as yesterday when it is past, and as a watch in the night." These expressions are not given us to suggest that God measures time on a ratio of one day per thousand years, but simply to show us that he is a timeless God. Time has no measure with One who has no beginning and no ending. With him it is one eternal *now*, one unending *present*.

Some, in attempting to speak of God's eternity have described it as the "unreckonable ages of duration." But we are lost for words when we undertake to deal with such a fathomless subject. Even divine inspiration leaves us with much yet to be discovered. Some things are reserved for the next world.

Oh, what a refuge for his people is this blessed and only Potentate (1 Tim.6:15), "Who only hath immortality, dwelling in the light which no man can approach unto; whom no man hath seen, nor can see!" and what mighty arms are underneath them! How appropriately is the question posed in Romans 8:31, "If God be for us, who can be against us?"! The answer is obvious.

July 26

"Blessed is the people that know the joyful sound" (Psalm 89:15)

What could this *joyful sound* be other than the old gospel bell ringing from the lips of God-called ministers with not a discordant note? There are people who are able to discern this unique sound, and there are people who are *not* able. Those who know this soul-cheering strain are blest indeed for they possess hearts and ears that have been tuned and prepared by divine experience to receive the good news of a finished salvation wrought by a risen and triumphant Savior. They have been taught to worship God in the spirit, to rejoice in Christ Jesus, and to have no confidence in the flesh (Phil. 3:3). They have seen the utter futility of seeking to establish their own righteousness and have been brought to depend solely and alone upon the shed blood and imputed righteousness of Christ for life and salvation.

From earliest youth we have heard many repugnant and loathsome sounds coming out of the Arminian camp, such as: "Jesus wants to save you if you'll *let* him"; "*Let* Jesus into your heart before it is too late"; "So live that in the Judgment your good works will outweigh your bad works and you will escape torment"; "Accept Christ as your personal Savior and *let* him give you life"; "God is trying to save the lost and is wringing his hands because so many refuse his offer of salvation," etc. But no such sentiment can be found in God's word. All such is a foreign tongue to heaven-taught souls and is a distressing and troubling sound. It depicts our Lord and Savior as a total weakling and gives man control over him. There is nothing joyful about such utterances.

The true gospel gives all glory to God, and declares that God's people are saved and called with an holy calling, not according to their works but according to his own purpose and grace which was given them in Christ Jesus before the world began (2 Tim. 1:9). It bases their obedience to his precepts upon the foot of grace, and shows that they do not act in order to have life, but because they already have it, and consequently desire to honor and serve him. It shows that poor fallen man is undeserving of the least of His mercies and declares eternal salvation to be all of grace from first to last. Do these things strike a pleasant note in your heart? If so you are a blest character indeed. You know the joyful sound.

July 27

"The eyes of all wait upon thee; and thou givest them their meat in due season" (Psalm 145:15)

I have often reflected upon the providence of God and marveled at how all his creatures are supplied with sustenance. The earth is over-spread with innumerable life forms and yet there is provision made for all of them, and they are perpetuated from generation to generation. I can look out my front window and watch the tiny little bluebirds as they busily gather their food, and I observe that their supply never runs out. It is always there for them. And this brings to mind the fact that even the little sparrows that we think of as being so insignificant, cannot fall on the ground without the Father taking notice. "Not one of them is forgotten before God" (Matt. 10:29; Luke 12:6). To me this is wonderful to think about. And then how comforting to consider that God's children are of more value to him than many sparrows and that the very hairs of their head are all numbered. Well might he tell us not to fear.

It also comforts me to consider what the Lord said about the lilies of the field. "They toil not, neither do they spin: and yet...even Solomon in all his glory was not arrayed like one of these" (Matt. 6:28). And then what a wonderful lesson he teaches us from this, and how reassuring it is to know that if he so clothes the grass of the field, which to day is, and to morrow is cast into the oven, he will much more clothe us who so often manifest so little faith in his providential care and keeping!

We learn from Genesis 22:14 that one of the names of God is *Jehovah-jireh*, which means, *the Lord will see, or, provide*. And can we not all acknowledge that he has always been a faithful and bountiful Provider? We may not have always had everything we wanted, but he has provided us with the necessities of life until this good hour. All the days of our lives he has not allowed us to go hungry or to suffer for lack of sustenance. I feel confident that it will always be thus with his people, as it has been with those before us. The Lord has mercifully given us our daily bread, both natural and spiritual. What a wonderful Provider he has been and still is! Let us not be fearful, but believing.

July 28

"Then spake the Lord to Paul in the night by a vision, Be not afraid, but speak and hold not they peace: for I am with thee, and no man shall set on thee to hurt thee: for I have much people in this city" (Acts 18:9-10)

If modern religionists were not so prejudiced against the truth, and in many cases *blinded to* the truth, they would be able to see that Paul was not sent to Corinth, or anywhere else, because God wanted him to *make* him some children, but *because there were already many of his children there*. He obviously was sent *to the people of God* in that city, not to the other crowd to whom the gospel is foolishness. The gospel is not sent to anyone for the purpose of regenerating them or to change goats into sheep, but rather to enlighten God's people who are in error, to convert them to the truth and to comfort, edify and instruct them so that they may be better equipped to serve God in spirit and in truth.

Our text shows clearly that not all the inhabitants of Corinth were God's people. If they had been then there would have been no point whatsoever in the Lord telling Paul, "I have much people in this city." If it were true, as modern religionists believe, that everybody is a child of God, then Paul would have automatically known that everybody in Corinth and every other city in the world were children of God, and God would not have said, "I have much people in this city." It would have gone without saying.

God has a people "*out of* every kindred, and tongue, and people, and nation," who have been redeemed by the blood of Christ (Rev. 5:9). These will all live with him in Glory by and by, whether they ever hear the gospel or not. All that God the Father gave to Christ *will* come to him, without the loss of a single one (John 6:37-39). God's people are known of him, and this is a part of the seal that the very foundation of God bears—"the Lord knoweth them that are his" (2 Tim. 2:19). They are "out of" every kindred and language throughout the earth. God at the first did visit the Gentiles to "take *out of* them" a people for his name (Acts 15:14). And he got everyone he went after. This is the way the God of the Bible works. He is not the little weak, puny being that the religious world makes him out to be. He is omnipotent (Rev. 19:6).

July 29

"I have finished the work which thou gavest me to do"
(John 17:4)

The work that the Father gave his Son to do was to save his people from their sins, which the angel said he *would* do (Matt. 1:21). He was *not* given the work of *trying* to save *anyone*, especially those who "are none of his" and who are *children of the devil*, and whom he "never knew" (Romans 8:9; John 8:44; Matt. 7:23). He came into the world to save those that the Father gave him, and he says: "This is the Father's will which hath sent me, that of all which he hath given me I should lose nothing, but should raise it up again at the last day" (John 6:39).

Will he do that, or will he not? If he does not, then he will not have done the will of his Father—it's just that simple. And if he does not do the will of his Father, then he and the Father both are a failure. The truly Christian mind can give no sanction to such a foolish and God-dishonoring notion.

The beloved apostle Paul declared it to be a faithful saying, and worthy of all acceptation, that Christ Jesus came into the world to *save* sinners (1 Tim. 1:15). Now, he either saved them and finished the work that the Father gave him to do, or he did not save them. Popular religion says he did not actually *save* them, he just made their salvation *possible*. Paul said he came to *save* them. Who will we believe, popular religion or the apostle?

A great part of the work that the Father gave Christ to do was to fulfill all the requirements of his holy law by being obedient to it in every particular. In doing this he wrought out a perfect righteousness which is imputed to every heir of grace "without works" on their part (Rom. 4:6-8). By being born of a virgin, living a perfect life, and dying as a perfect sacrifice for the sins of his people, he satisfied divine justice and finished the work that his Father gave him to do. He arose from the dead, and is now ascended back to the Father where he ever liveth to make intercession for the same people that he died for. The work he was given to do, is the work he performed—to a jot and a tittle, with nothing added and nothing left off. He did a perfect work that does not need anything attached to it by the feeble hands of men. What a consolation it is to know that Christ *finished* the work he was given to do, and how we ought to praise him!

July 30

"If a man think himself to be something, when he is nothing, he deceiveth himself" (Galatians 6:3)

Humility is one of the greatest and most becoming of Christian virtues, while pride and self-exaltation are some of the most unbecoming traits anyone can possess. Christ, our Great Example, said, "I am meek and lowly in heart." Therefore if we would be like him we must follow in his steps, both in the spirit and in the letter.

The great apostle Paul, who stated that if any man thought he had whereof he might trust in the flesh, he had more (Philippians 3:4), was also a very humble man. He spoke of himself as "less than the least of all saints," and as the chief of sinners. He acknowledged that in him, that is, in his flesh, dwelt no good thing, and he lamented the fact that he was a "wretched man." He had been highly favored of the Lord, but he was always keenly aware of the fact that he was what he was "by the grace of God," and he declared that though he preached the gospel, he had nothing to glory of. And though he was not behind the very chiefest apostles in anything, yet he realized that in and of himself he was *nothing*.

Galatians 6:3 makes it very clear that a self-exalter is a self-deceiver, but such a person does not deceive most of those around him, and he *certainly* does not deceive God. In Proverbs 8:13 we are taught that the Lord hates pride and arrogance, and he will bring low every one that is proud (Job 40:12; Isaiah 2:12). "Whosoever exalteth himself shall be abased; and he that humbleth himself shall be exalted" (Luke 14:11).

It greatly behooves all God's people not to think of themselves more highly than they ought to think (Romans 12:3) for when they think themselves to be something, when they are nothing, they are not thinking soberly. There is only one acceptable posture before God for fallen creatures such as we, and that is at the feet of our brethren, esteeming each of them better than ourselves.

What a difference it would make in our world and in our churches if everyone maintained such a posture! There would be no one bringing in troubling things or doing things to others that they would not want done to themselves. May we as individuals strive to remember that we are but flesh and blood and may we seek to always be meek and humble before God and men.

July 31

"In whom are hid all the treasures of wisdom and knowledge"
(Colossians 2:3)

The Deity of Christ is clearly set forth in the Scriptures, and here is one of many such instances. If he were not God then it could not be said of him that all the treasures of wisdom and knowledge are hid in him. In the prophecy of Christ in Isaiah 11, it was declared that the spirit of the Lord would rest upon him, the spirit of wisdom and understanding, the spirit of counsel and might, the spirit of knowledge, etc. This wisdom, knowledge and understanding was clearly manifest throughout his earthly ministry. We find him "sitting in the midst of the doctors" of the law when he was but a child of twelve years, "both hearing them, and asking them questions. All that heard him were astonished at his understanding and answers" (Luke 2:46-47). And how easily he confounded all those who sought to ensnare him in his speech, no matter what the degree of their education.

What a marvelous experience it must have been for his disciples to sit at the feet of One who knew all things—One who was the very repository of all the treasures of wisdom and knowledge! How blest were those, such as Mary, who eagerly availed themselves of every opportunity to absorb as much of himself as he was willing to impart to them, and how blest are we if we drink in as much of his word as he is pleased to unveil to us! How gloriously does it reflect his power and might and all His other marvelous attributes, and how needful it is for his people to hide as much of it in their hearts as they are able (Psalm 119:11; Col. 3:16)!

How beautiful is the declaration of Paul as he contemplated these things: "O the depth of the riches both of the wisdom and knowledge of God! how unsearchable are his judgments, and his ways past finding out" (Rom. 11:33)! It is to him alone that we are to apply for wisdom

(James 1:5), and who among us does not feel a great lack in this respect? Who among us does not feel that they could use a great deal more of this precious commodity? Our greatest wisdom is to always be "looking unto Jesus, the author and finisher of our faith." What a wonderful source of supply!

August 1

"Blessed is the man whom thou chastenest, O Lord, and teachest him out of thy law" (Psalm 94:12)

It is indeed a blest man who is chastened of the Lord, for there are many benefits derived from such chastisement. Chastisement is one of the ways God has of teaching His people. If it were not accompanied with *teaching* then of what profit would it be to them? It may be clearly inferred from His chastisement of us that He loves us, for He does not chastise those whom He does not love (Heb. 12:6-8). The chastisement of His people is a necessary function of His Fatherly relationship with them He deals with them as sons. Proverbs 13:24 tells us that "he that spareth his rod hateth his son: but he that loveth him chasteneth him betimes."

What if God had not smitten David's conscience for his transgressions? What if He had never sent the prophet to him with a story of a wretched act of wickedness. David would never have pronounced the ultimate sentence upon himself, and he would never have been convicted of the fact that *he himself* was "the man" who deserved that very sentence (2 Sam 11, 12). And in such a case how different would David's case have been? If his missteps had never been openly condemned of the Lord, how haughty and high-minded might he have been, and how unfit to lead God's people and to rule over them as their king? No man can truly be a great leader without a good measure of humility, and God's afflicting providences are necessary to that humility. We have only to observe those who are "without chastisement" to see the wretched results. Their arrogance and lack of principle is plain for any discerning eye to see.

The chastening of the Lord is nothing to be despised (Job 5:17; Heb. 12:5). Where would we be without it? It keeps us reminded that we are frequent and persistent transgressors. "In many things we offend all" (James 3:2), that is, in many things we all offend. We all come short in many respects and need divine correction. Notice that Psalm 94:12 combines chastisement with instruction from God's word. There is nothing we will ever be chastised for that has not already been condemned in the Scriptures. And what we fail to learn from the Scriptures we most likely will learn from bitter experience. Let us humble ourselves under the mighty hand of God.

August 2

"For thou hast created all things, and for thy pleasure they are and were created" (Revelation 4:11)

The question has often been asked, "Why did God create man?" and the verse above is the only clear answer I know of that we find in the Bible. Do you know of a better one? I gather from the nature of God, as it is set forth in the Scriptures, that he does not *need* anything (Acts 17:25). Therefore we conclude that he did not create either men or angels or anything else because he *needed* them. I believe we may rightly say that he created man for the same reason. He hides his truth from some and reveals it to others—*because it seemed good in his sight* (Matt. 11:26). That is the only reason I know of that he does anything he does. And if it seems good in his sight, then it *is* good, whether we understand it or not.

I reflect with wonderment upon the thought that the God of heaven could find pleasure in anything beneath the indescribable tranquility and peacefulness and the unsurpassable felicity of the glory world. But this is one of the great mysteries of Godliness. All things were created for his pleasure, but I am left to wonder how some of these things could bring him any pleasure at all.

We are told that the Lord takes pleasure in his people (Psalm 149:4), in those that fear him, and who hope in his mercy (Psalm 147:11). It seems not so difficult to see how he could take pleasure in those principles of holiness and grace that he has planted within the hearts of his people, and in the outward manifestation of them, but in what sense or senses he takes pleasure, for instance, in inanimate things may never be ours fully to know. I do believe, however that in some way he takes pleasure in such things as that the heavens declare his glory and the firmament showeth his handiwork (Psalm 19:1), even though this silent declaration is made in a passive sense.

This is a deep subject to me, as are many others, and I am lost in wonder as I contemplate God's great and glorious works. For the present I must strive to be content to know that whatever he does, or has done, is a product of the highest possible wisdom. I notice that as God performed his creative work we are told repeatedly that he "saw that it was good." I have often wondered how much more we will know in heaven than we are presently capable of grasping.

August 3

"I believe God, that it shall be even as it was told me"
(Acts 27:25)

During the apostle Paul's voyage to Rome a tempestuous wind arose that he had previously warned the crew of, but the centurion gave no heed. The situation looked hopeless, but the apostle had been assured by an angel of God that there would be no loss of life, only the ship. In the language above Paul told them that he believed it would be even as it was told him. His belief was based upon his past experience of the faithfulness of God. God had never failed to keep his word.

What a wonderful thing it is to have an infallible source of information upon which we can absolutely rely, with no fear that it might be wrong—namely, the written word of God, the Bible— accurately rendered in English in the King James Version. Whatever he has left on record in his inspired Book, we can depend upon, and say with full assurance that *It is even as it was told us.*

There are many "exceeding great and precious promises" given unto us by the Lord (2 Peter 1:4), and our past experience of his faithfulness to his word assures us that those promises shall all be fulfilled without fail. He has assured us that he will never leave us nor forsake us (Heb. 13:5), and we believe it shall be even as he has told us. He has assured us that he will come again and receive us unto himself, that where he is, there we may be also (John 14:1-3), and we believe it shall be even as he has told us. He has told us that there shall be a resurrection of the dead, both of the just and unjust (Acts 24:15), and we believe it shall be even as he has told us. In a word, if he has said he will do it, we believe he will do it. Over and over His word tells us that he is faithful. "Faithful is he that calleth you, who also will do it" (1 Thess. 5:24).

Nothing he has ever done has given us any reason to doubt his word. Everything he has done has given us every reason to believe he will always be faithful. Always and in every case, it shall be even as it was told us. He is immutable, and it can be no other way. What a blessing!

August 4

"Hitherto hath the Lord helped us" (1 Samuel 7:12)

As a monument to the victory that the Lord gave to Israel at Mizpeh over the Philistines, Samuel set up a stone and called it Ebenezer, which means "the stone of help" and he said, "Hitherto hath the Lord helped us." And thus may we, at any point in our lives, appropriately say the same. No matter what our age or what we have experienced in life, it is only by the help of the Lord that we have made it to the present hour. One of the verses of "Come, Thou Fount" says, "Here I raise my Ebenezer, Hither by Thy help I've come; And I hope by Thy good pleasure, Safely to arrive at home." Each day of our lives we may likewise set up our own *Ebenezer* and declare that "Hitherto hath the Lord helped us."

Just as Israel of old always had their enemies and were only victorious when the Lord helped them, so it is with his true followers today. They are constantly faced with the conflicts of life and with ever-present dangers, and must be always looking to the Lord for help. The devil, like a roaring lion, goeth about seeking whom he may devour, and the Lord's little ones need to be always watchful and prayerful lest the evil one should get an advantage of them.

It was a comfort to David to consider that though he was poor and needy, yet the Lord thought upon him, and he looked to him as his help and deliverer (Psalm 40:17). Some of the most beautiful language in the Bible is found in Isaiah 41:10 where the Lord says, "Fear thou not; for I am with thee: be not dismayed; for I am thy God: I will strengthen thee; yea, I will help thee; yea, I will uphold thee with the right hand of my righteousness."

And let us never forget that wonderful promise in Hebrews 13:5 and the words that follow in verse 6: "Let your conversation be without covetousness; and be content with such things as ye have: for he hath said, I will never leave thee, nor forsake thee. So that we may boldly say, The Lord is my helper, and I will not fear what man shall do unto me." May we go from day to day leaning upon the arm of the Lord, oft repeating those precious words, "Hitherto hath the Lord helped us."

August 5

"We do not present our supplications before thee for our righteousnesses, but for thy great mercies" (Daniel 9:18)

It is music to my longing ears to hear a man pray as did Daniel, confessing his sins and the sins of the people, and asking nothing on the basis of human merit or creature righteousness, but all in the name of the Lord and for his mercy's sake. In our old carnal flesh we have no glory of our own and no goodness we can claim, as one of the songwriters has indicated, and as the Scriptures so clearly proclaim. Not only must we make our petitions and supplications in the name of the Lord, but we must also have his mediation and intercession in order for our prayers to be acceptable to God. "For there is one God, and one mediator between God and men, the man Christ Jesus" (1 Tim.2:5). It is not the *woman*, Mary, but "the *man* Christ Jesus." *He* ever liveth to make intercession for *his* people (Heb. 7:25).

The text in Daniel brings to mind the fact that the Lord did not set his love upon Israel nor choose them because of anything in them, but based solely upon that which was in himself (Deut. 7:7). They were brought out of Egyptian bondage in such way as to clearly demonstrate that it was entirely by God's mercy and not anything in themselves. It was not because of any righteousness on their part or because of the uprightness of their hearts that the Lord drove out the heathen nations before them. It was because of the wickedness of those nations and because of God's faithfulness to his oath to the forefathers of the Israelites, Abraham, Isaac, and Jacob (Deut. 9:5).

As sinful creatures, having fallen in Adam, we can never expect access to God or blessing from his hand on the basis or our own righteousness or meritorious works. We must come empty-handed before him, pleading naught but Jesus' blood and righteousness. We must ask all things in the name of Christ and for his sake. His imputed righteousness is the only thing we, as his children, can plead. We are truly blest if we have been so dealt with of the Lord that we can come before him in this way, laying our souls prostrate before him and asking nothing but his mercies, realizing that we are all as an unclean thing, and all our righteousnesses are as filthy rags (Isaiah 64:6).

August 6

"Are not two sparrows sold for a farthing? and one of them shall not fall on the ground without your Father" (Matthew 10:29)

To me, this is a profound thought! The great creator of the universe takes notice of the fall of sparrows! Another amazing thought is that he has even numbered the hairs of our head. These things are given as reasons why we should not fear those who would persecute us, or even destroy our bodies. If God takes notice of sparrows, that are so numerous and so worthless in the eyes of men, shall he not take care of his people who are of more value than many sparrows? Shall he not take special notice of their afflictions? Shall he not be particularly mindful of their ill treatment, their heartaches and concerns? What a comforting thought!

It is more than my limited mental faculties can take in to think of the Lord taking notice of every sparrow that falls to the ground. Sparrows are so plentiful, and at times such a pest, that I have seen people trapping them in order to cut down on their population. Yet God is aware of each one of them, and is conscious of them when they fall. It was he who gave life to every one of them, and he knows when that life departs from them. And if he takes notice of such things as sparrows, shall he not much more take notice of those to whom he has given a never-dying soul. If he has so beautifully clothed the lilies of the field, shall he not much more clothe his people, even though they may often demonstrate little faith (Matthew 6:26-30).

If God takes notice of the fall of sparrows, what reason do we have to think that he does not likewise take notice of all his other creatures? It is he that causes the grass to grow for the cattle, and herb for the service of man (Psalm 104:14) and it is he that giveth food to all flesh (Psalm 136:25). The eyes of all wait upon him, and he gives them their meat in due season. He opens his hand and satisfieth the desire of every living thing (Psalm 145:15-16). How marvelous it is to consider that even though there are untold billions of living creatures upon the earth, the Lord still looks upon each of them as individuals and takes special notice of their own particular needs! Such a God is far beyond our comprehension, but it is just such a God to whom we look, and whom we embrace by faith and look upon as our all in all.

August 7

"As ye would that men should do to you, do ye also to them likewise" (Luke 6:31)

This is commonly referred to as "the golden rule," and Matthew says, "this is the law and the prophets" (Matt. 7:12). In other words, if we comply with this one directive, we will have essentially complied with all of God's precepts (Rom. 13:8; Gal. 5:14; 1 Tim. 1:5; James 2:8).

On one occasion a lawyer asked Christ, "Which is the great commandment in the law, and his reply was, "Thou shalt love the Lord thy God with all thy heart, and with all thy soul, and with all thy mind. This is the first and great commandment. And the second is like unto it, Thou shalt love thy neighbor as thyself. On these two commandments hang all the law and the prophets" (Matt. 22:35-40). We cannot violate the law with regard to our treatment of our fellow man without also violating the law with regard to our devotion to God.

A good example of this is found in 1 John 3:17; "But whoso hath this world's good, and seeth his brother have need, and shutteth up his bowels of compassion from him, how dwelleth the love of God in him?" It will avail us nothing to claim that we love the Lord if we treat our brother in this way. If we do not love our neighbor as our self, then obviously we do not love the Lord with all our heart.

If all men were to always comply with the directive set forth in Matthew 7:12 and Luke 6:31 this would be an almost perfect world. Of course that is a big *if,* and a great many people do not and will not observe this instruction, but if they did it would solve all the major problems in the world. Wars would cease, all locks would be removed from all doors, and there would be no crime, no prisons, no broken marriages and no quarrels between neighbors. If no one ever did anything unto others that they would not want done to themselves there would be no lawsuits and litigation and no problems too big to be settled privately among friends. Such is the divine superiority, and worthiness of the law of Christ. Oh, that men would abide by it!

May the Lord help us to examine all our steps before we take them, and to consider well all our words before we voice them, to be as sure as we can that we are not doing or saying anything to others that we would not want done or said to ourselves. It is a very serious matter to offend one of God's little ones (Mark 9:42; Luke 17:2).

ॐॐ

August 8

"Even so then at this present time also there is a remnant according to the election of grace" (Romans 11:5)

The apostle Paul asserted here that just as there was an elect remnant in Elijah's day, so there was also an elect remnant in his day. And we may safely conclude that in every period of man's history some of the elect family has lived. God chose them in Christ "before the foundation of the world" (Eph. 1:4), and he has a people "out of *every* kindred, and tongue, and people, and nation, whom Christ has redeemed to God by his blood and made them unto him kings and priests (Rev. 5:9-10). Even among those tribes and nations that long ago went out of existence, God had a people that were a part of the "remnant according to the election of grace." In all ages of time there have been "two manner of people" upon the earth—the righteous and the wicked. The first two people that were born into this world were on opposite ends of this spectrum. One was righteous and the other was "of that wicked one" (Matt. 23:35; 1 John 3:11).

All of God's elect, at some point in their lives, are born of the Holy Spirit, and therefore one reason we know that there are always some elect living upon the earth is because Christ said, "The hour is coming, *and now is*, when the dead shall hear the voice of the Son of God: and they that hear shall live" (John 5:25). That process is going on at all times, among God's elect throughout the earth. Because of his great love for them he is, and as long as the world stands will continue to be, quickening his people from death in sins into divine light and life at his own appointed time and according to his own will (John 1:13; 5:21; Eph. 2:1, 4-5).

A world in which there were no children of God would be a world that was too wicked to sustain life. Look how wicked it is even with them in it. What would it be without them? We see examples almost every day of men who count it their greatest glory to hurt, maim or kill others. What if these were the only kind of people in the world? We should be everlastingly thankful that "at this present time also there is a remnant according to the election of grace," and that the hour "now is" when the dead are hearing the voice of the Son of God and hearing with a hearing ear. If it were not so, all of us would be in a lot of trouble.

August 9

"Behold, I am the Lord, the God of all flesh: is there anything too hard for me?" (Jeremiah 32:27)

According to the religions of men there are many things that are too hard for the Lord. They proclaim a god who is doing his best, *trying* to do this and *trying* to do that, but failing at least as often as he succeeds. Every time I hear popular religionists speak they invariably bring up something the Lord *wants* to do or is *trying to do* but can't without man's cooperation. They seem to think that the God who created the universe with a word has somehow lost control over his creation. They appear to believe that the Christ who says in (John 17:2) that he has "power over all flesh" has somehow lost that power, and now all flesh has control over him. They speak as though they think the God that Paul said was "able even to subdue all things unto himself" (Phil. 3:21) cannot now subdue anyone without their permission.

They say Christ *wants* to save all mankind but can't because they won't let him. Therefore according to them, the answer to the question, "Is there anything too hard for the Lord," is *Yes*. For one thing, saving those that he has purposed to save is too hard for him according to them. If there was *anything* the Lord *wanted* to do and *couldn't* do, then there would be something that was too hard for him. But the Bible plainly tells us that his hand is not shortened that it cannot save (Isaiah 59:1). It also declares that "He doeth according to his will in the army of heaven, and among the inhabitants of the earth: and none can stay his hand, or say unto him, What doest thou?" (Dan. 4:35). The true God is yet in the heavens: "he hath done whatsoever he hath pleased" (Psalm 115:3), and "He shall not fail nor be discouraged" (Isaiah 42:4).

When Sarah laughed in unbelief at the message of the Lord that she would bear a son in her old age, he asked the question, "Is any thing too hard for the Lord?" (Gen. 18:14). The answer of course is *No*. God is omnipotent, and he still rules and reigns (Rev. 19:6). His power has not diminished one iota. His council shall stand, and he will do all his pleasure. If he has spoken it, he will also bring it to pass, and if he has purposed it, he will also do it (Isaiah 46:10). In view of such Scriptures, it is indeed strange that anyone would speak disparagingly of God.

August 10

"Lord, I believe; help thou mine unbelief" (Mark 9:24)

These were the words of the man who brought his son to Christ, desiring that he might be delivered from the foul spirit that had tormented him since he was a child. There appears to have been some uncertainty on the part of this man as to whether Christ was able to help his son. But when Christ turned the tables one him, so to speak, and said, "If thou canst believe, all things are possible to him that believeth," he wept and said, "Lord, I believe; help thou mine unbelief." I have thought that there was a possibility that the man was not so much guilty of unbelief as he was ignorant of how to express himself. At any rate, he was humble enough to acknowledge that his faith was not what it needed to be and to ask Christ to strengthen it.

Today we would think of the man's statement as being rather quaint, but I believe the context clearly indicates that he not only was aware of the defects in his faith but was also aware of the fact that Jesus was able to help him in that matter. Perhaps his faith was stronger than he knew. Only God can give us faith, and it is he alone to whom we should look for the increase of it.

I believe the apostles felt the same need this man did when they besought the Lord to increase their faith (Luke 17:5). It is contrary to nature for men to confess faults in themselves. It is also disagreeable to most men's temperament to weep. The man who besought Jesus to help his unbelief not only acknowledged his weakness, but he did it through tears. This makes me feel a kinship with him in Christ. I wish I had more tears such as those he shed.

I have always thought that some of the greatest unbelievers in the world are those who argue that belief is essential to obtaining eternal life. Such people do not believe in the total depravity of man. They do not believe in election and predestination. They do not believe in special atonement. They do not believe in irresistible grace or effectual calling, nor do they believe in the final preservation of the saints. Neither do they believe in church government as taught by Christ and his apostles. That is an awful lot of unbelief if you ask me, and they seem to be totally oblivious to the fact that they are unbelievers in that regard. I never hear any of them expressing a desire to have their faith increased. They seem to feel that they have enough of it as it is.

August 11

"Thy people shall be willing in the day of thy power"
(Psalm 110:3)

Many times we have heard it said that God will not save anyone against his or her will. If that were true, then he would never save anyone, because by nature man's will is only bent toward evil. His heart is "desperately wicked and deceitful above all things" (Jer.17:9), and therefore he cannot will or desire that which his very nature is opposed to and abhors. The things of the Spirit of God are foolishness unto him (1 Cor. 2:14), and his carnal mind (which is the only mind he has) is enmity against God. "It is not subject to the law of God, neither indeed can be. So then they that are in the flesh cannot please God" (Rom. 8:7-8). This being true, how long would it take such persons to desire spiritual things? The answer is obvious. Their only desire where God is concerned is that he depart from them, for they desire not the knowledge of his ways (Job 21:14).

God saves his people sovereignly. Because they *are* sons, he sends forth the Spirit of his Son into their hearts, crying, Abba, Father (Gal. 4:6). He does not do this in order to *make* them his sons, but as it is said, *because they* are (already) *sons*. They are his in the covenant of grace, which was established in eternity, and he cannot, and will not, lose any of them. He begins a good work in them and performs it until the day of Jesus Christ (Phil. 1:6).

The reason he can make his people willing at any time he pleases is because he has power over all flesh and gives eternal life to everyone of his elect (John 17:2). He is able to subdue all things unto himself (Phil. 3:21), and that includes the most obstinate, and hardhearted sinner who every lived. It is nothing to him to subdue a man's will. He can do it in an instant. What more striking example of this do we need than his taking a persecuting Saul and instantly laying him in the dust, and changing him into a devoted follower? Even the king's heart is in his hand, and, like the rivers of water, he turneth it whithersoever he will (Prov. 21:1).

August 12

"Except the Lord build the house, they labor in vain that build it"
(Psalm 127:1)

This verse and the following teach us that all our efforts, without exception, are vain if the Lord is not in them and adding his blessings. Some men have high ambitions of building up the numbers on their church rolls by methods that are not sanctioned in God's word. They labor in vain, for he will not bless that which he does not sanction. That which he has not authorized in his church is abominable to him, and he will not prosper that which he hates. For instance, drawing people into church membership by entertainment, and other such carnal methods, can never replace their being added to the church by the inward work of the Holy Spirit and his providential leadings. Nothing we do will ever prosper unless the Lord approves of our efforts, and he will not approve of those efforts unless they are in compliance with a correct understanding of his word.

One of the most common methods of those who refuse to be guided by God's word, is to claim, and avow, the blessings of the Lord upon their efforts. They speak glowingly of how wonderfully the Lord is showing his approval of what they are doing. They publicize their meetings and speak of what glorious times they had, what powerful preaching they had, etc. Those Israelites who danced around the golden calf that they had insisted Aaron make for them, would also have said they were having a wonderful meeting and a very good time, but their abomination was nonetheless displeasing to God. Their actions were in willful violation of his word and therefore were detestable.

"Be not deceived; God is not mocked: for whatsoever a man soweth, that shall he also reap. For he that soweth to his flesh shall of the flesh reap corruption..." (Gal. 6:7,8). And it does not matter how much he may talk about how blest his actions are, that will not alter the miserable consequences. If God is not in it, no matter what it is, it will not and cannot prosper spiritually, though it may appear ever so successful outwardly.

August 13

"For as often as ye eat this bread, and drink this cup, ye do show the Lord's death till he come" (1 Corinthians 11:26)

It is interesting to observe that the Lord nowhere instructed anyone to commemorate his *birth*, yet the world makes the supposed remembrance of that occasion the most celebrated time of the year. On the other hand, he *did* institute an ordinance that commemorates his *death*, and the world makes little of it. And generally when they do pretend to observe it they refuse to do so according to the instructions he gave his disciples. They substitute crackers for unleavened bread, and grape juice for fermented wine. But crackers and grape juice were not used in the Jewish Passover supper. Bread and wine were the substances used in *that* supper and these were the substances Christ used in instituting *his* supper. Those Corinthians mentioned in 1 Corinthians 11:21 did not get drunk on grape juice.

Our text tells us that someone will be observing this ordinance of Christ "till he come." Many people live in constant fear of some cataclysmic event prematurely bringing an end to this earth. I suppose all of us have known of those who predict the end of the world and then when the predicted date draws near they flee to the mountains and hide, as though that would do them any good. But this world will not end until Christ returns, and until that time there will be a faithful remnant still keeping the ordinance of the Lord's supper and thus "showing his death" in the use of those emblematic substances that he has authorized.

We of course rejoice in the fact that Christ was born into this world, but the end for which he came was to suffer, bleed and die for his people. They were not reconciled to God by the *birth* of Christ, but by his *death* (Rom. 5:10; Col. 1:21-22). And it was by his resurrection that he became "the firstfruits of them that slept" (1 Cor. 15:20). When we partake of his supper we express our faith in the efficacy of his shed blood and broken body. We declare our confidence that his death accomplished everything it was designed to achieve and that ultimately every heir of promise will live with him in Glory. It is good to know that he will always have his faithful followers, still showing his death, *till he come.*

August 14

"If any man love the world, the love of the Father is not in him"
(1 John 2:15)

There are two entirely different kinds of love mentioned here. One consists of an infatuation with, and craving for, the vain, sinful and degrading things of this "present evil world," and the other consists of a longing for, and devotion to, God and godliness. And it is an undeniable and unalterable truth that if a person's affections are set upon ungodly things, he does not at one and the same time love God and the things of God.

In an unregenerate state, men do not have a duel nature. They have not been made partaker of the divine nature and therefore they only have a *corrupt* nature. This is reflected in the fact that they *walk according to the course of this world*, and continually seek to fulfill the desires of the flesh and of the mind (Eph. 2:2-3). They have no interest in divine things because the love of God is not in them.

Let us look at the text from a positive standpoint. If we do *not* love the world, then the love of the Father *is* in us. If we have been killed to the love of sin, if our souls are vexed from day to day by the filthy conversation of the wicked, if we detest the counsel of the ungodly, etc., then we are blest characters indeed. If we are a lover of the humble followers of Christ and their fellowship is sweet to us, it is a very strong evidence that we have been begotten of God. "Whosoever believeth that Jesus is the Christ is born of God: and every one that loveth him that begat loveth him also that is begotten of him" (1 John 5:1). This is another way of saying that if we love the Begetter (God), we will also love those whom he has begotten (his people). Or, said another way, if we love him that gives spiritual birth, we will love those to whom he has given that birth.

The entire world is made up of those on the one hand who love the world, and those on the other hand who love God—those who do *not* have the love of the Father in them, and those who *do*—those who have divine life and those who do not. What a wonderful thing it is "to know the love of Christ, which passeth knowledge," and to "be filled with all the fulness of God" (Eph 3:19)! We have reason to be everlastingly thankful if we have been brought to love his great name.

August 15

"In hope of eternal life, which God, that cannot lie, promised before the world began" (Titus 1:2)

God would not have promised eternal life without having particular persons in mind to whom he was directing that promise. And if we can determine to whom he *gives* it, then we will know to whom he *promised* it. Christ himself gives us the answer when he says, "My sheep hear my voice, and I know them, and they follow me: and I give unto *them* eternal life; and they shall never perish," (John 10:27-30). Also in John 17:2 he tells us that he gives eternal life "to as many as" the Father has given him. These are "the children of promise" spoken of in Galatians 4:28 and to whom eternal life is assured.

God would not, and could not, promise eternal life to someone and then renege on the promise. That would make him a liar, which is an utter impossibility. What he has promised he is able also to perform (Rom. 4:21). Not only is he *able* to do what he has promised, but his faithfulness and impeccability *dictate* that he do so. Nothing he has promised can fail of fulfillment. Fortunately for his people, he is a God of stability and certainty; a God of purpose and design, determinate counsel, and immutability. "He is in one mind, and who can turn him? and what his soul desireth, even that he doeth" (Job 23:13). "Our God is in the heavens: He hath done whatsoever he hath pleased (Psalm 115:3).

It is very comforting and reassuring to think upon God's divine certainties. Let us look at a few more of them. "The counsel of the Lord standeth for ever" (Psalm 33:11). "There are many devices in a man's heart; nevertheless the counsel of the Lord, that shall stand" (Prov. 19:21). "The Lord of hosts hath purposed, and who shall disannul it?" (Isa. 14:27). "Thy counsels of old are faithfulness and truth" (Isa. 25:1). "My counsel shall stand, and I will do all my pleasure" (Isa.

46:10). "If it be of God, ye cannot overthrow it" (Acts 5:39). "Being predestinated according to the purpose of him who worketh all things after the counsel of his own will" (Eph. 1:11).

Popular religion paints a much different picture of God and makes him out to be less than his creatures, but we may be sure that if we are among those to whom he promised eternal life, we shall surely have it. It cannot be otherwise, for he cannot lie and his decrees cannot be altered. He does not change, and "therefore ye sons of Jacob (*ye chosen ones*) are not consumed" (Mal. 3:6).

August 16

"Christ hath redeemed us from the curse of the law, being made a curse for us" (Galatians 3:13)

The "us" in the text are the children of God. The apostle was writing "unto the churches of Galatia," not to the general populace. He is telling them that they have *been* redeemed. In other words, the work of redemption is done. Nothing can be added to it or taken from it. It is a finished work that Christ accomplished on the cross. There is no part of it left for man to do.

The elect have been redeemed by virtue of the fact that Christ took their sins upon himself and put those sins away. They had "sold themselves for nought," and were promised that they would be "redeemed without money" (Isaiah 52:3). Christ paid the price in full, and the transaction is done. They *have* redemption "through his blood." They *have* forgiveness of sins, "according to the riches of his grace" (Eph. 1:7). And *having* it, they cannot lose it. What Christ has done cannot come undone.

It is not possible that he should redeem someone and then those persons come unredeemed. If he has redeemed them they are redeemed forever, otherwise *he* would be a failure and his *work* would be a failure: "For the redemption of their soul is precious, and it ceaseth for ever" (Psalm 49:8).

The idea of people doing something in order to get themselves redeemed is ludicrous. But if they have *been* redeemed, and if they have been made aware of it, then they ought to behave in such a way as to show their gratitude to the Lord for his mercies. They ought to honor him by obeying his precepts and conforming their lives to his teachings. His word should be more precious to them than their necessary food, and they should worship him according to the pattern laid down therein. "He hath visited and redeemed his people" (Luke 1:68).

August 17

"As it is written, He that glorieth, let him glory in the Lord"
(1 Corinthians 1:31)

Men have nothing in themselves to glory in, for there is nothing good in their flesh (Romans 7:18). If they have any good in them God put it there, and he is due all the credit for that good. "Every good gift and every perfect gift is from above, and cometh down from the Father of lights" (James 1:17). "It is He that hath made us, and now we ourselves" (Psa. 100:3). He formed man of the *dust of the ground*, so that no one can glory in the substance from which he was made. He became corrupt in Adam and now even at his best fleshly state he is "altogether vanity," so he has no justifiable basis for glorying in his nature. His heart "is deceitful above all things, and desperately wicked" (Jer. 17:9) and consequently his glory is in his shame (Phil. 3:19).

Nothing is more unbecoming of poor fallen mortals than glorying in themselves and their own abilities and achievements. It is God who makes each of us to differ from others, and we do not have anything in the way of gifts and graces that we did not receive from his merciful hands (1 Cor. 4:7). "A man can receive nothing, except it be given him from heaven" (John 3:27). Therefore to glory in those things as though we had not received them is a great affront to God. If the works of our hands enjoy a measure of prosperity, God is due all the praise, for it is owing to his blessings. We are not sufficient of ourselves to even *think* anything as of ourselves; but our sufficiency is of God (2 Cor. 3:5).

The only legitimate glorying we may do is "in the Lord" and what he has done, in us, through us, and for us. If he had not lifted us out of the horrible pit of unregeneracy and placed our feet upon the solid Rock of our salvation, we would have remained forever in a state of death in sins and would have been forever ruined. We had no ability or desire whatsoever to lift ourselves out of that wretched state. If the Lord had not provided himself an offering for the sins of his people they could never have seen heaven. For these and all other blessings God is due *all* the glory. Indeed, "He that glorieth, let him glory in the Lord."

August 18

"Cast down but not destroyed" (2 Corinthians 4:9)

In the context the apostle shows us that it is possible to be troubled on every side, perplexed, persecuted, and cast down, and yet not be distressed, in despair, forsaken or destroyed. God's people need to remember that ultimate victory over all imaginable foes is theirs, and the last enemy that shall be destroyed is death. The final outcome will be inconceivably glorious, and consequently they may view their present afflictions as light and of comparatively short duration.

Their outward man is perishing, but their inward man is being renewed day by day. The Lord is on their side and will never leave them nor forsake them. "Weeping may endure for a night, but joy cometh in the morning" (Psalm 30:5). Hence, they should strive to keep their eye of faith upon the things that the natural eye cannot see—the things that are eternal. Temporal things often look terribly bleak and disheartening, but the things of God are always glorious and uplifting.

The Lord will not allow one of his children to totally and finally fall away and perish. It is an utter impossibility because they are preserved in Christ Jesus and called. Let those of us who have been raised with Christ in regeneration be always seeking those things which are above, "where Christ sitteth on the right hand of God," and let us set our

affection on things above, not on things on the earth. We'll be much
happier that way.

᭞᭞

August 19

"His epistles…in which are some things hard to be understood"
(2 Peter 3:16)

In view of the fact that the Bible is divinely inspired and that it
contains "the *mysteries* of the kingdom of heaven," it is somewhat
strange that so many people think it can be rewritten so as to be easily
understood by everyone. Those who are in an unregenerate state do not
receive the things of the Spirit of God at all (1 Cor. 2:14), and no matter
how clearly those things are expressed, that still remains true. But even
those who have been born of the Spirit find much of God's word "hard
to be understood." As much as the apostle Paul himself had been
shown, and as much divine revelation as he possessed, he was still
overwhelmed as he considered the depth of the riches both of the
wisdom and knowledge of God, and exclaimed, "How unsearchable are
his judgments, and his ways past finding out, for who hath known the
mind of the Lord!" (Rom. 11:33-34).

On one occasion Paul was caught up into paradise, and heard
unspeakable words, which it is not lawful for a man to utter (2 Cor.
12:4). If such things as he heard were couched in "unspeakable
words" do you suppose we could have understood them if we had heard
them? In these mortal, unglorified bodies, I don't think so. But be that
as it may, the apostle did not attempt to give us any details as to what
he heard, and I am sure that if the Lord had determined that we needed
to know, he would have told us.

As I read the epistles, I find a certain degree of consolation in the
fact that even the apostle Peter found some things in Paul's writings
that were "hard to be understood." It makes me realize that my failure
to fully comprehend certain things is not merely due to my own
personal dullness and lack of discernment alone, but that there are

actually some things in the Scriptures that are hard for anyone to grasp the depths of—even inspired apostles.

We read in various places where the desire is expressed that the Lord would give "wisdom and understanding" (1 Chron. 22:12; Psalm 119:125, 144, 169; 2 Tim. 2:7). The Ethiopian Eunuch (Acts 8:27) acknowledged to Philip that he could not understand what he was reading in Isaiah unless some man should guide him. Have we not also felt that way many times as we have studied God's word?

August 20

"Trust in the Lord with all thine heart; and lean not unto thine own understanding" (Proverbs 3:5)

What wonderful instruction! Oh that we may always have grace to heed its clarion call! How prone we fallen mortals are to turn to God only as a last resort rather than living in constant reliance upon him! How subject we are to forget, at least momentarily, that his ways and his thoughts are high above ours, "as the heavens are higher than the earth" (Isaiah 55:8). In view of this vast difference, why would we ever substitute our own understanding in the place of trust in God?

What a terrible sin Abraham and Sarah committed when they *leaned unto their own understanding* in the matter of trying to produce the child that God had promised them. God did not tell them to produce the child by another woman, but he had promised Abram that from his own loins he would be given a child in his old age. All that Abraham and Sarah produced by Hagar was a mocking Ishmaelite, and look what suffering their carnal plan has brought upon the world, from then until now. We are presently at war with the Ishmaelites. The Lord told Hagar before Ishmael's birth that he would be a wild man. "His hand will be against every man, and every man's hand will be against him" (Gen. 16:12), and so it has ever been. So much for trying to get ahead of the Lord rather than wholly relying upon him to fulfill his promise. We will always create trouble for others and ourselves when we fail to trust in him with all our heart.

August 21

"And this is the name whereby he shall be called, THE LORD OUR RIGHTEOUSNESS" (Jeremiah 23:6)

What a beautiful name! *Jehovah-tsidkenu,* The Lord Our Righteousness. He is our righteousness by imputation. The apostle Paul tells us that Christ is *made* unto us "wisdom, and righteousness, and sanctification, and redemption" (1 Cor. 1:30), and it is for this reason that the only glorying we are justified in doing is *"in the Lord."*

We have no righteousness of our own that would justify us in the eyes of God in an eternal sense. In that sense "we are all as an unclean thing, and all our righteousnesses are as filthy rags; and we all do fade as a leaf; and our iniquities, like the wind, have taken us away" (Isa. 64:6). If Christ had not fulfilled all the requirements of God's holy law in our behalf, we would all have been doomed to eternal misery. If he had not met all the demands of Divine Justice, and then if God had not made that obedience ours by imputation, we would never see his face in peace.

Christ taught that if the righteousness of his people did not exceed the righteousness of the scribes and Pharisees, they would in no case enter into the kingdom of heaven (Matt. 5:20). And why must their righteousness exceed that of the scribes and Pharisees? Because the only righteousness those people had was a self-righteousness, or a creature-righteousness, which as we have shown is as filthy rags in the sight of God. No amount of works or human merit can ever supply a righteousness that will stand us in good stead with him as the basis for our justification before his judgment bar.

David has beautifully described the blessedness of the man to whom the Lord "imputeth righteousness without works" (Psalm 33:1-2; Romans 4:6-8), saying, "Blessed is he whose transgression is forgiven, whose sin is covered. Blessed is the man unto whom the Lord imputeth not iniquity, and in whose spirit there is no guile." Those to whom the Lord imputes righteousness can never have their sins imputed to them, for those sins were imputed to Christ and were thus "cast into the depths of the sea" (Micah 7:19).

God chastises his people in a parental way, lovingly and correctively, because they are his sons, but Christ took upon himself the penalty that justice demanded of them, and which they could never have paid. Very truly and rightly is He called, THE LORD OUR RIGHTEOUSNESS! Praise his holy name!

August 22

"I have planted, Apollos watered; but God gave the increase"
(1 Cor. 3:6)

Paul had observed that the Corinthian brethren were showing divided sentiments toward the ministers that God had sent them— esteeming one above another. Consequently he reminds them that though these different servants had their own particular gifts, fitting them for the places to which God had called them, yet it was the Lord alone who made their labors useful and beneficial. It is *he,* and he alone, who makes us to differ one from another (1 Cor. 4:7) and none of us have anything worthwhile that we did not receive from him.

If we will always keep this in mind it will greatly assist us in maintaining a proper perspective as to what our feelings toward one another and toward our ministering brethren ought to be. No matter how gifted a man may be, no matter how great his gifts of oratory, no matter how keen his mind, no matter how amicable his disposition, if the Lord does not prosper his efforts, he will not be profitable. *God alone* gives the increase.

Paul also pointed out to the Corinthian brethren that since neither they nor their preacher brethren had anything of any value that they did not receive from the Lord, then it was very unbecoming of them to glory as though they had not received those things. As we consider these things, it becomes very obvious that jealousy and partiality among brethren is one of the most unreasonable things in the world. Why should I be jealous of my brother's gifts, when it is the Lord who gave them to him? Should I not rather rejoice that he has those gifts, and that he is using them to the glory of God and to the edification of

the church? God gives to each as seemeth good in his sight, and if each
servant properly uses what God has given him, it will redound to the
glory of God and will accomplish that for which it was given. His
labor will be just as important, and useful, in its place, as is anyone
else's.

May the Lord help us to always keep in mind this vital and important
truth, that there can be no increase unless he grants it. He is due all the
glory—*all* the glory—for any good that comes of anything we poor
mortals do. The proper attitude for us, when we have done all those
things which we are commanded to do, is to humbly acknowledge that
we are unprofitable servants (in and of ourselves), and have only done
that which was our duty to do (Luke 17:10).

August 23

"One day is with the Lord as a thousand years, and a thousand
years as one day" (2 Peter 3:8)

I have never known of any reason to think that the Lord operates on
the basis that it takes a thousand of our years to make one of his
days. I believe this is verified by Psalm 90:4, which tells us that a
thousand years in his sight are but as yesterday when they are past, and
as a watch in the night. Notice that in that text a thousand years in
God's sight is also *as a watch in the night*, which is not the same as *one
day*. Hence, it seems to me that these verses are simply telling us that
with God time has no significance from the standpoint of his
duration. When he refers to his pre-existence he does not says, "Before
Abraham was, I was," but rather "Before Abraham was, I AM" (John
8:58). He is the same "yesterday, and today, and forever" (Heb. 13:8).

I see no reason for an eternal God to have any use for time except as
it relates to his dealings with his creatures. He has made men of one
blood and has "determined the times before appointed, and the bounds
of their habitation" (Acts 17:26). And, it is not for us to know "the
times and seasons, which the Father hath put in his own power" (Acts
1:7). Even the devils are aware that there is a time appointed for their

torment (Matt: 8:29), and Satan knows that "he hath but a short time" (Rev. 12:12). We also read of a day when there shall "be time no longer" (Rev. 10:10).

The eternity of God is one of those characteristics or attributes that makes him incomprehensible to our finite minds. We know that he has always existed and ever shall exist but how this can be we know not. To our rational minds it seems impossible that such could be true, but by faith we believe him when he tells us in his word that he is "from everlasting, and to everlasting" and we add our "Amen, and Amen" (Psalm 41:13). If we could explain him or comprehend him, he would not be God. David expressed it well when he said, "Great is the Lord, and greatly to be praised; and his greatness is unsearchable" (Psalm 145:3).

August 24

"He shall save His people from their sins" (Matthew 1:21)

This is the proclamation of the angel of the Lord with regard to the salvation of God's people. There can be no uncertainty about the matter for it is founded upon the unalterable foreknowledge, choice, and predestination of God (Romans 8:27-39; Eph. 1:4-12). Not one of those who were given to Christ in the Covenant of Grace "before the foundation of the world" can ever be lost in an eternal sense, for they are "kept by the power of God through faith unto salvation" (1 Peter 1:4-5). Each one of them are saved, and called with an holy calling, not according to their works, but according to God's own purpose and grace, which was given them in Christ Jesus *before the world began* (2 Timothy 1:9).

In reply to these plain and undeniable declarations some will say, "But this would be unfair. What about those who want to be saved but cannot because they were not chosen?" To this illogical question we reply that the Bible makes it plain that it is only the wicked who will be eternally damned. The Bible says nothing about good people wanting to go to heaven but being prohibited because they were not elected. It is only those who are called with an holy calling who want to go to heaven, and even *they* must be saved by God's *mercy* and *grace*—and mercy and grace cannot be bestowed upon *meritorious* creatures. These words clearly imply a *lack* of merit.

Again, someone will say, "If God only saves *his people*, and their salvation is guaranteed, why should they not simply enjoy all the sin they desire while they live, for they will be saved anyway." This question implies that God's regenerated, born again people desire to sin, which is not the case. The grace of God in their hearts teaches them that "denying ungodliness and worldly lusts, (they) should live soberly, righteously, and godly, in this present world" (Titus 2:11-12). In the new birth they are killed to the love of sin and wish that they could avoid it altogether. They certainly have no desire to dishonor that precious One who called them, and they do not wish to pour contempt upon his name by sinning against him. Rather, they feel that they owe him their all in service and devotion for his great goodness toward them.

August 25

"For as by one man's disobedience many were made sinners, so by the obedience of one shall many be made righteous"
(Romans 5:19)

The two men mentioned in this verse are clearly Adam and Christ. It was Adam's disobedience by which many were made sinners, and it is the obedience of Christ that shall make many righteous. The *many* that were made sinners were all that Adam represented as their federal head; in other words, the whole human race. By the same token, the *many* that will be made righteous are those whom Christ represents as their federal Head; or, in other words, all those that were given to him by the Father (John 6:37; John 17:2). Therefore, "as in Adam all [i.e. that he represented] die, even so in Christ shall all [i.e. that he represented] be made alive" (1 Cor. 15:22).

Just as all of Adam's race, or the whole human family, had the consequences of his fall imputed to them, and thus were "made sinners," so, in like manner, the consequences of Christ's obedience is imputed to all the members of his elect family, and thus they are "made righteous." How clearly this is set forth, and yet how generally it is denied by the religious world!

Popular religion will not have it that the obedience of *one man* shall make many righteous. It maintains that righteousness is only acquired by the obedience of anyone who will have it. In other words, it argues that men can gain heaven only by their own obedience to certain conditions, and that it is left to each individual's discretion as to whether they will have it or not.

But what did mankind have to do with being made sinners in Adam? Nothing whatsoever. Adam's posterity was not consulted to see if they wanted to be made sinners by his *disobedience*. And so, by the same token, God's elect family, who likewise fell in Adam, are not consulted to see if they want to be made righteous by his *obedience*. The latter case is exactly like the former in that regard. Just as Adam's sin was imputed to his posterity, so also is the righteousness of Christ imputed to his people (Romans 4:6), and that "without works" on their part. It is only *believers* (already made righteous) who are exhorted to "maintain good works" (Titus 3:8), because unbelievers cannot please God (Heb. 11:6).

August 26

"The Lord knoweth them that are his" (2 Timothy 2:19)

The religious world speaks of Christ knocking at the door of men's hearts seeking entrance and promising that if they will open unto him, he will give them eternal life. They base this false idea on a total misunderstanding of Revelation 3:20, which has nothing at all to do with the unsaved but is dealing with a church.

If God were appealing to unregenerate sinners for entrance into their heart, that would indicate that God did not know whether they were going to respond or not. This cannot be true, for God knows all things. What would be the purpose of his appealing to someone that he knew was not going to respond?

The very foundation of God stands sure and it bears a seal. And part of that seal is that "the Lord knoweth them that are his." In his own time he visits each one of them and quickens them into divine life. In this life-giving work there is no powerless appeal to them for entrance, but rather an exertion of almighty power, sending forth the Spirit of Christ into their hearts, crying, Abba, Father (Gal. 4:6). Any open minded reader will observe here that God does not send His Spirit into their hearts in order to make them his sons, but he does that work *because they are sons.* They are his by divine election. He foreknew them in the covenant of grace before the foundation of the world and predestined them (Rom. 8:29-30). You see, he knows those who are his sons and those who are not, and he does not send his Spirit into the hearts of those who are not his. Clearly there are some who are "none of his" (Rom. 8:9) and whom he "never knew" in a covenant sense (Matt. 7:23). There are some who are "of their father the devil" (John 8:44). Such characters clearly are not members of God's elect family whom he chose in Christ Jesus before the world began (Eph. 1:4).

David said, "In thy book all my members were written, which in continuance were fashioned, when as yet there was none of them" (Psalm 139:16). And John said, "Jesus knew from the beginning who they were that believed not, and who should betray him." He knows those that are his, and these he exhorts to "depart from iniquity." Notice the latter part of that "seal" in 2 Timothy 2:19.

August 27

*"Most men will proclaim every one his own goodness: but a
faithful man who can find?"* (Proverbs 20:6)

Most men fall in the category of those who are spoken of in
Matthew 6:2,5,16 as hypocrites, who want others to see those
things they are doing that they think are good. They do this because
they like to call attention to themselves and want others to think they
are good. We would like to believe that such characters are in the
minority, but God's word declares them to be in the majority. "Most
men," means the majority of men. And in contrast to these, it is
difficult to find a "faithful" man.

Self-righteous men are not content to merely *think* of themselves as
good, but they feel that they must *proclaim* their supposed
goodness. They want the world to know how good they are. They can't
be quiet about it. But God's view of them is that they are "whited
sepulchres" who "appear righteous unto men, but within they are full of
hypocrisy and iniquity" (Matt. 23:27-28).

The only thing that can make a man see his own wretchedness by
nature, and to realize that he has no goodness in and of himself, is an
illuminating work of grace within his heart. This will quickly strip him
of his supposed merit and worth and lay him low in the dust of self-
abasement. It will enable him to understand such statements as Isaiah's
when he declared, "Woe is me! for I am undone; because I am a man of
unclean lips, and I dwell in the midst of a people of unclean lips: for
mine eyes have seen the King, the Lord of hosts" (Isaiah 6:5).

One such view of the King is all it takes to make a man lose all
interest in proclaiming his own goodness. When Job was blest with
such a view he said, "Behold, I am vile," and, "I have heard of thee by
the hearing of the ear: but now mine eye seeth thee. Wherefore I abhor
myself, and repent in dust and ashes" (Job 40:4; 42:5-6).

August 28

"My kingdom is not of this world" (John 18:36)

If this one fact were rightly taken into consideration by the religious world most of their erroneous notions with regard to the church and heaven would be eliminated. The true church is not a worldly organization. How could it then have a worldly headquarters?

Organized religion operates on worldly principles, and is like any other big business. It requires a worldly plan of operation and a worldly headquarters, from which all its worldly edicts are issued and through which all its worldly programs are funded and directed. This requires thousands of employees, tremendous office space, and millions of dollars, much of which is consumed in keeping up the bureaucracy.

The true church has never required any such machinery. It is a *spiritual* kingdom. Its *Head* (the Lord Jesus Christ) is in heaven and thus its *headquarters* are in heaven. It is governed by his inerrant Word, which was given by divine inspiration (2 Tim. 3:16; 2 Peter 1:21), and is a thorough furnisher unto all good works.

If the religious organizations of the world were driven into the dens and caves of the earth by persecution, most of their works (which they account good and necessary) would have to be left behind, for they could not drag along their organization with them. All their human means and instrumentalities would be effectively stymied. But not so with the Lord's church; it would continue to function essentially as it had before. Its simple form of worship, consisting of preaching, praying, and singing, would continue the same, as would the ordinances of baptism and the Lord's Supper. Truly, this is a kingdom that none can see, nor enter, except those who are born of the Spirit (John 3:3,5), and even among that class there are many who never live in this militant institution, though some of them are not far from it (Mark 12:34).

❦

August 29

"These little ones" (Matthew 10:42)

It is sobering to consider what the Lord has said about the little ones. He loves them with a love that is beyond all comprehension, and is so careful of them that even the very hairs of their heads are all numbered. The text shows that there is a reward for doing them kindness, and elsewhere we find that there is an awful curse for doing them injury (Matt. 18:6). God forbid that we should ever be guilty of offending them or despising them, or in any way abusing them! May he help us to always love and nurture the little ones and never do anything that would cause one of them to sin. What care must the Lord take of them if he attends them with angels? (Matt. 18:10).

Who are "these little ones"? They are such as have been converted and have become "as little children" in their humility and meekness, their felt weakness, and their total dependence upon their heavenly Father. It is of such as these that the kingdom of heaven consists (Matt. 19:14), little ones who are constantly looking to the Lord to provide all their needs and to lead them in the way of righteousness. The apostle John referred to these as "little children" numerous times in his epistles. He had a tender affection for them and nothing brought him more joy than to see them walking in truth (2 John 4).

A long time ago I believe the Lord began a work of grace in my heart that I hope has resulted in my becoming one of the little ones. So often I feel my weakness and my utter helplessness and need. Like the apostle Paul I feel to be the chief of sinners and less than the least of all saints. And since the Lord has stripped me of all dependence upon the feeble and fickle arm of flesh and laid me low in the dust of self-abasement, I must frequently and reverently prostrate myself before him and plead for his constant provision, compassion, love, mercy and watch-care. Without his constant attendance upon me and my countless needs I am ruined and undone. Dear reader, can you not witness with me in these feelings? May we always be kept little in our own eyes.

August 30

"My sheep hear my voice, and I know them" (John 10:27)

Contrary to what multitudes claim to believe, the Lord most assuredly knows, and has always known, those that are his. He does not have to wait to see who will believe on him in order to know who are his. He "knew from the beginning who they were that believed not, and who should betray him" (John 6:64). The very foundation of God has a seal with this inscription affixed to it, "The Lord knoweth them that are his" (2 Tim. 2:19).

It necessarily follows, then, that he is also fully aware of those who are *not* his (John 8:44). And because he knew his people in a covenant sense from all eternity, he is said to foreknow them (Rom. 8:29; 1 Peter 1:2). Hence, he chose them in Christ "before the foundation of the world" (Eph. 1:4).

When Paul was in Corinth abiding in the home of Aquila and Priscilla and his preaching had met with rejection from the Jews, he then went to the home of Justus. While there the Lord spoke to him in a night vision and said, "Be not afraid, but speak, and hold not thy peace: for I am with thee, and no man shall set on thee to hurt thee: for *I have much people in this city*" (Acts 18:1-10). This shows clearly and powerfully that "the Lord knoweth them that are his."

Corinth was a wicked city, yet the Lord had "much people" there, and it was to them that the apostle was sent. It is obvious that God did not direct Paul to Corinth in order to try to get some of them to become children of God because He *already* had "much people" there, even though the gospel had never been preached to them. Paul was sent to instruct those people in the truth and to save them from the religious ignorance and idolatry that abounded there and to establish a church there. The gospel ministry has never been intended to increase the number of God's elect family which he foreknew (Rom. 11:2).

Zacharias, filled with the Holy Ghost, prophesied, saying, "Blessed be the Lord God of Israel; for he hath visited and redeemed *his people*" (Luke 1:67-68). This is an accomplished work for a particular (peculiar) people—God's people—and it clearly shows that any efforts by modern religionists to increase his family constitutes a gross rejection of his word and a blatant refusal to believe that God has a foreknown and predestinated people.

August 31

"Because they have no changes, therefore they fear not God"
(Psalm 55:19)

The first and most vital change that the children of God undergo that the vessels of wrath never experience is the change from nature to grace. This change is wrought when the Lord takes up his abode within the hearts of his elect and imparts divine life into their souls, or quickens them by his Spirit. This is when they become new creatures in Christ, old things pass away and, behold, all things become new (2 Cor. 5:17). This change drastically affects them for the rest of their lives. It causes them to love the things they once hated and to hate the things they once loved.

God's people undergo many changes in their feelings and emotions as a result of the indwelling of the Spirit. Sometimes their love for the Lord flames high, and at other times it seems to flicker. He seems so close at times and on other occasions it seems that he is "clean gone forever." Their lives are indeed a mixture of joys and sorrows. They have a conflict between the flesh and the Spirit (Rom. 7:14-25; Gal. 5:16-17), and this is often a source of trouble to them and is the root of many of their changes.

The wicked know nothing of such things. "They are not in trouble as other men; neither are they plagued like other men" (Psalm 73:5). They are strangers to that soul-trouble that arises from a work of grace within the heart, and they have never known anything about the plague of sin. Neither have they ever known anything about the joys of communion with Christ.

There will be one final and glorious change for God's people when their vile bodies will be raised and fashioned like unto the glorious body of Christ. There will also be a change for the wicked, but it will be a dreadful and unalterable change—a change from which they can never escape. We who have a hope in Christ should be exceeding thankful for our changes.

September 1

"For ye know the grace of our Lord Jesus Christ, that, though he was rich, yet for your sakes he became poor, that ye through his poverty might be rich" (2 Corinthians 8:9)

This is a beautiful thought, beautifully expressed. And what Paul wrote to Timothy about it cannot be improved upon: "Without controversy great is the mystery of godliness: God was manifest in the flesh, justified in the Spirit, seen of angels, preached unto the Gentiles, believed on in the world, received up into glory" (1 Tim. 3:16).

Our Lord came from the shiny courts of heaven where he owned all things and condescended to take upon himself a sinless human nature into union with his divine nature and to assume a state in which he "had not where to lay his head" (Matt. 8:20). All this was done in order that his people, who have nothing of themselves, might one day possess heaven as "heirs of God, and joint-heirs with" himself (Rom. 8:17).

The life of every child of God is a rags-to-riches story. What wretched paupers they are in and of themselves! And yet, after a short stay here upon the earth, they will enter into riches beyond description and all the glory and beauty of heaven will be theirs. This will all be owing to what the Lord has done for them, dying for their sins, imputing his righteousness unto them, and at last changing their vile bodies and fashioning them like unto his own glorious body.

God's people are made rich in a spiritual sense when the Lord takes up his abode within their hearts in regeneration, but how much more glorious will be the riches of their eternal home! These riches will not consist of such things as silver and gold but in those indescribable pleasures that will attend the glorified state. They will be made perfect and will be totally absorbed in the inexpressible joy of the praises of their Lord forever. What wonderful riches!

September 2

"Many are my persecutors and mine enemies; yet do I not decline from thy testimonies" (Psalm 119:157)

As I reflect back upon the many years of toil and danger through which I have come I am filled with gratitude that the Lord has sustained me through it all and I have not become disenchanted with his precious truth. Many hardships and trials have arisen as a result of my striving to follow him in precept and example, but none of them have so disheartened or discouraged me as to make me decline from the dear old doctrines of grace. I have met with much mistreatment and strong disfavor in consequence of my refusing to compromise God's word and because of my unwillingness to conduct the affairs of his church on worldly principles and precepts, but none of these things have moved me. I still hold firm to God's precepts and desire no other. For this steadfastness in his truth I give him all the credit and thank him for his sustaining grace.

It strikes me as self-evident that the Lord's way has to be the best way, and to true believers it is the *only* way. And it also appears strange to me that anyone who claims to be a follower of Christ would want any other way. If the Lord's way is the best way, why then should they seek, or desire, another way? Why should anyone "decline from" a *perfect* way in preference to a very *imperfect* way.

The history of the Lord's church is fraught with untold examples of faithful servants whose persecutors, with all their seemingly limitless arsenal of ungodly means of distressing the saints, were not able to draw them away from God's testimonies. In fact, God's people have always prospered most in the Spirit when they have been most pressed and harassed by their enemies. The enemies of the church have often been the means, in God's hands, of drawing her into a more sacred nearness to Him. The more Israel's taskmasters afflicted them, the more they multiplied and grew (Ex. 1:12). The persecutions of men against the early church (overruled by the providence of God) was the means of dispersing her throughout the world in a way that nothing else ever did, and affliction and hardship has often been a means of purging dross from her ranks.

September 3

"No man can serve two masters" (Matthew 6:24)

No man has ever lived who loved the Lord with all his heart and served him with devotion and dedication, and at the same time loved the world and worldliness and served it with the same devotion and dedication. Our Lord made it very plain that no man can serve two masters, God and mammon. "Mammon" in the days of Christ was a common word for riches. This would encompass all material things of any natural value. Those persons whose hearts are set on such things are not, and cannot be, servants of the Lord. "Where your treasure is, there will your heart be also" (Matt. 6:21).

Mammon is a *master* over those who serve it, just as the Lord is *Master* over those who serve him. "To whom ye yield yourselves servants to obey, his servants ye are to whom ye obey; whether of sin unto death, or of obedience unto righteousness" (Rom. 6:16). Those who serve mammon, or the things of the world, are total slaves to those things. This *master* has full control over them and will continue to hold them in its firm grasp until or unless the Lord delivers them from its bondage. And it is certainly a great *bondage*. Those who are bound by it do not think so, yet it is true that they are in complete enslavement to it and have no desire to be freed from its ruthless grip.

God's people are taught not to be conformed to this world, but to be transformed by the renewing of their minds, that they may prove, or discern or show, what is that good, and acceptable, and perfect, will of God (Rom. 12:2). They are to set their affection on things above, not on things on the earth (Col. 3:2), for the "fashion of this world passeth away" (1 Cor. 7:31). The grace of God teaches them that "denying ungodliness and worldly lusts," they should live soberly, righteously, and godly, in this present world (Titus 2:11-12). And they are clearly told that the friendship of the world is enmity with God. Whosoever therefore will be a friend of the world is the enemy of God (James 4:4; 1 John 2:15-16). Oh, may he help us to serve him, and him alone!

$\wp\!\!\prec\!\!\wp$

September 4

"It is not in me" (Genesis 41:16)

Pharaoh had heard that Joseph could understand dreams so as to interpret them, and had brought him from the dungeon where he had been unjustly held. Pharaoh had dreamed the same dream twice and none of the magicians of Egypt could tell him what it meant, and when he approached Joseph about interpreting it, Joseph told him, *"It is not in me*: God shall give Pharaoh an answer in peace." In this we see the faithfulness of Joseph as a true servant of the Lord. He was quick to give God all the glory for the gifts and abilities he possessed. He took no credit to himself but said, "It is not in me."

Daniel did the same when he came before king Nebuchadnezzar and was asked by the king, "Art thou able to make known unto me the dream which I have seen, and the interpretation thereof?" Daniel too was faithful to give the credit to the One to whom it was due, saying, "There is a God in heaven that revealeth secrets" (Dan. 2:26-28). No true servant will take to himself the glory that is due only to his Lord. First of all he loves his Lord and desires nothing but his glory and honor; and secondly, he knows that God is a jealous God and will not give his glory to another (Isa. 42:8).

The same spirit is seen in Peter when Cornelius met him and fell down at his feet and worshipped him. Peter would have no part of it but took him up, saying, "Stand up; I myself also am a man" (Acts 10:25-26). It is also seen in Paul and Barnabas at Lystra when through them the Lord healed the man who had been crippled from his mother's womb and had never walked. When they realized that the people were making preparations to offer sacrifices to them, they rent their clothes and ran in among the people, crying out, "Sirs, why do ye these things? We also are men of like passions with you" (Acts 14:8-18).

All God's servants should always be careful to give God all the glory for any good that they are able to accomplish. They do not have anything worthwhile that they did not receive of the Lord and therefore they should never glory as though they had not received it (1 Cor. 4:7). And when commended for the fruitfulness of their labors let them always remember to say, "The Lord is due all the glory; *It is not in me.*"

September 5

"Fear not: for they that be with us are more than they that be
with them" (2 Kings 6:16)

These were the words of Elisha the prophet to his servant when they were in Dothan and surrounded with the hosts of Syria's armies. Benhadad, the king of Syria, had sent his hosts to apprehend the prophet because he had been disclosing all of Benhadad's secret counsels to the king of Israel and thus thwarting his evil designs against Gods people. All Elisha's servant could see was the Syrian army, and with great consternation he asked the prophet, "Alas, my master! How shall we do?" Elisha then prayed that the Lord would open the servant's eyes, and when he did so the servant saw that "the mountain was full of horses and chariots of fire roundabout Elisha." Hence, those that were with Elisha and his servant were more in number than the Syrian armies that surrounded them.

You will recall that when the great multitude came to the Garden of Gethsemane with swords and staves to arrest Christ, Peter whipped out his sword and cut off the ear of one of the servants of the high priest. Christ put the man's ear back on and told Peter, "Put up again thy sword into his place...thinkest thou that I cannot now pray to my Father, and he shall presently give me twelve legions of angels?" (Matt. 26:53). One legion of Roman soldiers consisted of about six thousand men. But the truth is that Christ could have overcome any number of soldiers by himself, as is shown in John 18:1-6.

We can only wonder how many times we may have been delivered from various dangers and never knew that the Lord's angels were around us. What awesome sights might we behold if our eyes were opened to see the spirit world! It is no doubt a great blessing that we cannot see the fowl and loathsome spirits that would destroy us if they had leave of God to do so. And it is likewise a blessing that we normally cannot see the angelic spirits, for we have instances in the Scriptures when even the saints were frightened by the appearance of angels until they were told to "Fear not." But what a comfort it is to know that no matter how great our enemies may be, nor how much we may seem to be in the minority, if God is on our side we are in the majority! "They that be with us are more than they that be with them."

September 6

"Emmanuel, which being interpreted is, God with us"
(Matthew 1:23)

There is no other way to view this interpretation other than that Jesus is God. "The Word was God," and "the Word was made flesh, and dwelt among us" (John 1:1, 14). The apostle Paul described this wonderful transaction thus; "Great is the mystery of godliness: God was manifest in the flesh" (1 Tim. 3:16). The thing that most irked the religious leaders of the Jews with Christ and most inflamed their hatred of him was the fact that both in his words and his deeds, he showed himself to be "equal with God" (John 5:18). And the apostle tells us that Christ "thought it not robbery" to occupy that exalted position (Phil. 2:6).

Christ himself very plainly declared his deity on numerous occasions. Without any reservation he asserted that he and his Father were one, and that the Father was in him and he was in the Father (John 10:30, 38). He said, "he that seeth me, seeth him that sent me" (John 12:45). "Philip saith unto him, Lord, show us the Father, and it sufficeth us. Jesus saith unto him, Have I been so long time with you, and yet hast thou not known me, Philip? He that hath seen me hath seen the Father; and how sayest thou then, Show us the Father?" (John 14:8-9). The apostle Paul declares that "in him dwelleth all the fullness of the Godhead bodily" (Col. 2:9); that he is the brightness of his Father's glory, and the express image of his person; that he upholds all things by the word of his power, and that he, by himself, purged our sins (Heb. 1:3).

How clearly and powerfully do the works of Christ prove his Godhood. He restored sight to the blind, raised the dead, stilled the tempest and many other miracles too numerous to mention, even if we had knowledge of all of them. And he was, and is, "God with us." He was, and is, the representative of God unto us. That is, in our present state he is as close as we can come to looking upon the Father himself, for he, in his person, represents to us all that God is, or all that we are capable of comprehending of God. What a blessing it is that we have such a beautiful picture of him presented to us in his blessed word. May we dwell much in it and hide it in our hearts.

September 7

"Jesus Christ the same yesterday, and today, and forever"
(Hebrews 13:8)

How wonderful a subject for contemplation is the immutability of Christ. One of the poets once wrote, "Change and decay in all around I see," and thus it is with all of us. Hence it is impossible for us to fully comprehend a being who *does* not change and *will* not change because he *cannot* change. A being who is perfect in all his *works*, perfect in all his *ways*, perfect in all his *knowledge*, and perfect in all his *law*, never has any *reason* to change (Deut. 32:4; 2 Sam. 22:31; Psalm 18:30; Job 37:16; Psalm 19:7). He does not have to adapt to events and circumstances because he has known all things from all eternity; hence, no contingency can take him by surprise.

With him there is no variableness, neither shadow of turning (James 1:17). This is true because any change on his part would reflect imperfection. Even a *shadow* of turning would prove him to be changeable and would show that his original course was not what it should have been. Anything in the Scriptures that might appear to us to represent a change on God's part is simply a change in his dispensations toward men and is not a change of mind or purpose on his part. God's purposes, no matter who or what they relate to, are, like him, eternal. Hence, for him to make new decrees or establish new aims would be for him to change. It would be for him to vary or turn from his previous course of action.

"I am the Lord, I change not; therefore ye sons of Jacob are not consumed" (Malachi 3:6). If the salvation of God's people were not "according to the purpose of him who worketh all things after the counsel of his own will" (Eph. 1:11), then it would not be sure to any of them. However, the Scriptures make it very clear that the final abode of the heirs of promise is an inheritance (1 Peter 1:4), not a reward for good works. And that inheritance is "reserved in heaven for (those) who are kept by the power of God *unto* salvation." Not only is that inheritance *reserved* for them, but it is *incorruptible*. That is, it cannot be *corrupted*. It cannot be *defiled*, and it cannot *fade away*. It other words, it cannot be changed in any way. What a blessing it is that we have an unchangeable God and Savior!

September 8

"I will put a new spirit within you" (Ezekiel 11:19)

What a glorious change is wrought in a child of grace when the Lord visits him with irresistible power and quickens him into divine light and life! He takes out the stony heart and gives him "a heart of flesh," or, in other words, a soft and tender heart, made so by his indwelling Spirit. This is such a miraculous operation that only God can perform it, and it is altogether without human input or instrumentality in any way, shape, form or fashion. It is so obvious and profound an instance of divine power that it is spoken of as *a new creation* (2 Cor. 5:17). And its effect upon the subjects of it is so profound that the things they had previously loved lose their former appeal, and the things they had despised become the most precious things in their lives. "Old things are passed away; behold, all things are become new." It is indeed a life-changing experience.

Multitudes have been deceived into believing that this spiritual birth (John 3:5-6) is obtained simply by mouthing the words of a prayer that some unenlightened person has written, saying that they realize their sinfulness and have accepted Christ as their Savior. This cheapens it and makes it into a weak and beggarly thing and a path that the most wicked, filthy and abominable creatures on earth may traverse. Such a thing is far beneath the perfect integrity and infinite majesty of the eternal God. He would never associate himself in any way with such an abomination. The new birth is strictly a divine transaction in which he alone is active and his people are totally passive. The vile and detestable sons of Belial will never be able to approach unto the hallowed courts of the Lord, nor will they ever have any holy desires or aspirations.

There is a good reason why the new birth is always spoken of in terms that exclude all actions or contingencies on the part of those upon whom the Lord chooses to bestow it. "You hath he quickened (or given life), who were dead in trespasses and sins" (Eph. 2:1, 5). The new birth is a resurrection; a *giving of life to the dead.* It is a moving of God toward men who are incapable of moving toward him. It is a translation from the power of darkness into the kingdom of God's dear Son (Col. 1:13). Hence, it is the work of God alone—bestowed, in every case, upon undeserving characters.

September 9

"The gospel of your salvation" (Ephesians 1:13)

In a word, the gospel tells God's people how they were saved. The word *gospel* means *glad tidings,* or, *good news.* The apostle could have said, "The *glad tidings* of your salvation." But it cannot be the good news of your salvation unless you have been saved. There are no glad tidings for you if the Lord has not saved you. The thing that makes the gospel good news to God's people is the fact that it tells them how, and by whom, they were saved.

If the views of popular religionists were correct, then it would have to have read, "The news of how you may *get* saved," or, "The news that you have been *offered* salvation." And this could never be good news to spiritually dead folks, because they are not sensible of any need for salvation. That is why the "good tidings" are only preached (effectually) to the *meek.* It is why the gospel only binds up *"the brokenhearted,"* and proclaims liberty only to "the captives," and only comforts *those that mourn* (Isaiah 61:1). It is why only "the poor" (the *spiritually* poor) have the gospel preached *to them* (Matt. 11:5). No one else is interested in it. No one else can understand it.

If a person feels a need of salvation they are already born of the Spirit. In fact, such a sense of need arises from the new birth rather than being the *cause* of the new birth. The Lord told Israel that he would leave in the midst of them an afflicted and poor people, and that *they* would trust in the name of the Lord (Zeph. 3:12). Those are the only ones who have ever truly trusted in the Lord. They are the only ones who can.

There is a timely sense in which the gospel saves "the brethren" (1 Cor. 15:1-2), but it is never instrumental in the eternal salvation of anyone. That is alone by the grace and mercy of God. The gospel will save us from many errors and other hurtful things, *if we keep it in memory,* but it was never intended as a tool to save us eternally.

September 10

"He hath done all things well" (Mark 7:37)

These words were uttered by those who witnessed Christ's healing of a person who was deaf and who had a speech impediment. They expressed a great truth, but as I meditate upon them I view them also as a great *understatement.* Christ not only did all things well, but he did them perfectly. By virtue of the fact that he was, and is, perfection personified, everything he has done, or will do, is done the very best way it can be done, and he always gets it right the first time. His perfection leaves no room for trial and error; no room for correction or later improvement; no room for regret that it was not done a better way. Perfect knowledge of all things, past, present and future, (omniscience) will not allow for any flaws or defects, and infallibility will not allow for any imperfection. Hence, Christ went far beyond simply doing all things *well*—He did all things transcendently, immaculately, and superlatively, so that those who witnessed his works of healing "were beyond measure astonished."

Even His own countrymen, who were loath to believe him, were astonished at his teachings and said, "Whence hath this man this wisdom, and these mighty works?" (Matt. 13:54). We, even as weak mortals, may perform many tasks *well,* but we cannot perform the "mighty works" that Christ performed, and neither can we do anything *to perfection* in the same sense as he.

I have always subscribed to the old adage that if anything is worth doing, it is worth doing well, and in all things I strive to measure up to that maxim, but sometimes I succeed and oft times I fail. Christ never failed. He never even came close to failing, because all power was given unto him, in heaven and in earth (Matt. 28:18; John 17:2). Where omnipotence dwells, imperfection must flee away.

Christ did not merely accomplish our redemption *well,* but he accomplished it to perfection. He did it gloriously and completely, and God was well pleased with the performance of all that he gave the Son to do. As a glorious testimony to that fact he received him again into heaven where he ever lives to make intercession for the saints. And he is doing *that* to perfection too. Yes, true enough, he did all things well, but he did them *extraordinarily* well and we marvel at his greatness and glory.

September 11

"But ye believe not, because ye are not of my sheep"
(John 10:26)

Popular religion puts it just the other way around and says, "You are not of the Lord's sheep because you won't believe," but the Bible always gets things in their proper order. In the case of these unbelieving Jews, they did not believe because they were not children of God. In other words, they were not members of the family of God.

Those who are not of God's sheep, or his elect, are never given divine life, and therefore never possess true faith. Christ said of this class, "Ye are of your father the devil, and the lusts of your father ye will do" (John 8:44). Hence, as the Scriptures declare, they are known by their fruits (Matt. 7:16). They are evil, and therefore their fruits are evil. Faith is one of the fruits of the Spirit of God (Gal. 5:22), and therefore those who do not have the Holy Spirit abiding within them are incapable of bearing spiritual fruit.

The apostle Paul says to the Galatian brethren, "Because ye *are* sons, God hath sent forth the Spirit of his Son into your hearts" (Gal. 4:6). Notice how clearly the order is stated here. It was because they *already were* sons of God that he sent forth the Spirit of his Son into their hearts. It was not *in order to make them sons,* but *because they were sons.*

God does not send forth His Spirit into the hearts of those who are "none of his" (Rom. 8:9). And if God never sends forth the Spirit of Christ into a person's heart, that person will forever remain dead in trespasses and sins (Eph. 2:1,5) and will never embrace, comprehend, or discern spiritual things (1 Cor. 2:14). He will never *believe* in God, *love* God, or desire the *things* of God. Like Jesus said to the non-elect Jews, they will die in their sins (John 8:21), and they will suffer the just penalty for their wretchedness and iniquity, which is eternal punishment and damnation (Matt.25:46; Mark 3:29). Only God's chosen people will ever believe onhHim in the sense of trusting in him and viewing him as their all in all. Happy are we if the fruits of the Spirit are visible in our lives, for that indicates that we are the sons of God.

September 12

"I have spoken it, I will also bring it to pass" (Isaiah 46:11)

This verse makes it very clear that if God has said a certain thing will come to pass, it *will* come to pass. It also makes it clear that he will do whatever he has purposed to do. "He will work, and who shall let [or hinder] it?" (Isaiah 43:13). This speaks of the future, but with regard to the past we are told that "He hath done whatsoever he hath pleased" (Psalm 115:3). Therefore, not only has he done whatsoever he was pleased to do in the past, but he will do whatever it pleases him to do in the future. He is not the failure that the religious world declares him to be—trying to save everybody, but unable to save anybody unless they let him. "He shall not fail nor be discouraged" (Isaiah 42:4). He has never failed at anything he undertook to do, and he never will. He is incapable of failure. Neither does he, nor can he, get downcast and distraught. He is immutable, all-wise and all-powerful, and therefore never has any occasion to become discouraged. "He is the same yesterday, and today, and forever" (Heb. 13:8). In other words, he changes not (Malachi 3:6).

This is the God that the Bible describes, and this is the God that Primitive Baptists have rejoiced in and trusted in down through the centuries. They will not acknowledge any other. Their experience has taught them that they cannot put their confidence in the flesh (Phil. 3:3) and it has convinced them of the vanity of the gods of men. Like the three Hebrew children, they will not serve those gods (Dan. 3:18). They will not because they know those gods are the inventions of men and have no power to reach their case.

The God of the Bible is a God of purpose. He does nothing "at a venture" but "worketh all things after the counsel of his own will" (Eph. 1:11). Both the salvation and the calling of his elect are "according to his own purpose and grace, which was given (them) in Christ Jesus before the world began" (2 Tim. 1:9). Therefore there can be no uncertainty about it. It is not "according to their works" but according to his own eternal decrees and edicts. He has purposed it, and we may rest assured that he will bring it to pass. He does not operate on the basis of any degree of indecision, vacillation or shadow of doubt.

September 13

"Thou only, knoweth the hearts of all the children of men"
(1 Kings 8:39)

The apostle tells us in Hebrews 4:13 that "all things are naked and opened unto the eyes of him with whom we have to do." And the Lord asks the following very interesting questions in Jeremiah 23:24,

"Am I a God at hand, and not a God afar off? Can any hide himself in secret places that I shall not see him? Do not I fill heaven and earth?" Not only does God see what we do, but he knows why we do it, and no thought or deed can be concealed from his all-seeing eyes.

What a vain thing it is when men think the Lord will not see what they do (Job 22:13; Ps. 10:11)! What a vivid illustration of the sad effects of Adam's transgression that he would try to hide himself from the Lord in the Garden! Whether naked or clothed with fig leaves, we are fully exposed to the view of our Maker. "Hell and destruction are before the Lord: how much more then the hearts of the children of men?"

It was very clear when Christ walked among men that he knew their thoughts (Matt. 12:25; Luke 6:8; 11:17). No man can explain how the Lord could do this, but not only did he know their thoughts when he was with them, but it is obvious to me that he knew the thoughts they would have before they existed. How could he *declare* the end from the beginning (Isaiah 46:10) unless he *knew* the end from the beginning? No thought can be withheld from him (Job 42:2). "Known unto God are all his works from the beginning of the world" (Acts 15:18).

It is a solemn thing to realize that the Lord knows our heart, but to the child of God it is also a very comforting consideration. Many a time men may misjudge us, and they may even attribute the worst of motives to us even when we have nothing but the purest of motives, but we take comfort in the knowledge that the Lord fully knows our hearts and will deal with us accordingly. "I the Lord search the heart, I try the reins, even to give every man according to his ways, and according to the fruit of his doings" (Jer. 17:10). How amazing and wonderful is this great Creator of heaven and earth!

September 14

*"Women received their dead raised to life again: and others
were tortured, not accepting deliverance; that they might obtain
a better resurrection"* (Hebrews 11:35)

Many have wondered what the "better resurrection" of this
text is. I will here give my thoughts on it for the reader's
consideration.

W. E. Vine, in his Dictionary of New Testament words gives us one
of the first meanings of the word *resurrection* as, "A raising up, or a
rising up." As the resurrection of the bodies of God's people is a ri*sing
up*, or *deliverance* from corporeal death, I believe the "better
resurrection" of Hebrews 11:35 is speaking of a deliverance that those
who were tortured for their faith viewed as being much better than the
deliverance they would have received if they had recanted or
denied their faith in order to escape torture.

In the 37th verse we read of some who were stoned, sawn asunder,
and otherwise slain, but these who are mentioned in verse 35 are only
said to have been *tortured*, **not put to death**. The reason they did not
accept deliverance from that torture was because they knew that it
would be a far better "rising up" or deliverance, or resurrection, to have
the peace of mind and conscience that came with knowing that they had
not denied their God and their faith but had remained faithful to Him
and His cause. This should be a great encouragement to God's people
of all ages to be faithful to God no matter what they may have to suffer
for it.

September 15

"The love of money is the root of all evil" (1 Timothy 6:10)

Many times we have heard it said that money is the root of all
evil; but that is not what the apostle said. He was not speaking
here merely of money, but of the *love* of money. The *love* of money is
the root of all evil. An inordinate desire for material wealth is the root

of all evil, or in other words, all *kinds* of evil. There are *acts* of evil that are not related to the love of money. For instance, in the case of Cain slaying Abel, we find no way in which this evil deed involved the love of money, however, the love of money may be found to underlie all *types* or *classes* of evil. It is not necessarily involved in *every act* of evil or in every evil thought.

Covetousness may be defined as an inordinate or excessive desire for material possessions. Such possessions are usually obtained with money. Hence a great many people are caught up in this terrible vice, even though it is strongly warned against by Christ and his apostles. The apostle Paul said, "Let your conversation be without covetousness; and be content with such things as ye have: for he (*the Lord*) hath said, I will never leave thee, nor forsake thee" (Heb. 13:5).

I believe that when the apostle says, "Be content with such things as ye have," he simply means for us to be content with what we have until we can legitimately, and honorably improve our lot—if it needs improving, materially or otherwise. He is not saying that it is all right for us to stay in a state of poverty and not try to improve our situation if we can, but he is saying that in our present state we should be happy, thankful and reconciled to what the Lord has blest us with and not be coveting what others have or lusting for more of this world's perishable goods. He himself had learned, in whatsoever state he was in, therewith to be content (Phil. 4:11). What a wonderful lesson that is, and how we all need to learn it, if we have not already done so!

What a powerful reason the Lord gives us in Hebrews 13:5 for not being covetous or desiring more and more of this world's goods! He has assured us that *he will never leave us nor forsake us.* This being true, why should we inordinately trouble ourselves about how much wealth we have laid up for the future? One of the names of God is *Jehovah Jireh*—meaning, *The Lord will Provide* (Gen. 22:14). Let us trust his word explicitly and never be found *loving* money.

September 16

"He that knoweth God heareth us; he that is not of God heareth us not" (1 John 4:6)

John draws a clear distinction here between those who are of God and those who are not. He begins the chapter by declaring that many false prophets are gone out into the world, and he tells us that these prophets are of the world. Consequently they *speak* of the world and the world *hears* them. In other words, their ministry is a worldly ministry that is received and embraced by worldly people.

In contrast to this, John says, "We are of God: he that knoweth God heareth us; he that is not of God heareth us not. Hereby know we the spirit of truth, and the spirit of error." Using this test the followers of Christ still today may determine those who are motivated by the spirit of truth and those who are motivated by the spirit of error.

A person who is "not of God" simply cannot hear the "joyful sound" of that gospel which was preached by Christ and his apostles, and which is still preached today by those that God has *put into the ministry* (1 Tim. 1:12). Some of those to whom Christ himself preached were "not of God," and to them he said, "Why do ye not understand my speech? even because ye cannot hear my word. Ye are of your father the devil, and the lusts of your father ye will do" (John 8:43-44). Spiritual hearing requires spiritual discernment, or understanding, and natural men (those who are yet spiritually unborn) have no such discernment (1 Cor. 2:14). It requires an "ear to hear" (Rev. 2:7, 11, 17, 29), and without that spiritual "ear" there can be no hearing of spiritual things. The things of the spirit of God are hidden from the wise and prudent and revealed unto babes (Matt. 11:25). And, it is given unto some to know the mysteries of the kingdom of heaven, but to others it is not given (Matt. 13:11).

The apostle Paul said, "We speak the wisdom of God in a mystery, even the hidden wisdom, which God ordained before the world unto our glory; which none of the princes of this world knew..." (1 Cor. 2:7). If everyone had the ability to receive the gospel, such scriptures would have no place.

৩৯ৎৎ

September 17

"He taught them as one having authority, and not as the scribes"
(Matthew 7:29)

The scribes were for the most part Pharisees, and were looked upon by the Jewish people as being highly educated in the Law of Moses. However, they mainly taught the traditions of the elders and they wasted a great deal of their time in trifling disputes and debates about things that were of no benefit to anyone. But Christ possessed the authority of heaven and everything he did or said was directly to the point and was useful and instructive. He wasted not a moment in idle chatter or in any other pointless activity. There was no area in which he was lacking in wisdom and knowledge. He was perfectly attuned to the mind and will of his Father in heaven, and consequently he never misspoke or erred to any degree whatsoever. He always spoke the truth, and therefore could never be successfully contradicted or refuted. Even at twelve years of age he astounded the doctors of the Law with his understanding and answers (Luke 2:42-47).

The scribes could not speak with the authority that Christ spoke with because they were neither sent of God nor did they abide strictly by the authority of the Scriptures. But Jesus was given all power, in heaven and in earth (Matt. 28:18), and many hearing him were astonished, saying, "From whence hath this man these things? and what wisdom is this which is given unto him..." (Mark 6:2). Others said, "Never man spake like this man" (John 7:46). His divine authority was clearly manifest by His power over even the unclean spirits, who were compelled to obey him when he commanded them (Mark 1:27).

We have heard many men professing to speak in the name of the Lord, but who gave no evidence that they spoke with authority. There is a power and unction that accompanies the words of those who has been called of God to the ministry that does not attend the words of those who have not been called. If a man has been divinely called he will at least at times speak "in the demonstration of the Spirit and of power" (1 Cor. 2:4). He will not use enticing words of man's wisdom nor the wisdom of this world, but he will speak the wisdom of God in a mystery, even the hidden wisdom which God ordained before the world unto our glory (vs. 5-7). He, like Jesus, will stay within the bounds of God's revealed will and his inspired word and not fool around with vain speculation or with man's uninspired ideas and notions.

September 18

"God be merciful to me a sinner" (Luke 18:13)

Unless the mighty hand of God has touched a man and shown him what a wretch he is by nature, he will never understand this prayer. Such a prayer can only arise in the heart of one who has been brought to the end of his own strength and made to realize that he is empty handed so far as possessing anything that he might plead before the bar of God as a justifying righteousness. Notice the contrast between the poor publican who prayed this prayer and the self-righteous Pharisee who was also in the temple praying.

The publican stood afar off and would not so much as lift his eyes unto heaven, but smote upon his breast, saying, "God be merciful to me a sinner." But the proud Pharisee stood and prayed *with himself,* saying, "God, I thank thee, that I am not as other men are, extortioners, unjust, adulterers, or even as this publican. I fast twice in the week, I give tithes of all that I possess." The publican was *bowed,* a consciousness of his guilt and unworthiness preventing him from even looking upward. The Pharisee *stood* and *prayed with himself,* egotistically feeling himself to be too pure for the defiling company of others. The publican did not rely upon one tiny spark of merit, but simply pleaded for *mercy.* The Pharisee proudly boasted of his good character and all his honorable deeds, and never showed the slightest indication of soul-trouble or feelings of need, or any awareness whatsoever of his corrupt state by nature.

But what was the standing of these two men in the eyes of God? The publican went down to his house justified, but the Pharisee did not. And what man on the planet could have convinced this Pharisee that he was not one of the greatest men the earth ever produced? He is like many others that we have known. God forbid that we should ever fill his self-exalted shoes! Rather, let us ever be humble, realizing as did Jacob, that we are not worthy of the least of all the mercies, and of all the truths that God has shown unto us, his servants (Gen. 32:10). If we feel otherwise, we are sure to be brought down in God's own time.

ა

September 19

"Who hath first given to him, and it shall be recompensed unto him again?" (Romans 11:35)

Such a thing can never be, yet men in their native blindness and ignorance have such a high opinion of themselves that they think they can bring God under obligation to them to give them eternal life. They fancy that they can first give their hearts to God and as a result he must then recompense them with salvation. Their notions in this regard arise from the vain assumption that their hearts are so good that surely God must want them.

But let us weigh this argument against what his word says of man's heart. The prophet Jeremiah said, "The heart is deceitful above all things, and desperately wicked: who can know it?" (Jer. 17:9). Christ spoke of it as the fountainhead of all kinds of evil (Matt. 15:19; Mark 7:21). Solomon said, "The heart of the sons of men is fully set in them to do evil" (Ecc. 8:11); and again, "The heart of the sons of men is full of evil, and madness is in their heart" (Ecc. 9:3). What would a pure and holy God want with such a vile and corrupt heart?

God's blessings flow from grace and mercy, not from a debt on his part. The only merit anyone has is that which God puts within them. He does not bargain with them, but he takes the stony heart out of his people and gives them an heart of flesh, or a soft and tender heart (Eze. 11:19). He makes them willing in the day of his power (Psalm 110:3). While they are yet dead in trespasses and sins he quickens them into divine light and life (Eph. 2:1-5) and they then become new creatures in Christ, "old things are passed away; behold, all things are become new (2 Cor. 5:17).

Prior to this new birth God's people live just like the rest of mankind. They walk according to the course of this world, fulfilling the desires of the flesh and of the mind, and are by nature the children of wrath, even as others. They have nothing God wants; nothing he would have if they could give it. It is not they who take the first step in their salvation, but he. Not only does he take the first step, but he takes all the other steps in their translation from the kingdom of darkness into the kingdom of light. After this divine transaction takes place, it is *they* who are brought under obligation. It then becomes their privilege, and duty, to walk in obedience to the parental laws of Christ.

September 20

"When I would do good, evil is present with me" (Romans 7:21)

The conflict within the children of God between the flesh and the spirit is a very real phenomenon, and we should view it as a great blessing that we are told about this conflict in the Bible. How would we feel if the only kind of characters we found in the Scriptures were people who never reflected any faults, failings or shortcomings? We would not be able to witness with them and would feel that we were either of a different nature than them or else we were great failures when compared with them.

But seeing that even the most outstanding characters in the Bible had a warfare between the flesh and the spirit, it makes us know that we are not alone in this struggle. David, for example was a man after God's own heart, yet in a weak moment he committed the sin of adultery, and then, what amounted to the sin of murder in his effort to hide his adultery. This not only shows us that he had a sinful nature, but it also shows us the depths to which even a child of God may sink if left to himself and the vile inclinations of his own heart. What sobering thoughts!

Jesus summed up this inward conflict very well in a few words when he told his disciples that "the spirit indeed is willing, but the flesh is weak" (Matt. 26:41). It could not be stated better. This in no wise justifies sin, but it explains why it can be that even when we would do good, evil is present with us.

Paul breaks it down so well in Romans 7, when he speaks of being carnal, sold under sin, and doing things that he hated, and failing to do things that he desired. He acknowledged that in his flesh dwelt no good thing, and confessed that though there was a willingness on his part, yet many times he could not find how to do that which was good: "For the good that I would, I do not: but the evil which I would not, that I do." Have we not all keenly felt this conflict from time to time—some of us more than others no doubt?

Again Paul mentions this inward warfare in Galatians 5:16-17 where he speaks of the flesh lusting against the Spirit, and the Spirit against the flesh. He tells us there that these are contrary the one to the other, and this explains why we so often find ourselves unable to live up to the standard that we so much desire to maintain. The only hope of a measure of success is to walk in the Spirit. As long as we are doing that, we will not fulfill the lusts of the flesh. May the Lord help us in our efforts to live close to him.

September 21

"In my flesh shall I see God" (Job 19:26)

The apostle Paul tells us that in the resurrection the Lord will "change our vile body, that it may be fashioned like unto his glorious body" (Phil. 3:21). This is a *change*, not an *exchange*. It will not be another body, as some contend, but it will be a *changed* body.

Job makes this very clear. He says, "I shall see him for myself, and mine eyes shall behold him, and not another." The destruction of both his skin and his body would not prevent him from one day seeing God *in his own flesh* and *with his own eyes*, not somebody else's flesh and somebody else's eyes. Nor would the destruction, or consuming, of all his early hopes prevent this. In spite of all his present misery and anguish and the dissolving of his earthly house (2 Cor. 5:1), he was assured of the ultimate resurrection and glorification of his own body. What a precious hope is this!

Nothing is testified to more plainly in the Bible than the resurrection of the body. It is true that our body is vile by nature and it will consequently die and be "sown," or buried, in that corrupt state, yet *it* (the same *it*) shall be raised in a non-corrupt state; a state in which it cannot be corrupted (1 Cor. 15:42). It is likewise true that it will be raised "a spiritual body," but it will not be *another* body, only a *glorified* one.

In other words, the same process that makes it a *glorified* body, will, in that same process, make it a *spiritual* body. It will still be a body of *flesh*, but it will be a glorified, or spiritual, flesh. And in that flesh we shall see God, and it will be *us*, not somebody else. Thus, "It is sown (buried) a natural body, *it* [the same *it*] is raised a spiritual body" (1 Cor. 15:44). We will not be raised as "a spirit," but we will be raised spiritual, and will therefore be free of sin and impurity. A spirit does not have flesh and bones (Luke 24:39).

The apostle Paul spoke of his hope toward God, "that there shall be a resurrection of the dead, both of the just and unjust (Acts 24:15). God's people will come forth unto the resurrection of life, and those that are not his people will come forth unto the resurrection of damnation. How sweet is the hope that in that glorious morning we shall hear our Lord say, "Come, ye blessed of my Father, inherit the kingdom prepared for you from the foundation of the world" (Matt. 25:34)!

September 22

"Ever learning, and never able to come to the knowledge of the truth" (2 Timothy 3:7)

This language perfectly fits a great many religionists, for no matter how much they learn they never arrive at a sufficient knowledge of the truth to become a viable part of the true Church. Some of them come so close that it may be said of them that they "are not far from the kingdom of God" (Mark 12:34), but they can never make the necessary transition. Many of them are indeed children of God, but their knowledge is sufficiently defective that they can never wholeheartedly identify themselves with those meek and lowly and despised followers of Christ who make up the true militant kingdom of Christ here in the world.

Only the stripping work of the Holy Spirit can so crucify a person to the world as to make him willing to cast his lot with "that way which the world calls heresy" (Acts 24:14). And only that inward work can bring them to the place where they are not only willing but desirous of being identified with that sect that is "every where spoken against" (Acts 28:22).

There are truths taught in God's word that a man simply will not accept and embrace unless the light of the Spirit shines upon it and applies it to his heart with power. This is confirmed by 1 Corinthians 1:26: "Not many wise men after the flesh, not many mighty, not many noble, are called: but God hath chosen the foolish things of the world to confound the wise..." Christ thanked his Father that he had hidden these things from the wise and prudent and had revealed them unto babes (Matt. 11:25-27), and he told his disciples that it was given unto them to know the mysteries of the kingdom of heaven, but to others it was not given (Matt. 13:11).

The Lord must open the hearts of men in the same sense that he opened the heart of Lydia before they will attend unto the things that are taught by Christ and the apostles (Acts 16:14). Otherwise it matters not how much they may learn intellectually of the letter of the Scriptures, they will never be able to come to a knowledge of the truth. This is a great mystery to some, but that is exactly the point.

September 23

"Few and evil have the days of the years of my life been"
(Genesis 47:9)

Jacob viewed his days as being *few* in comparison with those of the patriarchs, and especially as compared to eternity. And he viewed them as *evil,* not just as it related to his own weaknesses and failings, but chiefly with regard to the many troubles and trials he had endured. He was not blinded by the vain philosophies of the world but was keenly aware of the brevity of life and of his own mortality. He looked at life realistically and did not seek to put any false veneer on things, as do the purveyors of modern thought. He was one hundred and thirty years old when he arrived in Egypt, and he lived another seventeen years, but at the end of his days I feel certain that he would still have referred to his life as brief and troubled. How much more momentary is our own life now in this day when the average person lives not much more than seventy-five years?

When I was a young man I never dreamed that it would seem to take such a short time for me to grow old, and the fact that my days would be filled with so much trouble was something I had little knowledge of. It is a blessing that we do not know the future, for who could face it if they could view in the beginning all that they would ever have to suffer or endure during their lifetime? God does not require us to face more than one day at a time, and he meets out our trials and troubles in merciful doses, so that we may not be overcome with more than we can bear. He also sanctifies our afflictions so that we may learn from them and become better prepared to cope with possibly greater trials down the road. His grace is always sufficient, no matter how great our conflicts.

As we reflect upon the brevity of our stay here upon earth let us make good use of our limited time, and may we never lose sight of that wonderful city that awaits us—that "city which hath foundations, whose builder and maker is God" (Heb. 11:10). And let us ever keep in mind that there is a "better country, that is, an heavenly" (v. 16). Our hope is that we will soon be there. If so, all will be well. For the children of God this present life is just a pilgrimage to that better land. This world is not our home.

September 24

"Without me ye can do nothing" (John 15:5)

Our Lord speaks here of those things which are pleasing to him and which bring honor to his name. No man should ever entertain any notions that he can do anything of that nature in his own strength or without an existing relationship with Christ. The apostle Paul stated it very well when he said, "Not that we are sufficient of ourselves to think any thing as of ourselves; but our sufficiency is of God" (2 Cor. 3:5). Those things that are pleasing to him are spoken of as the fruit of the Spirit. And just as there must be a tree before there can be fruit, so also a man must be possessed of the *Spirit* before he can bring forth spiritual *fruit*.

What a glaring contrast there is between the fruit of the Spirit and the works of the flesh, as set forth by the apostle in Galatians 5:19-23! The works of the flesh consist of such things as adultery, fornication, uncleanness, lasciviousness, idolatry, witchcraft, hatred, variance, emulations, wrath, strife, seditions, heresies, envyings, murders, drunkenness and revellings. But the fruit of the Spirit consists of such things as love, joy, peace, longsuffering, gentleness, goodness, faith, meekness and temperance.

These latter fruits, which are good, are only performed by those who have undergone a spiritual or heavenly birth and who are seeking the Lord's guidance and direction in their daily conduct and conversation. No man is sufficient for these things in and of himself but they are performed under a divine influence and from a heart made tender by the inward work of the Holy Spirit. Without Christ they cannot be performed at all.

To the ears of a humble child of grace how distressing do the words "without Christ" sound, and how much they long to live close to him. We read of those who have no hope and who are without God in the world (Eph. 2:12). These are those who are "in the flesh" and consequently "cannot please God" (Rom. 8:8). What a blessing to be delivered out of that dreadful condition and to have the love of God abiding within our heart! Having been thus delivered, we can do all things, i.e. all things pleasing to God, through Christ who strengthens us (Phil. 4:13).

September 25

"Whatsoever is not of faith is sin" (Romans 14:23)

A companion text to this is Hebrews 11:6, which tells us that without faith it is impossible to please God. The reasons this is so is because those who do not possess faith have no godly principle whatsoever abiding within them, and consequently nothing they do arises from a principle that honors God. None of their actions have God's glory in view but rather they are based solely upon fleshly impulses and motivations.

They may do many things that appear good outwardly and which are quite acceptable socially, but if those things do not spring from grace in the heart then they are not pleasing to God. "The carnal mind is enmity against God" (Rom. 8:7). It is not merely disinterested or indifferent, but it is actually *antagonistic* to God, and therefore has nothing in it that can meet with his approval or acceptance. The fact that not all men possess faith is the reason the apostle Paul prayed to be delivered from unreasonable and wicked men (2 Thess. 3:2).

Herein lays one of the great fallacies of popular religion. It says that a man must "have faith," and thus please God, in order to receive divine life. But as we have shown, the Scriptures teach that prior to divine life a man *cannot* please God. Faith is one of the *fruits* of the Spirit (Gal. 5:22), and therefore cannot precede the Spirit's indwelling. God's people do not receive his Spirit in order to become his sons, but he sends forth the Spirit of his Son into their hearts *because they already are sons* (Gal. 4:6). Nothing could be made any plainer with human language than this vital point, yet the vast majority of Bible readers miss it. Life always precedes action, both in the natural and spiritual realms.

Those of us who have a hope in Christ should ever be mindful that whatsoever is not of faith is sin. We should strive to the best of our ability to see that all we say and do has faith at its base. Before we do anything we should ask ourselves why we are doing it and whether or not it has God's glory as its object, for if it arises merely from selfish or fleshly motives, then it will not, and cannot, be pleasing to him. Following this course will not only prevent us from willfully inflicting injury upon others, but it will greatly facilitate our efforts to stay in that narrow way that leads to life, a way that is found by relatively few (Matt. 7:14).

September 26

"As many as were ordained to eternal life believed" (Acts 13:48)

Arminianism maintains that men must determine their own eternal destiny, and that no one was predestinated to be conformed to the image of Christ (Rom. 8:29) or to the adoption of children by Jesus Christ (Eph. 1:5, 11). It affirms that God's people were not "afore prepared unto glory" (Rom. 9:23) and that they were not "chosen in Christ before the foundation of the world" (Eph. 1:4), but that all men are left to decide for themselves whether they want to be children of God or not. It declares that no one is saved and called according to God's own purpose and grace which was given them in Christ Jesus before the world began, totally apart from their works (2 Tim. 1:9), but that, on the contrary, men must believe, repent, pray, etc., in order to *have* eternal life. But of course, the Scriptures do not support such teaching.

On the occasion mentioned in Acts 13:48, all those Gentiles who had been ordained to eternal life believed. But this was a unique occasion. It was by no means typical. There are many that are embraced in the electing love of God who do not believe the gospel when they hear it. The apostle Paul made it very clear that there were some who were even *enemies* of the gospel, yet "as touching the election" they were beloved of God (Rom. 11:28). This shows that simply being ordained to eternal life does not guarantee that a person will believe the gospel. The vast majority of God's people never believe the true gospel. Most of them never even *hear* it preached, but on the occasion of Acts 13:48, all those who were ordained to eternal life, did indeed believe it.

The names of God's people were written in the book of life of the Lamb slain from the foundation of the world (Rev. 13:8; 17:8). Our Lord Jesus Christ came into the world to bleed and die for them. He asserted that they were given unto him of the Father and that he would give unto them eternal life and they would never perish. He further said that they would all come to him and that he would lose none of them but would raise them up again at the last day. Modern religion denies all these things, but some of us still hold them near and dear to our hearts and rejoice that they are true.

September 27

"What do ye more than others?" (Matthew 5:47)

In the context the Lord is pointing out the contrast between the ideas and notions of men and the actual truth of those matters. Some of the old adages that have been passed down through the years may have a lot of truth in them, but often they do not express the *whole* truth of the situations they address, and frequently they are totally in error. Many of the things the Lord's disciples were accustomed to hearing stated by the religious leaders of the day, and which the society around them unquestioningly took for truth, were indeed very much in error and were nowhere taught in God's word. It is that same way today.

If we believe every popular religious sentiment we hear, what do we more than the generality of the society in which we live? The Lord pointed out the popular teaching of the Pharisees that we should love our neighbor and hate our enemy. Where did they get such a notion? They got it from somewhere other than God's Book.

Christ taught his disciples to love their enemies, to bless those who cursed them, to do good to those that hated them, and to pray for those who despitefully used them and persecuted them (Matt. 5:43-44). But is that the way most people act? Is that the admonition they follow? Certainly not. They come much closer to following the teachings of the Pharisees in such matters. How then can we be any different from them if we behave the same way they do? What do we *more* than they?

The Lord has called us out from the world and he teaches us to come out from among them and be a separate people. He has shown us what the general course of this evil world is. He has shown us what the world loves and what it seeks to attain. Therefore if we would do *more* than them, we must avoid that which they delight in. Christ said, "That which is highly esteemed among men is abomination in the sight of God" (Luke 16:15).Consequently, it is a good policy for us not to imitate the world's customs and fashions, nor to involve ourselves in their much-loved pleasures and ways. Otherwise, what do we more than others?

September 28

"In all thy ways acknowledge him, and he shall direct thy paths"
(Proverbs 3:6)

Just as we should trust in the Lord with our whole heart at all times and constantly avoid the sin of leaning unto our own understanding instead of his, so we should acknowledge him in everything we do. In so doing we have his assurance that he will direct our paths. The clear implication is that if we do not acknowledge him in all our ways, then we cannot expect him to direct our paths. But Oh! How we do need his providential leadership and direction.

The prophet Jeremiah said, "O Lord, I know that the way of man is not in himself: it is not in man that walketh to direct his steps" (Jer. 10:23). Man is too weak by nature to seek out the course that is most honoring to God and most to his own benefit and to the service of others. There is nothing we should desire more than that the Lord would direct our steps, and lead us in paths of righteousness for his name's sake. And there is nothing we should desire less than to be left to chose our own paths and to be guided by our own feeble judgments.

How needful it is that we "acknowledge" the Lord in all our ways! And how do we do that? By recognizing our constant need of him in all things and by giving our continual assent to the fact that without him we are nothing, yea, less than nothing. The apostle Paul said that we are not sufficient of ourselves to think anything as of ourselves; but our sufficiency is of God (2 Cor. 3:5). And our Lord said, "Without me ye can do nothing" (John 15:5).

Without divine strength, guidance and direction we can do nothing that is pleasing to the Lord or that will bring praise and honor to his holy name. Without his directing our paths we are sure to go astray, and are certain to be out of the way of righteousness. In all we do we need to always acknowledge that he is our all in all, and we should always have the attitude of Moses when he said to the Lord, "Show me now thy way," and, "If thy presence go not with me, carry us not up hence" (Ex. 33:13, 15). There is only one way we should desire, and that is the Lord's way, and we should never want to go anywhere that his presence will not go feelingly with us. As much as in us is, let us acknowledge him in each step we take. It is the path of peace.

September 29

"And he gave some, apostles; and some, prophets; and some, evantelists; and some, pastors and teachers; for the perfecting of the saints, for the work of the ministry, for the edifying of the body of Christ" (Ephesians 4:11-12)

The Scriptures make it abundantly clear that none of the gifts God has given to the church are for the purpose of *making* saints or *producing* a body for Christ. If popular religion were true, then the major part of the work of the ministry would be to make living saints out of dead sinners and thus determine whether Christ has a body or not, but we do not find a whisper of such things in the Bible.

There is a sense in which the preaching of the true gospel can *perfect* the saints, but it cannot *create* the saints. It can and does *edify* those who are a part of the body of Christ, but it cannot bring the body of Christ into being. It can nourish, build up, and instruct those to whom it is the power of God and the wisdom of God, but it provides no spiritual benefit to those who are dead in sin and who consequently view it as foolishness. In a word, it can feed the living, but it cannot raise the dead.

To edify a person is to build them up, establish them, instruct and improve them, and in a scriptural context it refers to doing those things in a *spiritual* sense. The *saints* are the only ones who can be thus improved in moral and religious knowledge and enlightenment. It is in that sense that they are *perfected* or thoroughly furnished. It has nothing to do with fleshly perfection, but rather it involves spiritual growth and development, and a kind of godly and gracious maturity or completeness. The gospel is a "preparation" and is well suited, under the influence of the Holy Spirit, to accomplish these ends in the lives of those whose hearts have been touched and tendered by the grace of God.

If any of God's gifts to his church had been intended to populate heaven, then the apostle Paul had an excellent opportunity to say so in his instruction to the Ephesians concerning those gifts. But he was as silent as the grave with regard to any such ends or purposes. In many instances the silence of the Scriptures speaks volumes.

September 30

"They loved the praise of men more than the praise of God"
(John 12:43)

Many of the chief rulers of the Jews believed on Jesus but they did not openly acknowledge him to be the promised Messiah because they greatly feared being branded as heretics by the Pharisees and "put out of the synagogue." Excommunication from the Jewish religion, because of all the dreadful restrictions, penalties, and curses attendant upon it, was a thing greatly feared by the Jews. Therefore many who were indeed convinced that Christ was the Son of God chose to deny him rather than suffer the consequences of being recognized as his followers. They preferred to have the applause and approval of men rather than to endure any of the hardships associated with a public profession of faith in Christ.

There are multitudes in this day who are of the same mindset as those cowardly Jews. They prefer to "go with the flow" and identify themselves with popular opinion rather than to be stigmatized and condemned as true followers of the meek and lowly Lamb of God and to worship him strictly according to the Scriptures. We have known of a number of Arminian preachers who have acknowledged that the Old Line Primitive Baptists have the true doctrine and practice, but that if they preached those things among their own people they would be cast out and lose their lucrative positions. How weak, unstable, and undeserving must a person be to know the truth and yet be afraid to preach it or confess it! "We ought to obey God rather than men" (Acts 5:29). And if we do not there will be grave consequences.

The difficulties attendant upon being a true follower of Christ may seem too severe to some and they may look upon it as being far too much to require of anyone. However, if following Jesus was easy how could there be any test of true sincerity, dedication and devotion? As it is, only the most genuine, honest and devoted of men are willing to identify themselves with the humble and despised followers of Christ; embrace those teachings that the world speaks of as "hard sayings" and "dangerous doctrines," and walk in "the way which they call heresy" (Acts 24:14). Christ was faithful to let his disciples know that being his follower would not be an easy road. We have seen many start out very well, but they soon fell by the wayside when they ran into tribulation or persecution. True Christianity, so to speak, separates the men from the boys.

§∞§

October 1

"The hour is coming, and now is, when the dead shall hear the voice of the Son of God: and they that hear shall live"
(John 5:25)

This verse speaks of the work of regeneration that the Lord performs in the hearts of all His children at some point in their lives; but this work always occurs when the subjects of it are "dead in trespasses sins" (Eph. 2:1,5) and consequently have no spiritual discernment or ability. They have neither the will nor the faculty to "accept Christ," "pray through," "let the Lord into their hearts," or any other of the various and sundry things they are told by popular religionists that they must do in order to be born again and live with God in glory. This is why their spiritual birth cannot be "of blood, nor of the will of the flesh, nor of the will of man," but must of necessity be "of God" (John 1:13). It is why Christ told Nicodemus that "The wind bloweth where it listeth (that is, *where it wills,* or *is minded to blow*), and thou hearest the sound thereof, but canst not tell whence it cometh, and whither it goeth: so is every one that is born of the Spirit" (John 1:13).

It is said here that the hour in which the Lord performs this work of the new birth "is coming, and now is." That simply means that the Lord is doing it now, and that he will do it in the future as long as the world stands. He will not miss a single one of his people. All that the Father has given unto him will, positively come to him, and he will in no wise (under any conditions) cast them out (John 6:37). At any point in time the Lord is *quickening,* or regenerating, some one, or some ones, of his people, whether it be *now* or an hour from now, or years from now. It goes on from day to day, and ultimately every member of the elect family will be brought into "newness of life" and this change will result in old things passing away and all things becoming new (2 Cor. 5:17).

In a word, *regeneration* or the *new birth,* consists of the spiritually dead hearing the voice of Christ (*inwardly, and usually inaudibly*) and thereby being brought to life spiritually. It consists of being "created in Christ Jesus unto good works, which God hath before ordained that we should walk in them" (Eph. 2:10). It cannot be "of man." Neither the *will* of man nor the *works* of man can have any say in it. It has to be "of God," and "by grace."

ೞ∾ಌ

October 2

"They that be whole need not a physician, but they that are sick"
(Matthew 9:12)

The crux of this verse is that those who think they are righteous to not feel the need of the grace and mercy of Christ. It is only those who are aware of their innate lack of righteousness and who feel themselves to be guilty and undeserving who are the proper subjects of the infinite mercy of God. As long as a person thinks he can justify himself before God by his own efforts, Christ is of no effect unto him (Gal. 5:4). That is, Christ provides no benefit to him.

If men could be justified in any other way than by the shed blood and imputed righteousness of Christ, then of course they would have no need of him whatsoever. Neither his life nor his death would be of any value or effectiveness to them, and actually their employment of any other method of justification would be an outright rejection and repudiation of him and his work of redemption. The apostle Paul states it this way: "I do not frustrate the grace of God: for if righteousness come by the law, then Christ is dead in vain" (Gal. 2:21). In other words, he might as well not have died if men can save themselves by their own efforts, and his grace has no part or place in their deliverance—it is not wanted or needed.

It is only from a posture of a feeling of utter helplessness and unworthiness that a man will cry out to the Lord as did the poor publican and say, "God be merciful to me a sinner" (Luke 18:13). As long as a person feels as did the Pharisee who condemned this publican and boasted of his own goodness (Luke 18:11-12), he feels no need of Christ whatsoever. In his own mind he is perfectly whole and has no need of the Great Physician, Jesus Christ. The only reason Isaiah saw the Lord "high and lifted up" (Isa. 6:1) was because he saw himself as "undone" and "a man of unclean lips" (v. 5). And look at Job 42:5-

6. When he saw the Lord in a proper light, he exclaimed, "I abhor myself, and repent in dust and ashes." This is the only posture from which a man will truly feel his need of Christ.

If we can can see ourselves as Paul saw himself—*a wretched man* (Rom. 7:24), and *less than the least of all saints* (Eph. 3:8), and *the chief of sinners* (I Tim. 1:15), we should greatly rejoice, for that puts us in a position where we realize our need of the Lord. It is a great blessing to be humbled under the might hand of God!

October 3

"Come, ye blessed of my Father, inherit the kingdom prepared for you from the foundation of the world" (Matthew 25:34)

Modern religion boldly proclaims that every man determines his own destiny, and they make this assertion in spite of the plain declarations of the Scriptures to the contrary. God's people were chosen in Christ before the foundation of the world (Eph. 1:4); predestinated to be conformed to his image (Rom. 8:29), and "afore prepared unto glory" (Rom. 9:23). In God's book all their members were written, "when as yet there was none of them" (Psalm 139:16). The very foundation of God stands sure, having this seal, "The Lord knoweth them that are his" (2 Tim. 2:19). He foreknew them in covenant love and he puts his law in their inward parts, and writes it in their hearts" (Jer.31:33) and assures them that he *will* be their God and that they *shall* be his people. He gave them to Christ, and Christ will give eternal life to each and everyone of them (John 17:3). All of them will come to him and he will in no wise cast them out (John 6:37). In other words, he will lose none of them but will raise them up again at the last day (v. 39).

If men could determine their own final destiny then there could be no such thing as "pre"-destination and God's word could not be relied upon, for it plainly teaches that he *predestinated* his people. The apostle Paul affirmed that *all* scripture is given by divine inspiration and is profitable "…that the *man of God* may be perfect, *throughly* furnished unto all good works"(2 Tim. 3:16). But how could it be a thorough furnisher to God's people if it taught them things that were not true?

We read in Revelation 17:8 of some whose names were *not* written in the book of life from the foundation of the world, which clearly implies that there are some who *were* written in that book from the foundation of the world. And if so, then they didn't determine their own destiny. And the same goes for those who were "predestinated," and "*afore* prepared unto glory." But the truth is that if fallen men, dead in trespasses and sins, were left to determine their own final destiny they would, in every case, make the wrong choice. In that corrupt state they are only interested in fulfilling the desires of the flesh and of the mind (Eph. 2:2-3).

October 4

"When I am weak, then am I strong" (2 Corinthians 12:10)

The apostle Paul knew that the weaker he felt himself to be in the flesh, and the more conscious he was of his own innate weakness and insufficiency, the stronger he was in the Lord. God's people are never so weak as when they are relying upon the feeble arm of flesh and trying to deal with life's problems in their own strength. And conversely, they are never so strong as when they are keenly aware of their own weakness and are fully relying upon the Lord for grace and strength to worship and serve him properly. What a wonderful blessing it is when we are able to fully and completely cast our care upon him, with the full assurance that he cares for us (1 Peter 5:7)! It is a peaceful feeling that no one can truly appreciate unless they have experienced it.

This is what enabled Daniel to go into the den of lions, and the three Hebrew children to face the flames of a fiery furnace. It is what enabled numerous others of God's people to face the wrath of kings and to endure torture and death at the hands of their persecutors. It is what enabled David to face a man in battle who was physically much larger and stronger than he. These men, along with many others of the saints, were *strong in the Lord* when they did such things. Hebrews 11 gives us a veritable catalog of such feats, all wrought by a God-given faith.

How strong Elijah was when he faced the opposition of over eight hundred of the idolatrous prophets of Baal and the prophets of the groves (1 Kings 18:19), and yet how weak he was a little later when he hid himself in a cave and feared for his life (1 Kings 19:9-10)! In the first instance he was trusting wholly in the Lord, and in the second instance he was looking too much at his outward circumstances. And again, consider the case of Peter, who momentarily had such a burst of faith that the Lord enabled him to walk on the water, but very quickly his attention was diverted to the boisterous waves around him, and he began to sink.

How typical these instances are of our own vacillating conditions. Sometimes we are strong in the Lord and at other times we are spiritually low! The only times we are truly strong is when we are totally relying upon the Lord and are fully conscious of our own weakness.

October 5

"The flesh lusteth against the Spirit, and the Spirit against the flesh: and these are contrary the one to the other: so that ye cannot do the things that ye would" (Galatians 5:17)

When God's people are quickened into divine life they are "made partakers of the Holy Ghost" (Heb. 6:4) and "the divine nature" (2 Peter 1:4). This brings about a conflict or warfare between the flesh and the Spirit. When the disciples of Christ could not even watch with him for the short space of one hour, he said unto them, "The spirit indeed is willing, but the flesh is weak" (Matt. 26:40-41). It was the Holy Spirit within them that made them want to follow Christ, but it was their frail and fickle flesh that made them yield to their fatigue and sleep instead of standing watch.

It was the spiritual nature in Peter that fully intended never to deny Christ, and to go with him even unto the death, but it was the fleshly nature in him that prompted him to curse and deny that he even knew Christ. Then, a little later, when he was powerfully reminded of his weakness and disloyalty, he "went out, and wept bitterly." It was the spiritual nature in him responding to the convicting work of the Holy Spirit that brought him to repentance in this matter. The inner conflict between the flesh and the spirit was never more clearly illustrated than in his case. It was the old fleshly nature in Peter and the other apostles, left to itself, that made them flee in the face of the threat of death, but it was by the aid of the Holy Spirit that most of them were later enabled to die as martyrs for the cause of Christ.

David also may be pointed out as a vivid example of a child of God who, in weak moments, and when temporarily left to himself, acted in a manner that was altogether inconsistent with the principle of grace that had been implanted within him. But there is one common thread that runs through the experiences of the children of God, and that is that they sooner or later feel deep remorse for their transgressions and confess them to the Lord with broken hearts. Those who feel no godly sorrow for their transgressions obviously are strangers to the conflict described in Galatians 5:17 and Romans 7. They only have a carnal nature and therefore experience no warfare between the flesh and the Spirit.

October 6

"And they sung a new song, saying, Thou art worthy to take the book, and to open the seals thereof: for thou wast slain, and hast redeemed us to God by thy blood out of every and tongue, and people, and nation" (Revelation 5: 9)

Look closely at what the text is saying. Those for whom Christ died were "redeemed to God"—not just redeemed, but redeemed to God. That shows the work to be complete.

All the multiplied millions of God's people, the world over, were redeemed to him when Christ was slain. That is, he bought them back. They had "sold themselves for nought" (Isaiah 52:3), and he redeemed them. By this "one offering" of the precious Lamb of God they were "forever perfected" (Heb. 10:14). He gave himself "for the church" (Eph. 5:25), that is, his elect. He laid down his life "for the *sheep*," again, his elect (John 10:15), and nowhere do we find where he laid down his life for a single one of the goats. The only thing the goats will ever hear from God is, "I never knew you: depart from me, ye that work iniquity" (Matt. 7:23), and, "Depart from me, ye cursed, into everlasting fire, prepared for the devil and his angels" (Matt. 25:41).

And now, look closely at the redemption price—"the blood of Christ." Modern religion says, "Give us your silver and gold so that we may save the perishing hordes," but divine inspiration says money has nothing to do with it: "Forasmuch as ye know that ye were not redeemed with corruptible things, as silver and gold...but with the precious blood of Christ" (1 Peter 1:18). His blood did not merely make redemption possible, but it brought redemption to all the elect. "In whom we have redemption through his blood, the forgiveness of sins, according to the riches of his grace" (Eph. 1:7). Could language be any plainer?

Lastly, look again at who were redeemed—a people "out of every kindred, and tongue, and people, and nation." Anyone who looks at this honestly and without prejudice, will have to admit that "*out of* every nation" does not mean "every nation." *Out of* every kindred is not the same as every kindred.

Look at Peter's words at the counsel at Jerusalem, "God at the first did visit the Gentiles, to take *out of* them a people for his name" (Acts 15:14). It is plain, then, that God never intended to take all the Gentiles as his people, but a people *out of* the Gentiles. If words mean anything, and they do, then this plainly overthrows the popular notions that "God loves everybody," and "God is trying to save everybody." Let us always take God's word rather than men's.

October 7

"For ye see your calling, brethren, how that not many wise men
after the flesh, not many mighty, not many noble, are called"
(1 Corinthians 1:26)

In order to understand what the apostle means here, or anywhere else as to that, it must be realized that he is addressing the Lord's church. He is not directing his teachings to the world at large but to the Lord's true disciples. "For ye see *your* calling, *brethren...*"

"Now I beseech *you*, *brethren...*" (1 Cor. 1:10); "Moreover, *brethren*, I would not that ye should be ignorant..." (1 Cor. 10:1); "Moreover, *brethren*, I declare unto *you* the gospel..." (1 Cor. 15:1); "Now this I say, *brethren*, that flesh and blood cannot inherit the kingdom of God..." (1 Cor. 15:50); "Therefore, *my beloved brethren*, be *ye* stedfast..." (1 Cor. 15:58); "I beseech *you*, *brethren...*" (1 Cor. 16:15). In these and in numerous other references Paul addresses the *brethren* just in this one book. Go through all the epistles and see to whom they are written. They simply cannot be applied to those who do not qualify as *brethren*.

Now, the apostle appeals to the brethren's own experience and observation. He tells them that they can see by looking at their own situation as a body of believers that God does not call many of those who are viewed by the world as wise, mighty and noble. In other words as they considered the background of each individual member of the church it would be plain to see that there were very few among them who had come among them from the "upper crust," so to speak. They were made up primarily of the poorer and more common class. The apostle does not say there are none of the notable or so-called elite class called from nature to grace, but he does assert very clearly that God does not call *many* of that class of people. This is totally contrary to popular religion's claim that God calls everybody and that it is left to them how they respond.

We find Peter, on the day of Pentecost, saying to the brethren, "The promise is unto you, and to your children, and to all that are afar off, even as many as the Lord our God shall call" (Acts 2:39). This clearly shows that God does not call everybody. The promise, whatever that entails—whether it be eternal salvation, the remission of sins, or the special outpouring of the Holy Spirit during that apostolic period—applies only to those that the Lord calls. In other words, it applies only to God's elect. No man can make it apply to anyone else without willfully wresting the Scriptures.

October 8

"The love of God is shed abroad in our hearts by the Holy Ghost which is given unto us" (Romans 5:5)

Let the reader pause for a time and consider a Being so great that he can, in a moment's time, put his love within the heart of the most obstinate sinner. And when he does so, what a miraculous change it produces in their life and conduct. Among a number of other things it makes them ashamed of the things in which they previously found pleasure (Rom. 6:20-21). It makes them love the things they once hated, and hate the things they once loved. It actually makes them new creatures in Christ. Old things pass away and all things become new (2 Cor. 5:17). It puts them into a condition in which sin no longer has dominion over them (Rom. 6:14).

The love of God is not in a man's heart until the Lord puts it there. And if a person does not have it, he does not want it, for he knows nothing about it. Consequently he has neither desire nor ability to initiate any kind of process in which he would come to love God and his people and what they stand for. If a person does not love God (and none do by nature), how are they to go about doing any of the things that modern religion tells them they must do in order to be a child of God? That Arminian system tells them that they must believe on Christ from the heart, sincerely accept him, honestly believe on him, etc. But how can they do such things when they do not love him? And how can they love him when his love has not been "shed abroad" in their heart?

We who love God, do so because he first loved us (1 John 4:19). It was because of his "great love wherewith he loved us," that "even when we were dead in sins," he quickened us together with Christ (Eph. 2:1,

4, 5). And this alone is salvation by grace. The religious theory that says we must love God in order to get him to love us is as foreign to the Scriptures as light is to darkness. It is just the opposite of the truth.

Elder John R. Daily expressed in very beautifully in song when he wrote:

> *His love from eternity fixed upon you,*
> *Broke forth and discovered its flame,*
> *When each with the cords of his kindness he drew,*
> *And bro't you to love his great name.*
> *Oh had he not pitied the state you were in,*
> *Your bosoms his love had ne'er felt;*
> *You all would have lived, would have died too in sin,*
> *And sunk with the load of your guilt.*

Oh, may we ever praise his precious name!

October 9

"But the very hairs of your head are all numbered"
(Matthew 10:30)

I am told that in the Greek language each letter has a numerical value, and that in the ten words of this text there are over forty aspects of the factor seven, a number that in the Scriptures represents completeness or perfection. Yet, if we were to ask a Greek scholar to compose a sentence in which there would be as many as three such aspects of the factor seven, he would be hard pressed to do so.

Is this not an astounding fact? Is it not a wonderful proof of the divine inspiration of the Scriptures, and, apart from this, is it not a wonderful thought that God has such care for his people that he even numbers the hairs of their heads? These are "great matters," and they are "too high for me" (Psalm 131:1). "Such knowledge is too wonderful for me; it is high, I cannot attain unto it" (Psalm 139:6). How could poor mortals such as we, ever comprehend a God so great?

The Lord is teaching us here against the fear of man. He would have us to be assured of his care for his people. He who takes note of the death of sparrows, will much more regard the affairs of those whom he chose in Christ before the foundation of the world and whom he has loved with an everlasting love. He who has so elegantly clothed the grass of the field will much more attend to the temporal needs of his elect family. If he regards the least matters in our lives, will he not much more regard the weightier matters.

How blessed it is to know that men can only do harm to the inferior part of our body! It should greatly comfort us to consider how limited our enemies are in what they can do to us. They may take our natural lives but they cannot take our higher lives. They may kill our bodies, but they cannot kill our souls. We are already dead to the world and the world unto us, and our life is hid with Christ in God (Col. 3:3). He who knows the number of our hairs also knows the number of our days. May they all be devoted to him.

October 10

"Verily, verily, I say unto you, He that heareth my word and believeth on him that sent me hath everlasting life, and shall not come into condemnation; but is passed from death unto life"
(John 5:24)

This verse is frequently used by unenlightened religionists to try to prove that spiritually dead sinners, dead in sins, must hear and believe the gospel in order to have divine life and to escape eternal hell. However, in order for it to teach that idea, it would have to read as follows: Verily, verily, I say unto you, If those of you who are devoid of divine life, and do not have 'ears to hear' will hear my word, and if you who have no faith will believe on God, then you will never be cast into hell but will pass from death in sin into life eternal.

Of course the text teaches no such mumbo-jumbo. Rather, it is clearly saying that those who *are* (already) *hearers* of the word of Christ and *are* (already) *believers* in the heavenly Father, *already possess* ("hath" or "have") everlasting life, and consequently they shall not come into eternal condemnation because they have already *passed* ("is passed" or "are passed") from death unto life.

The hearing and believing of this verse are *evidences* of divine life, not the *causes* of divine life. If we make the hearing and the believing conditions unto life, then we make eternal life contingent upon the works of men who are incapable of performing the works. We thus make it contingent upon the works of men who are dead in trespasses and sins. This is an unworkable theology.

Salvation by grace is described very clearly in the second chapter of Ephesians and it involves the *quickening* of God's people into divine life "even when they were dead in sins," and the *creating* of them in Christ Jesus *unto* good works—not *because of* good works. It also has to do with those who "were far off" being "made nigh by the blood of Christ" so that they are "no more strangers and foreigners, but fellow-citizens with the saints, and of the household of faith." Even the faith through which they are saved by grace is *not of themselves*, but is "the gift of God" (Eph. 2:8), so that their works are entirely eliminated from the picture "lest any man should boast." God will not share his glory with another (Isaiah 42:8,11).

October 11

"And my speech and my preaching was not with enticing words of man's wisdom, but in demonstration of the Spirit and of power" (1 Corinthians 2:4)

The apostle Paul would have us know that there was far more to his preaching than mere oration. His gospel labors were accompanied by the power, unction and fervor of the Holy Spirit. It was in fact a *demonstration*, or a manifestation of those things. When we witness a man of God being delivered from all worldly hindrances and lifted up to preach the gospel of his grace to the comfort, instruction and edification of his people, we are beholding a miraculous display of God's power. It is something that is not within the natural ability of any man to do, and it can never be done apart from the almighty aid of the Holy Spirit.

We have never believed that God was at work in that preaching which lacks this power, unction and aid. Why would he bless that which he does not choose to accompany, and sanction, with his divine Spirit and power? The apostle tells us that he knew the Thessalonian brethren were included in the number of God's elect because of the fact that the gospel he preached unto them was received by them, not in word only, "but also in power, and in the Holy Ghost, and in much assurance" (1 Thess. 1:4-5). When the preacher is blest to proclaim it in power, and in the Holy Ghost, and in much assurance, we may be certain that someone, or ones, within hearing of it will receive it in the same manner. And when they receive it in this way it is always profitable.

Remember those beautiful words in Isaiah 55, "So shall my word be that goeth forth out of my mouth: it shall not return unto me void, but it shall accomplish that which I please, and it shall prosper in the thing whereto I sent it." Notice, there are four *shall's* in this verse. Those *shall's* are placed there to emphasize the certainty of God's word accomplishing the purpose for which he sends it.

Paul shows us very plainly in 1st Corinthians 1:17, 2:1-5, and 2:13, that his purpose was not to impress the brethren with outward things such as flowery words and phrases, but to point them to Christ and to build them up in the most holy faith. Man's wisdom is never to be put on display in the preaching of the gospel, but rather Jesus Christ and him crucified. All God's ministering servants should earnestly desire that the faith of their hearers might rest in the power and wisdom of God, rather than upon poor, feeble men such as themselves.

October 12

"He that knoweth God heareth us; he that is not of God heareth us not" (1 John 4:6)

I believe it may rightly be said that, among other things, the Bible is an expose' on the fallacy of Arminianism. And what is known as Arminianism did not have it origin with James Arminius in the sixteenth century, but it began with Satan and the first lie in the Garden of Eden when he told Eve that in the day she ate of the fruit of the tree in the midst of the Garden she would not die but her eyes would be opened and she would be as gods, knowing good and evil.

Modern Arminianism is essentially the belief that certain conditions are necessary to be met by unregenerate sinners in order for them to obtain eternal life (salvation by works). In Eve's case Satan presented her with only one condition in order to supposedly raise herself to a higher order of life, but in the case of modern religion it is whatever conditions a particular denomination decides is necessary. We have heard and read a rather lengthy list of things advocated by the various religious organizations as being essential to the obtaining of eternal life and salvation. But whatever conditions are set forth, whether they be many or few, it all boils down to eternal salvation by works, which the Bible clearly refutes.

One of the fallacies of worldly religion is that it requires those who are not of God to perform certain acts that they neither *can* nor *will* perform in order to become children of God. In a word, it requires spiritually dead men to do what they cannot do, in order to get what they do not want. Hence, it just simply *does* not work, and *cannot* work. Those who know God will give heed to what the true servants of God preach, while those who are not of God will not. Christ clearly taught that no one can come to him except those who are drawn by the Father (John 6:44).

According to popular religion those who are not of God must hear the gospel, but according to the apostle John they *hear it not*, and Christ said they *cannot* hear it. Modern religion says they must come to Christ, but Christ says they cannot come unless they are drawn by the Father. In a nutshell here is the situation: popular religion says the wicked (those who are not of God) must seek God in order to be saved, but Scripture says, "The wicked, through the pride of his countenance, *will not seek after God* (Psalm 10:4). Therefore the only conclusion that can reasonably be reached is that Arminianism *is not a workable theology.* "The preaching of the cross is to *them that perish* foolishness; but unto us *which are saved* it is the power of God" (I Cor. 1:28).

October 13

"His greatness is unsearchable" (Psalm 145:3)

I love to think about the greatness of God, though I realize it is an inexhaustible subject and I know we finite beings can never begin to fathom that which is infinite. Our efforts to delve into it are poor at best, but I enjoy wading along the edge of that vast ocean, gathering from the beautifully polished pebbles of truth that I am occasionally blest to discover there.

From the morning of time saints of every generation have related to their children some of the glorious things God has done, and great minds have meditated upon the splendor, majesty and glory of his miraculous works. His awe-inspiring deeds have been on many a tongue through the centuries and untold volumes have been written about his greatness and the wondrous examples thereof. I often think of the unspeakable magnitude of his love, mercy and kindness to a wretch like me, and have marveled at how gentle and tender his chastenings have been. His compassion has been intermingled with everything he has ever done in behalf of his people, and he is good to all.

This greatness is seen in everything around us—the sweetness of a baby's smile, the twinkle of a billion stars, the flowers of the field so perfectly arrayed, the birds that are painted with the Master's brush and whose songs are given by Heaven's Musician. It is felt in the gentle touch of a soothing breeze, and the light and warmth of the glowing sun. These and countless other things gloriously declare the greatness of God, and this is to say nothing of the untold spiritual blessings with which he has graciously loaded us.

Unenlightened men may speak disparagingly of him and talk of all he would do if we would only allow him, but this is as a foreign tongue to those who have been laid low in the dust of self abasement and blest to see him "high and lifted up." They cannot speak so meanly of him, but must ever say, "The Lord is a great God, and a great King above all gods" (Ps. 95:3), "clothed with honor and majesty" (104:1), "the Great, the Mighty God" (Jer. 32:18). May he help us to magnify his glorious name.

October 14

"Who maketh thee to differ from another? (1 Corinthians 4:7)

This question and those that follow it was addressed to those who were not giving proper consideration to the source of the gifts that their ministers possessed and were failing to realize that no man's efforts will prosper unless the Lord blesses them. But please allow me to address some thoughts here that are along a somewhat different line than is the main thrust of the context. The fact that the Lord makes each of us to differ from all others is a very interesting subject for meditation.

God is a being of infinite variety. We see this in almost all things around us. No two trees grow exactly alike, though they may look ever so similar. Observation, and science, tells us that no two snowflakes are precisely the same in their design, though there are untold billions of them. No two sunsets are the same in every particular of their various shades and hues. And no two people are exactly the same in their composition, disposition and personality. Even so-called identical twins have distinguishing marks and differences if we look closely enough for them, and they often have very different attitudes, sentiments and interests. We as individuals are different in some ways, however minute the variance, from every other person who has ever lived upon the earth, for God is not in the business of making clones. As a general rule when we look at a person we can instantly tell whether or not we have ever seen them before.

I realize that there are instances in which cosmetic surgery is needed to correct, if possible, defects that are a serious hindrance to a person's physical and emotional well being. However, there is a lot of such surgery that is a product of mere vanity, and some people have suffered results that left them in worse shape than they were originally. Much of this sort of thing is a result of people being unduly dissatisfied and displeased with the physical appearance the Lord gave them. I cannot believe the Lord is pleased with this. I think most of us need to simply dress and groom ourselves in as modest and presentable a way as we can, and then conduct ourselves in such way that whatever our physical construction may be, those around us who really matter will love us anyway. There is a lot of truth in the saying that, "Pretty is as pretty does."

October 15

"Our God whom we serve is able to deliver us...and he will deliver us" (Daniel 3:17)

What a wonderful faith it is that through the ages has allowed the dear saints, such as Shadrach, Meshach, and Abednego, to confidently rely upon the Lord in their most trying hours with the full assurance that he not only is *able* to deliver them but that in some way he *will* deliver them! Whether or not they are delivered from present perils or even death at the hands of their persecutors, they will yet be delivered, for either way, whether they are in the body or out of the body, they are still totally in the hands of the Lord and ultimate victory is theirs. If God be for them who can be against them? No power on earth can touch their never-dying souls, and therefore, to be absent from the body is to be present with the Lord. For them to depart this life, whether by natural death or at the hands of others, is for them to be with the Lord in a far better place.

It appears from Daniel 3:18 that the three Hebrew children were not certain that the Lord would deliver them from the fiery furnace, but they seemed perfectly assured that in one way or another they would be delivered out of the hand of the king. I believe that from their viewpoint God would either deliver them from death by a miracle, or else he would deliver them from the king by taking them home to glory. Either way, they were assured of a glorious deliverance, and were thus given courage to defy Nebuchadnezzar's evil decree that they worship his golden image. Even death was preferable to their worshipping an idol.

There are still men and women today, and I hope I am among them, who have the same confidence in the Lord as Shadrach, Meshach, and Abednego, and who would refuse to bow their knee to the image of Baal even in the face of possible death. Oh! What a comfort is such a faith as we face the trials and difficulties of life! How blest are we if we have that threefold assurance of God's deliverance that the apostle Paul had: "Who delivered us from so great a death, and doth deliver: in whom we trust that he will yet deliver" (2 Cor. 1:10)!

October 16

"We know that all things work together for good to them that love God" (Romans 8:28)

I believe the "all things" mentioned here are the same "things" mentioned three verses later in verse thirty-one. These *things* are predestination, calling, justification and glorification, and they "work together" for our good. It does not seem reasonable to me to say that *good* things *work together* with *evil* things, and that consequently everything we do and everything that happens to us during our lifetime, whether good or bad, turns out for our good. I am fully aware that God can bring good to his people out of things that were intended by men to hurt them. We have instances in the Bible where he did exactly that, but that was not a case of *evil* "working together" with *good*, but rather of God *overruling* evil and bringing good to his people instead. Good things and evil things do not "work together." On the contrary, they are always opposed to each other.

Romans 8:28 confirms to us that there are people in this world who "love God" and who are "the called according to his purpose." And it is *these* for whom the "all things" mentioned above *work together* for good. It is clear that anyone who is called of God is called "according to his purpose" and not as a result of anything they did in order to get called. The promises of God are not to everybody in general, but to "as many as the Lord our God shall call" (Acts 2:39)—no more and no less.

It is clear from verse thirty-one that if God be for us there is no one that can be effectually against us. His purposes and decrees cannot be defeated or overthrown. A person who has been predestinated, will most certainly be called into divine life here in time. They will be justified in time, and they will finally be glorified. There is no power in heaven or in earth or in hell that can prevent it. It is as sure to come to pass as if all of it were already done. Evil men and evil spirits may be suffered to go far in distressing God's people here in this time world, but nothing is more sure than the ultimate safety and security of the saints.

October 17

"The secret of the Lord is with them that fear him" (Psalm 25:14)

I will not dwell long here, for there are mysteries surrounding the text that are too wonderful for me. However we are not left to question the fact that there are some things God-fearing people know that others do not know. There are truths known by such people that flesh and blood cannot reveal. The apostle Peter, for instance, had a heart-knowledge of Christ that no one but the Father in heaven had revealed to him (Matt. 16:15-17). And thus it is with all those who have that same kind of knowledge. "There is a path which no fowl knoweth, and which the vulture's eye hath not seen" (Job 28:7), and this knowledge is part of that path. Those who have no reverence for God cannot view this beautiful path, but Peter and many other trusting souls have been blest to do so. God will not cheapen his glories by allowing the ungodly to look upon them.

The text gives us to know that there are special things reserved for those who truly fear God. The *fear* of God in the sense of the text is a reverence of him, a veneration of him, an adoration of him, and a childlike trust in him. To those who have been blest to have such feelings toward him it is given "to know the mysteries of the kingdom of heaven," but to those who are not of that class it is not given (Matt. 13:11; Luke 8:10). This, within itself, is a blessing of immense proportion, and how distinguishingly favored are those upon whom it is bestowed!

There can be no doubt but that God has hidden some things from one class, "the wise and prudent," and revealed them unto another class described as "babes" (Matt. 11:25). Sometimes those *babes* wish they could share those things with unbelievers, and occasionally they have attempted to do so, but with hurtful results. The Lord taught his disciples not to give that which is holy unto the dogs nor cast their pearls before swine (Matt. 7:6). These are not *literal* dogs and swine, but unenlightened and unprincipled people who will only trample the precious things of God under their feet and insult and ridicule those who treasure them. Only those *to whom it is given* can enter into the joy of such high and holy things. In Malachi 3:16 we read that *they that feared the Lord* "spake often *one with another*." That's what true believers have to do today. There's no one else they can talk to about these things.

October 18

"Alas, my master! how shall we do?" (2 Kings 6:15)

These are the words of Elisha's servant when he saw the hosts that the king of Syria had sent to Dothan to apprehend the prophet. The city was surrounded with horses and chariots and a great host of soldiers, and no doubt the scene appeared awfully bleak to the servant. But Elisha comforted him and said, "Fear not: for they that be with us are more than they that be with them." Then Elisha prayed and asked the Lord to open the servant's eyes that he might see the defenses that the Lord had provided them. "And the Lord opened the eyes of the young man; and he saw: and, behold, the mountain was full of horses and chariots of fire round about Elisha."

How many times have our own outward circumstances appeared extremely dark and gloomy and we have fearfully wondered, "How shall we do?" How shall we overcome what seems to be insurmountable odds? How shall we make it through this unfriendly world that is filled with constant hardships and difficulties?

Have we not many times felt that our path was strewn with so many obstacles that we surely would not be able to deal with all of them? Well, at such times all it would take to put our mind at ease would be for the Lord to open the eyes of our soul to see the deliverance that he has already prepared for us. Even before we call upon him, he will answer (Isaiah 65:24). He has already seen the obstacles that face us and has taken care of all the contingencies so that none of them will overcome us when we get to them.

We know not how many times the Lord may have sent his angels to watch over us in times of danger. I am confident that we have many times been delivered from evils that we never even knew were near us. How Elisha's servant must have rejoiced when he was blest to see the protection that the Lord had provided his master! We, like him, may sometimes wonder how our circumstances are going to turn out, and we may cry as did he, "Master! How shall we do?" But God's humble poor need not fear the outcome, for they will ultimately do well. "Say ye to the righteous, that it shall be well with him" (Isaiah 3:10). "If God be for us, who can be against us?" (Rom. 8:31). If the Lord is on our side, we are in the majority, no matter how outnumbered we may sometimes feel. May he strengthen our faith and help us to keep these things in mind.

October 19

"When the Son of man cometh shall he find faith on the earth"
(Luke 18:8)

If even one percent of all the people who are identified with the various religions of the world possessed the kind of faith that the Lord spoke of here, he would never have posed this question. The question itself implies that there will be very little true faith when he returns.

There has always been comparatively little genuine faith at any given time in history. It is a relatively "little flock" to whom the Lord is pleased to *give* his kingdom (Luke 12:32). He has hidden these things from the wise and prudent (who make up the vast majority of religious professors), and has revealed them unto babes (Matt. 11:25). And the "babes" that he speaks of here are members of the "little flock" who possess true faith.

How many people do you know who are willing to turn their backs on popular religion and endure the stigma associated with being identified with a "little flock" that is looked down upon by the world and despised as ignorant and unlearned and behind the times? How many do you know who care nothing for all the worldly forms of entertainment that is provided by the popular churches, and who view it as an abomination in the sight of the Lord for such things to be done in his name and in the name of religion? How many people do you know who have the same kind of dedication to Scriptural principles and practices that was reflected in the lives of many of the characters of the Old and New Testaments? I suspect that, even now, there are very few relatively speaking.

Will the Lord find faith on the earth when he returns? Yes, he will, because he will always have some faithful followers. Just as in Elijah's day God had "reserved unto himself" a people who have not bowed the knee to the image of Baal, Paul says, "Even so at this present time also there is a remnant according to the election of grace." Once the Lord has begun a good work in his people he will perform it until the day of Jesus Christ" (Phil. 1:6). But the question asked in Luke 18:8 seems to clearly imply that, when Christ returns, true and genuine faith will be relatively scarce.

October 20

"Have mercy on me, O Lord; for I am weak" (Psalm 6:2)

What a blessed word is *mercy* to those who have been enabled to see and feel their true condition by nature. They know that if God dealt with them strictly on the basis of *justice* it would spell their doom. Like the Publican of Luke 18:10, 13, they realize that there is no relief from a sense of guilt and sin to be had in a plea of one's own righteousness and merit. There has been a conviction ingrained deeply within their hearts by the Holy Spirit that tells them their eternal condemnation would be entirely just—hence it is obvious to them that God's mercy is their only hope. They know that the only right way to plead with him is from a posture of absolute demerit and weakness. David could not urge his own goodness or greatness when supplicating God, but could only acknowledge his sin and unworthiness by begging for mercy.

Any plea for mercy is a tacit admission of demerit. There can be no such thing as deserved mercy or merited grace. By Divine inspiration the apostle Paul has related to us that if we are a subject of mercy it is strictly God's doing: "It is not of him that willeth, nor of him that runneth, but of God that showeth mercy...Therefore hath he mercy on whom *he* will have mercy, and whom he will he hardeneth." He is the Divine Potter, and he can take of the same lump and make one vessel unto honor and another unto dishonor.

In the final analysis it will be seen that God has shown his wrath and made his power known by enduring with much longsuffering the vessels of wrath fitted to destruction, and he has made known the riches of his glory by showing compassion upon the vessels of mercy which he afore prepared unto glory (See Romans 9). And let it be remembered that for anyone to reply against God in this or any other matter is for the creature to argue with the One who created him. Disputing with

God is one of the most futile exercises anyone can engage in. When
vying with him, man can only be the loser. Why God does what he
does may not always be understood, but of one thing we can be
certain—the Judge of all the earth will, in all cases, do right (Gen.
18:25).

October 21

"I delight in the law of God after the inward man"
(Romans 7:22)

If God has taken up his abode within our hearts in regeneration then
we are composed of what the apostle Paul speaks of as *the inward
man* and *the outward man* (2 Cor. 4:16; Eph. 3:16), *the old man* and *the
new man* (Rom. 6:6; Eph. 4:22; Col. 3:9; Eph. 4:24; Col. 3:10). These
references deal with the *old nature* with which we are all originally
conceived, and to the *new nature* that is imparted to us when the Lord
gives us divine life, or, the heavenly birth. This shows us that the old
nature is not removed from us in regeneration, however it is greatly
subdued by virtue of the fact that our new nature wars against it and
tends to keep it under and bring it into subjection (Gal. 5:17; 1 Peter
2:11; 1 Cor. 9:27). Though sin continues to have a *being* within us, we
are nevertheless assured that it shall not have *dominion* over us (Rom.
6:14). Through the Spirit we are able to *mortify* the deeds of the body
(Rom. 8:14).

Those whom God has not visited by His Holy Spirit do not delight in
his law, for they have no *inner man* by which to do so. Rather, they
desire not the knowledge of his ways and prefer that he would depart
from them (Job 21:14).

If we find comfort in his word and find ourselves longing to know
more about it and to grow in the knowledge of it, we have a sweet
evidence that we have within us more than just the *old* man, or the
outward man, and that our interest in godliness arises from the *inward*
man.

Very early in life the word of God found a place in my heart, and I
desired to be guided by it. Like Paul, I found a conflict between the

flesh and the spirit, so that I could not measure up to the standard I desired to reach, but I still tried. I tried then and I try now. I fell short then and I fall short now, but I still *delight in the law of the Lord.* I hunger and thirst after righteousness. I long to walk in the ways that please the Lord and to experience fresh manifestations of his love and presence. Much of the time I struggle with the blunting and dulling influence of the old, outward man and I long for the day when that conflict will cease forever, but until then that inward warfare tells me that I am a child of God. It wouldn't be there if I were not, and for that I am thankful. Give us, dear Lord, a greater delight in thy law.

PART 2

MUSINGS

October 22

Musings #1

S ome time ago I read of an afflicted person who, upon being asked how he bore his sufferings so well, replied; "It lightens the stroke to draw near to him who handles the rod." I immediately thought of those occasions when as a child my older brother and I were chastened by one or the other of our parents with a switch from a nearby tree. I would humble myself and stand as quietly and as near to them as possible. This made it more difficult for them to apply the switch in their hand. But my older brother would always protest loudly and try to evade the instrument of punishment and ward it off with his hands and arms. This only made his chastisement more severe, which he highly resented. Let us then remember that when chastened of the Lord it will go much easier on us if we humbly acknowledge our guilt and draw as close to him as we can.

October 23

Musings #2

S ome of the enemies of the Bible doctrine of Eternal and Unconditional Election have described it as "a dangerous doctrine." But what honest and true believer in the pure and holy God of heaven and earth could stoop to accusing him of incorporating into his precious Word a dangerous doctrine?

It is unthinkable that he would have done such a thing; and even if it were possible, many good and godly men would have long ago discovered such an abomination. The truth is, the doctrine of election cannot be harmful to anyone in any way because it is not a negative act. It is not *reprobative* (conveying or expressing disapproval, or reprobation), but *approbative* (conveying approbation or approval). It is an act of glorious grace toward those who, by nature, were children of wrath even as others, and who, in themselves were equally unlovable with those who were not loved, and every whit as underserving as those who were not elected.

Notice, the Lord does not say, "I will bestow good upon those who are deserving," but, "I will have *mercy* on whom I will have *mercy*" (Rom. 9:15). *Mercy* clearly implies a total lack of desert or merit on the part of the one who receives it. There is nothing dangerous about mercy.

October 24

Musings #3

S omewhere in my studies over the years I found it said that the Jews would not willingly tread upon the smallest piece of paper in their path, but would take it up and look at it because they thought the name of God might possibly have been written on it and they didn't want to tread upon his name. It is highly likely that there was some superstition involved in that practice but none of us should ever do or say anything that would in any way tread upon the precious name of our God.

Many people tread on God himself by thinking that he is "altogether such an one as themselves" (Psalm 50:21) and by placing limits on him in the sense of thinking he cannot do all his pleasure. Multitudes do this very thing when they argue that God cannot save anyone unless they *let* him or when they speak of his *trying* to do thus and so. How they arrive at such conclusions I do not know, in view of the fact that he is omnipotent (Rev. 19:6) and that "He hath done whatsoever he hath pleased" (Psalm 115:3; Dan. 4:35).

But as for treading on the Deity, let us also be very careful not to tread upon any of our fellow men either, for in so doing we might thus be treading upon precious souls so dear to Christ that he endured the most indescribable sufferings, and died the most ignominious of deaths, in their stead.

October 25

Musings #4

To the children of God one of the sweetest assurances in all the Bible is that "there shall be a resurrection of the dead" (Acts 24:15). Not all will sleep in the grave, because some will be alive at the second coming of Christ (1 Thess. 4:15), but all the saints will be changed, for their corruptible bodies must be made incorruptible, "this mortal must put on immortality" (1 Cor. 15:53). This is when their "vile bodies" will be fashioned like unto the *glorious body* of Christ (Philippians 3:21). Then they will be "caught up together" in the clouds, to meet the Lord in the air, and so shall they ever be with him.

What a source of joy and comfort this is to those who "love his appearing" (2 Tim. 4:8) and what a blessing it is to live each day in this precious hope! Many professed atheists have died with words of hopelessness and dread on their lips, but I have never known of the last words of a true believer to express anything but sweetness and assurance.

The well known Christian Edward Perronet said as he was dying, "Glory to God in the height of his Divinity! Glory to God in the depths of his humanity! Glory to God in his all-sufficiency. Into his hands I commend my spirit." On the other hand when the famous Voltaire was dying he said, "I am abandoned by God and man."

Though we should never join Balaam in his evil works, we may legitimately voice the same desire as he when he said, "Let me die the death of the righteous, and let my last end be like his" (Num. 23:10).

October 26

Musings #5

The apostle James says, "Faith, if it hath not works, is dead, being alone" (James 2:17), and he shows by the context that the only way anyone can prove that he possesses true, God-given faith is by his works. This visible demonstration of genuine trust in and reliance upon

God is spoken of as one's "*work* of faith" (1 Thess. 1:3; 2 Thess. 1:11). In like manner, the proof of one's *love* by his actions is called his "*labor* of love." And likewise, the proof of one's hope is called his "*patience* of hope."

Patience is not only a *virtue*, but it is also a *work*. "Let patience have her perfect work" (James 1:4). Our works will in no way make our home in heaven any more secure or certain than God's decrees have already made it, but if we were to take works out of the Christian religion all we would have left would be the empty shell of a dry, lifeless, and powerless dogma; which is just another way of saying, "Faith without works is dead" (James 2:20).

By the same token, works without true faith are "dead works" (Heb. 6:1; 9:14). Multitudes have boasted of having done "many wonderful works" in the Lord's name (Matt. 7:22-23), but obviously their works were "dead works," and there was nothing wonderful about them *or* their works because the Lord rejected them.

October 27

Musings #6

The thought of a Being so great that he could, and did, create this huge ball upon which we live by simply commanding it, is, in itself, far beyond our ability to rationalize or fathom, and we could never believe such a thing without a God-given faith. If this earth had been the only thing he had created, then that one work alone would have been far too much for finite minds to comprehend. In fact, a Being who could do no more than create a *gnat* by the mere exertion of his will, would still be altogether beyond understanding.

None of *us* can create a gnat. None of us can create *anything* in the sense of producing *something* out of *nothing*. But not only has God created the world we live in, and all it holds, but he has also created other heavenly bodies so numerous no man can count them.

The size of the sun boggles our little minds, but there is a star, called *Zeta Aurigae*, which we are told is about *ten million times* larger than the sun. Who are we poor mortals compared to our great Creator? The apostle Paul said, "If a man think himself to be something, when he is nothing, he deceiveth himself" (Galatians 6:3). How foolish are those who think more highly of themselves than they ought to think (See Romans 12:3)!

October 28

Musings #7

The Lord has pleasure in seeing his people walk together in unity and love, each esteeming their brethren and sisters better than themselves. He takes delight in seeing them bear long with one another, overlooking one another for good and not for evil; striving together for the unity of the faith in the bonds of peace; doing unto others as they would have others do unto them in all the various relations of their lives.

He also has pleasure in seeing them putting him ahead of all things else and seeking first his kingdom and his righteousness in all they do; being kind and gentle unto all men; humbling themselves under his mighty hand and bearing his meek and lowly image; letting their light shine before men in such way as to bring glory and honor to his great and good name. If all of them would do these things, what a vast difference it would make in their lives and in that glorious church which is of his own building!

Let us all strive more zealously and sincerely to spend more time in his blessed word, in prayer and in meditation upon those things which are true, honest, just, pure, lovely, of good report, virtuous, and praiseworthy (Philippians 4:8). If we do these things the apostle assures us that the God of peace will be with us.

October 29

Musings #8

It greatly comforts me to know that God visits each of his people some time between their conception and their death and quickens them into Divine light and life (John 5:21; Eph. 2:1-5); brings them up out of an horrible pit, out of the miry clay, sets their feet upon a rock, establishes their goings, puts a new song in their mouth, even praise to him (Psalm 40:3); and kills them to the love of sin (Romans 6:2). I am thankful that he sheds abroad his love within their hearts; upholds them by his grace and shields them from myriad evils and dangers that constantly surround them, and that he will never leave them nor forsake them (Heb. 13:5).

I also find great comfort in the fact that he will raise each one of them again at the last day without the loss of one. We should all thank God daily from the depths of our hearts that he continues to send forth his Spirit into the hearts of his people at his own appointed time. What an unlivable environment this old world would be if none of us had any of the principles of righteousness guiding our thoughts and actions!

Where there is no grace, there is no godliness! Where there was no Divine love there would be no tenderness, compassion, and caring, and no society could function where those qualities were totally absent.

October 30

Musings #9

As we are constantly faced with vexing circumstances around us we need to continually remind ourselves that God is still on his throne; that he possesses all power both in heaven and in earth, and that he is still ruling and reigning according to his infinite wisdom and knowledge. Things will never get out of control from his viewpoint, even though it may sometimes appear to us mortals that all is lost.

This is why Christ could calmly sleep in the ship when his disciples were fearing for their lives (Mark 4:35-41). We poor worms of the dust could face the storms of life much more calmly and confidently than we sometimes do if we trusted in God more devotedly, humbly, and submissively.

Oh how weak we feeble souls are, and how prone we are to try to deny our shortcomings and to lean unto our own strength, wisdom, and understanding! When we do that it always causes us trouble and distress of soul. We are often compelled do as Christ's disciples and beg him to increase our faith in the sense of giving us greater dependence upon his promises and greater confidence in his mercies. Like Israel of old, we often forfeit timely blessings and deny ourselves a number of sweet privileges by our failure to fully cast our cares upon the Lord as we should and to humbly submit ourselves to his divine will.

October 31

Musings #10

I am sure the apostle Paul was accused of a great many evil things during his years of service, and I draw this conclusion, not only from the Scriptures but simply by virtue of the fact that he preached the truth. Being an honest, faithful, and sincere, proponent of the doctrines of the gospel is all it takes for a man to be, at times, the object of false accusations, misrepresentations, and distortions. It appears to me that one of the most abominable falsifications ever leveled at Paul was that he taught that we should do evil in order that good might come (Rom. 3:8). Very appropriately did Paul rebuke these unsavory accusers and tell them that their damnation was just.

Someone has said that such an accusation is the mark of a reprobate sinner and that those who thus turn God's mercy into an excuse for sinning have something within them that is much worse than a heart of stone. I say they surely must have a conscience that has been *seared with a hot iron* (1 Tim. 4:2). Any person who would in any way be encouraged to break God's laws and defame his name simply because he is so good to them, has to be a most wretched creature. As the apostle so aptly put it, the damnation of such characters is most assuredly just and right! The goodness of God leads humble souls to *repentance*...not to *sin and wickedness* (Romans 2:4). His grace teaches us just the opposite of ungodliness. It declares unto us that "*denying ungodliness and worldly lusts, we should live soberly, righteously, and godly in this present world*" (Titus 2:11-12). It is an abominable error for anyone to think that God's abounding mercy gives them any excuse whatsoever for their sins!

November 1

Musings #11

When the Lord condescended to take up his abode within our hearts, to reveal himself unto us, and to give us a sweet hope in his mercy, he changed our lives forever. From that point forward we have had a treasure that far exceeds anything this world has to offer.

But along with that treasure comes a responsibility to be true and faithful to the Giver. And just as the *gift* will never be taken away, neither will the *responsibility* as long as we live in this world. We never know when we might be called upon to be faithful even unto death for the cause of Christ, and actually surrender our natural lives; but whether we are ever called upon to do that or not, we should ever be ready to lay down our lives for our brethren in the sense of not counting our lives dear unto ourselves (Acts 20:24) in comparison with our being obedient and faithful to our Lord, and putting the kingdom of God first, although it sometimes requires us to go and do even when we feel that it takes a heavy toll on us physically and emotionally.

This is particularly true of the Lord's ministering servants, but it applies to all God's people. Spiritual maturity is reflected in a willingness to "spend and be spent" for our brethren, even though in some cases it might be that the more abundantly we love them, the less they love us (2 Cor. 12:15). This requires grace such as was given to the apostle Paul, the three Hebrew children, Abraham, and many others we read of in the Scriptures. May the Lord give us a similar strength of faith, especially in the face of trial and tribulation.

November 2

Musings #12

If there is any good in any of us it is a product of the Spirit of God alone. Such good is not, nor *can* it ever be, a product of the flesh. Even the apostle Paul, as a regenerated child of God, asserted that there was "no good thing" *in his flesh* (Rom. 7:18).

Sometimes we hear it said that there is a little good in everybody, but such things are said by those who are unaware of the fallen nature that all men inherited from their first father, Adam. In their native state men consist of nothing but the flesh (Romans 8:9), and therefore there is nothing in them that God approves of or looks upon as "good."

Unregenerate men may do things that are counted good by other men, but God sees the motive behind the deeds, and he knows whether those motives are honorable or not. "The Lord seeth not as man seeth; for man looketh on the outward appearance, but the Lord looketh on the heart" (1 Samuel 16:7). The deeds of men may issue in a measure of good to certain other persons and yet those deeds be motivated by altogether selfish, or possibly even sinister, motives.

It is also not uncommon for men to come into great wealth and through certain charitable donations reach a high standing in their communities, when in reality those gifts may put the donors into a lower tax bracket, or provide other fringe benefits, so that they actually make money by giving. But a careful observation of such persons reveals that, oft-times, they never seem to give any conclusive evidence that there has ever actually been a work of grace wrought in their hearts by the Holy Spirit. In the old carnal flesh of men alone, there is nothing of any worth in the sight of God. In that sense "the flesh profiteth nothing" (John 6:63).

November 3

Musings #13

These are decadent times, and from my viewpoint there are not as many true believers as there were in former days, though there is a much larger population. There are some who have made a profession of faith in Christ but who have not done the works thereof and have been of little or no worth in the kingdom of Christ, while others have held out faithful and have been great pillars in the church. Sadly, there have been others who have departed from the faith altogether.

It therefore behooves the faithful followers of the Lord to be especially vigilant that they bear much fruit unto holiness and shine as lights in the world. Those who have been favored with an experiential knowledge of the truth are greatly and distinguishingly blest, and since much has been given *to* them, so also is much required *of* them (Luke 12:48).

Upon them rests the duty, and the privilege, of supporting to the utmost of their ability all those efforts that promote the glory, honor and praise of God, the edification and upbuilding of his saints, and the furtherance of their joy. In all such efforts they greatly need divine light, leadership, and direction. They need *courage* to stand firmly for truth and right, regardless of the opposition they meet with, and they need *wisdom* to so fulfill their responsibilities as to promote the general welfare of our beloved Zion.

November 4

Musings #14

It has grieved me much over the years to see the decline of America both in church and state. Some no doubt would say things are as good as they have ever been, and I wish I could believe it to be true, but I cannot. We do not see the degree of godliness even among our leaders that we used to see, or that existed long before we were born.

It is a fact of history that in 1787, eighty-one-year-old Benjamin Franklin addressed Congress over the question of whether small states should have the same representation as large states. He stated he was convinced that Scripture is right when it says, "Except the Lord build the house, they labor in vain that build it" (Psalm 127:1). Then he said, "Gentlemen, I have lived a long time and am convinced that God governs in the affairs of men. If a sparrow cannot fall to the ground without his notice, is it probable that an empire can rise without his aid?" He then made a move that prayer, imploring the assistance of Heaven be held every morning before Congress proceeded with business; and the motion carried.

It is greatly to be regretted that so many in our day seem to so flagrantly deny the power of prayer and very seldom, if ever, implore the Lord's blessings in a meek and submissive way. General Eisenhower said of prayer, "It gives us courage to make the decisions we must make in crisis and then the confidence to leave the result to a Higher Power." And Charles H. Spurgeon said, "Groanings which cannot be uttered,* are often prayers which cannot be refused."

May the Lord help us to pray, often and earnestly, even if it is only with groans that we cannot put into words.

November 5

Musings #15

The Lord's church is a "little flock" in the sense of her meekness, humility, and simplicity, but she is also a little flock in the sense of her numbers, relatively speaking. God could have made her the largest church in the world if he had chosen to do so, but he did not so choose.

From time to time some of those associated with the Old Baptists have gotten the idea that by the exertion of enough human endeavor and the employment of enough means and method they can add to the church numerically. I've never known of a case where any such efforts have been truly successful. The only means and methods I've ever found that we are authorized to use in the Lord's church are those found in his holy Word.

John the Baptist was authorized to "make ready" a people prepared for the Lord, but neither he nor anyone else can make the preparation. The Lord alone adds to the church (Acts 2:41, 47). If men add them, then they are *on* the church and not *in* the church. The first thing that must be done in order for anyone to even be able to *see* the kingdom of God is for the Lord to give them Divine life (John 3:3). Men cannot perform that work.

The next thing then is that they must be made humble enough to be willing to, and desirous of, being identified with the Lord's humble and persecuted church, and men can't do that either. His believing people can and should be kind and loving toward outsiders and his called ministers can and should preach the truth to them when opportunity is presented, and they should exhort them to obey it, but they cannot give them spiritual life, nor instill in them a meek and lowly spirit, nor put within them a hunger and thirst after righteousness. The pure gospel of the Lord Jesus Christ can only be received and delighted in by such as "the meek, the poor, the broken-hearted" (Is. 61:1; Matt. 11:5; Luke 4:18).

November 6

Musings #16

How thankful I am to have lived all my life (at present 73 years) among a people called Primitive, Original, or Old School Baptists who believe in the doctrines of Unconditional Election, Predestination, Irresistible grace, Effectual Calling, the Redemption of all the Elect of God, and the Final Preservation of that same blessed number, just as the Bible teaches them in the King James Translation! All God's people would do well to inform themselves as to what is said there about these precious old truths and leave the doctrines of men behind and serve the Lord as the inspired Scriptures teach them to do.

How much better it is when they can begin at the beginning with the assurance that they were "chosen in Christ Jesus before the foundation of the world" (Eph. 1:4) and that Jesus *delivered them* (past tense) from the wrath to come" (1 Thess. 1:10)! It is sad that so many of them simply will not accept what is said in 2 Timothy 1:9 showing us that we were both saved, and called, with an holy calling, and that this saving and calling was not based upon our own works but upon *God's own purpose and grace which was given us in Christ Jesus before the world began.*

How sweet it is to rest in Jesus, assured that our eternal salvation is already secured in him and that our service here is not to work our way to heaven, which is a slavish, and selfish, service, but to honor and glorify him to the best of our ability and to serve him out of love for all the wonderful things he has done for us! This is where true joy is found, and it is indeed a strait and narrow way that is only found by a few, relatively speaking (Matt. 7:13-14). It is not a popular path but it is a path wherein is found the abundant life that Christ promised to his faithful and obedient sons and daughters!

November 7

Musings #17

How often do we take the blessings of the Lord for granted and fail to thank him for the favors that we daily, hourly receive? We miss a great deal of joy by our failure to meditate frequently upon the unfailing providence of God. We need to always be aware of the fact that it is he who *keeps* Israel (his people) and that he never slumbers nor sleeps (Psalm 121:3-5).

In one of the most beautiful portions in all the Inspired Volume we are told that God's people are "kept by the power of God" (1 Peter 1:5); and the result of their being thus kept is found in Romans 8:31, namely, "If God be for us, who can be against us?" He is in, through, and around us at all times, and if we were as keenly alert and perceptive as we long to be, we would see him in all the affairs and concerns of our lives.

If we had been a companion of the apostle Paul, what do you suppose we would have thought of the awful persecutions and abuses that were heaped upon him? Would we not have wondered how God could be in those things in any way whatsoever? Yet, he said he would have his brethren to understand that those things had "fallen out rather unto the furtherance of the gospel" (Philippians 1:12). We mostly view things on their surface, but there were a number of wise purposes that Paul's sufferings served, and there are likewise often unseen benefits that we derive from our own trials and tribulations, but until we learn what those benefits are we often wonder why we have to endure them. May the Lord give us greater discernment in these and all other matters.

November 8

Musings #18

We observe a great variety among the vast number of things God has created. No two snowflakes exactly alike have ever been documented, and the same is true of fingerprints. We also observe the same kind of variety among the planets and stars.

For instance, the star *Zeta Aurigae* consists of a substance that is 1,200 times less dense than air, but another star, called *Wolf 457*, is so dense that if we could place a cubic inch of it on the surface of the earth it would weigh nine hundred tons. A number of stars have been discovered called "radio stars," and in terms of radiation output these are the strongest bodies ever discovered. The strongest of these has an energy output equal to 30 billion of our suns.

Now, do not such amazing considerations strongly impress us with our smallness compared with our great Creator? There is a vast difference between *our* strength, and *his* strength, *our* nature and *his* nature, *our* ability and *his* ability, *our* wisdom and *his* wisdom, etc. Yet, in view of all this isn't it astonishing to hear otherwise intelligent people talking about what God *wants* to do but *can't* unless we poor mortals *let* him. It would be well if such people would read Daniel 4:35, Psalm 115:3, and Psalm 135:6, and adjust their religious views to the teachings of the Scriptures rather than continuing to conform them to the misguided opinions and notions of men.

November 9

Musings #19

In the creation God made Adam of the dust of the ground; not of precious metals or beautiful jewels, or costly pearls, but of *dust,* which is among the lowliest of substances (Gen. 3:19). Just as he established a method of recovery for his people from the dreadful results of Adam's fall, totally excluding the works of man, in order to leave no grounds what ever for him to boast of having saved himself (Eph. 2:9), so also he created man in such way as to leave no grounds for him to boast of having had anything at all to do with his own creation.

The epitaph to all man's earthly prospects has already been written; "Dust thou art, and unto dust shalt thou return." In a word, all men may rightly say that, in and of themselves, they are "a worm, and no man" (Psalm 22:6). So then, "Where is boasting?" Paul says, "It is excluded" (Rom. 3:27). With regard to us poor, weak, and sinful mortals, would it not be fitting if we all constantly wore these words upon the breastplate of our heart, "Boasting is excluded! Boasting is excluded! Boasting is excluded!"

Men are by nature inherently very inclined to boast of their own achievements, even though they have nothing in themselves of which to boast. Paul made it exceedingly clear that God the Father made Christ unto his people wisdom, and righteousness, and sanctification, and redemption, so that "according as it is written, he that glorieth, let him glory in the Lord" (1 Cor. 1:26-31). May the Lord burn these words into our minds and write them upon our hearts.

November 10

Musings #20

As I consider the indescribable sufferings our blessed Lord endured on behalf of his elect, I lift the following lines from that dear man of God, the late Joseph Charles Philpot of England (1802-1869). He said, "Let us ever bear in mind that the sufferings of the holy soul of Jesus were as real, that is, as really felt as the sufferings of his sacred body, and a thousand times more intense and intolerable. Though beyond description painful and agonizing, yet the sufferings of the body were light indeed compared with the sufferings of the soul. Surely never was there such a pang since the foundations of the earth were laid as that which rent and tore the soul of the Redeemer when the last drop of agony was poured into the already overflowing cup, and he cried out, 'My God, My God, why hast Thou forsaken Me?' Nature herself sympathized with his sorrow and was moved at his cry, for the earth shook, the sun withdrew his light, and graves yielded up their dead."

I have often thought that my own *soul-sufferings*, as miniscule as they have been compared to those of our blessed Lord, were *far worse* than any physical pains I have ever endured; hence, I have no difficulty believing that the soul-sufferings of Christ were far greater than the physical pain he experienced during his life and death. Who can tell what our Lord was enduring when he said in the Garden of Gethsemane, "My soul is exceeding sorrowful, even unto death" (Matt. 26:38) or when he spoke so plaintively of the feeling departing of his precious Heavenly Father from his human nature. Oh, what an unspeakably enormous debt of love we owe to this gloriously precious Savior for what he endured in our behalf!

November 11

Musings #21

The apostle Paul tells us that we presently "see through a glass darkly," and shortly follows with, "Now I know in part" (1 Cor. 13:12). Here is something amazing to think about: an apostle to whom a great abundance of revelation was given, yet acknowledging that he now only knew "in part." When we consider the wonderful things Paul was blest to leave on record for us, and when we observe his fellow apostle, Peter, confessing that some of those things were "hard to be understood," it is truly astonishing.

We ask this question: If Paul had such a great amount of knowledge and wisdom, and yet confessed that he *knew only in part*, how much is there yet to be revealed and known? What wonders the Lord must still have in store for us when "that which is in part shall be done away!" If we now "see though a glass darkly," how will it be when we are able to view things through glorified eyes and to "know even as also we are known?"

I once knew an old Elder Smith who often spoke of God's people one day seeing heaven, "in all its full-orb glory." We can but faintly imagine the splendid scenes of inexpressible beauty that will unfold before us there, and oh, what will it be to see Jesus "face to face" without the veil of nature marring our view and to rejoice in him without any interruptions, distractions, or diminishings! How wonderful it will be for those of us who "hunger and thirst after righteousness" to be eternally furnished with that divine nourishment for which our souls so strongly yearn! The store will never be exhausted, and neither will our rapt attention to, and enjoyment of, that which the store contains.

November 12

Musings #22

Men do not have a free will when it comes to either believing in Christ or not believing in him. The *true* believer can no more decide that he will lay down his faith and despise God than he can create a universe. He has been "delivered from the power of darkness, and translated into the kingdom of Christ" (Col. 1:13), and the love of God has been shed abroad in his heart by the Holy Ghost which is given unto him (Rom. 5:5), and it is an impossibility for him to will, or decide, to start *disbelieving* in that power which has made him a new creature in Christ Jesus (2 Cor. 5:17).

The *unbeliever* has never experienced this inner work of grace, and he thinks those who speak of such a work are simply deluded and hoodwinked. He could no more believe in God in the same sense that the saints believe in God than he could raise the dead to life or drink the ocean dry. The *believer's* will is not free to decide that he will go back into a state of godless unbelief, and the *unbeliever's* will is not free to decide to become a true and devoted *believer*. Christ told Peter, "I have prayed for thee, that thy faith fail not" (Luke 22:32), but to the unbelieving Jews he said, "Why do ye not understand my speech? even because ye *cannot* hear my word" (John 8:43), and again, "Ye believe not because ye are not of my sheep" (John 10:26).

If men had a "free" will in the strictest sense of the term then neither good *nor* evil could control it. If their will were entirely free, then they would possess the ability to will to love God one minute and to will to hate him the next minute. But any *wicked* person knows very well that he has no *desire* to love God, and he has no desire *for* such a desire. And, by the same token, any *righteous* person is fully aware that he has no desire to *hate* God, and he has no desire *for* such a desire. So, when men speak of "everybody having a free will," they simply show that they are untaught concerning the limitations of fallen humanity.

❧❧

November 13

Musings #23

There is no way to express the magnitude of the blessing of eternal life. One of the things that makes it so inexpressibly precious is the fact that it is "the gift of God...through Jesus Christ our Lord" (Romans 6:23); and the fact that it is a *gift,* not only shows us how we came by it, but it also shows us that it will never be taken from us, because "it is of the Lord's mercies that we are not consumed, *because His compassions fail not"* (Lam. 3:22).

In view of this great truth the only way God could take back the gift of eternal life would be for him to revoke his own mercies and default on his compassions and thus turn them into a complete failure and himself into a false god. This is exactly what the religious world is teaching when they argue that a child of God may lose his eternal life if he does not hold out faithful to the end. God forbid that we should ever embrace such a God-dishonoring doctrine or give any credence at all to such a distressing thought! God *promised* his people eternal life before the world began, and *he cannot lie* (Titus 1:2); therefore to argue that the salvation of the saints is not secure in Christ Jesus is to say that God may break his promise and become guilty of one of the most horrendous lies that could be told.

Christ taught his disciples that all those that the Father gave him would without fail come to him and would be raised up at the last day (John 6:36-39), thus securing their salvation for all eternity. This does not in any way override the fact that they may bring much misery upon themselves in this time world because of disobedience to his word, but that does not affect God's promises to them concerning their security in Christ.

November 14

Musings #24

We Primitive Baptists are the only ones I know of, with the exception of a few small Calvinistic groups here and there, who believe the words of Christ when he said it is given unto some to know the mysteries of the kingdom of heaven, but to others *it is not given* (Matt. 13:11). It doesn't matter how clearly that truth is stated, those who are without "ears to hear" just simply cannot hear it.

Without divine light in the soul men will always view this as an act of unfairness on God's part, so they will not accept it, even though it comes straight from the mouth of Christ himself (Luke 10:21). We, in our fleshly weakness, would often by-pass God if we had the power, and *make* others see it and embrace it whether they wanted to or not, imagining that our love for them is greater than God's. But that cannot be, and it is not his way of bringing his people into the mysteries of His kingdom. He will not put that power into the hands of his poor, feeble creatures. If we had such power we would misuse it and we would boast of it.

The Lord knows what he is doing and why he is doing it. And, whether we understand it or not, *and very often we don't,* everything he does is done the very best way it can be done, because he is perfect in wisdom and he would never do anything in less than the best way. It has pleased him to hide the truths of the gospel from the wise and prudent and reveal them unto babes; and he did it because it seemed good in his sight (Matt. 11:25). No other reason is required or needed. If it seems good in his sight, then that is sufficient, and we poor mortals cannot improve on it (Please read Daniel 4:35; Rev. 4:11).

Then let us all bow before the Lord in humble submission to his perfect will and way. "He *shall* save his people from their sins" (Matt. 1:21) and he never has asked or needed the help of men in that work or in any other.

৵৽৻

November 15

Musings #25

Oh that all our churches had always followed the admonitions of Paul to all "speak the same thing"...and "be perfectly joined together in the same mind and in the same judgment" (1 Cor. 1:10)! If all of us had the proper care and love for one another and for the cause of Christ, and were all united upon the common ground of preserving the body (church) from schisms (1 Cor. 12:25) we would not have any strife and confusion among us.

Division is the product of carnality (1 Cor. 3:3), not of selfless devotion to the glory of Christ and to the up-building of his timely kingdom. If we have the kind of love for the Church that the woman who came before Solomon had for her new-born baby (1 Kings 3:25-26) we will not do or say anything that will divide it. Just as the woman was willing to give up her child altogether rather than see it mutilated and destroyed, so will we be willing to give up our part in the Church rather than see it divided or thrown into confusion.

This is the only attitude that will preserve the Church from those ugly, God dishonoring schisms that have so frequently plagued it. None expose themselves to greater timely judgments than those who disturb the peace of our beloved Zion. Christ loves his church with a love that human tongue cannot express and no mortal can conceive, and those who do it harm are in for divine retribution that they cannot imagine.

November 16

Musings #26

When we use the term "Total Depravity" we do not mean that every man is as bad as he can possibly be in every respect, but we mean that "in his flesh" there is "no good thing" (Rom. 7:18) and that so far as recovering himself from the devastating effects of Adam's fall in the Garden of Eden, he is totally void of any such ability. He doesn't even have a will, or desire, to be recovered from his carnal condition. In that sense he is like a sow that wallows in the mire (2 Peter 2:22). He is perfectly satisfied to clothe himself in the filth and corruption of this "present evil world" (Gal. 1:4) and to take in as much of its carnal pleasures as possible. Just as swine enjoy wallowing in mud-holes because it is their nature to do so,   likewise men love to wallow in sin and corruption for the same reason; it is their nature to do so.

Man's depravity is so pervasive that it once resulted in the whole human race, except for eight souls who were mercifully spared, being destroyed in the flood of Noah's day. And even so today, if it were not for the mercies of God we would all be consumed (Lamentations 3:22). If it were not for the exceeding sinfulness of sin, it would not have required the agonizing, and infinite, death of the very Son of God to redeem the elect family from their fallen condition by nature. If any allowance whatsoever could have been made for sin, something less than the blood of Christ could have sufficed. But there is no such allowance. May   we   ever   adore   the   inexpressibly   blessed, and efficacious, sacrifice of Christ in behalf of his children!

November 17

Musings #27

It was only a short time ago that one of the newscasts reported that there was an outcry from the Jews that they did not crucify Christ; that it was the Romans who did it. Well, it is true that Roman soldiers carried out the crucifixion, but it was because the Jews wouldn't have it any other way.

This whole affair is made very plain in the Gospels. Others of the New Testament writers also leave no doubt about the matter. In the apostle Peter's sermon on the day of Pentecost he addressed the men of Israel and plainly told them that they had "by wicked hands" crucified Jesus of Nazareth (Acts 2:22-23). And the apostle Paul declared the same in 1 Thessalonians 2:14-15; saying that the Jews "both killed the Lord Jesus, and their own prophets" and that he also had been persecuted by them. They had greatly displeased God and were contrary to all men.

When Christ was before Pilate they had cried out over and over, "Let him be crucified!" (Matt. 27:22-23); and then when Pilate said, "I am innocent of the blood of this just man," then all the people (all the Jews present) answered, "His blood be on us, and on our children" (vs. 24-25). Then in Acts 5:28 notice how they had changed their tune about that blood when they had commanded the apostles not to speak in the name of Christ. They then cried, "Ye have filled Jerusalem with your doctrine, *and intend to bring this man's blood upon us.*" But of course the apostles had not brought Christ's blood upon them; they had brought it upon themselves, and the rest is history.

The Jews, *and their children,* as a people, are still suffering the consequences; and this divine retribution will only be lifted from their shoulders when they, as a people, truly repent of this great crime of crucifying their own promised Messiah: "(According as it is written, God hath given them the spirit of slumber, eyes that they should not see, and ears that they should not hear;) unto this day" (Romans 11:8).

November 18

Musings #28

Through all the thousands of years of the Old Testament dispensation, Satan kept up his incessant efforts to overthrow the purpose of God, but of course he was never successful. He could not stop God's centuries-old blessings upon the human race nor his special favors to his chosen people.

In spite of all the wretched idolatry and the numberless other forms of corruption and wickedness that he suffered to exist throughout the world for many ages, he never suffered Satan to gain control over creation. And when the appointed time of the Lord came to send his only begotten Son into the world to redeem his people from their sins, Satan could do nothing to stop it, though he tried mightily. And what he thought was the end of Christ when he died on the cross, was, in reality, his own defeat and ruin in the sense of putting him and his angels under a certified and unavoidable sentence of eternal damnation in that lake of fire which is prepared for him and all those who worship at the shrine of evil.

Satan can only function within the limits under which God has restricted him, but with all the restraints God exerts upon him he is still suffered to distress us from time to time. Hence we are compelled to flee to the throne of grace and beseech his help in that age-old struggle called living; but for now, we can rest in the assurance that Satan is already defeated, and that defeat only remains to be made manifest in the final day. The saints, on the other hand, are already victorious, so that they may now sing, "Thanks be to God which giveth us the victory through our Lord Jesus Christ" (1 Cor. 15:57).

November 19

Musings #29

The apostle Paul tells us that God's people; those who were embraced in His covenant foreknowledge (Rom. 8:29) were predestinated; and that this predestination (the determining of the ultimate destination of this foreknown people) is "according to the purpose of him who worketh all things after the counsel of his own will (Eph. 1:11).However, the advocates of free-will religion cannot embrace this grand truth because it contradicts their persuasion that a person's eternal destiny, in the final analysis, depends upon the exercise of their own will rather than upon God's own purpose and grace, which was given to His people in Christ Jesus before the world began (2 Tim. 1:9). Nevertheless, it appears plain that those of us who are of the Primitive, or Original, or Old School Baptist faith, have the divinely inspired Word of God very much in our favor.

We feel great gratitude that our eternal destiny is in God's hands rather than in our own feeble and fickle hands, because our experience tells us that if it were left to us to attain a steadfast and unwavering level of holiness sufficient to qualify us for heaven, we, together with everyone else, would be doomed. May the Lord open the eyes of those who do not believe the above principles and bless them to honor him as they ought by readily and happily acknowledging that "He *shall* save his people from their sins" (Matt. 1:21). May he bless us all to bravely go against the massive tide of popular opinion and to openly stand for the truth as it is in Christ Jesus, regardless of the consequences.

November 20

Musings #30

Many years ago when there were no motels or hotels along the dirt roads navigated by travelers of that day, a man and his son were traveling in the west. When night overtook them, they had to ask for lodging at a place where the surroundings did not look at all appealing. When they went to bed they did so with their pistols in their hands, not knowing but that they might be in the home of very bad people. Soon after they laid down they heard the man of the house reading in the Bible and then offer prayer. The traveler then confidently said to his son, "Go to sleep, my son; no trouble will befall us here tonight."

The way he knew they were in a safe home was by listening to their host's Bible reading and prayer. It made him aware that the gentleman was a humble follower of Christ and it satisfied him that he and his son need fear no harm from him.

It was the same with the early Christians who had not heard of Paul's conversion and were very fearful of him until they were told that, "behold, he prayeth" (Acts 9:10-22). All they needed to know in order to feel safe in receiving Paul into their number was to know that God had changed him into a truly praying man; not just a praying man but a very humble, contrite, sincere, and pentitential man. They then knew that Paul would never be persecuting them again. Such a person does not represent a danger to those around him. He, or she, will do the church no harm.

November 21

Musings #31

Christ never spent an idle moment, for he was always in communion with his heavenly Father. He never spoke an idle word, for he always knew exactly what to say and what not to say. He never had an idle thought, for being eternally omniscient "He is in one mind, and who can turn him?" (Job 23:13). And, he never did an idle deed, for he always knew exactly what was the right thing to do. In a word, he *always* did those things that please the Father (John 8:29).

Many people think that "Christ stands at the door of the heart of every man trying to get them to let him come in." And obviously one of the reasons they think Christ does this is because they think he does not know who *will* believe on him and who *will not* believe on him. But this cannot be true for John said, "Jesus knew from the beginning who they were that believed not, and who should betray Him" (John 6:64).

This "knocking" that such people are referring to is not at the heart of all mankind but was directed to the church of the Laodiceans, giving them the opportunity to respond to his voice and commune with him (Rev. 3:20). It had nothing whatsoever to do with Christ trying to get into someone's heart. Christ was not, is not, and never has been, the weak and puny personality that unenlightened religionists often make him out to be, and I think many of them do not even realize they are doing it.

November 22

Musings #32

One of the many lessons the Lord taught his disciples was the true spirit of prayer. What he told them *not* to do is very significant. They were told *not* to imitate the hypocrites in making a display of themselves for the purpose of being seen of men. He told them *not* to use vain repetitions like the heathen do, and *not* to think that they would be heard if they prayed long enough and loud enough. None of these things would have been either appropriate or needful. Neither a vain show, a vain desire to be seen and heard by others, nor a vain multiplying of words, can, or will, impress the Lord.

Not only that, but he knows very well what we have need of before we ask him (Matt. 6:5-8). The only kind of petitions he will respond to favorably are those that are uttered with genuine sincerity, humility, and submission to his divine will. In this as well as in all things else, let us follow the Lord's example in prayer and say, "Not my will, but thine, be done."

God's way is always far better than our way, even though it is often displeasing to our flesh. Most likely one of the greatest ways in which God shows his mercies to his people is in his *not* giving them all that their fleshly nature desires. We are reminded that it did not go well with the Israelites when they complained of the manna God had provided them and desired flesh to eat instead (Psalm 78:25-31).

November 23

Musings #33

Popular religion makes an offer it cannot deliver, and offers it to those who cannot receive it (John 6:65). It asks those to believe the gospel who view it as foolishness (1 Cor. 1:18), and encourages those to accept Christ who have no interest in him. It urges them to meet conditions they cannot meet, in order to get what they do not want, so they can go where they don't want to go, in order to do what they cannot do. It requires them to love that which they hate, and to hate that which they love. Under such a system as this, how many people could ever be expected to reach heaven?

On the other hand, under God's way of saving his people from their sins (Matt. 1:21), he is one hundred percent successful in every case. In this matter he is the supreme, and sole, actor, from beginning to end. His first action toward them was to foreknow them in covenant love from all eternity, and to predestinate them to be conformed to the image of his Son. In time He calls them from nature's darkness into divine life and imputes his righteousness to them. This work, in the old English manner of speaking is called *quickening*. We see this in John 5:21: "For as the Father raiseth up the dead, and quickeneth them; even so the Son quickeneth *whom He will*" (cf. John 1:13; Eph. 2:1, 5, etc.). He keeps them by his power (1 Peter 1:5) and at last he raises them from the graves and glorifies them, making them fit for the glory world (Rom. 8:29-30).

Clearly, man's will has no place in these transactions, but after they are thus given divine life they are then called upon to maintain good works in honor to the One who has thus had such great mercy upon them (Titus 3:8). The way of salvation that is popular among men would never save a single soul, but God's way saves every one of his people without a single loss (John 6:37-39) and it populates heaven with an innumerable host.

November 24

Musings #34

When we look into the face of a precious little child, especially when it is smiling and cooing, it is difficult to realize that within its little heart resides all the existing seeds of evil, and that unless God in mercy intervenes in the course of its life and imparts a principle of grace in its soul, its ultimate end will be one of great misery. We know that some infants only live for a short time, and some are even stillborn, but the apostle Paul tells us that the wages of sin is death (Rom. 6:23); therefore we learn that those who die in infancy are a testimony to the fact that they came into the world with a sinful nature.

If there were such a thing as "infantile purity" (which many people profess to believe) then no infant would die in that state of fleshly perfection. On the other hand, all of us who survived infancy have grown up to be sinners by practice (there are no exceptions), and this is likewise a positive proof that we were born with a sinful nature. We do not become sinners because we sin, but we sin because we are sinners by nature. We have the sinful blood of our fallen parent,

Adam, flowing through our veins, and we pass that blood along to our children.

This is what David was referring to when he said, "I was *shapen* [Hebrew for *"brought forth"*] in iniquity; and in sin did my mother conceive me" (Psalm 51:5). Many people either cannot or will not embrace this truth, but no truth has ever been nullified by the fact that some did not believe it. "The scripture cannot be broken" (John 10:35).

November 25

Musings #35

To an humble child of God, one of the sweetest of blessings he can experience in this life is the evidences he receives from time to time that he is a child of God. Such evidences are no part of worldly religion, because that kind of religion teaches that if people will make a profession that they have "accepted the Lord as their personal Savior" then they will immediately become a child of God and therefore they have no reason to need any evidences of grace in their souls that they are his children. However, those who have learned something about what they are by nature and who have been brought to know what the apostle Paul meant when he said, "O wretched man that I am" (Rom. 7:23), crave assurances along the way that they are embraced in the covenant of grace.

To them such scriptures as 1 John 3:14 are very comforting, namely, "We know that we have passed from death unto life, because we love the brethren." In other words, if we have been brought by the grace of God to love his believing people, it is a sweet evidence that we have been born of God's Holy Spirit and have been called from a dead state in sin into Divine light and life.

In Matthew 5:3-12 we are given an excellent list of things that can only be said of those who have passed from death unto life and to whom the kingdom of heaven belongs. "Whosoever believeth that Jesus is the Christ *is* born of God," not *will get* born of God, but *is* born of

God. We are shown very plainly in John 1:13 that the new birth is not
of the will of man, but is solely *of God*. When a person gets that point
straight in his mind, he is then not far from the kingdom of God (Mark
12:34).

November 26

Musings #36

Our journey here is but a short span. It will not be long till that
happy day will dawn when we shall know no more pain or
sorrow, and all distress of every kind will be forever done
away. Though our years here come to an end, there is coming an eternal
day that will *never* end, but all will be joy forevermore. O what a
blessed hope is ours!

We cannot begin to imagine how sweet it will be on the other
side. Would it be amiss to say that the greatest joy we have ever known
in this life will there be multiplied by thousands? The apostle Paul has
told us by divine inspiration that it will be "far better" than anything we
presently know (Philippians 1:23), and David gives us to understand
that when we awake with the likeness of our Lord we "shall be
satisfied" (Psalm 17:15). He also tells us that in the Lord's presence is
fullness of joy, and at his right hand there are pleasures for
evermore (Psalm 16:11).

Some people's notions of heaven, if they were true, would rule out
our being completely satisfied there, but if we were not satisfied then
heaven would not be heaven. We cannot now conceive of being totally
and completely satisfied, but that is the way heaven must be in order
for us to be eternally happy. If we could fully remember the times
when we were most joyfully lifted to the mountain tops of rejoicing in
the Lord, then add to that the idea of freedom from all pain and
trouble, joined with eternal duration, we would then have at least a
reasonable concept of what heaven is.

November 27

Musings #37

Laban said to Jacob, "It is in the power of my hand to do you hurt" (Gen. 31:29); but what Laban did not know was that he could do nothing against Jacob unless the Lord suffered it to happen. God warned Laban not to speak to Jacob either good or bad, and Laban knew he was bound by that caution, and whatever his intentions may have been prior to that warning, he did not attempt to do any harm to Jacob but agreed to a covenant of peace.

Though many do not realize it, even their hearts and minds are under the complete control of God. He has not made robots of them, but he does have power over them so that if he chooses to do so he can *restrain them from* doing what they intended to do, or he can *compel them to do* what they had not desired or designed to do. This is so beautifully illustrated in the case of Pilate who said to Christ, "Knowest thou not that I have power to crucify thee, and I have power to release thee?" But Pilate did *not* have the power he thought he had, or that he *claimed* to have, and this was clearly shown by Christ's answer to him: "Thou couldest have no power *at all* against me, except it were given thee from above" (John 19:10-11).

It was further shown in the next verse, for from that moment on Pilate *sought* to release Christ but *could not* because of the demand of the Jews that he be crucified. How well this illustrates the truth of Proverbs 21:1; "The king's heart is in the hand of the Lord, as the rivers of water: he turneth it withersoever he will"! Let no man, no matter how great he may be, or deems himself to be, think that he can function independently of God.

November 28

Musings #38

From time to time we have observed those who seemed to have great ambitions of making a big name for themselves, but the humble followers of the blessed Lamb of God should never entertain any such aspirations. They should always be keenly conscious of the fact that when they have done all those things that God's word commands them to do, they are still to acknowledge that they are unprofitable servants and have nothing of which to boast, but have only done that which was their *duty* to do (Luke 17:10). They should all remember that they are *servants*, not masters. They are not lords over God's heritage (1 Peter 5:3), and they should ever keep in mind that it is their responsibility to further the joy of God's people, not to lay undue burdens upon them. And, they are not just *servants*, but in and of themselves they are ***unprofitable servants***, and therefore any success they enjoy in their labors is owing entirely to the blessings of the Lord.

No matter how much they may labor, it is God, and he alone, that *gives the increase* (1 Cor. 3:7). They will do well to keep these things ever in mind and acknowledge them in all they do. God forbid that any of his servants should ever claim for themselves any particle of the glory that belongs to him. He must *increase* but they must *decrease* (John 3:30).

November 29

Musings #39

Often some of life's most vitally important lessons are couched in just a very few words of Inspiration. One such instance of this may be found in Romans 12:2, "Be not conformed to this world." What a life-changing effect it would have on many of God's people if they would truly and faithfully observe this one simple rule! They should not fashion themselves after the ways of the world or in any manner copy its wicked ways, but they should watch the world in a cautionary way with a view to avoiding its evils and the dreadful consequences of its unwise and unbecoming behavior.

The directive in Romans 12:2 clearly implies that the saints will have ample opportunity to see how such people live, and to observe the devastating results. They should take particular notice of the misery and unrest the followers of evil bring upon themselves as a result of running after iniquity. It behooves them to notice how worldlings ruin their health and destroy their happiness; how they suffer from drunkenness and other drug abuse; how they disregard God's laws concerning marriage and many other aspects of life, and observe how they make a hell on earth for themselves; how often they destroy themselves financially and otherwise. It is not a pretty sight.

The devil paints a very appealing picture of worldly pleasures and pursuits, but he *never* addresses the ruinous consequences of foolishly following the pernicious ways of godless humanity (2nd Peter 2:2). No, a thousand times no! Such behavior should never be thought of as anything but destructive and ruinous. It should only be noticed with a view to shunning it.

How those powerful words of Romans 12:2 should ring in our ears from hour to hour and from day to day, "Be not conformed to this world!" Avoid the ways of the world as you would avoid the ways of death, for such they truly are!

November 30

Musings #40

The much-loved old song "God of love, O hear our prayer" has a line that says, "Save us from the great and wise, till they sink in their own eyes." The enemies of the old church are those who have never been made to sink in their own eyes. They have never seen themselves as poor, wretched sinners by nature. They have never had a view of themselves as justly condemned by the pure and holy Law of God, and they have never been given a sweet hope in Christ as the only Savior of poor, lost and undone sinners.

But at the point when an enemy of truth is brought down in the dust of self-abasement by an inner work of the Holy Spirit, he is no longer a threat of any kind to the humble followers of the Lord. After that work is done the Old Church then need not beseech the Lord to save her from such a person, just as the apostolic Church was no longer fearful of Saul of Tarsus once the Lord had struck him down on the Road to Damascus, made him to sink in his own eyes, and to confess that he was a wretched man in and of himself.

Prior to such a conversion a man may think himself great and wise, just as did king Nebuchadnezzar (Daniel 4), but once the Lord strips him of his self-righteousness and shows him what a vile and filthy creature he is by nature, he can no longer vaunt himself nor fight against the meek and lowly followers of the Lamb. The apostle Paul himself, once he was brought to sink in his own eyes, was almost immediately compelled to pray to God for protection from those who had not been thus brought down. That great work turned him from being a persecutor to an object of persecution. And all those who would live godly in Christ Jesus shall likewise suffer unjust treatment in one way or another for the truth's sake (2 Tim. 3:12).

December 1

Musings #41

If, as some say, Christ does not know who *will* believe on him and who *will not* believe on him and therefore he stands knocking at the door of every man's heart *hoping* they will let him in; how, then, could he have *foreknown* his elect people (Romans 8:29; 2 Timothy 2:19; 1 Peter 1:2)? And, if then, he *does* know them, how is it that some deny that he "knew from the beginning who they were that believed not, and who should betray him" (John 6:64)?

And if he knew these things, why would he be trying to get someone to open the door of their heart if he knew full well that they *would not* believe on him? We find where Christ stood at the door of the seven churches of Asia (Revelation 2-3), giving those who heard his voice, and opened the door, the privilege of having him come in unto them and enjoying spiritual communion with him; but we find nowhere in the Scriptures where Christ was ever knocking at an individual's heart, knowing full well that there was not going to be any response. If that sort of thing had been the case, then it would have proved Christ not to be possessed of any of those attributes that would have shown him to be both all-knowing and all-powerful.

It is amazing how determined some people are to have a little god over whom they wield full control. Perhaps it makes them feel more comfortable in their religion. There has to be a reason why so many say of Christ, "We *will not* have this man to reign over us" (Luke 19:14).

December 2

Musings #42

How awful and degrading is the notion, so widely and popularly promulgated in our day, that many of God's people will be eternally lost and ruined in hell in spite of all the efforts of the Deity to save them! To argue in favor of such a proposition requires the open denial of a significant number of scriptures clearly taught in God's word. It requires the picking and choosing of a few *reference texts* and putting contradictory interpretations upon them which are in direct opposition to the many *proof-texts* with which we are supplied in the Holy Scriptures.

For instance, the "whole world" spoken of in John 3:16 and 1 John 2:2 cannot possibly refer to the whole *Adamic world,* for that would require us to take one of two heretical positions; the first being the doctrine of Universalism, which necessitates No-hell-ism, and the other being the Eternal Apostasy of multitudes for whom Christ suffered and died. This second position entails the idea that even though Christ put their sins away as far as the east is from the west (Psalm 103:8-13), they will nonetheless be eternally lost, which is an awful affront to the eternal will, wisdom, and purpose of God.

Both John 3:16, First John 2:2, and any other such *reference-texts,* are speaking of *the whole world of God's elect,* not the whole world of humanity. John 6:37-40 (a proof-text) shows us, as clearly as language can make any point, that *all* the Father gave to Christ *will* come to him and that he will not lose a single one of them. He will in no wise cast them out of his eternal covenant love and mercy. How clearly this refutes, denies, and exposes the fallacy of freewill religion!

December 3

Musings #43

If God had intended for us to save ourselves in an eternal sense by meeting various conditions, why did he make a choice of certain ones in Christ Jesus *before the foundation of the world* (Eph. 1:4)? And, in such a case, why did Paul tell Timothy that God has "saved us, and called us [his people] with an holy calling, not according to our works, but according to his own purpose and grace, *which was given us in Christ Jesus before the world began*" (2 Tim. 1:9)? And why did Paul tell Titus that God promised eternal life to his people "*before the world began*"?

The answer is obvious; God did not base the eternal salvation of his people on their feeble and fickle, vacillating and uncertain will, but he based it upon his own eternal, settled, steady and immutable purpose and decree. "The foundation of God *standeth sure,* having this seal, "The Lord knoweth them that are his..." (2 Tim. 2:19). The "everlasting covenant" that God confirmed in David, is said to be "ordered in all things, and sure," and David counted it as being "all his salvation, and all his desire, and he was assured that *it would neither grow larger nor smaller* (2 Sam. 23:5). In other words, it has from all eternity embraced a fixed number, and no man or set of men can alter it in any way, although they wear themselves out trying. It embraces every soul that loves God and longs to be with him, and it leaves those in their sins who by their own choice prefer a life that does not include God and godliness.

Numbers of people reject these truths, but we should remember that it has pleased God to hide these things from the wise and prudent, and reveal them to babes (Matt. 11:25), and Christ gives us the only reason we need to know as to why he did it, saying; "Even so, Father: for so it seemed good in thy sight." And, if it does not seem good in *our* sight, it is because we are at odds with God and we need to beg him to give us greater understanding.

PART 3

BITS & PIECES

December 4

Two Different Choices

The reason the rich young ruler, mentioned in Matthew 19:16, Mark 10:17 and Luke 18:18, did not want to share his wealth with the poor, was because he loved that wealth more than he loved God. He preferred treasure on earth to *treasure in heaven*. He went away sorrowful. If following Christ meant parting with his wealth, then it meant more than he was willing to perform.

There are many today who, no doubt, would make the same choice. What a great contrast is this to the choice of Moses, who preferred to suffer affliction with the people of God rather than to enjoy the pleasures of sin for a season; esteeming the reproach of Christ greater riches than the treasures in Egypt (Heb. 11:25-26)!

The rich ruler made a bad choice, but Moses made a good one. Moses, like Mary (Luke 10:42), chose that good part, which was not taken away from him. What wondrous things he was blest to perform and accomplish by the hand of the Lord! What glorious displays of the power of God he witnessed! What a useful place he filled in the ancient church, none of which would have been so if he had made the same choice as the rich young ruler! Who can tell what temporal joys the young ruler would have experienced if he had done what the Lord directed?

December 5

Sheep in the Midst of Wolves

Were not the providential mercy and grace of God ever in exercise toward his chosen family, the plight of the Christian would be miserable beyond expression. The apostle Paul said, "All that will live godly in Christ Jesus shall suffer persecution" (2 Tim. 3:2). "But evil men and seducers shall wax worse and worse, deceiving and being deceived." The apostle John said, "And we know that we are of God, and the whole world lieth in wickedness" (1 John 5:19).

Paul and John had no illusions about the dangers the humble servants of Christ are exposed to in this wretched and unfriendly world. Christ himself had told John and the other apostles, "Behold, I send you forth as sheep in the midst of wolves" (Matt. 10:16), and that is a very apt analogy. Wolves have a natural instinct to attack and destroy sheep at every opportunity, and unless the sheep have a shepherd to protect them from these natural predators they will soon be devoured. If left to fend for themselves they are virtually defenseless. It is their nature to *fear* the wolves, not to *fight* them.

Likewise, the meek and lowly followers of Christ would soon be swallowed up and devoured by their enemies if it were not for the ever watchful eye of their loving Savior. Paul was vividly aware of this fact when he prayed that he might be delivered from unreasonable and wicked men (2 Thess. 3:2). May we all be thus delivered.

December 6

Headed Toward Home

When I was a boy we had a big horse named Maude. She was as gentle as a lamb but she was lazy and very, very slow, unless she was either forced or encouraged to speed up. In fact, we used to say Maude had three speeds, slow, slower, and stopped. When I would saddle her up and ride her away from the house she was very reluctant and made it quite clear that she didn't want to go. But then when I would head back toward home her step would become much more lively and I could almost hear her thinking about that rich, green grass in the pasture that awaited her return.

Through the years, as I have gone about the duties of the ministry, I have often thought of Maude and of how much I sometimes reminded myself of her. I have many times reluctantly left the safety and comfort of home and the little family I loved so much and have gone on distant journeys, not knowing what lay ahead and not knowing whether the Lord would bless my labors when I reached my destination. How hard it has sometimes been when I reflected on the fact that I was getting further and further from home all the time, and that at best I would not return for several days. As a general rule the Lord has blest me to feel that he was with me on those journeys, but there have also been times when I surely was thankful when I finally got headed back toward home, and then it was hard to stay within the speed-limit. Indeed, there is no place like home.

But there is another journey that I have been on ever since the Lord called me into the Christian race, and in this journey I have all the time been drawing *closer* and *closer* to home, my blessed *eternal* home. Every day and every step has brought me nearer and nearer to joys and pleasures unspeakable, and sometimes it seems I can hardly wait to see the lights of that great city not made with hands. Within my soul it seems I can almost see the outstretched arms of my dear Savior and hear him saying, "Come, ye blessed of my Father, inherit the kingdom prepared for you from the foundation of the world" (Matt. 25:34). It is indeed good to be headed toward home, and the older I get the brighter is the prospect of seeing my Lord face to face in that sweet abode called heaven.

December 7

Truth Resides with the Minority

The world likes to be on the side of the majority, for to their way of thinking this puts them on the side of *right*. Among worldly-minded men and women the argument that "everyone is doing it" seems to give license to any activity. But this certainly runs counter to the teachings of the Scriptures. Our Lord taught us that the broad way that leads to destruction is *always* where you will find the multitudes (Matt. 7:13), and there have always been *few* comparatively who found the narrow way which leads to life. I cannot think of a single instance in the Bible where the *majority* was right, but it abounds with instances in which the minority was on the side of truth and right.

The apostle John was well aware of the ratio between those who are right and those who are wrong when he said, "We know that we are of

God, and the whole world lieth in wickedness" (1 John 5:19). True believers have always been very much in the minority. Look how many were gathered together in the upper room at Jerusalem at the close of our Lord's earthly ministry—"about an hundred and twenty" (Acts 1:15)—not many compared to the multitudes among whom he had ministered. The church enjoyed a great ingathering shortly after this, but even then the numbers were small comparatively speaking, and I suspect some of them did not remain faithful to the Lord and his Church.

A good rule of thumb, even if we had no Bible would be to observe what the world delights in and avoid it, or, in most cases, go just the opposite direction. This is not an idea that originated with us, but it is a principle that the Lord of glory expressed: "That which is highly esteemed among men is abomination in the sight of God" (Luke 16:15).

December 8

Abraham's Faith

In the twenty-second chapter of Genesis it is said that God did tempt Abraham. Many do not understand what is meant here by this tempting, but much of the mystery is cleared away when one is made aware of the fact that the same Hebrew word that is translated *tempt* in this place also means *to prove* or *to try*.

It cannot be allowed that God tempted Abraham to *sin*, for he never tempts any man in that sense (James 1:13), but he tried, proved, or tested him. And this testing of his faith was not in order that God might discover what was in Abraham, for he knows all things, but it was for Abraham's benefit and for ours.

As we consider the marvelous example of this godly man's faith, how we do admire the strength of it! How we do delight in the God-honoring nature of it! And how we do desire to emulate it! How far are we willing to go in obedience to what God requires of us? If we were commanded to give up something that was as precious to us as was Isaac to Abraham, would we as willingly and unhesitatingly comply as he proved he was ready to do? Could we confidently say within ourselves, "If God has commanded it, it has to be right, and I will do it even though I do not understand why he requires it?" Well, he will not require us to slay our beloved children, but there are many things he has taught us that we ought to do, and many things that we ought to either give up or avoid as his followers.

How well do we respond to his precepts and admonitions? Is our faith as strong as was Abraham's? We may never know for sure, but it is a good question to ponder.

ॐॐ

December 9

Christ Our Example

The apostle Paul admonished the saints to be followers of him, even as he also was of Christ (1 Cor. 11:1). Christ is our great example, and we should follow no man any further than he follows Christ. Just as our Lord was "meek and lowly in heart," so should we strive as much as we are able to reflect those same characteristics. Everything Christ did was done honorably and with great dignity. He was inherently holy and perfect, and we are inherently corrupt and sinful, and consequently our efforts to follow him must fall distressingly short of his flawless standard, but we should always aim at the mark and strive to keep it ever before us.

In our efforts to follow him we should be gentle and kind in all our dealings with others. We should be full of compassion and tender-heartedness toward them. We should ever strive to control our passions and never get "out of sorts" with those around us. We should be very longsuffering and forbearing toward those who slander us and otherwise mistreat us. We should always go leaning upon the everlasting arms of Jesus and constantly taking our cares and concerns to God in humble prayer and supplication. We should ever seek to do only those things to others that we would want done unto us.

These things represent a very high standard but that is precisely the point. If we would be followers of Christ these are the kinds of things it is necessary for us to humbly and sincerely strive for. Many people claim to be Christians, but one would never know it by the way they conduct themselves. All of us, to a more or less degree, fall short in our efforts to emulate our blessed Lord, but that does not excuse us from trying to the best of our ability. The more we try, the closer we will get to the perfect standard he set before us.

December 10

It is God that Showeth Mercy

Some have tried to explain God's election by saying that God foresaw those who would be good and he consequently elected them to salvation on that basis. However, not only does the Bible teach just the opposite with regard to what God foresaw (Psalm 14:2-3), but such an arrangement would base salvation entirely upon creature righteousness and human merit, which the Bible emphatically denies (Romans. 9:11; Romans 11:5-6; Eph. 2:8-10).

The example of Jacob and Esau clearly makes the point to anyone who is willing to see. The Lord loved one of them and hated the other without any consideration of their works, either good or bad, and without any unrighteousness or injustice on God's part (Romans 9:11-14). Neither Jacob nor Esau had any merit by nature, but were both sinners under the curse of God's holy law. God simply had mercy on one of them and not the other. Jacob became a godly person because of God's mercy. Esau was left in his sins.

The charge is often made against this doctrine that God would have been unjust to love one and not another, but this is a false conclusion based upon a false premise. God would have remained just and holy if he had never loved *anyone*. It is clearly his divine prerogative to have mercy on whom he will have mercy, and to have compassion on whom he will have compassion (Exodus 33:19). "So then it is not of him that willeth, nor of him that runneth, but of God that showeth mercy" (Romans 9:15-16, 18). The lesson is as clear as pure spring water.

The key word here is "mercy;" not the *just deserts* of men, but *mercy*. If mankind were *deserving* of God's love and compassion there would be no place for *mercy* whatsoever. All are enemies of God by nature (Romans 8:7-8), and all would have remained in that condition if he had not shown *mercy* to those he loved. Some of mankind are "vessels of *wrath*," and some of them are "vessels of *mercy* (Romans 9:22-23). If you have the love of God in your heart, it is because you are a vessel of mercy. If you *don't* have the love of God in your heart, then you are not interested in his mercy, and do not feel any need of it.

December 11

Spiritual Discernment Required

The Scriptures of the Old and New Testament were given by divine inspiration, not in part but in whole (2 Tim. 3:16). In other words, the Bible was not written by the will of man but it was written by holy men of God "as they were moved by the Holy Ghost" (2 Peter 1:20-21). The Lord breathed-out the very words, not just the thoughts (Psalm 12:6; Prov. 30:5). *Men* of God were inspired *of* God. They wrote of *spiritual things,* or "the things of the Spirit of God" which the natural man cannot receive (1 Cor. 2:14). Consequently an understanding of such things requires *spiritual* discernment. Without this discernment, or, "the mind of Christ" a man cannot know these things. They are only foolishness unto him.

Many efforts have been made to rewrite the Bible in an attempt to make it understandable to anyone who reads it. What a foolish and dangerous enterprise! God's word itself pronounces severe penalties upon those who add to it or take from it (Rev. 22:18-19). God never intended that those who love the filth and mire of this ungodly world should understand his precious word or find any comfort therein. "There is a path which no fowl knoweth, and which the vulture's eye hath not seen" (Job 28:7).

In response to a question from his disciples as to why he spoke to the multitudes in parables, Christ answered, "Because it is given unto you to know the mysteries of the kingdom of heaven, but to them it is not given" (Matt. 13:11). He himself thanked His Father because he had hidden these things from the wise and prudent, and had revealed them unto babes (Matt. 11:25). "Even so, Father," says he, "for so it seemed good in thy sight."

It is comforting to God's people to know that his word is a special Book, and a divinely inspired Book. It is also good to know that it is a preserved Book (Psalm 119:89; Is. 40:8; Matt. 24:35; 1 Peter 1:25). Therein is the righteousness of God revealed "from to faith," not from *faith* to *unbelief* (Romans 1:17). It is "revealed," which clearly shows that it is not automatically understood by everyone who reads it. Why should anyone expect a Book inspired by the all-wise and eternal Deity to be understood by ungodly and graceless men with no divine light or understanding? It cannot be reasonably expected that a Book inspired by the omniscient God should be understood even in part without the light of the same Spirit that inspired it.

In order for anyone to understand, and find comfort in, the spiritual import of any of the Bible, they must first be regenerated by the almighty power of God, and then given spiritual discernment. Much prayerful study of its wonderful pages will then enable those thus enlightened to uncover many of its precious gems of truth.

December 12

Preservation of the Saints

God's people, whom he chose in Christ before the foundation of the world (Eph. 1:4), are "sanctified by God the Father, and preserved in Christ Jesus, and called," (Jude 1) and this calling is by the Holy Spirit. Hence, all three persons in the Godhead are equally involved in the eternal security of the saints. In order for a child of God to be eternally lost, God the Father, God the Son, and God the Holy Ghost would all have to be defeated in their purpose and in their individual office-works.

The elect were foreknown, chosen in Christ, and predestinated. In consequence of this and because of the fact that God will do all his pleasure, they will all ultimately be called, justified and glorified (Isaiah 46:10-11; Romans 8:29-30). There can be no doubt as to their complete and total safety in Christ. All the purposes, counsels, and decrees of God are firmly united in securing their ultimate preservation and deliverance. Through the grace that is given unto them, "the righteous also shall hold on his way" (Job 17:9).

Christ possesses power over all flesh, and will consequently give eternal life to all that the Father gave Him (John 17:2). He says, "I give unto them eternal life, and they shall never perish." Not only that, but he goes further and declares that no man shall pluck them out of *his* hand or the *Father's* (John 10:28-29). Words cannot make anything any plainer.

Christ further says, "All that the Father giveth me shall come to me; and him that cometh to me I will in no wise cast out" (John 6:37). And then he goes on to show that he came to do the will of his Father, and that will was that of all which he had given him, he should lose nothing, but should raise it up again at the last day (vs. 38-39).

A case has never been more thoroughly and undeniably proven than that of the preservation and security of the saints. It is a great comfort to those who are blest to see it and embrace it, and it gives wonderful motivation for all their efforts to serve the Lord. As Paul expressed it, "I beseech you therefore, brethren, *by the mercies of God,* that ye present your bodies a living sacrifice, holy, acceptable unto God, which is your reasonable service" (Romans 12:1).

December 13

A Wonderful Change

I doubt that we could find a more remarkable example of the difference between an unregenerate and a regenerate than that of the thief who was brought to repentance while on the cross. In Matthew 27:44 and Mark 15:32 we observe that both the thieves who were crucified with Christ were joining in mocking and reviling him. But in Luke 23:40-43 we find one of them rebuking the other for railing on Christ, acknowledging their own just condemnation and confessing the innocence of Christ. We hear him asking to be remembered by the Lord when he came into his kingdom, and Christ telling him, "Today shalt thou be with me in paradise." There is only one thing that can account for this dramatic change in one of the thieves, and that is the work of the Holy Spirit in his heart, bringing him out of death in sins into divine light and life.

We notice again that before the Lord regenerated this thief he was mocking and railing against Christ just like the other one. He obviously had no love for Christ and no interest in his kingdom. These are obvious marks of an unregenerate state, but as soon as the Lord gave him the new birth, he began confessing his just condemnation, acknowledging the innocence of Christ and desiring to be with him in heaven. Such sentiments and desires can only come from the quickening of the Holy Spirit.

It should also be observed that neither Christ nor this new-born thief started "witnessing" to the other thief and trying to get him to "accept the Lord before it was too late." The Scriptures never mention any such thing. Christ could just as easily have given *both* these thieves spiritual life as he did the one, if it had been his purpose to do so. In fact, he could have instantaneously quickened the whole mob if he had chosen to do so.

We should often consider our own weaknesses and imperfections and remember that it was the Lord who brought *us* out of death in trespasses and sins. We should remember this thief on the cross and reflect on the fact that just as he had no fitness, either internally or externally, that would have commended him to God's grace, so neither did we. As Elder J. Harvey Daily once said, "If God had made choice of *characters* instead of *persons*, this thief would have never seen heaven," and neither would we.

Everyone who has ever been born of God was born in the same way this thief was born—entirely by the grace and mercy of God, and without the aid of a Bible or a preacher or a missionary. All of the heirs of grace are quickened into divine life at God's own appointed time. He never has needed man's help to do anything.

December 14

Meet for the Master's Use

If God's children will keep themselves from dishonorable men, from their bad company and their evil pursuits, they will be persons who are fitted to and suitable for the Lord to make use of in his service, for the glory of his name and for the benefit of others. They are thereby prepared to perform in a proper way all those good works to which he has called them.

This, it seems to me, is basically what the apostle Paul is saying in 2 Timothy 2:21. This of course refers to the born-again children of God behaving themselves in such way as to enjoy a close and comforting communion with the Lord, as opposed to the behavior of Phygellus and Hermogenes, mentioned in 2 Timothy 1:15. A child of God who is living in disobedience forfeits his right to be put to an honorable use by the Lord in his kingdom here in the world.

Those who have experienced the joy of being used of God to perform some good services in behalf of his people, know that nothing in this world brings the kind of fulfillment and satisfaction that this does.

We cannot make ourselves "meet (fit or suitable) to be partakers of the inheritance of the saints in light" (Col. 1:12) but after that condition has been established by the Lord, we then are called upon to live righteously, humbly, and soberly in this present evil world so that we might be useful servants employed in praising our Master and being devoted to the welfare of his children for so long as our sojourn here may last. May he lay the burden of this truth upon the hearts of all his people.

December 15

Christ is Precious to Believers

"Unto you therefore which believe he is precious" (1 Peter 2:7)

To those who believe that Christ has power over all flesh and that he will give eternal life to as many as the Father has given him, he is precious. To those who believe he came into the world to save sinners, and who have a sweet hope that they are among that blest number for whom he shed his precious blood, he is a most precious person; a most merciful and compassionate High Priest, a precious Prophet, a precious King, a precious Friend, a precious Elder Brother, a precious Leader and Teacher, a precious Example, a good and precious Physician, and a kind and tender Shepherd. He is all in all to those who view him thus.

It is only *believers* who view him as truly *precious*. However, he cannot be as highly valued by those who think they are saved because they accepted him as their Savior as he is by those who believe he saved them according to God's own purpose and grace (2 Tim. 1:9). He cannot be as precious to those who feel that they had *little* to be forgiven for as he is to those who feel that they have been forgiven an enormous sin-debt. This principle is set forth very clearly in Luke 7:41-47.

If a person thinks Christ cannot save anyone unless they *let* him, then he will not be as precious to that individual as he is to those who believe salvation is entirely by the grace of God and not by any of the deeds of men. If a man thinks Christ is *trying* to save sinners, then he will not be as precious to that person as he is to those who believe he does his will in heaven and in earth and none can stay his hand or question what he does (Dan. 4:35). If a man thinks that those for whom Christ died may reject him and be eternally lost, then Christ will not be as precious to him as he is to those who believe that his shed blood and imputed righteousness is sufficient to house everyone of his elect in heaven without the loss of a single one (John 6:37-40).

What we believe about Christ will determine the extent of his experiential value to us. May he help us, therefore, to always believe the right things about him, and may he grow more and more precious to us as we travel down this short pathway of life and as we learn more and more of his wonders and glories.

December 16

The Heart

It is a *sobering* thought that the Lord knows the secrets of the hearts of men (Psalm 44:21), and it is an *humbling* thought that some of the secrets of their hearts are such as God finds displeasing. And it is a *mortifying* thought that, viewed strictly from the standpoint of their natural corruption, apart from the grace of God, men's hearts are "deceitful above all things, and desperately wicked" (Jer. 17:9). Who can really *know* the heart? It is certain that no mere man knows it. None of us know our *own* heart as God knows it.

Have you not many times heard humble followers of Christ say, "If I know my heart"? They say this because they are aware that sometimes they might be deceived with regard to what they believe their heart is telling them. It is only as their heart is in harmony with "thus saith the Lord" that they can be assured that it is right in God's sight. We read of those whose hearts were not right with God (Psalm 78:8, 37). Sometimes we might think ours *is* right when it is not. How this thought should humble us! How few there are who really *know the plague of their own heart* (1 Kings 8:38)!

The natural man, or the man who has not been born of the Spirit of God, has a wicked heart that *always* deceives him, so that he calls evil good, and good evil; puts darkness for light, and light for darkness, and puts bitter for sweet and sweet for bitter" (Is. 5:20). Solomon speaks of this crossed up and perverted perspective when he says, "Every way of a man is right in his own eyes: but the Lord pondereth the hearts" (Prov. 21:2). But no matter how much a man is deceived by his own heart, it never deceives God. Oh that we might be blest with an "honest and good heart" and with greater spiritual discernment!

December 17

Apt to Teach

One of the qualifications of a minister, as given by the apostle Paul to Timothy, is that he be "apt to teach" (1 Tim. 3:2). Sad to say, I have known men who have been ordained to the ministry who were more apt to *confuse* and *misinform* than they were to *teach*. Poor judgment has often been used in ordaining men to the ministry (and to the deaconship, too, as to that matter). Prayerful consideration of their qualifications has been sadly lacking in many cases. This, probably as much as any other one thing, has contributed to the weakened condition of many of our churches.

The Greek words that our translators rendered "apt to teach" mean "skilled in teaching." When a man preaches, his hearers should *learn* something from his preaching. It should be instructive and edifying. It is the business of ministers to explain and expound the Scriptures, or to "open and allege" (Acts 17:3).

Some men give no forethought to what they want to talk about when they go into the pulpit, and no matter what text they take for a beginning point, they merely rattle off whatever shallow thoughts come to their mind, and the listener is left with nothing of any depth or substance but only a string of disconnected thoughts that do not necessarily have any relation one with the other. If they can *sound* like they are preaching that is all it takes to satisfy them that they are *doing* so.

What I am speaking of here may appear harsh to some, but I have been observing it for more than fifty years and it distresses me no less now than it did in the beginning. I am genuinely sorry for men who have been placed in the ministry in name only, for it is a difficult enough responsibility even for those who have been called to it. However, I grieve even more for the damage such a misstep as ordaining unqualified men does to the churches.

Skill in teaching requires, first of all, God-given abilities, and secondarily, but no less important, it requires prayerful and diligent study and meditation. How can a man teach what he does not know, and how can he preach in demonstration of the Spirit and of power without unction from on high? If a man has not studied sufficiently to even be able to *quote* or give the content and essence of a text correctly, how can he *expound* and *explain* it correctly? If he does not even know what it *says*, how can he know what it *means?*

Dear Lord, wouldst Thou lead, guide, and direct thy people as to whom they should ordain to the ministry, and then lead, guide and motivate those who are thus ordained to give themselves as wholly to the work as is necessary to qualify them to teach thy inspired word in such way that it will edify the hearers.

December 18

Faith

One of the things the Lord has revealed to his people concerning their walk with him is that it is necessary for them to walk "by faith and not by sight" (2 Cor. 5:7). It is natural for us to want to see the path clearly marked out before us prior to taking a single step, but it is a much greater honor to God, and gives him far greater glory, for us to step out by faith on his promises, trusting him implicitly to provide our needs and to open the way before us at the appropriate time.

Many people think they would like to have grace to die, or dying grace, long before they need it, so that they might feel comfortable about that approaching hour. But we will not wish for that or any other grace ahead of time if we really believe God will provide it when the need arises. We can then feel secure and at ease about our appointment with death, confident in the assurance that the Lord will not forsake us in that day, but will be as faithful to us then as he has been throughout our life.

True believers are blest above measure in that they are, by faith, as certain of God's existence and as assured of his divine attributes as if they had seen him face to face. "Faith is the substance of things hoped for, the evidence of things not seen" (Heb. 11:1). Men who are not in possession of the gift of faith may be surrounded with any amount of outward evidence of the things that believers rejoice in and still not see or find comfort in any of it. Spiritual sight goes far beyond natural sight.

Such unbelievers think the enlightened sons of God are fools, for because they themselves cannot see with their natural eyes the things that saints see by an eye of faith, they think those things do not exist. God has revealed enough just in the natural creation to leave unbelievers without excuse (Rom. 1:20), but that does not change the fact that they are spiritually blind. They have no *spiritual* light or discernment (1 Cor. 2:14). That is why many of them will not even acknowledge God in nature.

What a great advantage faith is to God's believing people, for it enables them to lay hold upon that which otherwise would mean nothing to them! May the Lord help us to use the faith he has given us to his glory and to our own comfort.

December 19

Better Than a Sleeping Pill

In a sermon several years ago an Elder mentioned a lady who was so troubled and disturbed about certain circumstances in her life that she could not sleep well. One night she worried so much that after she went to bed all she could do was roll and tumble. She finally got up and said, "I believe I will look in the Bible. Maybe I can find something there that will cause me to go to sleep." When she opened the Bible her eyes fell on the expression in Psalm 121:4, "Behold, he that keepeth Israel shall neither slumber nor sleep." She thought about it for a moment and said, "There is no use for both of us to stay awake: I will just go back to bed and go to sleep."

The next time we find ourselves unable to sleep, it might help us to relax if we too would remember that the Lord is always on the job. He is always looking out for his people and taking loving notice of their problems. He is our ever-present Shield and Helper (Psalm 33:20;

115:9-14). He is a Watchman who not only *sees* our troubles but is also able to *do* something about them, night or day.

Even if we are having problems that we can do something about, we usually can't do much about them in the night, so may the Lord help us to cast our cares upon him and sleep in the confidence that he is always awake and always aware of our circumstances. May he bless us to rest while it is night, so we will be in better condition to face the day ahead of us. There is no point in sitting up with the Lord. He is a faithful Guardian.

December 20

Sermon Without a Proof Text

A couple of years ago I saw a sermon title on a church sign that read: *The Qualifications For Sunday School Teachers*. The text given for that sermon was Hebrews 5:12. Well, I suppose we could say that Hebrews 5:12 is just as good as any other verse in the Bible to prove what the qualifications of Sunday School teachers are, because it says absolutely nothing on that subject. There is not a word of it in the entirety of the Bible because there is no such office or position mentioned anywhere in its pages.

Sunday Schools are a relatively modern invention and neither Christ nor his apostles ever mentioned them, authorized them, or advocated them. They had their origin in the late seventeen hundreds and were not even originally intended by their founder Robert Raikes of Gloucester, England, as religious institutions.

According to the Methodists, in 1784 John Wesley expressed the hope that these schools *would become* "nurseries for Christians." I think that is pretty much the way they are viewed now by popular religionists, and this man-made tool has become so commonly accepted that anyone who does not have them in their churches is viewed as strange, backward and ignorant. But it has come to the place in this modern age of so called enlightenment that *anyone* who conforms his or her worship strictly to the New Testament pattern is considered strange and ignorant. In spite of that "we ought to obey God rather than men" (Acts 5:29). In such a case, what men think of us is beside the point.

৽∾ఌ

December 21

Why Do We Worship God?

As I observe some people and the light and flippant way in which they approach their religion, I fear that there is nothing spiritual about it; that there is no real dedication and devotion to God or to his cause. It seems to me that their profession is little more than a business transaction between themselves and God. It is as though they are saying, "We will serve you, but only in order to bring you under obligation to us. We will pay homage to you, but only if you will give us life eternal." If this is their thinking, then theirs is a vain religion that does not bring any honor to God at all.

What would we think of a son who only complied with his father's will out of a sense of obligation, or to avoid punishment or to gain some reward, and not out of any love and affection? We would not think much of the character of such a son would we? Just so, in matters of religion; it does not seem at all respectable, or respectful, or proper for a person to serve God for no other reason than what they hope to get out of him.

The true worshipers of God worship him "in spirit and in truth" (John 4:23). They worship him "in spirit, and rejoice in Christ Jesus, and have no confidence in the flesh" (Philippians 3:3). They do not worship him in order to avoid torment, or in order to obtain some supposed obligatory blessings from him, but simply because they love him as a kind and benevolent Father. Theirs is an entirely unselfish service that arises from a heart tendered and softened by the mercy of God; a heart that desires nothing but his honor; a heart that says, "Though he slay me, yet will I trust in him" (Job 13:15). Oh, dear Lord, may we always have such a heart!

৽∾ఌ

December 22

Those Who Mind Earthly Things

There is a song that recently became very popular in which the country music star sings, "I love this bar; it's my kind of place." As I reflect on this I am filled with gratitude that I have never had any desire whatsoever to even go inside a bar, much less feel like it was "my kind of place." Even the thought of it is extremely abhorrent to me.

For a short time in my young days I had a job selling various kinds of nuts, chips, etc., and on my route there were a few bars that I had to go into in order to service the chip and nut racks. I always greatly dreaded going into those places, for a number of reasons. For one thing, most of them were kept so dimly lit that my eyes had to get adjusted to the darkness before I could see where I was going or what I was doing. (This always reminded me of John 3:19; "Light is come into the world, and men loved darkness rather than light, because their deeds were evil"). For another thing, I always felt very uncomfortable in the presence of the kind of people who frequented those places.

I once saw a man fall off a high barstool onto a cement floor because he had drunk himself into unconsciousness. When he came to and some of his drinking buddies helped him up, the first thing he did was to deny that he was drunk. They thought it was funny. I never could see where such foolishness could possibly bring anyone any pleasure. So, when anyone tells me that they love a bar, and that it is "their kind of place," I automatically assume that they are in love with the world and the things thereof (1 John 2:15). They are among those who "mind earthly things" (Phil. 3:19).

Thank God, a bar is not *my kind of place.* My kind of place is where the Lord shows his smiling face. I love the company of good, humble, sober people who seek to follow the Lord in precept and example. Of these kind of folks I need have no fear. Whither they go, I will go, and where they lodge, I will lodge. Their people shall be my people, and their God my God (Ruth 1:16). I hope they will never entreat me to leave them.

❧

December 23

Never Less Alone

People sometimes speak of being "alone with God," and we know what they mean, but actually, is this not somewhat of a misnomer? Is it not true that we are never *less* alone than when we are feelingly alone with the Lord? And is it not true that God's people are never alone, even when they do *not* feel his presence, for he says that he will never leave them nor forsake them (Heb. 13:5)?

I don't know how Daniel may have felt when he was cast into the den of lions, but I suspect that he never felt less alone in his life. All he had in the way of visible company was a pride of beasts that would have normally torn him to shreds but for the providential restraints that God had put upon them. Would not such a visible manifestation of God's providential care and keeping have been a source of great comfort to Daniel? Would it not have been a great confirmation of God's love to him, and would it not have deeply affected his heart and mind?

How must Shadrach, Meshach and Abednego have felt when the Lord appeared in visible form to them in the fiery furnace? The three of them had fallen down bound into the midst of the furnace, but when the king looked in he saw four men up and walking in the fire and he said, "The fourth is like the Son of God" (Dan. 3:25). Those faithful servants of the Lord experienced no harm because the Lord was with them. They not only did not feel any pain, but they did not feel alone either. What a wonderful experience this must have been, and what joy must have filled their hearts!

One of the most joyous times of my life was when I was alone in a two-room cabin with no thought of such a communion with the Lord as I was blest to experience for a few precious moments. I have never been lifted higher nor had a more delightful season of refreshing nor shed tears more freely, and it came upon me suddenly without any solicitation on my part, and I will remember it fondly for as long as I have a right mind. I was never less alone than in that blessed hour of seeming solitude.

December 24

Peace in the Midst of Adversity

It is one of the great mysteries of godliness that a child of God may have inner peace even when all outward circumstances seem totally opposed to it. I have read of many of the martyrs being blest with a calm and peaceful frame even while suffering the most cruel and tortuous of deaths. We see Paul and Silas praying and singing praises unto God at midnight in the inner prison with their feet bound fast in the stocks. Naturally speaking we would not think of their circumstances as being at all conducive to singing praises to God, but the secret of the matter is that they were blest with the felt presence of the Lord, and that was all it took to make their prison a palace. We think of Daniel and the peace he must have felt in the den of lions when he saw that the Lord had made those normally hostile beasts as gentle as lambs. What a joyful experience it must have been for Shadrach, Meshach, and Abednego to be preserved from harm in the midst of a burning fiery furnace, and to even have the very Son of God to appear there with them!

The children of God should not judge their future state by present circumstances. They may be downcast and discouraged one moment and exalted to the mountain tops the next. God is not in any way limited or bound by their circumstances. He can give his people a token for good at any time he may choose. He may at any moment cheer their hearts with his heavenly cordials no matter how bleak their present state may appear.

The Psalmist says, "Weeping may endure for a night, but joy cometh in the morning" (Psalm 30:5). How good it is to know that our *nights* of doubt and discouragement will ultimately, in God's own time, be followed by *mornings* of relief and uplifting! When we find ourselves low in the valley, we need to wait on the Lord, for he will not leave us there always. He knows when the best time for deliverance is, and the most efficient and beneficial way, to bring it about.

Some of the sweetest moments of communion with the Lord come in the midst of suffering, and when least expected. David tells us that the afflictions of the righteous are many, but that the Lord delivers them out of them all (Psalm 34:19). The afflictions are not pleasant but they serve needful purposes, sometimes perhaps known only to God, and, without them we could not experience the deliverances. The assurance of ultimate deliverance should make all trials easier to bear, and while we await the deliverance we will have times of refreshing and "a little reviving in our bondage" that will greatly help us in our struggles. God is indeed merciful, and is a rewarder of them that diligently seek him (Heb. 11:6). We cannot go wrong by doing so.

December 25

God is Immutable

The apostle James tells us that with God there is no variableness, neither shadow of turning (1:17). This attribute is spoken of as his *immutability* (Heb. 6:17-18). It is one of those glorious traits that make him what he is, and which makes him so precious to those who are blessed, as was Isaiah, to see him "high and lifted up" (Isa. 6:1).

Man is *mutable*; that is, he is *changeable*. Not only is he *capable* of change, but he is a *subject* of change. He is *ever* changing. Every moment of his life even his body is changing, making ready for the grave. But God is immutable, that is, he changes not.

He makes this assertion of himself in Malachi 3:6: "I am the Lord, I change not..." And Job says, "He is in one mind and who can turn him? and what his soul desireth, even that he doeth" (23:13). God put into the mouth of Balaam to say to Balak, "God is not a man, that he should lie; neither the son of man, that he should repent: hath he not said, and shall he not do it? or hath he spoken, and shall he not make it good?" (Num. 23:19).

It is to this grand attribute of immutability that we owe our preservation in Christ. "I am the Lord, I change not; *therefore* (for this reason) ye sons of Jacob (spiritual Israel) are not consumed." It is not because of any ability on our part to "hold out faithful" as some would mistakenly tell us, but it is owing to the fact that *God* does not change, and therefore, "having loved his own...he loved them unto the end"

(John 13:1). "Hath God cast away his people? God forbid...God hath *not* cast away his people which he foreknew" (Rom. 11:12).

We are very fickle, capricious, weak and unstable in our very nature, and if our home in heaven depended upon our steadfastness, none of us would ever inhabit that blessed abode. But because "the gifts and calling of God are without repentance," on *his* part (Rom. 11:29) none of his people will ever be cast away in a final and eternal sense.

December 26

A Downward Drift

In recent years the drift of our country away from the principles of godliness upon which it was founded seems to have become much more accelerated. There seems to be a very passionate desire on the part of many people to blur the distinction between right and wrong and to make almost any form of immoral behavior socially acceptable in our society. But as American colonist William Penn (1644-1718) is quoted as saying: "Right is right, even if everybody is against it, and wrong is wrong, even if everybody is for it."

God will not lower his standard to suit man's notions of what constitutes proper behavior. His laws, and the penalties for disobeying them, remain the same from age to age, and he will not be mocked. His word tells us that whatsoever a man sows, that shall he also reap (Gal. 6:7). Without doubt this applies to nations as well.

This is being borne out before our very eyes from day to day. Multitudes are sowing the seeds of ungodliness and are daily reaping the bitter fruits. Just as there are negative consequences connected with disobeying the laws of nature, so also there is a grievous aftermath associated with disobedience to the laws of morality and decency. I often wonder how far down the road to death, hell and destruction the Lord will allow our own nation to go. William Cowper who lived from 1731 to 1800 said, "My soul is sick with every day's report of wrong and outrage with which earth is filled." I feel the same way.

December 27

Brought to Love the Doctrine They Hated

I was born to a Primitive Baptist mother, and my father was converted to the Old Baptist doctrine soon afterward and when I was about two years old he started "preaching the faith which once he destroyed." Then when I was twenty-one I united with the Old Church and soon began to be called on to speak in the Lord's name. Less than a year later I was liberated, and then ordained about a year after that.

In those early years I did a lot of visiting among the churches around over the country and spent quite a bit of time in the homes of some of the most able ministers of that day, all of whom have passed on now. Consequently from early childhood I have heard a lot of the old preachers relate their experiences in coming to a knowledge of the truth, and one thing that stands out in my mind is that many of them were at first "enemies of the gospel." At the time my father and mother married he was very much opposed to the Old Baptist doctrine. He called it a "damnable doctrine" and wished that it would be made illegal to preach it in the presence of children.

I have often thought about the apostle Paul's hatred of the doctrine prior to his conversion and the extent to which his experience corresponds with that of a number of other Primitive Baptist preachers I have known, and others of them that I have read about. But what a contrast is this to those Arminian preachers who decide, of their own volition, to take up the religious world's version of the ministry as an occupation. They know nothing of such an experience as Paul's, and they know nothing experientially of that way that the world calls heresy (Acts 24:14) and which is everywhere spoken against (Acts 28:22).

True, God-called ministers do not volunteer for the post. I know I certainly did not seek it nor desire it. I never had any intention of ever occupying that station. One of the reasons was that I was convinced that the Lord would never call such an unfit and unworthy subject as me to that office. If I indeed have any part in it, I was *placed* in it by the Lord. Paul said the Lord *put* him into the ministry, and *enabled* him (1 Tim. 1:12). For forty-five years I have tried to labor in that capacity, and I hope this service has proven, at least to some small degree, my sincerity in the matter and my devotion to the cause.

December 28

Some Thoughts on Prayer

A little boy once asked his father if God knows all things. His father replied in the affirmative and then asked him why he wanted to know. The little boy said, "Well, every time our preacher prays, he tries to tell the Lord everything."

I, too, have many times heard those kinds of prayers. It doesn't seem to be as bad as it used to be, but when I was younger it was common for very lengthy prayers to be offered in our church meetings. It always seemed strange to me for men to pray much-too-lengthy prayers and then in the closing express their awareness that we are not heard for our "much speaking" (Matt. 6:7).

The verse following informs us that our heavenly Father knows what things we have need of "before we ask him." We should not pray as though we are trying to inform God of our circumstances. I believe prayer should consist primarily of praise, supplication, and thanksgiving; and our petitions should always be for such things as are honoring to God.

In my own prayers I always try to also remember to beg the Lord to keep me humble and make me submissive to his will in all things. If we are to enjoy any true, spiritual communion with our Lord in this life, we must be humble, and we must be reconciled to the patient bearing of whatever he allows to come into our lives. And in order to accomplish this it is not necessary for us to "make long prayers" (Mark 12:40; Luke 20:47).

December 29

Incorrect Views of Man's Ability

A godly man of the past has wisely stated the following: *"It cannot be said too often that a false theology finds it's source in inadequate views of man's depravity."* How true this is! It might well be said that all error, both in doctrine and in practice arises from this very inadequacy. If we are ignorant of man's native corruption and wickedness, it will inevitably follow that we will think man *can* do what God's word says he *can't* do. For example the Bible says, "Without faith it is impossible to please God" (Heb. 11:5). Yet those who deny man's depravity contend that those who are without faith *can indeed* please God. When the Bible says, "They that are in the flesh *cannot* please God," they say, "Yes, they *can* please God. In fact, they *must* please God in order to obtain eternal life."

When such totally opposite positions present themselves to us we are left with only two choices—we must either believe God or men. It is not a complicated proposition. We either believe God or we believe men. If we believe men instead of God we merely confirm our depravity. This brings about a situation in which people are *denying* their depravity with their mouths on the one hand, but *confirming* their depravity by their actions on the other hand.

If we do not believe God's word, at least one of three things is true: (1) we have been so deceived by false teachings that our minds will not allow us to embrace the truth, or (2) we have not yet been born of God's Spirit, or (3) we are not his children. Christ said to some of that class, "Ye believe not, because ye are not of my sheep," while of the sheep he says, "My sheep hear my voice" (John 10:26). This *cannot* be the same crowd, all with the same abilities.

Dr. Carolyn Dean's

Natural Prescriptions
for Common Ailments

ALSO BY CAROLYN DEAN, M.D., N.D.

Homeopathic Remedies for Children's Common Ailments
Menopause Naturally